The STANLEY Complete Step-By-Step REVISED Book of HOME REPAIR and Improvement

James A. Hufnagel

Revised and Updated by Edward Lipinski

A Round Stone Press Book

SIMON & SCHUSTER
New York London Toronto Sydney Singapore

SIMON & SCHUSTER
Rockefeller Center
1230 Avenue of the Americas
New York, New York 10020

A ROUND STONE PRESS BOOK
Directors: Marsha Melnick, Susan E. Meyer, Paul Fargis
Editorial Director: Nick Viorst
Editor: Judy Pray

General Editor: William L. Broecker
Design: Jeffrey Fitschen
Art Editor: Paul Colin
Editorial Consultant: Roy Barnhart
Illustration: Vantage Art, Inc., Robert Steimle

CONTRIBUTORS
Roy Barnhart
Francis Donegan
Merle Henkenius
Carol Hupping
Chris Peterson
Thomas F. Sweeney
Joe Truini

STANLEY REVIEW BOARD
Robert E. Allaire
James S. Amtmann
Scott A. Bannell
I. James Elmore
Ronald F. Gilrain
Francis E. Hummel
Joseph L. Jones
M. Michael Maznio
John L. Poccia
Carl C. Stoutenberg
Thomas J. Williams

Printed and bound in U.S.A.

1 3 5 7 9 10 8 6 4 2

Library of Congress Cataloging-in-Publication Data
Hufnagel, James A.
   The Stanley complete step-by-step book of home repair and improvement / James A. Hufnagel.—
2nd ed. / rev. and updated by Edward Lipinski.
      p. cm.
   Includes index.
   ISBN 0-684-87260-9
   1. Dwellings—Maintenance and repair—Amateurs' manuals.
   2. Dwellings—Remodeling—Amateurs' manuals. I. Lipinski, Edward R., 1943–
II. Stanley Works. III. Title.

TH4817.3 .H84 2000
643'.7—dc21   00-041292

CONTENTS

CONTENTS

CONTENTS

INTRODUCTION by Dean Johnson

Welcome to *The Stanley Complete Step-by-Step Revised Book of Home Repair and Improvement*. It's been seven years since the first edition of this book was published. Stanley remains one of the world's most recognized and trusted brand names in tools and hardware and the book has become an acclaimed bestseller in its own right. Due to the overwhelming success of the original Stanley book, it has now been revised to bring it up-to-date and to bring its readers even more how-to information. Inside you'll find several updated chapters covering a range of tools and techniques, a complete new section called The Homeowner's Inspection Guide, over 100 new illustrations, and a new look to the book as well.

As with the first edition, this is not a book for architects and contractors; it is a book for homeowners. It does not tell you how to design or build a new house. Instead, it tells you what to do with the house you have: how to maintain and repair it when necessary; how to upgrade, alter, and enlarge your living space; how to keep the primary operating systems—heating, ventilation, plumbing, electrical—in good order; how to inspect your home and keep it in working condition. It tells you how to do the things you can reasonably expect to do without special knowledge, experience, or ability—things that will save you a great deal of money if you do them yourself. There is a special joy and sense of accomplishment in learning how to do a job the right way and then doing it. That is the real aim of this book: to enable you to make your home more enjoyable and to add to its value.

Again and again, viewers who watch my "Hometime" show on public television ask me to recommend a reliable reference book that concentrates on around-the-house projects—a book in which they can quickly find accurate, easy-to-understand answers to the thousands of questions homeowners face. This is one of those at the top of my list that I'll enthusiastically recommend and use. Why? In a word: Stanley.

Since 1843, when Frederick T. Stanley and his brother William founded the Stanley Bolt Manufactory, the people at what is now called The Stanley Works have been committed to producing quality hardware, tools, and a wide range of other home products. The Stanley mission—and motto—is to "make something great." That means starting with the right tools, selecting the right materials, fasteners, and other hardware, and using the right techniques to ensure professional-looking results.

Making something great—and I cannot stress this enough—also means making things safely. Quality tools, hardware, and products, along with safety, have been Stanley's hallmarks for a century and a half. Stanley's sponsorship makes this book a homeowner's manual that enables you to make great things and make them safely at the same time.

The Stanley Complete Step-by-Step Revised Book of Home Repair and Improvement is unique in a number of ways. Many so-called do-it-yourself books fall short of giving all the information you need to complete a task successfully, and some are downright misleading. Others attempt to summarize highly technical or complex projects. Often these more intricate jobs require skills, equipment, and in some cases licenses that most of us simply do not have. *The Stanley Complete Step-by-Step Revised Book of Home Repair and Improvement* not only provides fully detailed, illustrated instructions for all the projects you can handle, but also warns you away from potentially dangerous or difficult jobs and suggests when to hire professionals for the tasks you don't feel qualified for or ones where you know you will need to meet codes. Sometimes a professional can save you time and money.

I've also learned from my "Hometime" audience that many of today's homeowners prefer a buy-it-yourself approach to typical do-it-yourself projects. Some buy-it-yourselfers shop for the materials or equipment needed and then hire a subcontractor and supervise the work. A growing number of buy-it-yourselfers, however, are discovering that manufacturers of home products now offer an astonishing range of kits that include in a single package everything you need to complete a project, along with instructions that guide even the unhandiest person through every step of assembly and installation.

The people at Stanley have designed many products, from doors to closet organizers to garage door openers to home security systems. They not only make the tools and hardware to do the job, but they also have been listening to what consumers want to know for over 150 years. They have distilled all that knowledge and put what most people want to know into this book.

Whether you're a do-it-yourselfer or a strictly hands-off buy-it-yourselfer, *The Stanley Complete Step-by-Step Revised Book of Home Repair and Improvement* introduces you to the latest home products, walks you through the steps involved in working with them, and enables you to decide whether you prefer to take on a project personally or pay for a pro's time. Finally, I think everybody will appreciate the visual clarity of the more than 2,000 drawings on these pages. All this ensures that you can count on *The Stanley Complete Step-by-Step Revised Book of Home Repair and Improvement* to help you make great things—and enjoy the results.

Every home project begins with an assessment of the tools that will be needed to get the job done. This opening section introduces you to those tools and shows how to use them safely and effectively. Chapters 1 and 2 cover hand and portable power tools. Chapter 3 explains the basics of setting up a workshop that might include one or more stationary power tools, and Chapter 4 tells about construction equipment, ranging from ladders to house jacks, that various home projects might call for.

In all, this section covers nearly 100 tools, but you can accomplish many repairs and improvements with fewer than two dozen hand and portable power tools. Dozens of other, specialized tools are discussed in subsequent chapters. Throughout the book, you will find recommendations for which tools you should get first. Use these recommendations to guide your tool purchases—and invest in the best quality you can afford. A handful of quality tools will outperform a wall lined with poor ones.

RENTING WHAT YOU NEED

As your skills and appetite for home projects increase, you will find yourself adding to your basic tool assortment. Before each purchase, ask yourself how often you expect to use the item. A power circular saw, for instance, is almost a must for a major construction project such as building a deck, but unless you anticipate a series of big construction jobs, you may be dollars ahead to rent specialized, expensive, and infrequently needed tools.

Just about any tool can be rented. Some rental dealers cater mainly to contractors. Others are accustomed to renting to homeowners as well. Homeowner-oriented outlets provide basic instruction in how to use the tool you rent and often supply printed materials you can refer to. Patronize only an established dealer who

I TOOLS AND EQUIPMENT

has a well-organized shop and yard and offers clean, properly maintained equipment. A good dealer will make sure the equipment is in good, safe condition, and that you have everything you need when you leave. He will also explain how to assemble and use whatever you rent, and will have instruction manuals and other support materials if you need them.

CARING FOR TOOLS

At the end of each project, make it a habit to clean your tools thoroughly before putting them away. This is also a good time to test cutting tools for sharpness and replace or sharpen dull edges. Dirty, dull tools do inferior work and could cause an injury.

IMPORTANT

The tools illustrated in this section and throughout the book may differ in design, operating controls, and other details from tools you may now have or may purchase. Always read the instructions that accompany any tool that you acquire and follow them exactly. It is especially important to read and follow all safety precautions given in tool instructions, as well as those given in the text of this book, in order to understand fully the proper and safe use of the respective tool.

1 HAND TOOLS

Quality hand tools, properly used and properly maintained, produce quality work. This chapter introduces you to the hand tools required for most around-the-house jobs, explains how to use them, and offers some buying and safety pointers.

Measuring and layout tools. In any project you must accurately measure and mark materials for cutting and assembly. Pages 13–15 explain how to use tapes, rules, squares, bevels, levels, chalklines, and plumb bobs.

Cutting and shaping tools. Marked stock must be cut precisely to size, and often shaped and smoothed as well.

Pages 16–27 cover saws, drills, knives, snips, chisels, planes, surface-forming tools, and abrasives.

Striking and prying tools. When the parts for your project are ready for assembly, you most often will need a hammer. There's more to choosing and safely using a hammer than most people think. Pages 28–31 will familiarize you with hammers, mallets, and related tools such as nail sets, punches, and prying tools.

Fastening tools. Screwdrivers are the most common and easy to use fastening tools, but you need to select the right type for the job at hand, and there are

many other fastening tools as well. Pages 32–39 deal with screwdrivers, pliers, wrenches, clamps, glue guns, staplers, riveters, and soldering guns.

Specialty tools. This chapter focuses only on the basic hand tools you will use for a wide variety of household repairs and improvements. Power tools are covered in Chapter 2, setting up a home workshop in Chapter 3, and equipment for construction work in Chapter 4. Many projects, such as taping drywall, painting, and masonry and electrical work, call for specialized tools. Those are discussed in the chapters dealing with the jobs for which they are used.

MEASURING BASICS

Whatever the project, precise measurements make the difference between success and a frustrating waste of time and materials.

READ DIMENSIONS ACCURATELY
Good quality flexible tapes, folding rules, and squares have measurement marks along both edges of the blade in various increments. On a tape or rule, the scale along one edge commonly divides inches into 16ths, while the scale along the other edge has 1/32-inch graduations for the first 6 inches or foot. Carpenter's squares are usually marked in 1/8- or 1/16-inch divisions on both edges, and combination squares in 1/8-inch divisions on one edge, 1/16- and 1/32-inch divisons on the other edge. Use the larger scale for rough work such as framing and the finer scale where close tolerances are critical, such as in cabinetry and finish work.

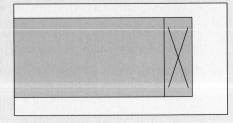

Tape

Combination square

START SQUARE AND PLUMB
Never assume that an end or edge you will be measuring from is truly square, horizontal, or vertical. Always check with a square, level, or other appropriate layout tool, as shown on pages 14 and 15.

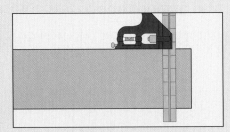

MARK MEASUREMENTS ACCURATELY
Mark framing and rough work dimensions with a sharp pencil. A pen mark can bleed or smudge enough to prevent accuracy. On hardwoods and for precision work, use a scratch awl or a sharp knife blade. Mark a V with its point exactly at a measured dimension. A dot is difficult to see; a short line can slant confusingly. To draw a line through a single mark, place a square or an accurately set bevel against an

edge you know is true. To join two or more marks with a line use a metal straightedge.

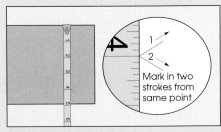

Mark in two strokes from same point

MARK SCRAP CLEARLY
Mark the waste on one side of a cutoff line with a large X so you can quickly determine on which side of the line the saw kerf should fall; see page 16.

MEASURING TOOLS

Just about every home project begins with measurements. You cannot measure accurately with a household ruler, yardstick, or cloth sewing tape. Instead, invest in a retractable *tape rule*, a tool you will use more often than any other. You might also want to add a *folding rule*.

TAPE RULES
A retractable tape rule consists of a 6- to 50-foot-long flexible metallic or fiberglass *blade* that rolls up into a *case*. Better tapes are equipped with a spring-driven return and a *thumb lock* that holds the blade in position when it is extended. The blade is coated for protection against abrasion and wear. *Top-reading* tape rules have a window that is especially useful in taking *inside* measurements such as the distance between

door jambs. The reading shown in the window compensates for the length of the case. With other tapes the case length is marked on the side and must be added to the length visible on the blade when making inside measurements.

A *hook* at the end of the tape enables you to take *outside* measurements, such as the length of a board, without a helper to hold the end of the tape. The hook slides slightly to make up for its own thickness in inside and outside measurements.

Besides foot and inch markings, the blade of a good tape rule has distinctive markings at 16-inch intervals, the standard spacing for wall studs and other framing elements in house construction. The tape's flexibility also enables you to measure the circumference of

round objects such as posts, but do not try to crimp it into a right angle.

Include a 12-foot-long tape rule among your first tool purchases. Later you might want to add a 25-foot or longer tape for big jobs.

FOLDING RULES
A folding rule, also known as a Zig-Zag® or boxwood rule, has a number of segments hinged together with metal pivot joints; the total unfolded length is 6 or 8 feet. The most versatile rule has a metal *extension slide* for making depth measurements and inside measurements that are up to 6 inches longer than any unfolded length of the rule. Square segment ends allow using the extension slide as a marking gauge. Because a folding rule is rigid, it is very useful in situations where a flexible tape might sag or fall, such as reaching up to measure ceiling height.

HOW TO USE TAPES AND RULES

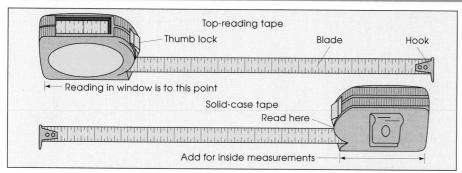

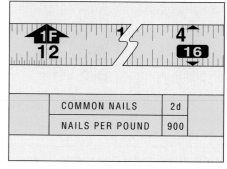

A RETRACTABLE TAPE RULE has a flexible blade and a thumb lock to hold the blade extended. A top-reading rule shows the distance to the end of the case. Solid cases are marked with the amount to be added to the blade measurement to obtain an inside dimension.

STUD SPACINGS are marked every 16 inches along a good tape rule. Many also have useful information on the back of the blade.

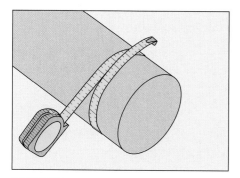

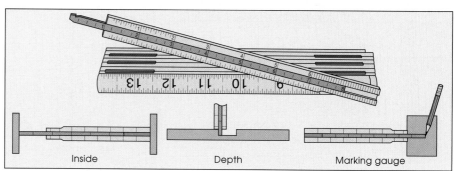

MEASURE THE CIRCUMFERENCE of a round object by wrapping the tape around it. To calculate the diameter, divide by 3.1416.

A FOLDING RULE provides rigidity for measurements where a flexible tape might sag or fall over, such as measuring overhead beyond your arm's reach. An extension slide is useful for making inside and depth measurements and as a marking gauge.

LAYOUT TOOLS

Layout tools are used to mark cutting and assembly lines, working from accurate measurements. *Squares* assist you in checking and marking 90- and 45-degree angles. *Bevels* can be set at any angle. *Levels* tell whether work is truly horizontal or *level*, and vertical or *plumb*. A *chalkline* marks long, straight lines, and a *plumb bob* indicates a point that is directly below another. A good worker uses these layout tools almost as often as a tape or folding rule.

USING A COMBINATION SQUARE

A *combination square* does many different jobs, making it the most versatile layout tool of all. Use it as a *try square* and a *miter square* to check and mark angles that are truly 90 or 45 degrees, a *marking gauge* to draw lines parallel to an edge, and a *depth gauge* to measure the depth of a cut. A built-in *level* shows whether a surface is level or plumb, and a *scratch awl* enables you to scribe lines with greater accuracy than is possible with a pencil.

Loosening a knurled knob on the handle of a combination square lets you slide the handle to any point along the blade, or you can remove the blade entirely and use it as a 12-inch rule.

USING A CARPENTER'S SQUARE

A *carpenter's square* or *framing square* is simple and rugged. It is a metal L with a 24-inch-long *body* and a 16-inch *tongue*.

Smaller squares are 6 × 8 or 8 × 12 inches. A full-size square is essential for large layout jobs. To use it, align the body along the edge of the work and the tongue across the face, then mark off the appropriate dimensions. Use either both inside edges or both outside edges, which meet at the *heel* of the square. You can also lay out 45-degree angles with a carpenter's square. To do this, position the tip of the heel at one edge of the work and align equal dimensions along the tongue and blade—6 inches and 6 inches, for example—at the other edge. Some squares have edge marks for laying out 30-, 45-, and 60-degree angles in this way. Many also have useful reference information engraved on the tongue and blade.

The Quick Square® layout tool is primarily used to give a 45- or 90-degree

HOW TO USE LAYOUT TOOLS

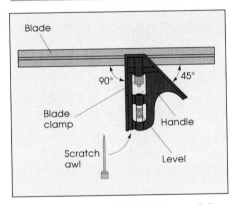

A COMBINATION SQUARE has a sliding 12-inch blade, 90° and 45° faces, a level, and a scratch awl for marking work.

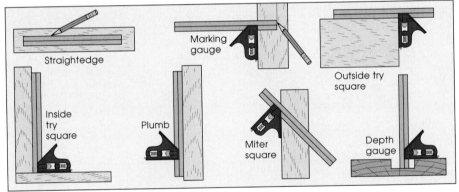

MANY DIFFERENT TASKS can be accomplished with the combination square, from checking corners and angles to making measurements and marking layouts. It is the layout tool you will probably use the most for small and medium-sized jobs.

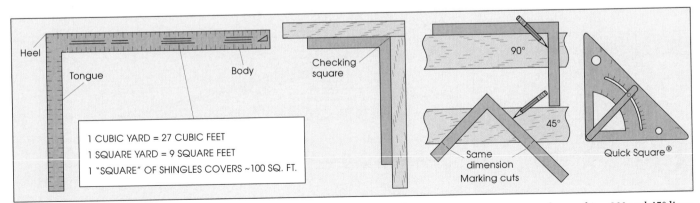

1 CUBIC YARD = 27 CUBIC FEET
1 SQUARE YARD = 9 SQUARE FEET
1 "SQUARE" OF SHINGLES COVERS ~100 SQ. FT.

A CARPENTER'S SQUARE is indispensable for large layout and framing work. Its most common uses are for marking 90° and 45° lines and checking for square corner alignment, but it also makes rafter and stair layouts and other complex tasks easier. Some have reference information on the blade. A Quick Square® indicates 90° and 45° angles directly.

angle directly. It is useful as a power saw guide, protractor, rafter square, or combination square.

USING A BEVEL

Mark angles of any degree with a bevel. Its blade can be set to lay out, duplicate, or check any angle. The setting is locked with a wing nut at the pivot or a knob at the base of the handle.

USING LEVELS

Levels include one or more *vials* each filled with a colored liquid and an air bubble. When you place the level against a surface that is level or plumb, the bubble comes to rest between lines marked on the vial.

A *carpenter's level* is from 18 to 96 inches long and should have at least three vials, one in the center for check-ing level and one near each end for determining if a surface or edge is plumb. A window that lets you see the level vial when looking down on the top edge is very convenient for checking floors and other surfaces where it would be hard to take a reading from the side. In some levels the vials can be replaced easily in case of damage.

A *torpedo level* is up to 9 inches long, handy in spots too tight for a carpenter's level. Some have three vials, for determining plumb, level, and 45 degrees. A new feature is lighted vials for working in dimly lit areas.

A *line level* has a single vial in a tubular case that has hooks so you can hang it from a taut string. It is especially useful for masonry work, outdoor projects, and wherever a level must be established between widely separated points.

USING A CHALKLINE AND PLUMB BOB

A modern chalkline has a cord that rolls up into a housing filled with powdered chalk. To mark a long, straight line, hook the cord to a nail at one point, pull the line taut just above the surface to a second point, then lift and release the cord to snap a line on the surface. New neon chalks provide high visibility. Some cases are shaped for use as a plumb bob when suspended from the cord.

A plumb bob is a heavy, pointed weight with a cord fastened to its axis at the top. When hung from a spot overhead it points to the spot directly below, no matter how the upper or lower surface may slant or curve. It is especially useful for transferring ceiling marks to the floor below, or establishing a true vertical for erecting the corner of a wall.

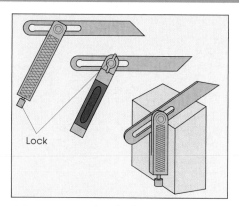

A BEVEL is used to duplicate and mark angles. Place the handle along one edge, adjust the blade to the angle, and lock it in place.

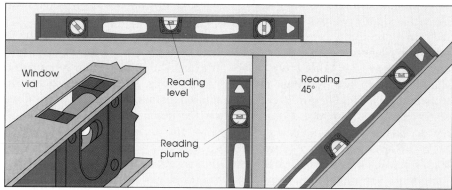

CARPENTER'S LEVELS of various lengths have vials for checking level and plumb. They are vital in carpentry, masonry, and many other around-the-house projects. A top-reading window and replaceable vials are desirable features.

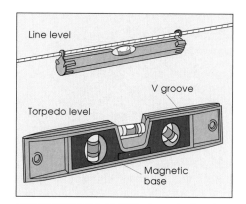

HANDY SMALL LEVELS are the line level, which can hang on a cord or be set on top of a surface, and the torpedo level.

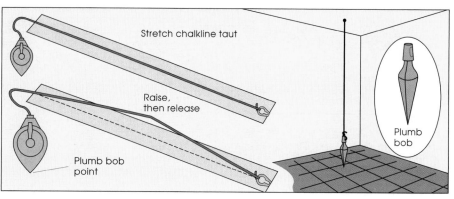

CHALKLINES AND PLUMB BOBS make it easy to mark long, straight lines and to find a point that is directly beneath another. Some chalklines can also be hung as plumb bobs to establish vertical alignment.

SAWS

Whether designed to cut across or along the grain of wood or through other materials, all hand saws have a blade with sharp chisel- or knifelike teeth that are counted in *points* per inch. The number of points and their size, angle, and sideways protrusion, called *set,* depend on the intended use of the saw.

The teeth slice or chip through material, creating a gap called a *kerf.* When sawing, the cut must be made just on the waste side of your marked cutoff line, to allow for the material removed in the kerf. Otherwise the work will end up a fraction of an inch short.

CROSSCUT SAWS

A *crosscut saw* works best cutting across the grain of lumber (or in any direction with plywood). It can also handle occasional *rip* cuts along the grain, so it should be the first saw you purchase. Good quality crosscut saws have teeth that are ground or bevel filed to put sharp edges on both sides for rapid cutting. *Aggressive-tooth* saws have sharply set teeth that are ground on the front and back edges to give 50 percent faster cutting performance, and usually a wider kerf, than conventional saws.

For all-around use with softwoods, get a crosscut saw with 8 or 9 points per inch. Later you might also want a 12-point saw for smooth cuts in hardwood or thin stock. A 26-inch blade is the popular length for most jobs. You can also purchase aggressive-tooth saws in 20- and 15-inch lengths that fit conveniently into a tool box.

RIPSAWS

A *ripsaw* has large chisel-like teeth designed for cutting along the grain of lumber rather than across it. There are usually 5½ points to the inch. They have a larger set, protruding farther to each side of the blade, and therefore cut a wider kerf than crosscut teeth.

USING A CROSSCUT OR RIPSAW

To saw a straight line, let the saw do most of the work. Make a few slow, short upstrokes to start the kerf. Use a piece of scrap lumber laid along the cutting line as a guide. That is much safer than placing a knuckle of your free hand against the blade, especially with an aggressive-tooth saw.

Once started, move your free hand to hold the work at a point well away from the blade and make long, full, up and down strokes. Traditional saw teeth are filed so that most of the cutting is done on the downstroke. Aggressive-tooth saws cut on both the down and up strokes. Apply only light pressure; let the saw cut under its own weight. Keep the flat side of the blade at a right angle to the surface. Point your index finger to help control the saw.

Keep the edge of a crosscut saw at a 45-degree angle to lumber, and at a 60-degree angle to plywood or paneling. Keep ripsaw teeth at a 60-degree angle to the surface of all work. If the saw strays from the line, bring it back with a slight twist of the handle as you cut. If the blade begins to bind in a long cut, insert a wedge or screwdriver near the beginning to keep the kerf open.

When you near the end of the cut, grasp the scrap end with your free hand so that the edge does not splinter as you make the last few strokes. You can expect some splintering along the underside of the cut because handsaws do most of their cutting on the downstroke. For this reason, cut plywood and lumber with the best face up, and remove the splinters on the back with medium-grade sandpaper. A strip of

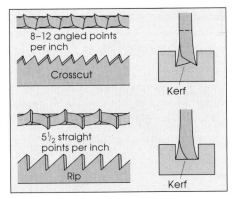

SAW TEETH are alternately set and bent outward to opposite sides of the blade. The more points per inch, the smoother the cut.

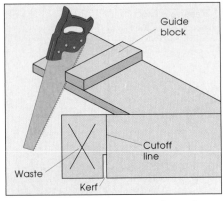

START A CUT with a scrap of wood as a guide. Keep the kerf on the waste side of the cutoff line.

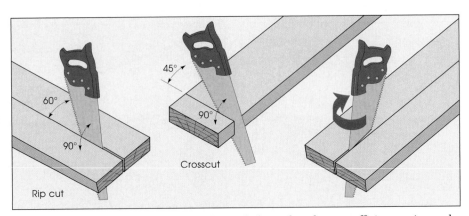

MAKE A CUT with full up and down strokes with the teeth at the most efficient cutting angle. For a square cut, keep the blade at a right angle to the surface. Use moderate pressure on the downstrokes; let the saw do the work. Twist the blade a bit to come back on line if necessary.

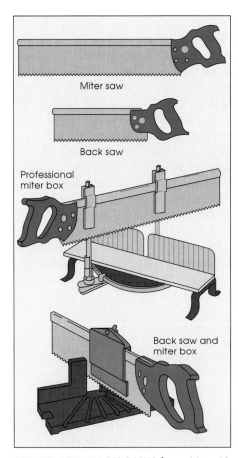

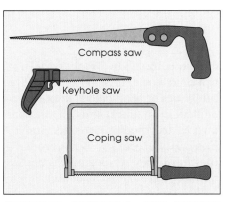

COMPASS, KEYHOLE, AND COPING SAWS are for making curved and inside cuts in a variety of materials.

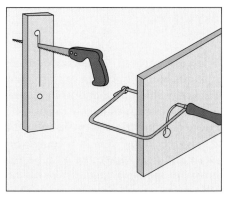

FOR AN INSIDE CUT, bore a starter hole first. Keep the teeth at a 90° angle to the work as you make the cut.

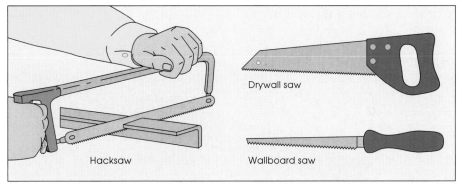

MITER AND BACK SAWS have 11 to 13 points per inch for smooth finish cuts. Use a miter box for controlled cuts at any angle.

CUT NONWOOD MATERIALS with the proper saw. Use a hacksaw for metals and other nonwood materials. Bear down on the forward, push stroke; ease up on the backstroke. Use only a drywall or wallboard saw to cut plasterboard; other blades will be ruined quickly.

masking tape along the cut line on the back side of an important workpiece will reduce splintering.

MITER AND BACK SAWS

For fine cuts in finish work, such as trim and cabinetry, use a 24- to 30-inch-long *miter saw* or a 12- to 14-inch *back saw*. Both have a rectangular blade reinforced with a stiffener along the back, and fine-set teeth, 11 to 13 points per inch, for a narrow kerf and a smooth cut. These saws can be used freehand, but they perform best when used in a miter box, which guides angle cuts.

SPECIAL-PURPOSE SAWS

Compass and *keyhole saws* have pistolgrip handles and are used to cut along irregular and curving lines. A compass saw has a narrow blade, usually less than 1 inch wide, that tapers to a point at the tip. A keyhole saw has an even narrower

blade and can cut tighter curves. A *coping saw* has a ⅛-inch-wide blade held in a deep U-shaped frame. It is used for curved and intricate cuts in wood and plastics less than ¾ inch thick.

To cut a shape out of the middle of a piece, bore a starting hole large enough for the tip of the sawblade or to thread a coping saw blade through.

A *hacksaw* is a strong frame that holds ½-inch-wide blades with 14, 18, 24, or 32 teeth per inch for cutting metals of different thicknesses and hardnesses, or almost any material other than wood. The blade is mounted with the teeth facing forward so they will cut on the forward stroke. Place one hand on the handle and the other on the front corner of the frame. Apply moderate pressure on the forward stroke and ease off on the return stroke to avoid dulling the blade. Protect your eyes with goggles when working with a hacksaw.

Drywall and *wallboard saws* have heavy-duty blades with coarse teeth that are specially designed to cut plasterboard without clogging or dulling, which would happen rapidly with a wood-cutting blade.

SAW SAFETY

Keep your fingers away from saw teeth at all times. Clean the teeth only with a brush. Use the sleeve that the saw was packaged in when you put the saw away. It protects you, and protects the saw teeth from damage.

Keep saw blades clean, and periodically wipe or spray the blades with oil to maintain them in good working condition.

Always provide support for the material you are sawing. Rest it on two sawhorses, secure it in a vise, or clamp it in place.

Never work with a dull saw. The blades of most special-purpose saws are inexpensive and easy to replace. Have crosscut, rip, and back saws professionally sharpened, or learn to do the job yourself.

FILES

Files are used to grind away excess material and to smooth a work surface. Files may either be *single-cut* or *double-cut*. Single-cut files have rows of teeth cut in one direction only—usually at a 65–degree angle to the centerline. Double-cut files have teeth that crisscross at opposing angles. Double-cut files grind away material faster than single-cut files but they create a rough surface that must be smoothed afterward. Use a single-cut file for this.

The number of *teeth* determine how coarse or smooth a file will be and, consequently, how smooth the final work surface will be. There are three categories of coarseness: smooth, second cut or medium smooth, and bastard cut or medium coarse. Smooth files have 60 teeth per inch, second cut files have 36 teeth per inch, and bastard files have 26 teeth per inch.

FILE SHAPES

Files have different shapes to allow them to adapt to a variety of work surfaces. The common shapes are flat, round, triangular, square, and half round. Flat files are general-purpose files and either single- or double-cut. Most flat files taper in width and thickness longitudinally (toward the end) and they have teeth on both surfaces and both edges.

A special kind of flat file called a *mill file* edge is always single-cut and is used primarily for finishing work and for draw filing. The mill file is also used as a sharpening tool for saw blades, knives, shears, and lawn mower blades.

Triangular files have only three tapering sides. They are used to cut material away from inside angles. A *knife file* is a type of triangular file that looks a lot like a flat file. It has three sides, two of

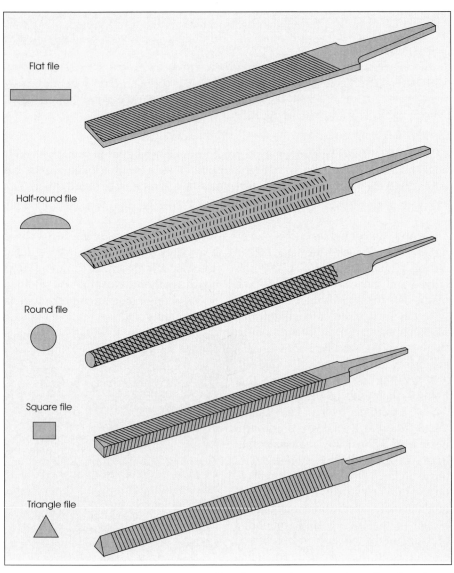

Flat file

Half-round file

Round file

Square file

Triangle file

FILES HAVE DIFFERENT SHAPES to allow them to adapt to a variety of work surfaces. The common shapes are flat, round, triangular, square, and half round.

CLEANING FILES

Files must be cleaned often to remove wood or metal particles that become lodged in the teeth. These particles can score the work surface unless they are removed beforehand. Use a combination file card to brush across and in line with the teeth. The file card has two sides: a wire brush on one side and a stiff-bristled fiber brush on the other. Use both sides to get a thorough cleaning.

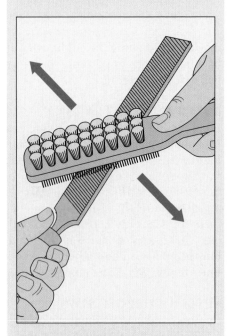

USE A COMBINATION FILE CARD to clean a file. Brush with the bristle side for general cleaning and the wire brush side to remove stubborn particles.

which are wide and taper to a point, like a knife. This file is primarily used by tool-and-die-makers to dress very narrow angles.

Round files have circular cross sections and are used to work inside holes and round slots. *Square files* look like flat files with four sides of equal width. They are used for clearing rectangular or square slots. The *half-round file* has one flat side and one rounded so it is useful for working on either curved or flat surfaces.

Most files are sold without handles, but they should never be used this way because the bare tang can cause injury. File handles are sold at most hardware stores and home centers. To mount the handle you only need to push or twist it onto the bare tang until it is secure.

RASPS

Rasps are files with very coarse teeth. They are used to quickly remove material from a work surface. They are usually available in flat, round, and half-round shapes. The terms "single-cut" and "double-cut" are not used for rasps because the cutting surface is composed of individual, and not parallel, rows of teeth. Rasps are designed primarily for wood, although some may be used on soft metals and plastics.

FILING TECHNIQUES

Learning to use a file is not difficult, but stroking the tool across the workpiece with correct hand and arm positions is essential to creating a quality job. The workpiece should be clamped at elbow height between blocks of soft wood in a vise.

The are two filing techniques: *cross filing* and *draw filing*. Cross filing has more applications, because it is used to remove material. In contrast, draw filing is a finishing technique used to smooth the work surface after cross filing.

To cross-file, grasp the file handle with one hand and grip the file tip with the fingers of the other hand, and hold it horizontally to the work surface. Push the file across the workpiece exerting minimal pressure to insure even cutting. A file only cuts on the *push stroke*, and not on the *return stroke*, so lift the tool after each stroke and return to the starting point.

Stop periodically to test the flatness of the work surface with a straight edge. Applying too much pressure at the beginning and end of the stroke will create a high spot in the center of the work. The opposite—a dished work surface— will make the center lower than the edges. In this case the starting and finishing pressure is too light. Apply even pressure throughout the stroke.

The draw-filing technique is used to remove saw and file marks and smooth the work surface. Choose a clean file with single-cut teeth and grasp it in two hands. Position the file so it is at right angles to the work surface and push it away from you across the work. To create an extra-smooth, polished finish, wrap the file in emery cloth and repeat the technique.

FILING TECHNIQUES

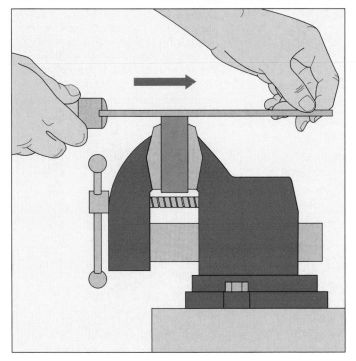

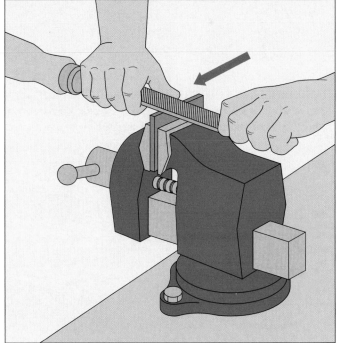

TO CROSS-FILE, grasp the file handle with one hand and grip the file tip with the fingers of the other hand, and hold it horizontally to the work surface. Push the file across the workpiece, exerting minimal pressure to insure even cutting.

THE DRAW-FILING TECHNIQUE is used to remove saw and file marks and smooth the work surface. Grasp the file in two hands, position it at right angles to the work surface, and push it away from you across the work.

DRILLS AND BITS

Often a hand drill or related tool can do a better job than a bulky power tool in starting screws or boring a few small holes, especially in tight spots.

AWLS AND GIMLETS

Awls are the simplest hole-making tools. A *scratch awl* resembles an icepick; you use the point to poke small pilot holes into wood. You can also use it to mark lines on wood or metal. A *brad awl* has a flat point, like a small screwdriver. You press the point into the wood across the grain and turn it back and forth to sever the wood fibers. A *gimlet* is a small-diameter auger bit with a T-handle. Use it to cut deeper holes than an awl makes.

PUSH DRILLS

A *push drill*, also known as a Yankee® drill, has a spirally threaded shaft with a snap-grip *chuck* on the end to hold a bit. Pushing on the handle turns the bit several revolutions. When you release the handle, a spring pushes the handle back for another stroke. A magazine in the handle holds an assortment of different-sized bits. A push drill makes short work of pilot holes.

HAND DRILLS

A *hand drill* works much like an egg beater. Turning its crank handle rotates bevel gears to turn the chuck. A hand drill accepts bits to bore holes up to ¼ inch in diameter.

Take care to keep a drill perpendicular to the work surface unless you specifically need an angled hole. Crank a hand drill slowly, and apply moderate pressure. If the bit seizes in the wood, turn the handle to back up a bit and try again. To drill a "blind" hole that does not go all the way through, wrap the bit with masking tape at the depth you want. Keep push and hand drills in good working order by periodically oiling the moving parts.

DRILL TYPES AND TIPS

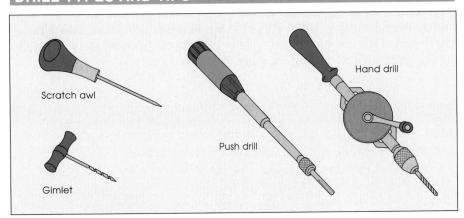

Scratch awl

Gimlet

Push drill

Hand drill

HAND DRILLING TOOLS offer greater control than a power tool when making small holes or working where there is little space. Because they are economical and take up little room, they are useful additions to a tool kit, even if you have an electric drill.

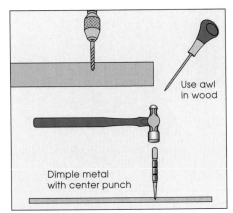

Use awl in wood

Dimple metal with center punch

GUIDE THE BIT with a tiny starting hole in wood or a dimple in metal exactly where you want to drill.

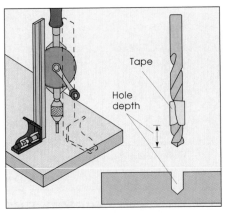

Tape

Hole depth

KEEP A DRILL PERPENDICULAR to the work by aligning it with a combination square. Recheck after several turns of the bit.

DRILL BITS

Bits for hand-operated drills are usually sold in sets that include an assortment of sizes, typically from 1/16 to 11/64 or 1/4 inch in diameter. *Twist drill bits* have spiral fluting that pulls the bit into the work and removes shavings. *Drill points* have straight fluting up the sides. They work best in push drills, but you can also use them in a hand drill. *Masonry bits* are tipped with carbide. Use them for drilling holes in brick and concrete. (To learn about bits for power drills, see pages 40–41.)

Although you can resharpen dull drill bits on a bench grinder, it is easier to simply throw away a worn bit and buy a replacement.

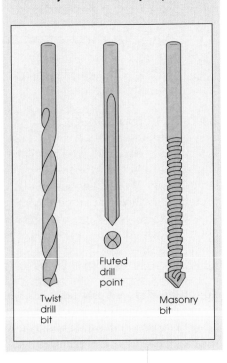

Twist drill bit

Fluted drill point

Masonry bit

KNIVES AND SNIPS

Knives and snips cut materials that are too thin or too flexible for sawing—everything from plastic laminate, shingles, carpeting, and resilient tile to drywall and sheet metal.

UTILITY KNIVES

A *utility knife* is an inexpensive but versatile cutting tool with a razor-sharp, replaceable blade mounted in a contoured handle. In a *retractable-blade* knife, the blade slides in and out of the handle and usually can be locked in three different positions. Extra blades can be stored in the handle. A *fixed-blade* knife uses the same blades as a retractable knife, but the blade is locked in position and cannot be slid back into the handle.

Other utility knives have *breakaway blades*. These have up to ten fresh points on a sectioned blade. When a point dulls, you break it off with pliers or a slot in the end cap of the knife, slide the blade forward, and lock a fresh point into place.

For general-purpose cutting, use a single-edged *standard blade* in a utility knife. This type is reversible: when the exposed half dulls, you open the handle and turn the blade around. A reversible *hook blade* has hooked ends that cut full thickness on a single stroke. Use a *scoring blade* to cut laminate and other plastics. Some scoring blades are reversible; others are not. Make clean cuts in resilient tile and sheet goods with a *linoleum blade*. This type is neither reversible nor retractable.

USING A UTILITY KNIFE

Change utility knife blades often. Dull blades make poor cuts and can cause dangerous slips. For safe, accurate straight cuts, lay sheet goods on a flat, protected surface and guide the knife with a metal straightedge. Do not bear down heavily or you could snap the blade. Instead, make several passes if necessary until the cut is all the way through the thickness of the material. Always dispose of dull blades or break off used blades in a safe manner. Do not leave blades lying around for others to find accidentally.

HOBBY KNIVES

A *hobby knife* does precision cutting. It consists of a pen-sized metal handle that holds a variety of curving and triangular blades in a chuck at the end. Use a hobby knife for cutting paper and other lightweight materials.

SNIPS

Snips have two opposing blades that slice through material from both sides. They are commonly used to cut sheet metal, but you can also employ them with screening, chicken-wire fencing, steel strapping, gaskets, and other metal stock. Do not, however, cut wire with snips. This can nick the blades, which will leave a ragged edge next time they are used on sheet goods. Instead, use pliers with appropriate wire-cutting edges (see page 34).

Single-action snips work like scissors. *Straight-pattern snips* cut straight lines and shallow curves. For tighter curves, use *duckbill snips*. *Compound leverage snips*, also known as *aviation snips*, have a double-hinged action that makes cleaner cuts with less effort. Different versions make left curve, right curve, and straight cuts.

> ### CAUTION
> Always wear work gloves when handling and cutting sheet metal. The cut edges are razor sharp. Also, thin slivers of cut metal can cause vicious punctures and cuts, especially in children's feet and animals' paws. Be sure to clean up all waste promptly and dispose of it safely.

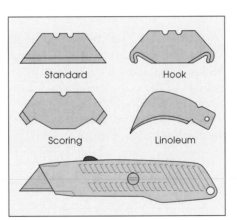

UTILITY KNIVES have blades for a wide variety of cutting tasks. A retractable-blade knife is safest.

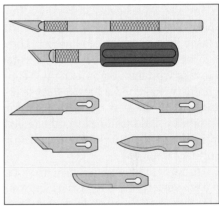

HOBBY KNIVES make precision cuts in thin, soft materials. They accept a variety of very sharp steel blades.

SINGLE-ACTION SNIPS cut light sheet metal. Use straight snips for straight cuts and large curves, duckbill snips for tight curves.

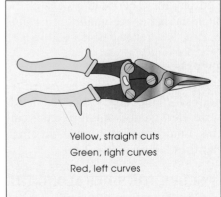

COMPOUND-LEVERAGE SNIPS offer increased power and control. Various types have color-coded handles.

CHISELS

Wood chisels cut by chipping and slicing away wood fibers. *Cold chisels* cut and chip "cold," untempered metals such as aluminum, copper, brass, and unhardened steel. Broad-blade *masonry chisels* such as a brick set fracture bricks and masonry blocks. Narrow, pointed masonry chisels chip out mortar and shape stone. They are similar to cold chisels but longer and narrower, and hardened to a different temper. For safety, never use a cold chisel for masonry work. (For more about using masonry chisels, see chapters 28, 29, and 32.)

WOOD CHISEL CONSTRUCTION

The high-grade tool steel blade of a *wood chisel* ends in a bevel. The bevel is ground and honed to a razor-sharp edge that does the cutting. Most chisels today also have bevels at the sides, but these are not sharp. Buy chisels with plastic or steel reinforced handles. They can be struck with the palm of your hand or with light hammer blows. Top-quality wood chisels have a steel striking cap at the end of the handle for durability. Old-fashioned wood-handled chisels must be driven with a mallet or soft-face hammer.

Home centers and tool dealers stock a wide variety of wood chisels, but you can accomplish most home projects with a basic set of four, ¼, ½, ¾, and 1 inch wide. Many packaged sets include a storage rack. Whether you buy chisels individually or in a set, you get what you pay for. The more expensive the tool, the better the quality of its steel and the longer it will hold a sharp edge.

CUTTING A MORTISE

Wood chisels excel at cutting *mortise* recesses for hinge leaves and other hardware. Here are the steps involved in cutting a mortise. (For more about hinge mortises, see pages 244–245.)

1 SCORE THE SIDES ALONG THE GRAIN with a utility knife. Do not try to cut to the full depth of the mortise; you can't judge it accurately from the surface. The purpose of this scoring cut is to keep the surface fibers from splintering when you chisel.

2 MAKE END CUTS across the grain with a chisel. Hold the chisel vertically on one of the end cutoff lines, with its bevel facing the mortise area. If you are working with softwood, tap the chisel handle with the heel of your hand. With hardwood, use gentle blows from a hammer or mallet. Make the cut at the other end in the same way, again with the bevel facing into the mortise area.

3 CUT A SERIES OF NOTCHES about ⅛ inch apart across the grain in the mortise outline. Hold the chisel at a 90-degree angle, with the bevel facing forward. Make the notches slightly shallower than the final mortise depth.

4 PARE OUT THE WOOD between the end and side cuts with the chisel held at a low, flat angle. If the mortise extends to the edge of the wood, as a hinge mortise does, make paring cuts from the edge, across the grain. Hold the chisel with its bevel up and the flat side parallel with the bottom of the mortise. Guide the chisel with one hand, and push or tap it with the other.

If the mortise does not extend to an edge, work from the center to each end, paring with the grain. Hold the chisel with the flat side up and the bevel face parallel with the bottom of the mortise.

5 SQUARE THE EDGES to the final depth with vertical cuts. At the corners, cut across the grain first, then along the grain. This way, the side cuts will not split beyond the ends of the mortise. Carefully scrape away wood with the chisel to take the bottom of the mortise to its final depth and make it flat.

BORE OUT DEEPER MORTISES

If you need a mortise deeper than ½ inch, first remove most of the material by drilling overlapping holes along its length. Wrap masking tape around the bit to serve as a depth gauge, as described on page 20.

Square up the ends and sides of the mortise with vertical paring cuts, first across the grain, then along the grain. Hold the chisel at and angle with the bevel facing into the mortise (last illustration at right). Make repeated cuts to

TYPES OF CHISELS

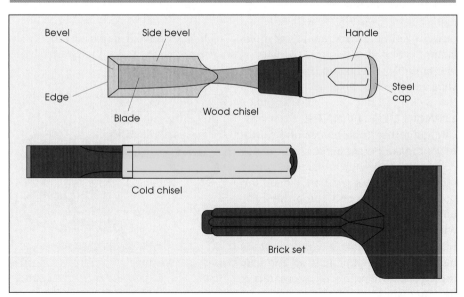

Bevel
Side bevel
Handle
Edge
Blade
Wood chisel
Steel cap

Cold chisel

Brick set

USE THE PROPER CHISEL for the material to be cut. You will need wood chisels for a great variety of jobs. Use a cold chisel only for cutting metal, where a hacksaw is insufficient. A brick set is only one kind of masonry chisel, but it is useful for many masonry projects.

shave away the waste and leave flat-sides. Scrape the bottom flat with a narrow chisel.

WOOD CHISEL SAFETY

Always keep both hands behind the cutting edge of a chisel and work it away from your body. Because operating a chisel requires two hands, secure the material you are cutting with clamps or in a vise. If you use a hammer with the chisel, wear safety goggles.

To avoid nicking the edge, never use a chisel as a screwdriver, pry bar, or anything else but a precision cutting tool. Guard the cutting edge whenever you put a chisel down, and store chisels in a rack or slotted container so the edges cannot hit each other or other tools.

Keep your chisels sharp. A dull edge not only does poor work, it will also soon need regrinding, and above all it is unsafe. Hone a chisel periodically as you work. For sharpening procedures, see the box on page 24.

COLD CHISELS

A cold chisel resembles a wood chisel, but it is thicker, with an octagonal shank that also serves as the handle. Cold chisels are available in widths from ¼ to 1 inch; some have vinyl grips to absorb shock. For around-the-house jobs such as cutting off rivets and rusted bolts, a single flat-edge cold chisel ½ inch or more wide will be sufficient.

Wear work gloves and safety goggles for protection against sparks and chips of material when using a cold chisel. Hold the chisel at a 45-degree angle to the work and strike it with a ball peen or a machinist's hammer, which have specially tempered heads. Never use an ordinary nailing hammer; its head can chip.

You can sharpen a cold chisel with a metal file, or more effectively with a power grinder. Keep a can of water at hand and cool the edge frequently when grinding, to avoid removing the temper. If the striking end of a chisel has become chipped or the edges have mushroomed out, it will be unsafe: a hammer blow can glance off, and chips of metal can fly off easily. Discard the chisel and get another; it is not an expensive item.

HOW TO CHISEL A MORTISE

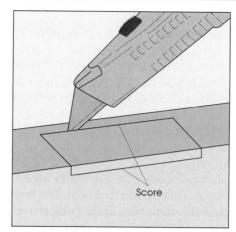

1. SCORE ALONG THE GRAIN with a knife to a depth of about ⅛ inch, to prevent splitting when you chisel.

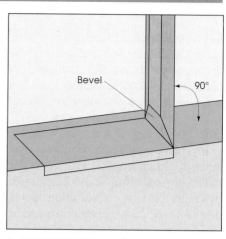

2. CUT THE ENDS of a mortise with the chisel positioned as shown. Tap lightly with a hammer or your hand.

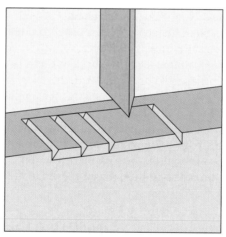

3. CUT NOTCHES about ⅛ inch apart across the grain with the chisel held vertically. Do not cut full depth.

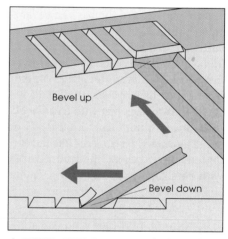

4. PARE OUT WASTE with short, light hand strokes—bevel up across the grain, down with the grain. Do not use a hammer.

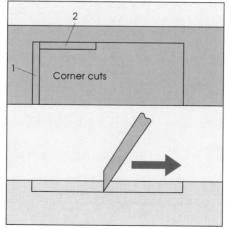

5. SQUARE THE CORNERS AND EDGES with careful downward strokes. Scrape the bottom to the final depth.

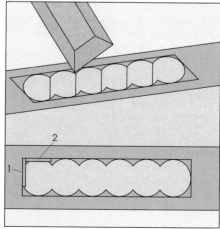

BORE HOLES for a deep mortise, cut corners, then shave the sides with the chisel edge at an angle.

PLANES

Use a plane to shave stock down to size, square and smooth its edges, or angle the edges with bevels and chamfers.

Planes are 6 to 22 inches long. For home use, buy a 9¼- or 9¾-inch-long *smooth plane*. Later, get a small *block plane* for cutting end grain and fine work.

In a plane a *cutter* blade protrudes at an angle through a slot or *mouth* in the machined, cast-iron *base*. The cutter is mounted with its bevel edge facing down. As the cutter peels off shavings, an arched *cap iron* on top of the cutter causes them to curl out of the way.

SMOOTH PLANE CONSTRUCTION

The smooth plane is a complex tool. A *knob* at the front of the base and a *handle* at the rear let you guide the plane with both hands and modulate pressure at the *toe* and *heel* of the base, or *sole*.

Near the center of the plane, the cutter and cap iron are secured to an angled *frog* by a *lever cap* with a *cam lock*. A *cutter adjust nut* changes the depth of the cut. A *lateral adjust lever* tilts the cutter to change the alignment of the edge with the sole.

ADJUSTING A SMOOTH PLANE

Deep cuts remove material fast; shallow cuts are slower and smoother. To adjust the cut, lift the cam and remove the lever cap. Lift the cap iron–cutter assembly off the frog. Loosen the screw holding the cap iron to the cutter. For coarse work set the cap iron about ⅟₁₆ inch back from the cutter edge. For finish planing, set it almost flush with the cutter edge. Tighten the screw and replace the assembly and the lever cap on the frog, but do not lock the cam yet.

Turn the plane upside down and sight along the sole from the toe. Turn the cutter adjust nut to bring the cutter edge to about a fingernail's thickness above the sole. Now snap the cam closed.

Finally, sight along the base from the toe again and use the lateral adjust lever to set the angle of the edge. For even cutting it should be parallel with the sole.

PLANING EDGES

Lock the work in a vise or clamp it with the edge to be planed facing up, about waist high. Always plane in the direction of the grain so the cutting edge will not snag grain ends. Rest the toe of the plane on the work and push the plane forward, with light pressure on the knob. When the base is completely on the work, apply equal pressure on the knob and handle to keep the sole flat on the surface. At the end of the pass, as the toe leaves the work, bear down lightly on the handle so the plane will not tip down and round the corner. Hold the plane at a slight angle across the work for easier, smoother cutting.

BLOCK PLANE CONSTRUCTION

A block plane is essentially a small smooth plane, but the cutter is inclined at a shallower angle, about 20 degrees, with the bevel facing up.

The block plane is excellent for smoothing end grain, trimming paneling and thin materials, fitting moldings, and working in tight spots.

PLANING END GRAIN

You can smooth end grain with a smooth plane, but a block plane, set for a fine cut, is less cumbersome. To avoid splitting, always plane from the corners toward the center—or clamp the work between two pieces of scrap and edge-plane across all three.

BEVELING AND CHAMFERING

A *bevel* is an edge angled across its entire thickness. A *chamfer* is an angle cut along just one corner of the edge. Use a combination square or bevel (see pages 14–15) to mark the desired angle on both ends of the piece, and draw lines along the length with a depth gauge. Hold a block plane at the desired angle and make repeated passes to plane down to these lines.

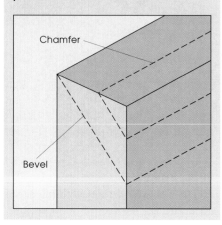

SHARPENING PLANE IRONS AND CHISELS

When a plane no longer shaves off continuous ribbons or a chisel splits wood instead of slicing through it, you need to touch up its edge on a whetstone or regrind the bevel and then hone it on the stone.

Check the edge carefully. If it is badly nicked or rounded, or not square across the width of the blade, it needs regrinding. A plane iron or chisel edge that is dull reflects light. A sharp edge does not.

Restore a dull edge by whetting it on a sharpening stone. Moisten the stone's surface with a few drops of sharpening oil, lay the blade's bevel against the stone, and move it back and forth. Bear down with both hands, exerting pressure only on the forward stroke. When the bevel is perfectly flat, lift it about 5 degrees from the surface of the stone and pull it across the stone once or twice.

You will know a blade is sharp when you can see or feel a slight burr along the flat, back side of the edge. Remove the burr by laying the back of the blade flat on the stone and stroking it a few times in a circular motion.

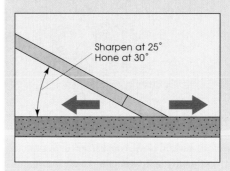

Sharpen at 25°
Hone at 30°

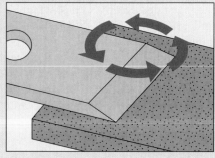

PLANE ACTION AND USE

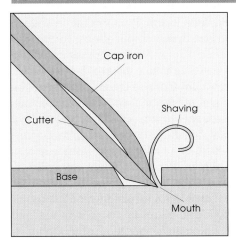

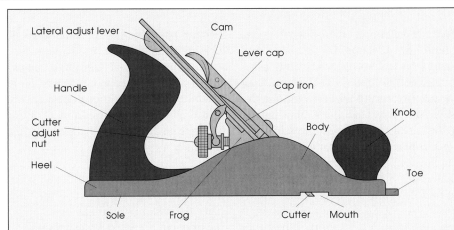

A PLANE CUTS by pushing the cutter edge into wood. Shavings enter the mouth and are curled by the cap iron.

A SMOOTH PLANE has a lever and cam mechanism that clamps the cap iron–cutter assembly against an angled frog. An adjusting nut sets the depth of the cut; a lateral adjust lever changes the angle of the blade to the sole.

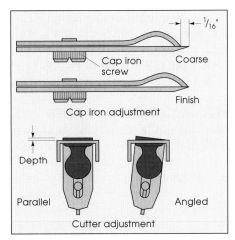

TO ADJUST A PLANE, set the cap iron position, then sight along the base to make cutter depth and angle adjustments.

START PLANING STROKES by pressing down on the front knob. During the stroke, apply even pressure front and back. At the end, press only on the back handle. Keep the plane angled slightly for easier cutting.

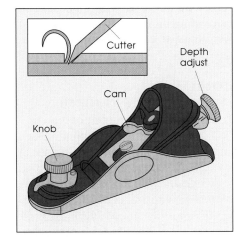

A BLOCK PLANE is only 6 or 7 inches long. The cutter is mounted at a shallow angle with the bevel facing up.

PLANE END GRAIN from the edges toward the center *(left)* to avoid splintering the edges. Or clamp scrap pieces to the edges *(right)* and plane across all three in the direction that resists the cutting action least.

SURFACE-FORMING TOOLS

Surface-forming, or Surform® tools, plane, shave, shape, file, smooth, and sand wood, plywood, soft metals, plastic, and other materials. The blade of a surface-forming tool has a unique design, much like that of a kitchen grater. It has hundreds of sharp teeth interspersed with holes through which shavings can pass. The holes enable surface-forming tools to shape and smooth better than traditional files and rasps, which clog and need to be cleared periodically. The blades mount on various lightweight metal bodies. In most of the tools the blades can be changed quickly and easily.

TYPES OF SURFACE-FORMING TOOLS

Surface-forming tools come in shapes to suit many applications. There are three *planes*. A full-size plane, having handles at both ends, combines the cutting action of a rasp with the control of a smooth plane. Use it for big shaping and smoothing jobs. A combination *file/plane* has a two-position rear handle that can be adjusted for either use. A short *pocket plane* fits in the palm of one hand for close work, trimming rough edges, and planing end grain (see page 25).

Two single-handled surface-forming files can replace a whole set of conventional wood rasps and files: a *flat file* and a *round file,* which can be used to rough out and smooth holes and other curves. A surface-forming *Shaver™* can get into curves and tight spots. The shaver tool cuts on pull strokes; all the other types of surface-forming tools cut on push strokes.

SURFACE-FORMING BLADES

Inexpensive surface-forming blades do not require sharpening. When one dulls, you can easily replace it with a new one. Blades for fine and regular (medium) cuts are available for the full-size plane, file/plane, and flat file. The regular-cut blades come in both flat and half-round versions for greater versatility. The flat version has a reverse tooth along one edge for working in inside corners. These tools and the pocket plane also accept sander blades that can be used in place of medium (80 grit) or coarse (46 grit) abrasive papers. The round file and Shaver™ take regular-cut blades.

USING SURFACE-FORMING TOOLS

To remove a large amount of material, fit the tool with a medium-cut blade and push or pull it along the surface at a 45-degree left angle to the grain, as shown at the left. Reduce the angle to remove less and leave a smoother surface. For further smoothing, switch to a fine-cut blade and direct it parallel to the grain. Using the fine-cut blade at a slight angle to the right produces almost a polishing action.

SELECTING AND USING SURFACE-FORMING TOOLS

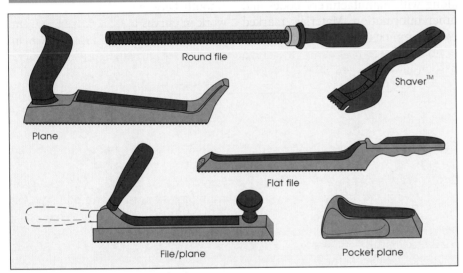

SURFACE-FORMING TOOLS are diverse and versatile. They produce different degrees of cutting, filing, and sanding action, depending on the blade used and its angle to the work (see below). Blades are replaceable.

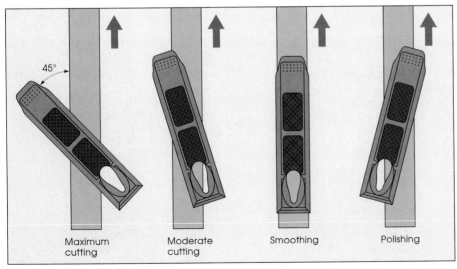

THE DEGREE OF CUTTING ACTION can be controlled by adjusting the angle of the tool to the axis of the work. Use only a fine-cut blade for fine smoothing and polishing, and with hardwood, end grain, plywood, chipboard, and drywall.

ABRASIVES

Abrasives—coated sheet materials, steel wool, and powders—can be used for rough cleaning and shaping, to remove tool marks, and to bring a project to a final state of smoothness.

COATED ABRASIVES
Sheet materials, commonly called sandpaper, are properly termed *coated abrasives*. They consist of a coating of abrasive particles—*grit*—bonded onto a backing of paper, cloth, fiber, or cloth laminated to paper or fiber. Coated abrasives typically come in 9 × 11-inch sheets that can be cut to size, in precut smaller sheet sizes, and in disks and belts for power sanders (see Chapter 2).

GRIT GRADES AND COATINGS
Abrasive grits are graded by particle size; the higher the grit number, the finer the particles. Grade categories and typical uses are:

Very coarse, 12–30 grit: very rough work such as removing thick coats of paint or other finishes.

Coarse, 36–50 grit: shaping and smoothing major imperfections in rough wood, removing rust from metal.

Medium, 60–100 grit: general wood smoothing and some finishing.

Fine, 120–180 grit: final finishing of bare wood.

Very fine, 220–600 grit: smoothing, polishing finish coats on wood and metal.

Open-coat abrasives have their grit particles spaced farther apart than *closed-coat* materials, which cut more quickly and produce a finer finish, but tend to clog more rapidly. Use open-coat abrasives for rough sanding or removing old paint and other finishing materials. Use the closed-coat type for final finish work.

The grit type, grade, and coating are marked on the back of coated abrasives, along with manufacturers' codes and other information. Materials marked *wet or dry* can be used on a surface moistened with water or oil, which keeps dust down, prevents scratching on smooth surfaces such as metal, and enhances the polishing action of the fine-grit grades.

GRIT MATERIALS
Abrasive paper grits have different cutting qualities.

Flint, yellow-tan in color, now seldom used, is the least expensive but cuts slowly, clogs easily, and dulls rapidly. It is suitable only for light-duty sanding.

Garnet, red-tan, is moderate in cost, harder and sharper than flint, and longer wearing. It does an adequate sanding job on hard and soft woods.

Emery is black and is commonly bonded to a cloth backing. Emery cloth is moderately priced and works best for removing rust and for polishing metals.

Aluminum oxide, brownish in color, does excellent sanding on most materials. It is more expensive than garnet but is more versatile and durable, and therefore a better buy in the long run.

Silicon carbide, bluish or greenish black, is the hardest and most costly grit. It can cut almost all materials, including glass and cast iron. It is a good choice for wet sanding and final finish work.

STEEL WOOL
Use steel wool to remove rust from metal, dull a surface prior to painting, smooth between finish coats, and to work in curves and carvings too tight for paper abrasives. Steel wool comes in seven numbered grades: 4/0 (0000), extremely fine; 3/0 (000), extra fine; 2/0 (00), very fine; 0, fine; 1, medium; 2, medium coarse; and 3, coarse. It can be used dry or with a solvent, but never without gloves.

ABRASIVE POWDERS
Pumice, rottenstone, and *emery* powders are most often used with oil or water and a soft pad to polish a finished surface (see Chapter 7).

> **CAUTION**
> Sanding produces dust that can be irritating or harmful to your eyes and lungs. Wear goggles, a face mask, and long sleeves when using abrasives. Gloves are a wise precaution and are essential when using steel wool.

Garnet   **100**
Paper   C wt.
Open Coat   **100**
_____
WARNING: WEAR EYE, FACE
     AND BODY PROTECTION

THE BACK OF ABRASIVE PAPER lists grit type, grade, paper weight, and other information. Obey the safety warning.

SANDING TIPS
Except for the roughest cleaning or shaping, always sand in the direction of the grain. For equal pressure on flat surfaces, clamp abrasive paper in an inexpensive sandpaper holder made of rubber, plastic, or metal, or wrap it around a scrap of wood. To avoid snags and tearing, sand against a wrapped edge of the block, not an exposed edge of the paper.

To sand round surfaces, tear a cloth-backed abrasive into strips and use it like a shoeshine cloth. Smooth the inside edges of a hole by wrapping abrasive paper around a dowel or your finger.

For some hand-sanding techniques, see page 92. To learn about power sanding, see pages 46 and 47.

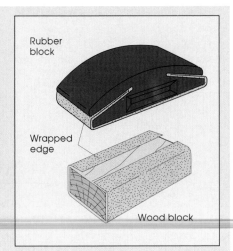

Rubber block

Wrapped edge

Wood block

STRIKING TOOLS

STRIKING AND PRYING TOOLS

Once the pieces of a project have been measured and cut, it is time to assemble them, a job often accomplished with a hammer or other striking tool. Hammers can also be used like prying tools (pages 30–31) to pull things apart.

HAMMER CONSTRUCTION

The everyday hammer is in reality a precision instrument. Good quality hammers have a *head* of fine-grain, high-carbon steel that has been heat treated for extra strength and hardness. The striking *face* is often tempered for additional hardness. *Chamfered edges* minimize the chance of chipping. A slightly rounded *bell face* is the best choice for general use. A flatter *plain face* provides greater control for driving nails at an angle, but less for straight-in nailing. A *checkered face* has a cross-hatched surface that will not slip on nail heads. All three types can be used for framing work.

At the other end of the head, a nail hammer has a *claw* with a sharp V notch that grips nails as you pull them loose. The common *curved claw* offers the best nail-pulling leverage. A *ripping claw* is straighter, for efficiency in prying boards apart as well as pulling nails. Nail-pulling techniques are described on page 30.

A hammer's *handle* provides leverage for swinging the head and pulling nails, and it absorbs shock from the impact when the head hits. Traditional *wood* handles, usually made of hickory, are tough, resilient, and very durable if given proper care. Buy only a first quality wood-handled hammer. A poorly made hammer can snap when you are pulling a nail or lose its head when you are swinging it.

A tubular or solid *steel* handle is mechanically locked into the head, so it cannot fly off. The stress of pulling nails or prying cannot break a steel handle, but steel has no shock-absorbing resiliency. So be sure a steel handle has a cushioned vinyl handgrip for comfort and safety.

Graphite handles have the strength of steel and the resiliency of hickory. Continuous fiberglass filaments, reinforced with graphite, are bonded with polyester resin for maximum shock absorption and durability. A vinyl grip further cushions blows. *Jacketed* graphite or fiberglass hammers offer superior overstrike protection over continuous fiberglass filament handles. A polycarbonate alloy jacket is molded over a solid fiberglass core rod. A mechanical wedge molded in the top of the handle, coupled with epoxy, provides a permanent head-and-handle assembly.

HAMMER BASICS

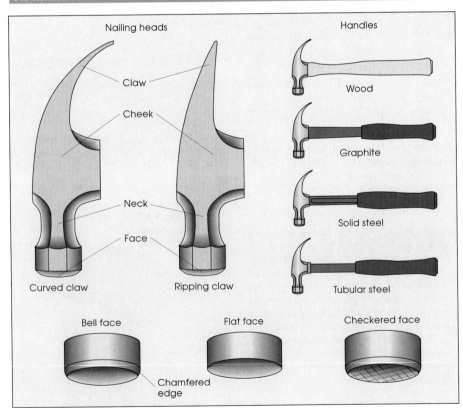

A NAILING HAMMER has a steel head with a curved or a ripping claw. A slightly rounded bell face is the most versatile. The type of handle is largely a matter of personal preference. A cushioned grip is essential on a nonwood handle.

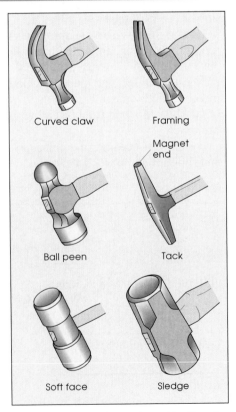

HAMMER TYPES match a wide diversity of applications. These are the most useful for home projects.

SELECTING HAMMERS

When you are evaluating any hammer, look for precision machining and workmanship. The claws on quality hammers have sharp, beveled edges so they can grip the head of a nail that is almost flush with the surface. The face should be well chamfered around the circumference. Avoid cheap, cast steel hammers, which can chip or snap in use. A cast hammer head is usually painted, has a rough texture, and a mold-line ridge in the middle.

Curved claw hammers drive and pull ordinary nails. Their heads weigh from 13 to 20 ounces. Include a 16-ounce curved claw hammer among your very first tool purchases. Later you might want to add a 13-ounce hammer for driving small nails and a heavier one for framing work. Do not use a claw hammer to strike masonry nails, cold chisels, or other metal; there is a danger of chipping. *Framing hammers* typically have 22-ounce heads with ripping claws and plain or checkered faces.

Ball peen hammers are used for striking cold chisels, punches, rivets, and other metallic items. Instead of a claw, the head has a rounded *peen* that you use to spread open a rivet. Do not drive nails with a ball peen hammer because its curved face will slip off the nail head. Ball peen hammer heads weigh from 4 to 48 ounces. A 16-ounce head is best for household projects.

Tack hammers typically have 5-ounce heads. A magnet at one end of the head holds tacks so that you can start and drive them with one hand while the other hand pulls upholstery or other material taut.

Soft-face hammers include wood and rubber mallets and the *dead-blow hammer* shown in the box on page 31. These tools have either permanently fixed or screw-on plastic faces that can be replaced when they become worn. You should use a soft-face hammer for knocking together tight wood joints and in any other situation where a steel hammer would mar the surface. (Otherwise, hit against a piece of scrap wood.)
Continued

DRIVING NAILS

Hitting nails squarely on the head is a very satisfying experience, once you get the hang of it. Here are the fundamentals.

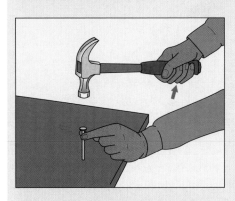

GET A GOOD GRIP. Hold the hammer firmly but comfortably at the end of the handle. Hold the nail near the head with the thumb and forefinger of the other hand. This way, if your aim is off, you will knock your fingers aside, instead of crushing them against the surface.

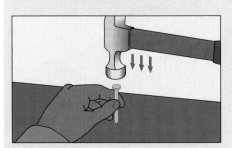

START THE NAIL. Use wrist motions to gently tap the nail head, taking pains to keep the nail perpendicular to the surface.

SWING THE HAMMER. After the nail is standing on its own, remove the fingers that were holding it, tap the nail once more to adjust your aim, then lift the hammer and let it descend in a smooth arc. Use your wrist and elbow as fulcrums, so that the hammer's weight and momentum do the work, not your muscles. If the hammer face does not hit the nail head squarely and solidly, it will likely skid off and bend the nail. To minimize bent nails, keep your eye on the nail, not the hammer.

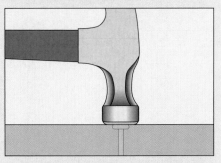

DRIVE THE HEAD FLUSH. In rough work, the final blow should make a dent that puts the nail head even with or just below the surface. In fine work, use a nail set, as shown on page 31.

HAMMER SAFETY

Hammering is high-force, high-velocity action. Protect yourself and bystanders in the following ways.

WEAR SAFETY GOGGLES when working with any striking tool. Chipping can cause an eye injury or permanent loss of sight.

HAMMER ONLY WITH THE FACE, never with the cheek of the hammer head, which is the weakest part.

NEVER STRIKE HARD METAL, such as a cold chisel, masonry nail, or another hammer head, with a nail hammer.

CLEAN THE FACE with steel wool periodically. Grease and dirt can cause the hammer to skid and bend the nail.

INSPECT THE HANDLE before use. If a wood handle is cracked or splitting, replace it. Similarly, if a fiberglass/graphite handle has been overstruck and has started cracking or splintering, replace it. Do not touch the splinters. They are sharp and cannot be easily seen to remove.

REPLACE ANY HAMMER if its striking face or bevel shows dents, chips, mushrooming or is excessively worn, if the claws show indentations or nicks inside the nail slot, or if the claw is broken.

USE A LARGE ENOUGH BALL PEEN HAMMER to strike another tool such as a chisel or punch safely. The hammer face should be at least 3/8 inch greater in diameter than the end of the tool being struck.

STRIKING AND PRYING TOOLS *Continued*

Sledgehammers drive cold chisels, masonry nails, stakes, and other items that require brute-force hammering. Sledgehammers range in weight from 3 to 20 pounds. Use a 3-pound "baby sledge" for driving jobs. If you will be breaking up concrete or doing other heavy masonry work you may also need a 10- to 20-pound sledgehammer.

PRYING AND PULLING TOOLS

A claw hammer combines striking and prying functions in a single tool. Tack claws, pry bars, and ripping bars are designed specifically for prying tasks, from pulling small nails to disassembling framing and demolishing walls. Center punches and nail sets are struck tools that extend a hammer's usefulness.

PULLING NAILS

A curved or ripping claw hammer can make short work of removing most nails. First, work the claw's edges under the nail head, lever up slightly to gain some space, and slide the head forward until the nail is gripped deep in the claw's V notch. Next, pull back on the handle until it is at a 90-degree angle to the surface. Slip a putty knife under the hammer head if you want to protect the surface. Do not try to pull beyond 90 degrees. That will bend the nail and place greater strain on the handle. Instead, slide a piece of scrap wood under the hammer head to raise it for greater leverage, then pry the nail up and out.

PULLING TACKS

A *tack claw* resembles a screwdriver, but it has a beveled and slightly curved notch at the end. Use it to remove tacks, brads, and nails that are too small for a claw hammer. You can also remove brads with long-nose pliers, as illustrated.

USING A PRY BAR

A flat steel *pry bar*, or Wonder Bar®, has many uses around the home. The beveled claws at each end are thinner than a hammer's claw, so you can slip or drive them where a hammer won't fit. A large bar can handle full-size nails and

HOW TO USE STRIKING AND PRYING TOOLS

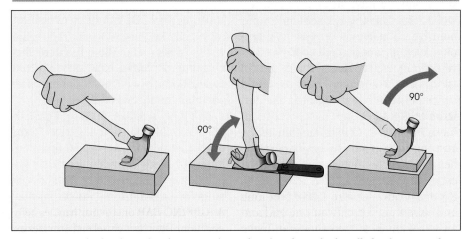

PULL A NAIL by hooking the claw onto the nail and rocking the handle back, perpendicular to the surface *(left)*. Protect the surface with a putty knife (center); use a scrap of wood for leverage to pull long nails *(right)*.

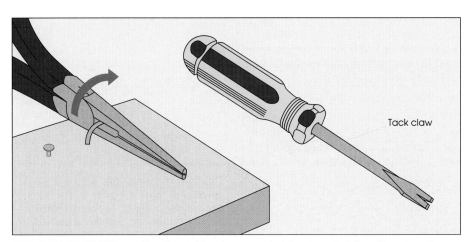

USE A TACK CLAW to pull tacks and brads, or to raise them enough for a hammer claw or long-nose pliers to get a grip. With pliers, pry the head up enough to grip it with the wire-cutting jaws, then roll them to one side.

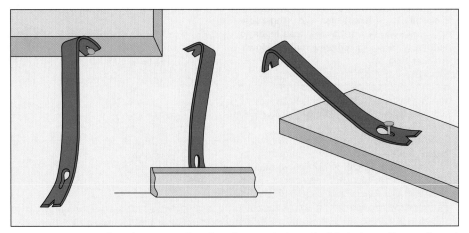

A FLAT PRY BAR has claws at each end and an eye hole in the blade for pulling nails and prying boards apart or removing molding and trim. A small-size bar is useful with brads, tacks, and delicate pieces of trim.

boards; a smaller size is appropriate for small nails, brads, tacks, and delicate wood trim. Use the hooked end or the hole in the blade to pull nails. To gently pry molding, paneling, or other materials you do not want to damage, slip the flat end in behind the work.

RIPPING BARS

Use a *ripping bar* (a *wrecking bar, crowbar,* or *pinch bar*) to pull large spikes, do heavy demolition work and, with a fulcrum underneath, to lift heavy objects. Ripping bars measure 1 to 3 feet long and have a curved claw at one end and an offset chisel at the other end. Use a ripping bar for prying and wrecking jobs where some damage is tolerable.

USING CENTER PUNCHES AND NAIL SETS

Center punches and *nail sets* resemble each other but perform different functions. Use a center punch's pointed end to mark and start holes in metal or wood. Nail sets have flat or cupped ends. Use them to drive the heads of finishing, casing, or flooring nails below the surface. Do not use a nail set as a punch or vice versa. Discard either if it is bent, cracked, or has a mushrooming head. Self-centering punches and nail sets have a hammer-driven shaft in an outer sleeve with a nose that fits into a hardware screw hole or over the head of a nail.

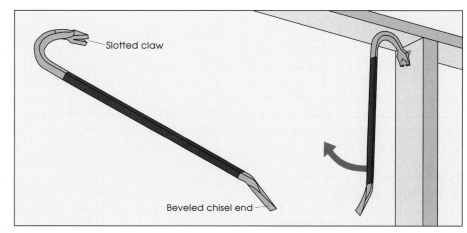

A RIPPING BAR or crowbar handles hefty prying and demolition jobs, such as removing a partition. The offset chisel end provides excellent leverage for prying. The claw is designed for removing substantial nails.

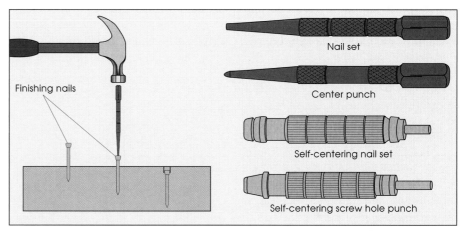

COUNTERSINK NAILS with a nail set. *Left:* Place the tip of the set on the nail head and drive it about ⅛ inch beneath the surface. *Right:* Center punches look like nail sets but have pointed ends for marking pilot holes.

DEAD-BLOW HAMMERS

One of the biggest problems with using a conventional hammer is that the head tends to bounce back, dissipating much of the blow's force. A *dead-blow hammer* has a hollow head loaded with shot that rebounds inside to absorb the recoil and help the head hit with more working force. It is especially useful in striking other tools, such as a cold chisel, with maximum effect.

Dead-blow ball peen hammers have steel heads; soft-face and sledge dead-blow hammer heads are made of hot-cast urethane. They all have metal rod handles encased in cast urethane. The urethane does not mar surfaces and reduces the noise of hammering.

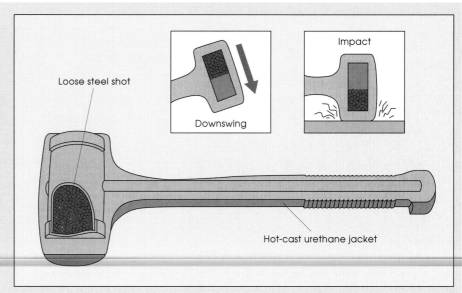

SCREWDRIVERS

Nails do a good fastening job in rough construction and some finish work, but many situations call for the superior holding power of wood screws. To properly install screws you must choose a matched screwdriver and use it effectively. If you prepare a suitable pilot hole for the screw, a hand screwdriver requires little more effort than a power driver and offers far more control.

SCREWDRIVER CONSTRUCTION

A screwdriver is a simple tool; it has a *handle* and a *blade*. The blade *tip* is shaped to fit into the head of a screw. Where the blade *shank* enters the handle, the best quality screwdrivers have a *bolster* for increased strength. It or the shank may have flat surfaces so you can use a wrench when you need extra turning power.

The most widely used screws have either a straight slot in the head or two crossed slots, called a Phillips head. Each requires a screwdriver with a tip of matching design. There are two tip shapes for straight-slotted screws. The *keystone* or *standard shank tip* flares slightly with *shoulders* above the tip for extra strength. It works well for driving or removing screws with heads that are flush with the surface.

The tip of a screwdriver with a *cabinet blade*, also called a parallel blade, narrow blade, or electrician's screwdriver, is no wider than the shank, so it can drive or remove screws recessed beneath the surface without damaging the hole.

A *Phillips head screwdriver* has a four-point tip that fits into the crossed slots in a Phillips head screw. Phillips head screws work especially well with electric or ratchet-driven screwdrivers. There are also several other tip shapes to fit the heads of specialty screws.

Today, most screwdriver handles are made of tough plastic. Some have a rubber grip that provides an extra-firm grasp. Handle shapes and grip designs differ somewhat. Choose whatever feels most comfortable to you.

SELECTING SCREWDRIVERS

Screwdrivers range widely in price and quality. You should definitely buy models that are at or near the top of the line.

SCREWDRIVER FEATURES AND TYPES

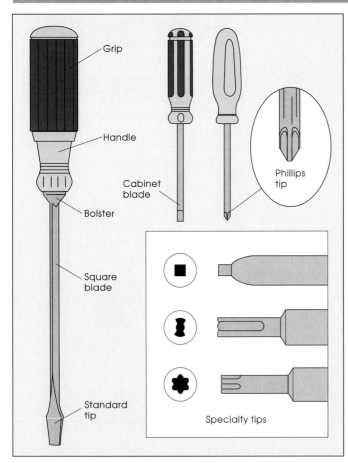

MOST SCREWDRIVERS have the same basic construction but can differ in handle shape, bolster, shank, and tip. All come in various blade lengths and tip sizes.

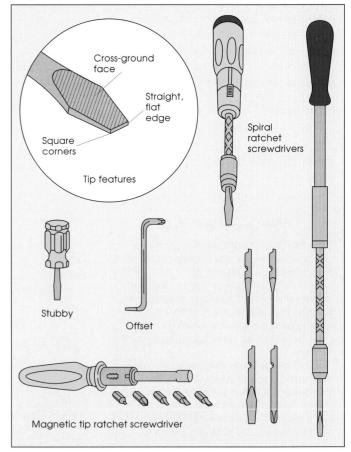

ADD TO A BASIC SET OF SCREWDRIVERS with some of these specialty versions. Tip quality is very important in all types. Choose a quick-return spiral ratchet driver for fastest, easiest operation.

Cheap screwdrivers are no bargain. They can damage the screw heads and will not last long. When choosing a screwdriver, inspect the tip. A tip for slotted screws should have a flat edge across both its thickness and width, have square corners, and be cross-ground (look for grinding traces on the face of the tip). These features will provide a secure fit and long working life.

You'll need a small assortment of screwdriver sizes and types. Many manufacturers offer them in sets.

Start with standard screwdrivers with 4- and 6-inch blades, cabinet screwdrivers with 3- and 6-inch blades, and two sizes of Phillips screwdrivers, 1-point and 2-point. Later, to work in tight spots you may want to add a pair of 1½-inch *stubby screwdrivers,* one with a standard tip and one with a Phillips tip. Or add an *offset screwdriver* with one standard and one Phillips tip. It will fit into even tighter locations and will provide up to ten times the turning power of an ordinary screwdriver.

If a project calls for driving a lot of screws, consider a *ratchet screwdriver* with magnetically held snap-in tips. Or choose a *spiral ratchet driver* with interchangeable tips, also known as a Yankee® screwdriver. As with a spiral-ratchet push drill (see page 20), a single stroke of the handle turns the tip 2½ times; releasing the pressure lets the handle return to position for the next stroke.

DRIVING SCREWS

Be sure the screwdriver tip fits the screw head perfectly. A tip that is too wide will scar the wood around the head and could easily slip off and gouge the wood. A tip that is too small could chew up the slot so badly that you might have difficulty removing the screw.

Hold a screwdriver handle firmly butted into the palm of your hand, with thumb and index finger pointed toward the shank. Use the other hand to grasp the shank and steady the tip in the slot. If you encounter strong resistance, slightly enlarge the pilot hole or coat the screw threads with paraffin. Do not use soap; it attracts moisture, which can cause rusting or staining.

DRIVING SCREWS

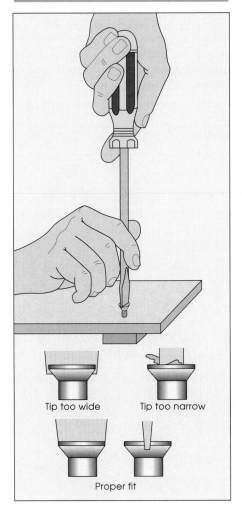

Tip too wide   Tip too narrow

Proper fit

DRIVE A SCREW by holding the screwdriver as shown. Be sure the tip fits the head properly, to avoid damage.

PILOT HOLES

Before driving any but very small screws into soft wood, bore a *pilot hole.* Otherwise, the wood could split or the screw be nearly impossible to turn. For screws such as pan head screws that are the same diameter from tip to head, drill a hole slightly smaller in diameter and slightly shorter than the screw. Other screws need holes that are sized for the shank and the threads, and that may also be *countersunk* or *counterbored* for the screw head—a total of three different diameters.

Rather than using two or three drill bits to make a pilot hole (see page 71), use a combination *drill and countersink.* It is shaped to bore the three different diameters in one operation and has a fixed or adjustable stop collar so the hole will be just the right depth. You can drill deep enough to countersink the screw head or not, as you choose.

A similar device, a *combination counterbore* bit, makes a hole that will recess the screw head completely below the surface. The screw head can be concealed with a plug cut from a matching piece of wood or from a dowel of matching diameter.

You can buy drill-countersink and counterbore bits individually or in sets to match popular screw sizes.

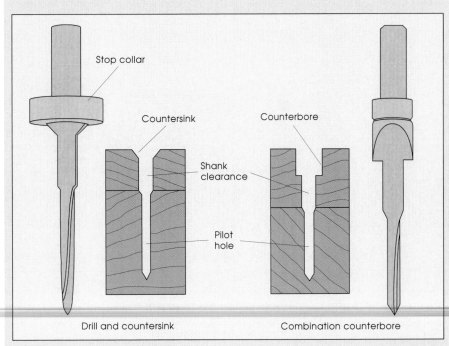

Stop collar

Countersink   Counterbore

Shank clearance

Pilot hole

Drill and countersink   Combination counterbore

PLIERS

When you need to get a good grip on something, pull a nail in close quarters, bend or snip a wire, or do any of a multitude of other around-the-home tasks, a pair of pliers is the tool you will reach for.

PLIERS CONSTRUCTION

Different types of pliers perform different jobs, but all have handles that operate scissors-fashion to open and close a pair of jaws that grip the work. *Slip-joint pliers*, the most common and versatile type, allow the jaws to be adjusted between two positions or widths of maximum opening. The jaws have fine serrations milled at the ends for gripping small objects. Coarser teeth toward the center grasp bigger work. Slipping the jaws to the wide opening position provides even more capacity.

Vinyl grips bonded to the handles of many pliers improve comfort and, if colored, make them easier to spot among an array of materials and other tools. However, the grips do not protect against electrical shock.

SELECTING PLIERS

A pair of slip-joint pliers is an indispensable tool for any do-it-yourselfer. Next most handy, for reaching into tight spots and holding, bending, or cutting wire, are *long-nose pliers*. These have slender, tapered jaws with fine serrations along part of their length. Sharp cutting edges just ahead of the pivot joint can snip through most wire. *Diagonal-cutting pliers*, which are sometimes called *side-cutting pliers*, cut wire and other thin metal items. Slip joint, long-nose, and diagonal-cutting pliers are often packaged in sets.

For bigger gripping jobs, use *groove-joint pliers*. These work like slip-joint pliers but are bigger, with angled jaws that adjust to several positions for several opening widths. Long handles provide increased leverage.

Locking pliers have either curved or straight serrated jaws. Other models have narrow or wide smooth, flat jaws to grip screening, canvas, polished metal, or other materials that might be marked by jaw teeth. You adjust the jaws to fit the work with a knurled screw at the end of one handle, then squeeze to lock the jaws in place. Flipping a lever on the tool's lower handle releases the jaws. Because they exert compound leverage, locking pliers are very powerful, and they can damage soft materials. The locking action means these pliers can be used for clamping as well as holding and turning.

There are several other types of pliers, such as needle-nose, bent-nose, linesman's or electrician's, and end nipper pliers. All are specialized tools. Along with some basic wrenches (next page) the five types of pliers discussed above and illustrated on this page will meet the needs of almost any household you will encounter. The only addition you might want to make is a pair of tweezers for handling tiny items.

SELECTING PLIERS

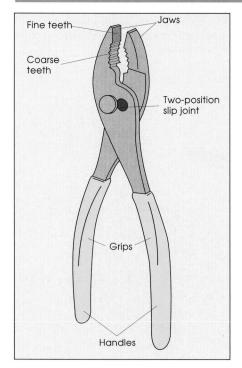

SLIP-JOINT PLIERS, the most common type, belong in every tool kit. Use them to grip small and medium-size objects.

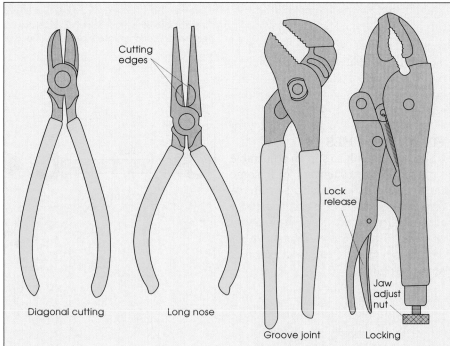

BASIC PLIERS, in addition to slip joint, include diagonal-cutting and long-nose types. To these add groove-joint pliers, for greater capacity and leverage, and locking pliers, for holding objects in a viselike grip.

WRENCHES

Wrenches are designed for turning square- or hex-headed screws and bolts, and nuts. Pliers can slip on these fasteners, and will almost certainly mar them. (Wrenches for plumbing projects are covered in Chapter 33.)

After inserting a bolt through a hole, you run a nut (usually with a washer) along the threads until both the bolt head and the nut/washer are against the work. You then use a wrench on the nut to apply twisting pressure called *torque* to tighten the fastener in place. (If the bolt enters a threaded hole, or you are using a bolt-headed screw, the wrench is used on the head of the fastener.) When removing a bolt or nut, you first apply pressure with a wrench to break the fastener loose, then run it from the threads. There are two basic types of wrenches, adjustable and fixed.

ADJUSTABLE WRENCHES

Make a pair of *adjustable wrenches* the first you own. An adjustable wrench has one fixed and one movable jaw that you tighten against the fastener with an *adjusting screw*. Adjustable wrenches come in lengths from 4 to 12 inches. With 6- and 8-inch sizes you can accomplish many light repair and adjustment projects. The advantage to having two wrenches is that you can hold a bolt head with one while turning the nut with the other.

FIXED WRENCHES

It is often difficult to slip an adjustable wrench into tight quarters, or in some cases to keep the jaws engaged with the fastener. For heavy torquing and easier accessibility, invest in some *fixed-jaw wrenches*. They are sized to match standard nuts and bolt heads and are commonly sold in sets.

WRENCH SAFETY

Never use a wrench as a hammer or strike one with a hammer, and do not slip a piece of pipe over a wrench handle for more leverage. Whenever possible, pull, don't push a wrench handle.

Open-end wrenches have different size C-shaped jaws on either end. They are very useful when you can get at a fastener only from the side. *Box wrenches* have closed ends of different sizes that fit over hex-shaped fasteners. Up to a dozen ridges or serrations, called *points*, on the inside surface grip the fastener all around so the wrench cannot slip. *Combination wrenches* have open jaws on one end and box jaws on the other, both the same size.

Although commonly considered an automotive tool, a set of *socket wrenches* has many household uses as well. The twelve-point sockets grip hex heads in the same way a box wrench does. They can be fitted with a variety of extensions and handles for use in almost any access situation.

Allen wrenches are used to tighten setscrews—small headless machine screws with a hex recess in one end that the wrench fits into. *Nut drivers* are like screwdrivers with hex or square sockets at the ends. There are sizes to fit fastener heads and nuts up to ½ inch across.

SELECTING WRENCHES

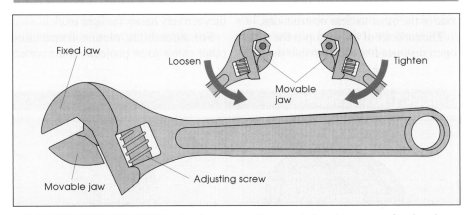

AN ADJUSTABLE WRENCH grips fasteners with smooth-faced jaws, one fixed and one movable. To avoid slipping, fit the wrench on the fastener so the direction of turning is toward the movable jaw.

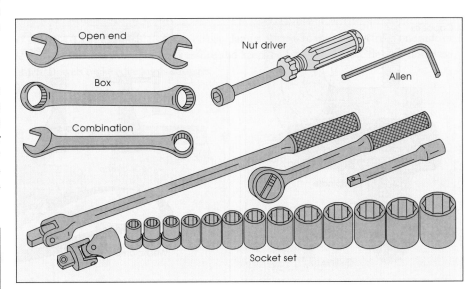

FIXED-JAW WRENCHES grip more securely than adjustable types. They come in individual sizes or in sets to fit standard nuts and bolt heads. Allen wrenches fit into recesses in the heads of setscrews. Socket wrenches have great versatility for use with hex-head fasteners.

STAPLING AND RIVETING TOOLS

Round out your collection of hand tools with a couple of specialized fastening machines. *Staple guns* make short work of installing insulation, putting up ceiling tile, securing carpet padding or plastic sheeting, picture framing, and other projects that involve fastening a thin material to wood. *Riveters* install fasteners to join thin pieces of metal, fabric, leather, and plastic.

STAPLERS

Staple guns drive staples that are ¼ to ⁹⁄₁₆ inch long. A manual stapler, the most useful and affordable type for home use, has a powerful double-action spring drive that minimizes recoil. With better models you can adjust the power so you can staple soft materials without crushing them. An electric stapler requires less effort than manual models. A manual *stapling hammer* is ideal for fastening foil and paper-faced insulation, building paper, plastic sheeting, and felt underlayment for roofing.

RIVETERS

Riveting produces a strong, permanent, tamperproof joint quickly and easily. A riveter has a pair of plierlike handles and a *nosepiece* that grips the *mandrel* on a special *blind rivet*. Better riveters have interchangeable nosepieces for setting rivets with different diameters, and a movable head to get into hard-to-reach places.

Choose rivets according to the *grip range*, which is the total thickness of the materials being joined, and the type of materials you are joining. Use steel rivets for fastening steel to steel. Aluminum rivets are for aluminum and soft materials, or wherever rusting might pose a problem. Rivets are available in diameters from ⅛ to ³⁄₁₆ inch, and with grip ranges from ¹⁄₆₄ to ½ inch.

USING A RIVETER

To rivet two pieces together, first align them and drill a hole through them the same diameter as the rivet you will use. Insert the rivet's mandrel all the way in-

to the riveter nosepiece and squeeze the handles slightly to get a grip on the rivet. Next, insert the rivet in the hole until its flange rests against the surface of one piece. Now squeeze the handles firmly. This pulls the mandrel from the rivet and causes the rivet to pop open into a mushroomed head that locks the pieces together.

If the material on the head side of the rivet is soft, slip a backup washer over the nose of the rivet before popping it to its final shape. The washer will spread the gripping power of the rivet over a larger area of the soft material. Be sure to add the thickness of the washer when choosing the grip range.

STAPLERS AND RIVETERS

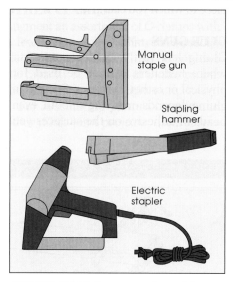

STAPLE TOOLS use a variety of heavy-duty staples. Some electric staplers can also drive brad nails.

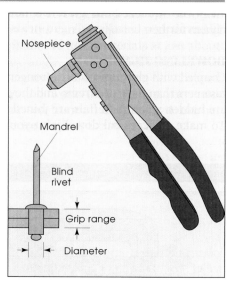

A RIVETER fastens thin materials with blind rivets. Rivets have various grip ranges and diameters.

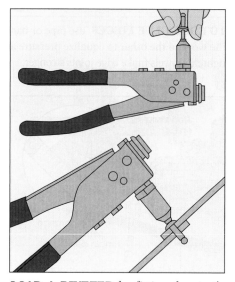

LOAD A RIVETER by fitting the rivet's mandrel into the nosepiece. Then insert the rivet in a predrilled hole.

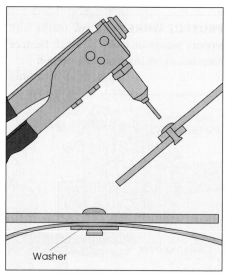

SQUEEZE THE HANDLES to pop the rivet head into a mushroom. Use a backup washer with soft material.

SOLDERING TOOLS

Solder, a metal alloy that can easily be heated to a liquid state, quickly and permanently joins wires, pipes, and metal components without drilling or fasteners. A *soldering iron, soldering gun, or propane torch* provides and directs the heat required for the job.

SELECTING SOLDERING TOOLS

Soldering irons and soldering guns use electricity to produce heat and are used mainly for making electrical and small mechanical connections. A gun heats up almost instantly when the trigger is pulled. A slower-heating iron offers greater control and can heat a somewhat larger area than a gun.

A propane torch is the tool to use for soldering pipes, sheet metal, and other large components. A torch consists of a burner and valve assembly that screws onto a replaceable canister charged with propane (or sometimes butane) gas. The intense heat of a propane flame, shaped by an accessory *spreader tip*, can also be used to soften putty and flooring adhesive, burn off paint, thaw a frozen pipe, and other applications. The easiest and safest way to light a torch is with an inexpensive *striker*, which has a flint that makes a spark when you squeeze the wire handles.

Various jobs call for different types of solder and *flux*, a paste that allows the solder to flow evenly. *Soft solder*, the type used for household work, once was mostly lead but now contains 95 percent tin and no lead. It commonly comes as a soft, silvery wire on a spool.

For electrical work, use *rosin-core solder*, which fluxes and solders in one operation. To join copper, brass, or bronze pipes you will need a container of rosin flux and a spool of *solid-core solder*. For galvanized steel use *acid flux* and solid-core solder. Solder is also available in bar form.

SOLDERING BASICS

To make a successful solder joint, first buff the metals shiny clean with emery cloth or steel wool. Apply a liberal amount of flux (if the solder does not contain flux), then heat the metal, not the solder. When the metal is hot enough, simply touch the solder to it. The solder will instantly melt, permeate the joint, and reharden as it cools. (Also see page 277.)

SELECTING AND USING SOLDERING TOOLS

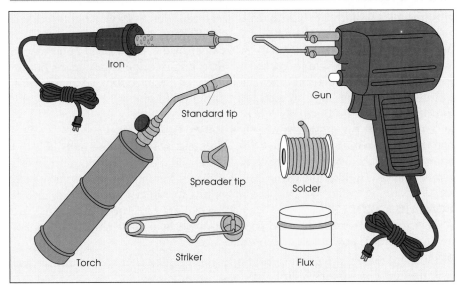

SOLDERING TOOLS include electric irons and guns and gas-fueled torches. A spreader tip broadens a torch's flame. A striker lights it. Solder typically comes wound around a spool, or as a bar of metal; flux is a paste.

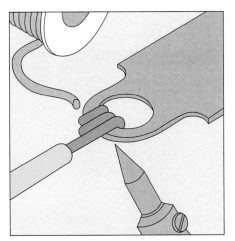

CLEAN METALS to a shiny state before soldering. Heat the metals, then touch solder to them. Twist wires in place for a physical grip before soldering.

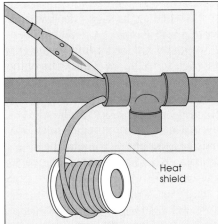

SWEAT-SOLDER PIPES with a torch. Heat the joint, then touch solder to the gap at the edge of the fitting. Capillary action will pull molten solder into the joint.

CAUTION

Melting solder requires a temperature of 750°F or more. Let the tip of an iron or gun cool before putting the tool away. If you use a torch, protect any combustible surface wherever you point the flame. Extinguish the torch every time you set it down. A burning torch could tip over or ignite your clothing. Relight the torch with a striker, which is safer than matches. If you are doing wiring, be aware that many building codes prohibit soldering house wiring. Instead, use solderless connectors (see page 429).

2 PORTABLE POWER TOOLS

Portable power tools are indispensable for all sorts of home repair and improvement projects. They can provide a quick and accurate way to drill, saw, shape, and sand virtually any building material. However, you must learn the proper and safe use of each tool. Read the instructions and the maintenance manuals for your tools before attempting to use them. This chapter covers six of the most useful tools and their accessories: the electric drill, circular saw, saber or hand jig saw, reciprocating saw, sander, and router.

PORTABLE DRILLS

The electric drill is by far the most popular and versatile power tool. Used primarily to bore holes in wood, metal, and masonry, a drill can also drive screws, sand wood, polish surfaces, remove rust, and strip paint.

The essential parts of a drill are a *housing* of metal or high-impact plastic, a *chuck* that holds the bits, and a comfortable *handle* with an integral *trigger switch*. Holding the trigger depressed operates the drill motor. A *chuck key* opens the chuck jaws for a bit to be inserted and closes them to lock it in place. Popular work-saving features include a variable-speed motor (speed increases as the trigger is depressed), a forward/reverse switch, a lock-on button for continuous operation (as when sanding or polishing), an auxiliary side handle, and a keyless chuck.

Drills are sized by the largest diameter bit shank their chucks can accept. The most common sizes are ¼, ⅜, and ½ inch. For most homeowners, the best all-around drill is a ⅜-inch, variable-speed, reversing model. An alternate choice, for added convenience and portability, is a cordless drill/driver. Powered by a rechargeable battery, it has many of the features found on corded drills, plus a slip clutch that lets you drive screws without bit slippage, which can strip the screw head and damage the workpiece. For convenience, buy an extra battery to be sure of having a fresh power pack.

BASIC BITS

The best way to bore small holes in wood and metal is with common twist-drill bits. Similar bits with nonslip brad points for precise hole placement are for use only in wood. Both types are available in diameters up to ½ inch. For economy buy bits in sets. Sizes from 1/16 inch to the maximum the drill chuck accepts will meet almost all your needs. For safety, always unplug a drill before changing bits, in case you accidentally hit the switch.

You can get large-size bits on cut-down shafts—for example, a ⅜-inch bit on a ¼-inch shaft. However, when drilling in wood it is better to use *spade bits* to make larger holes up to 1½ inch diameter. To prevent tear-out when a spade bit cuts through the far side of a board, back up the work with scrap wood. For boring very deep holes, such as through floors and walls to run wiring, you can get twist bits and spade

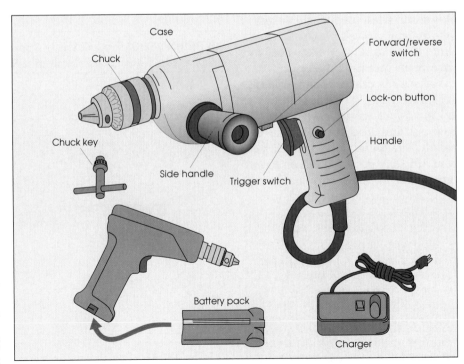

AN ELECTRIC DRILL can bore holes, drive screws, and do many other jobs. A ⅜-inch model is the best choice for homeowners. Highly convenient cordless models require at least one battery pack and a charger.

bits with extralong shafts. Or you can use an extension shaft with standard-length bits.

To drill very large holes, up to about 3 inches in diameter, use a hole saw. The best type consists of individual cup-like saws that fit onto a mandrel with a pilot bit. A hole saw tends to splinter the workpiece as it breaks through the back surface. Prevent this by drilling from one side until the tip of the pilot bit just comes through. Then drill back from the other side, using the pilot hole to get the saw properly lined up.

No tool kit is complete without a few tungsten-carbide-tip masonry bits for drilling into concrete, brick, stone, and plaster. Always operate masonry bits at the drill's highest speed and back the bit out of the hole often to pull out clogging dust that can overheat the bit. To drill into ceramic tile and glass, use spear-point carbide bits. Make an X of tape over the point where you want to drill and start the bit through that, to keep it from slipping on the hard, smooth surface. To cut large holes in ceramics, plastic, fiberglass, and sheet metal, use a carbide-grit hole saw.

DRIVING SCREWS

Any electric drill can be used for power driving screws; bits are available to fit almost all kinds of screws. The most flexible method is to use a short magnetic extension shaft that accepts screwdriver tip inserts. Tips for No. 6, 8, 10, and 12 slotted screws and for 1- and 2-point Phillips head screws are the most useful. A variable-speed drill is best, so you can start slowly to maintain control. An accessory slip clutch, or "screwdriver attachment," is very useful, especially with a fixed-speed drill.

When driving wood screws, first drill a pilot hole with a combination drill and countersink or a combination counterbore, as explained on page 33, or use standard twist bits of appropriate size (see page 71) and a separate countersink or counterbore.

There are many accessories for using an electric drill with increased precision, and for more than just drilling holes and driving screws. The most valuable accessories are shown on page 42.

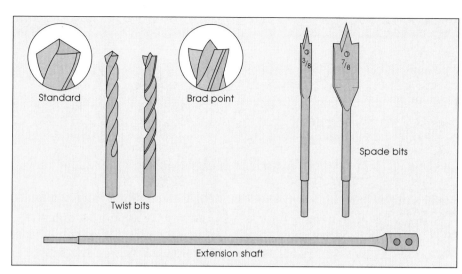

BASIC BITS are twist bits with standard tips for wood or metal, or brad points for wood only. Spade bits are best for oversized holes up to 1½ inches in diameter. An extension shaft provides extra reach with normal-length bits.

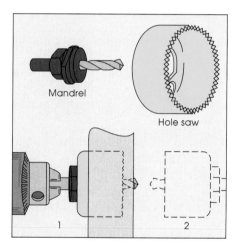

HOLE SAWS that fit on a mandrel cut large-diameter holes. Drill from both sides to avoid splintering.

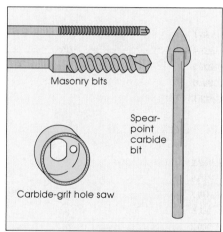

DRILL HARD NONMETALLIC MATERIALS with masonry bits. For tile and glass, use spear-point bits or carbide-grit hole saws.

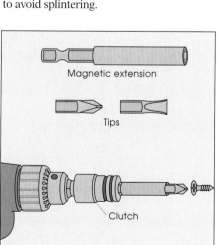

TO DRIVE SCREWS, use an extension shaft with screwdriver tips. An accessory clutch is very useful.

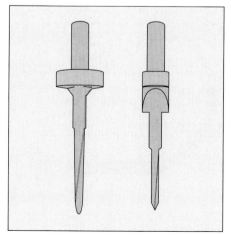

MAKE PILOT HOLES FOR SCREWS with a combination drill and countersink (*left*) or a combination counterbore (*right*).

ELECTRIC DRILL ACCESSORIES

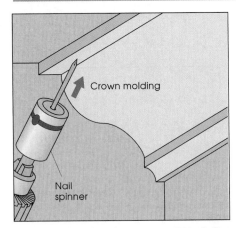

A NAIL SPINNER drives 1½- to 2½-inch finishing nails. Use it to fasten moldings, assemble frames, or wherever hammering might cause damage.

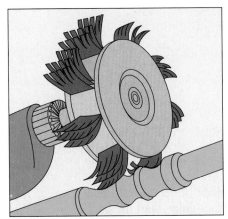

A FLAP SANDER makes it easy to smooth turned balusters, ornate moldings, and other irregularly-shaped pieces without destroying contours or surface detail.

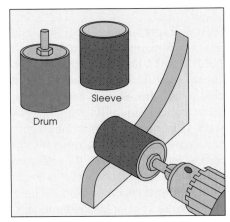

DRUM SANDERS take replaceable abrasive sleeves. Use them to sand, grind, and polish corners, curves, and flat surfaces on metal and wood.

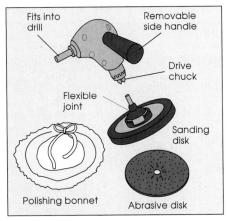

A RIGHT-ANGLE HEAD can accept bits or a sanding disk. Abrasive circles stick onto the disk, and a polishing bonnet ties on for buffing wax or fine finishes.

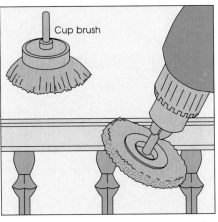

WIRE WHEELS AND BRUSHES make short work of removing paint, grime, and corrosion from metal and wood. Wear safety goggles when using them.

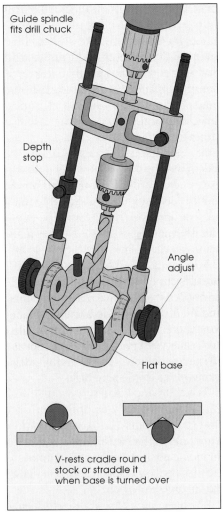

A DRILL GUIDE adjusts to bore perpendicular or angled holes with precision. V-rests accommodate round stock, and an adjustable stop controls hole depth.

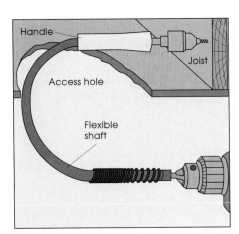

A FLEXIBLE SHAFT lets you work in spots the drill can't fit into. Use it with drill and screwdriver bits, sanding accessories, or wire wheels.

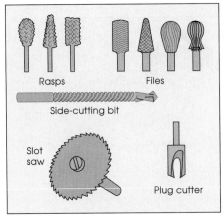

OTHER ACCESSORIES include rotary rasps and files, a side-cutting bit, a slot-cutting disk saw, and plug cutters to cut hole-filling inserts.

CIRCULAR SAWS

For fast, straight cutting, a portable circular saw is hard to beat. Saws are commonly identified by blade diameter. A 7¼-inch saw offers a good combination of power and cutting capacities.

The saw is operated by a *trigger switch* in the handle. A retractable *blade guard* covers the teeth below the base plate or *shoe*. The shoe can be raised or lowered to adjust the depth of cut, and tilted for angle cuts. The blade is held on the motor spindle by a nut and lock washer. A *blade lock* prevents turning when the wrench supplied with the saw is used to change a blade. Always unplug a saw before changing blades.

CIRCULAR SAW BLADES

There are rip, crosscut, and combination rip-crosscut blades for general use, and fine-tooth and hollow-ground blades for finish work and cabinetry. Specialty blades are available for cutting plywood and paneling, particleboard and similar materials, and plastic laminates. Blades for woodcutting are either high-speed steel or steel with carbide-tipped teeth. Carbide-tipped blades are more expensive, but they last much longer between sharpenings, which must be done by a professional. You can sharpen high-speed steel blades yourself with a file.

With the proper blade a circular saw can also cut other materials. Use an aluminum-oxide abrasive blade for metal and a silicone-carbide abrasive blade for concrete, brick, cement block, tile, and slate. With masonry, make repeated shallow cuts to get through materials more than about ¼ inch thick.

CUTTING WOOD

Because circular saw teeth rotate upward, place the workpiece good side down for cutting. To reduce splintering on the top (back) surface, first scribe the cut line with a utility knife.

Freehand cuts along a marked line are easy to make; you can see the blade through an opening in the shoe. For making controlled cuts up to about 6 inches wide, a removable *rip guide* can

be adjusted to run along the right edge of a workpiece. For better guidance and wider cuts, tack or clamp a wood or metal straightedge to the workpiece to guide the left side of the shoe. Set any guide so that the kerf of the cut is on the waste side of the cut line.

To start a *plunge cut* in the middle of a panel, place the toe of the shoe against the work with the heel raised to keep the blade above the surface. Retract the blade guide, start the saw, and lower the heel so the teeth enter the surface. When the blade has fully penetrated the wood and the shoe lies flat on the surface, move the saw forward to make the cut.

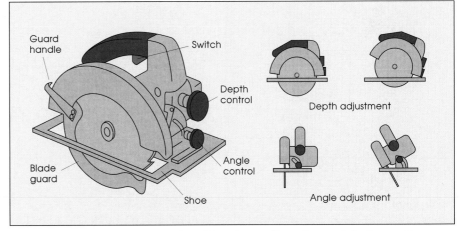

A CIRCULAR SAW is invaluable for all but the smallest jobs. Look for large adjustment control knobs, and a lock on the body for easy blade changing. An electromagnetic brake that stops the blade quickly is a valuable safety feature.

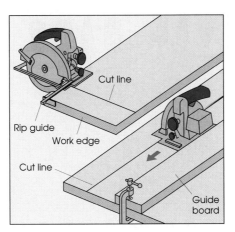

TO GUIDE A CUT, use the accessory rip guide on the shoe of the saw or, better, secure a straightedge to the workpiece.

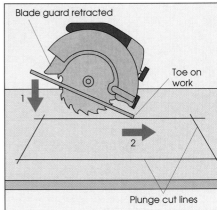

START A PLUNGE CUT with the toe against the work, heel raised. Lower the saw completely before moving it forward.

SABER SAWS

The versatile, easy-to-use saber saw or hand-held jig saw can make both straight and curved cuts in wood and metal. A standard saber saw has simple reciprocating action; the blade moves straight up and down. An orbital-action saw moves the blade forward into the wood on each upstroke for faster cutting. A scroll saber saw allows rotating the blade to cut tight curves precisely.

A saber saw is operated by pressing a *trigger switch* in the handle. In a variable-speed saw, speed increases as the switch is depressed. The saw rests on a flat *shoe*. The blade is located in an opening in the front of the shoe. It fits into a slot in the *shaft* and is secured with a *blade lock* or collar. In a scroll saw, rotating the *front knob* on top of the spindle changes the blade position.

BLADES

Saber saw blades differ in width and number of teeth per inch. Generally, more teeth produce a smoother but slower cut. When cutting curves, choose a narrow blade. For straight cuts, use a wide blade. Specialty blades include a knife-edge blade to cut cork, leather, sheet rubber, vinyl, and foam rubber; a carbide-edge blade to cut glass and ceramic tile; and a nail-cutting blade, for sawing wood that may contain an occasional nail—invaluable for home renovation work. Always unplug the saw when changing blades.

SAWING TECHNIQUES

A saber saw is most often used freehand. Because the blade cuts on the upstroke (unless you use a special reverse-tooth blade), the workpiece should be face down to avoid splintering the better surface. To make unwavering straight cuts, secure a straightedge to guide the shoe, or even two guides, one on each side of the shoe. At a knot, lift and lower the rear of the saw repeatedly to work through the knot with a rocking action. Additional sawing techniques are shown in the illustrations.

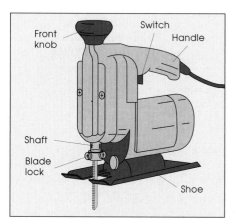

A SABER SAW is simple to use and accepts a great variety of easy-to-change blades. They are cheap enough to throw away when dull, rather than resharpen.

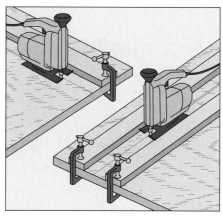

GUIDE STRAIGHT CUTS with a straight-edge, or two for long cuts. Make short straight cuts and curved and irregular cuts freehand.

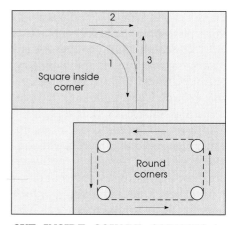

CUT INSIDE SQUARE CORNERS in three passes as shown. For round corners drill holes of the required radius and make straight cuts between them.

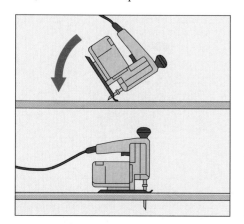

TO MAKE A PLUNGE CUT, put the toe down, with the blade above the work. Start the saw and lower the heel slowly until the blade penetrates the work.

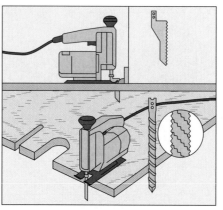

SAW UP TO A VERTICAL PIECE with a flush-cutting blade *(top)*. Use a spiral-tooth scroll cutter *(bottom)* to make tight cuts in any direction.

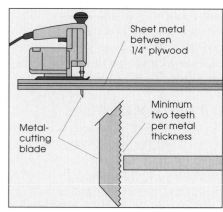

CUT THIN METAL by sandwiching it between plywood to prevent bending or tearing. The blade must have at least two teeth contacting the edge of the metal.

RECIPROCATING SAWS

A heavy-duty, rough-cutting tool, the reciprocating saw is essential for such tough tasks as taking down a partition, cutting through a wall to install a new window, or cutting a roof opening for a skylight. It can also be used to cut heavy timbers and prune large trees.

A reciprocating saw requires two-handed operation, one holding the body or a handle at the front, the other on the rear handle where a *trigger switch* controls a single-, dual-, or variable-speed motor. The *shoe* on the *nosepiece* pivots so it can be kept flat against the work. Blades can be mounted in the *spindle* with the teeth facing down, up, and in

some saws, right or left. The blade lock screw has a hex socket head that can be turned with an Allen wrench.

Blades of various types are 4 to 12 inches long. Most cuts are made with a 6- to 9-inch blade. Generally, it is best to choose the shortest, thickest blade suitable for the material to be cut. Always unplug the saw before changing blades.

SAWING HINTS

A reciprocating saw has a great tendency to vibrate and kick back when cutting. Keep both hands on the tool and hold the shoe pressed firmly against the surface of the work at all times.

With a variable- or two-speed saw, cut metal at low speed and wood at high speed. Use the following technique to start a plunge cut. Hold the shoe against the work with the blade tipped up. Start the saw and keep it at its slowest speed. Then very slowly lower the blade into the work. The saw will bounce some, so keep a firm grip.

Before cutting into a wall or floor, check for hidden pipes or wires. With the proper choice of blade, you can cut through plaster, metal lath, wallboard, wood framing, plywood, insulation, and all types of flooring and siding. If the blade tip strikes a hard surface, it may bend or break. You may be able to straighten a bent blade, but be sure to wear gloves in case it is hot.

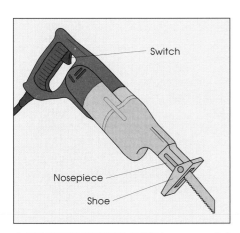

A RECIPROCATING SAW is a powerful tool requiring two-handed operation. The shoe must always be pressed firmly against the work.

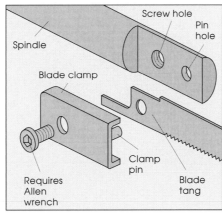

WHEN CHANGING BLADES, be sure the blade clamp pin engages the hole in the blade tang before tightening the clamp screw with an Allen wrench.

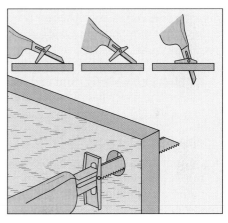

START A PLUNGE CUT with the shoe against the work, then pivot the saw upward. With long blades, drill a starting hole instead of plunging.

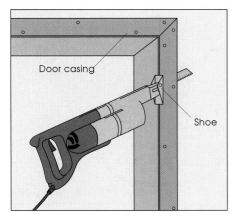

REMOVE CASINGS and similar trim by prying up enough to insert a metal-cutting blade to cut the nails. Keep the shoe tight to the work to avoid damaging the wood.

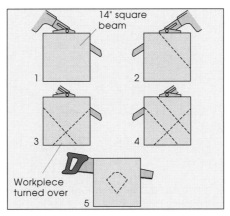

CUT EXTRALARGE PIECES such as timbers by rotating the workpiece, or by rotating the saw around them. Finish the cut in the center with a handsaw if necessary.

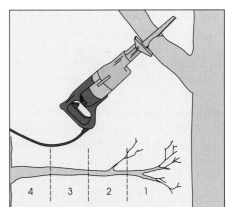

CUT TREE BRANCHES with a 12-inch pruning blade with six teeth per inch. For safety, remove large limbs in several short sections, not one piece.

SANDERS

The important task of sanding to prepare or finish surfaces goes quickly and easily with a portable electric sander. There are three types of sanders with the power and speed necessary to tackle any home or shop smoothing chore: belt, orbital, and random-orbit.

BELT SANDERS

Belt sanders are powerful tools used primarily to smooth rough surfaces and for heavy stock removal. They are also the best choice for removing paint, varnish, surface stains, and blemishes.

Belt sanders are most commonly available in three sizes: 3 × 21, 3 × 24, and 4 × 24 inches. The dimensions are the width and circumference of the abrasive belt. A 3 × 21-inch sander is big enough for most home repair and remodeling work. A dust collection bag is a valuable feature.

The sander is held by front and rear handles, and operated with a slide switch or a trigger switch with a lock-on button. To install a belt, unplug the sander and retract the front drum with the tension lever or by pushing the nose of the sander against a board. Remove the old belt and slip the new one over the front and rear drums and pressure plate. *IMPORTANT: Be sure the arrows on the inside of the belt point in the direction the belt will travel* (from rear to front across the bottom). Release the tension lever so the front drum snaps into operating position. With the sander held free of any surface, turn it on and adjust the tracking control to shift the belt slightly left or right so that it runs centered on the drums.

BELT SANDING TECHNIQUES

To avoid cross-grain scratches, sand parallel with the wood grain. However, when you need to smooth a very rough board, first hold the sander at a 45-degree angle to the grain to remove the surface roughness. Then sand parallel to the grain to remove cross-grain scratches. Switch to the next finer abrasive grade to smooth the board. Keep the sander moving at all times to avoid

forming a depression. Be very careful when sanding veneered wood; it doesn't take long for the abrasive to cut completely through the veneer.

ORBITAL SANDERS

Orbital sanders are used for final smoothing and finish sanding. They have rectangular or square pads that take a half-, quarter-, or sixth-sheet of

standard 9 × 11-inch abrasive paper. The paper is slipped in a clamp at the rear, stretched across the sanding pad, and secured by a clamp or tension roller at the front.

The small models are called *palm sanders;* half-sheet models are *finishing sanders*. They all vibrate the sanding pad in tiny circles—orbits—to produce a smooth surface. Most can be switched from orbital movement for the first sanding to straight-line movement for final smoothing.

TYPES OF SANDERS

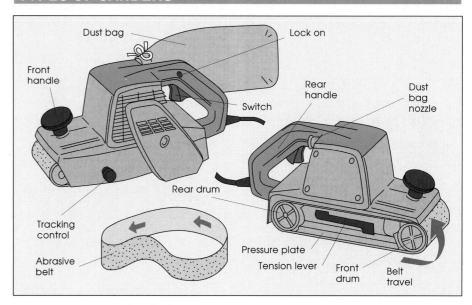

A BELT SANDER can handle the roughest jobs with a coarse belt, and finish sanding with fine-grit belts. Unplug the sander to change belts. Make sure the belt arrows point in the direction of travel, and adjust the tracking before using the sander.

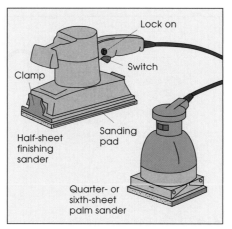

ORBITAL SANDERS are for light-duty and finishing work. They take ½-, ¼-, or ⅙-sheets of abrasive.

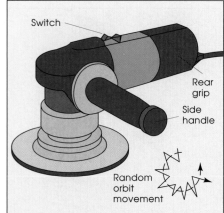

RANDOM-ORBIT SANDERS are the most versatile type. Abrasive disks are mounted with adhesive or have Velcro® backs.

Orbital sanders are ideal for rounding sharp edges, sanding between finish coats, and for smoothing hard-to-reach areas. Keep the sander oriented with the grain; turning it sideways risks snagging and tearing the exposed edges of the paper. For polishing and buffing, replace the abrasive sheet with an accessory lamb's-wool pad or several thicknesses of cheesecloth or soft cotton.

RANDOM-ORBIT SANDERS

The random-orbit sander is a unique tool that can handle both stock removal and finish sanding of both flat and contoured surfaces. Because the circular sanding pad rotates and orbits simulta-neously to produce a smooth, swirl-free finish, it is excellent for sanding across angled wood joints. Various models have pads of 4½, 5, or 6 inches diameter. Some take adhesive-backed abrasive paper; others take Velcro®-backed abrasive disks for quick, easy changes. For buffing and polishing, a polishing bonnet can be used on the pad.

ABRASIVES

Sheet, disk, and belt abrasives for power sanders are graded by type of grit and grit number (particle size), as explained on page 27. When sanding, start with the least coarse grade that will do the job. Then use progressively finer grades until you achieve the desired smoothness. At each change, sweep the surface clean of any grit from the previous, coarser abrasive. Otherwise the sander will go over the loose particles and scratch the surface.

> **CAUTION**
> Read the instructions for your sander carefully. When sanding, always wear a dust mask or, better, a dual-cartridge respirator, as protection against inhaling dust. To reduce the amount of airborne dust, use a sander equipped with a dust collection bag. Unplug the power cord before changing the abrasive sheet or belt.

SANDING TECHNIQUES

TO REMOVE WOOD QUICKLY, hold a belt sander at 45 degrees to the grain. Finish-sand parallel with the grain.

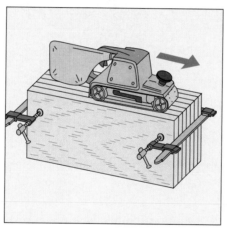

SPEED EDGE SANDING by ganging up several boards. Hold them with wood clamps or in a vise.

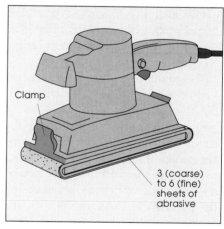

LOAD A HALF-SHEET SANDER with several pieces of abrasive. As one wears out, tear it off to expose the next.

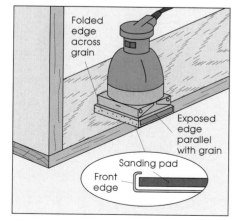

FINISHING SANDERS can work into corners, up to verticals. Sand as shown to avoid snagging the paper edges.

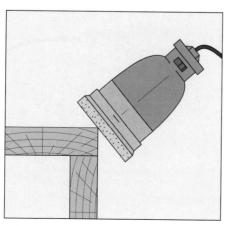

USE A PALM SANDER loaded with medium-grit sandpaper to ease sharp edges and corners. Move the sander rapidly.

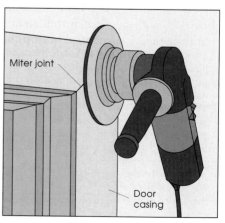

A RANDOM-ORBIT SANDER is ideal for angle joints because it will not leave cross-grain scratches.

ROUTERS

The router rivals the electric drill as the most versatile portable power tool. With a router and a variety of bits you can quickly and precisely shape decorative edges, cut wood joints, mill moldings, make frame-and-panel doors, trim plastic laminate, cut hinge mortises and dovetails, and more.

A router has a powerful, high-speed motor that spins cutting bits of various shapes. The bit is held in a *collet* chuck and protrudes through a flat, smooth base that slides over the surface of the work. The motor can be raised or lowered to adjust the depth of the cut. Routers are sized according to the maximum diameter bit shank the collet can accept and the horsepower of the motor. A ¼-inch, 1 hp (minimum) router will serve for most home projects. However, a ⅜- or ½-inch router with a more powerful motor can do much more.

There are two basic router designs. In a *fixed-base* router the bit protrudes from the base at a selected depth. To begin a cut in the middle of a piece, the router must be lowered into place freehand with the bit spinning. A *plunge* router holds the motor and bit retracted above the base. After the base is flat on the surface and centered over the starting point, the revolving bit can be lowered (plunged) into the workpiece and locked at the preset depth.

All full-size routers require two-hand guidance. There are handles on each side for a secure grip. Some routers have a switch on the motor body, others a trigger switch and lock-on button in one handle.

ROUTER BITS

Router bits come in literally hundreds of shapes and sizes. They are commonly made of high-speed steel or carbide-tipped steel. The latter type are more costly but stay sharp much longer. Bits fall into two categories: edge-shaping/trimming, and groove-making. An edge bit often has a ball-bearing pilot wheel that rides against the edge of the workpiece to guide the cut. Grooving bits have no pilot. They can be used freehand, or a guide can be used to control the router's path. A good basic set of bits is shown below.

As with any power tool, handle a router with care, and always unplug the power cord before changing bits.

TYPES OF ROUTERS

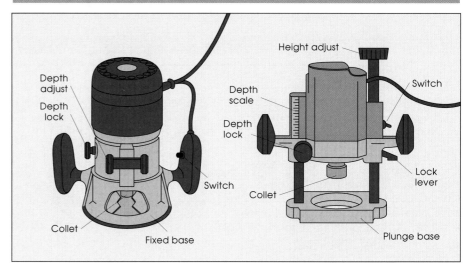

ROUTERS DIFFER in basic type—fixed base or plunging—bit shank size, motor horsepower, and handle and control details. These are only two examples. Collets are opened and closed with an end wrench to change bits.

BASIC BITS

Start with these bits for your router. Use straight bits to cut grooves and dadoes, core box and V-groove bits to cut flutes in columns, posts, and panels. Also get a mortising bit, used with a template (see next page). The edge-shaping bits are all piloted. The round-over and Roman ogee bits are the two most popular decorative edge shapers. The rabbeting bit cuts square lips; the cove and chamfering bits cut edges as shown.

If you will be making countertops or working with veneer, add a straight laminate trimmer, and one or more bevel trimmers. These are piloted bits made especially to cut plastic laminate edges without chipping, and without dulling rapidly. Ordinary bits will not do.

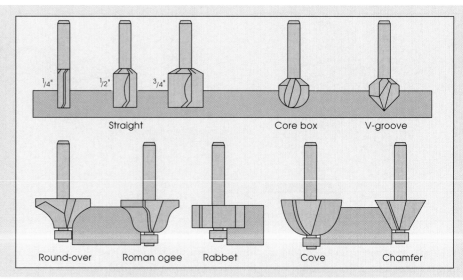

BASIC ROUTING

For a bit to cut properly its cutting edges must chop into the wood. Make cuts by moving the router as shown below. Moving in the opposite direction produces a gouging action that can rip out chips or tear edge grain. Allow the router to reach full speed before moving the bit into the work. Also, do not attempt to make a cut deeper than about ¼ inch in a single pass. Instead, make repeated, deeper cuts until the desired depth is reached.

Check that the ball-bearing pilot spins freely before using a piloted bit. Accumulated resin, glue, or dirt can jam the bearing and cause the pilot to burn the edge of the workpiece. To clean it, soak the bearing in lacquer thinner and scrub it with an old toothbrush, then lubricate with a light machine oil.

All routers accept an accessory edge guide for cutting grooves that are within about 6 inches of the edge of a board. The guide attaches to the router's base and slides along the edge of the board to control the cut. To rout grooves farther from the edge, clamp or tack on a wood or metal straightedge and press the edge of the base against it as you move the router. Measure from the cutting edge of the bit to set an edge guide or to find how far from the cutting line to place a straightedge.

When routing a narrow piece, increase its width with pieces of scrap wood to support the base of the router fully; otherwise the router can tip or slip.

ROUTING TECHNIQUES

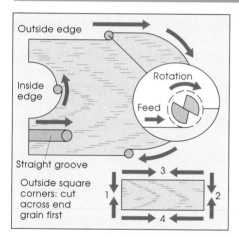

THE BIT ROTATES CLOCKWISE. Move the router so the bit edges chop into the wood rather than gouge it out.

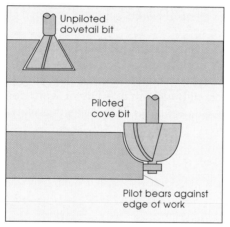

WIDTH OF CUT is determined by the diameter of an unpiloted bit, and by the bearing wheel of a piloted bit.

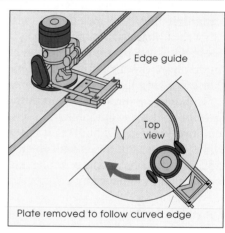

GUIDE CUTS with an accessory edge guide. Remove the guide plate to get two-point contact for a curved edge.

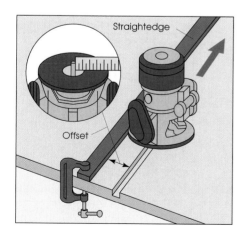

USE A STRAIGHTEDGE for cuts beyond the reach of an edge guide. Measure from the bit edge to get the offset.

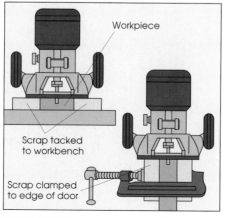

INCREASE THE WIDTH of a narrow workpiece with scrap to give full support to the router base.

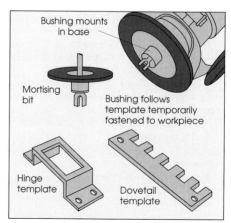

ATTACH A BUSHING to the router base to use templates for hinge mortises, dovetails, or other shapes.

3 A HOME WORKSHOP

A workshop provides space to work without interruption on projects that do not have to be done in place. It also provides a place to keep hand and power tools, and to safely store materials, paints, and solvents.

Whether located in the basement, garage, or a utility room, a home shop need not be large, but it should have certain features. They include:

• A separate electric circuit for power tools, with outlets located 40 inches or more above the floor for easy access. For safety, the lights in the shop area must not be on the same circuit as the outlets, so if a power tool trips the circuit breaker you will not be left in the dark. Discuss your needs with an electrician; generally, adding a 20-amp circuit should be sufficient.

• A window or a fan vented to the exterior if you plan on using paints or solvents in the workshop.

• Plenty of storage space for tools and equipment, lumber, and other materials.

• A door, or cabinets that lock, to keep tools and dangerous substances out of the reach of children. See chapters 36 and 37 for storage safety measures.

• A good workbench.

A HOME SHOP WORKBENCH

A workbench is the heart of a home shop. It should be large and sturdy enough for all the kinds of work you will want to do. You can buy a work-

bench or make your own at a considerable savings. The workbench shown here consists of a sturdy base with a double-layer plywood top and a storage shelf below. Study the drawings and parts list on these pages carefully, then follow the steps given below.

The major parts are fastened together with bolts or screws. The details in the figure below show pilot hole locations for attaching the rail and stretcher at one upper and one lower corner. Locate pilot holes similarly at all the other corners. Before attaching the shelf or top, check with a carpenter's square to make sure the joints are at right angles.

WORKBENCH PARTS

The pieces of the workbench identified in the illustrations should be cut as follows:

L: 4 legs, 4 × 4 × 32 1/2 inches
R: 4 rails, 2 × 4 × 58 1/2 inches
S: 4 stretchers, 1 × 4 × 25 inches
C: 2 cleats, 1 × 2 × 16 1/2 inches
1 shelf, 18 × 58 1/2 × 3/4-inch plywood
2 top pieces, 30 × 72 × 3/4-inch plywood
Q: 4 pieces, 3/4-inch quarter-round molding cut to fit between the legs
E: 4 pieces, 1/4 × 1 1/2-inch lattice cut to trim the top edges

Fasteners
8 angle irons, 3 × 3 inches
1 1/4-inch No. 8 and 2-inch No. 10 flathead wood screws
3/8 × 4 1/2-inch carriage bolts with washers and nuts
1 1/2-inch finishing nails
Wood glue

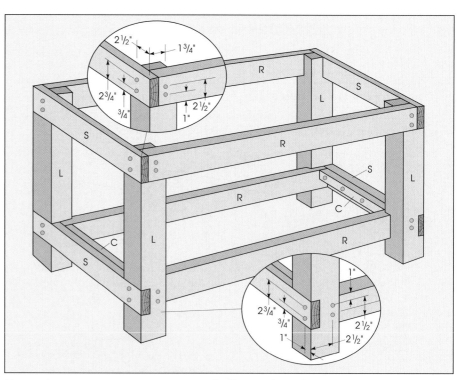

THE WORKBENCH BASE is constructed of legs, rails, and stretchers. Their number and sizes and the required fasteners are listed in the box at left. The top drawing on the opposite page shows how to cut the leg notches.

1 CUT THE LEGS. The 32½-inch length will give a 34-inch finished height with the top in place. Follow the drawing below carefully to get the notches (dadoes) for the rails and stretchers located properly. They are on the outside at the top of each leg. But the lower-rail dadoes are on the inside, and they are only ¾ inch deep so the shelf can rest on the exposed edges. The dadoes should be 3½ inches high for nominal 4-inch lumber, but measure your rails and stretchers to be sure; lumber widths may vary a bit.

2 CUT THE RAILS AND STRETCH-ERS. If you want a longer bench, make the rails longer than specified. The side stretchers could be cut shorter for a shallower bench if your space is limited, but greater depth would be impractical in most situations.

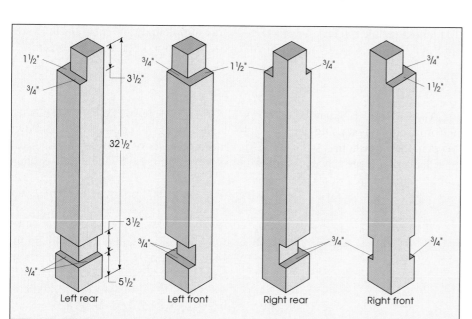

THE WORKBENCH LEGS are cut from lengths of 4 × 4 lumber. The notches for the rails and side stretchers must be located as shown and cut precisely to the size of the lumber used for proper support and assembly.

3 ASSEMBLE THE BASE. Build the ends by attaching the stretchers to the left and right legs with 2-inch No. 10 flathead screws. Then stand the ends up and place the back top rail between them. Drill holes through the rail and the leg for 4½-inch carriage bolts. Fasten the bolts with a washer under each nut, on the inside. Repeat for each of the other three rails.

4 CUT AND INSTALL THE SHELF. Cut 1 × 2 cleats and fasten them to the inside of the lower stretchers, top edges flush. Use glue, and 1¼-inch No. 8 flathead screws every 3 inches. Cut the shelf from ¾-inch plywood to fit between the legs and rest on the rails and cleats. Fasten it around the edges with 1¼-inch screws spaced every 6 inches. Finish the edges with ¾-inch quarter-round molding attached with 1½-inch finishing nails.

5 BUILD THE TOP. Cut two pieces of ¾-inch plywood to size. If you have changed the base dimensions, cut the top pieces to overhang 5 inches at each end and 2½ inches front and back. Fasten the pieces together with 1¼-inch No. 8 flathead screws driven up through the bottom panel. Space them every 6 inches around the perimeter and lengthwise down the center.

6 INSTALL THE TOP. Screw three angle irons to the inside of each top rail and one to each stretcher, as shown. Center the top over the base and drive 1¼-inch No. 8 screws up through the angle irons. Finish the edges with lattice strips fastened with glue and 1½-inch finishing nails every 6 inches.

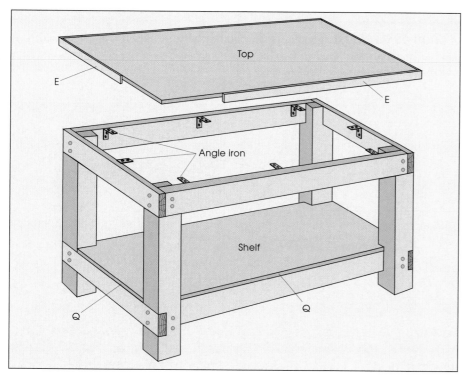

THE SHELF AND TOP are cut from ¾-inch plywood. Screw the top pieces together before attaching them to the angle irons. Trim the shelf edges with molding and the top edges with strips of lattice as shown.

VISES

Every workbench should be equipped with a vise to hold workpieces while you cut, sand, drill, solder, or do dozens of other jobs. The vise is like having an extra pair of hands so you can work without fear of the material slipping or moving out of place. Especially when using power tools, a vise is not just a convenience, it is an important piece of safety equipment.

There are two major types of vises suitable for a home shop, the *bench vise*, also called a mechanic's, metalworker's, or homeowner's vise, and the *woodworking vise*. Both consist of a *fixed jaw* and a *moving jaw* that travels on guide rods or a guide bar and is driven by a threaded rod with a handle to turn it.

BENCH VISES

A bench vise sits on top of the bench, secured by bolts or lag screws through mounting holes or by an edge clamp. The base may allow the vise to be swiveled left or right. The jaws have serrated or smooth metal faces that may be replaceable. Depending on the size of the vise, jaw face size (width × depth) ranges from about 2½ × 2 inches to 6 × 3 inches; the maximum opening or vise capacity typically ranges from 3 to 7½ inches. Often there is an *anvil* where work can be hammered, and a secondary set of *pipe jaws* to hold rods, pipes, and dowels.

If you will be doing much plumbing, electrical, or metal work, a bolt-on bench vise is a good choice. When working with wood, you can protect the surfaces by placing thin scrap over the metal jaws of the vise.

WOODWORKING VISES

A woodworking vise is fastened with bolts or lag screws to the underside of the bench top so that the top edges of its jaws are flush with the work surface. The flat jaws have tapped (threaded) holes so they can be faced with hardwood and countersunk flathead machine screws to protect workpieces. The jaw faces are larger than those of bench

vises—the greater area can hold a workpiece securely with less pressure. Capacity is greater too, for vises of the same relative size; it may be as much as 12 inches in some models. A useful feature is a pull-up *dog* in the top of the

movable jaw, for holding workpieces wider than the vise's capacity. The dog bears against the outer edge of the piece, pushing it against a temporary stop on the bench top.

If you will be working primarily with wood, select a woodworking vise. You can supplement it with a clamp-on bench vise for other work if necessary.

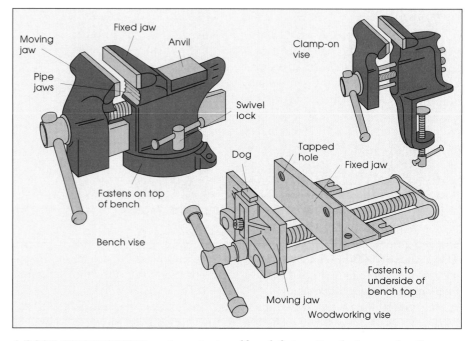

A GOOD QUALITY VISE is an important workbench fixture. Bench vises can handle many kinds of materials, but woodworking vises are much superior for holding boards and large workpieces securely and without damage.

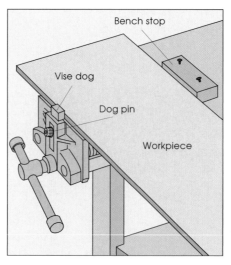

USE THE DOG in a woodworking vise to hold wide pieces. The bench stop can be tacked or clamped on, or inserted in a hole cut in the bench top.

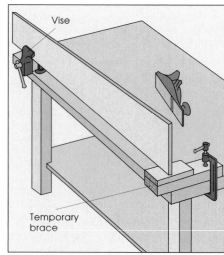

SUPPORT LONG PIECES by placing one end in the vise and resting the other end on a brace fastened to the bench top or legs. Clamp the work to the brace if necessary.

GRINDERS AND SHARPENING TOOLS

Only a sharp tool can cut cleanly and be used with safety. A home shop should have a grinder, flat stones with honing guides, and slip stones. With those at hand, it takes only a few minutes to keep chisels, planes, and other edged tools sharp.

GRINDERS

A bench grinder consists of a motor with a 4-, 5-, or 6-inch-diameter *abrasive wheel* at each end. The wheels may be coarse and medium grits, or medium and fine grits. Each wheel must have a *guard*, a shatterproof *eye shield*, and a *tool rest*. When the motor is turned on, both wheels revolve at up to 3,500 rpm, their edges moving down toward the tool rest. The tool is held firmly on the rest at an upward angle with its bevel facing the stone. For planes and chisels, use an angle of about 25 degrees; for pruning shears, 45 degrees; for carving knives, 10 to 15 degrees; and for scissors, 80 degrees.

Wear safety goggles whenever you use a grinder. Begin sharpening on the coarser grit wheel to remove nicks and restore the original bevel of the tool, then switch to the finer wheel. Keep a can of water at hand and quench the edge of the tool frequently to keep it from overheating. Finish by honing the edge on a fine-grit flat stone. You can replace one wheel with a wire wheel to clean metal, or a cloth wheel for polishing and buffing the edges and surfaces of tools and small workpieces.

HAND-SHARPENING TOOLS

Flat stones or *whetstones* are either water stones or oil stones. The fluid lubricates the stone and keeps particles of metal from clogging the pores. Stone grits run from very coarse (200 grit) to extrafine (1,200 grit). Some stones have a coarse grit on one side and a finer grit on the other. Water stones sharpen somewhat more quickly than oil stones, but wear out faster.

When sharpening chisels and planes on a whetstone, use a honing guide to hold the tool at the correct angle. Place the bevel on a coarse-grit stone and move the blade in loops or an S pattern. Continue until the bevel is shiny and a burr has formed on the back side of the blade. Remove the burr by rubbing the back flat on a fine-grit stone.

Slipstones come in a variety of shapes and are used to sharpen tools that do not have flat blades. They are rubbed against the tool, rather than moving the tool on the stone. Tools such as saws are sharpened with flat and triangular metal files. Many other tools can be sharpened with small grinding wheels or abrasive bits mounted in an electric drill.

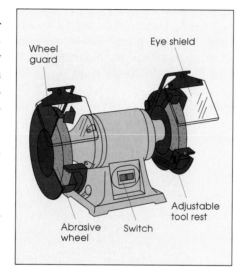

A BENCH GRINDER can be used to sharpen knives, scissors, and other edged implements as well as shop tools.

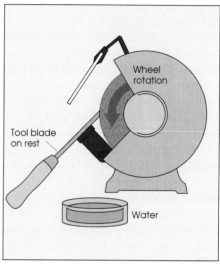

HOLD THE TOOL EDGE at an upward angle against the wheel rotation. Quench the edge in water frequently.

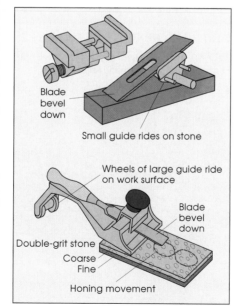

USE A HONING GUIDE to get the proper edge angle against a whetstone. Sharpen on a coarse or medium grit; remove the burr on a fine grit.

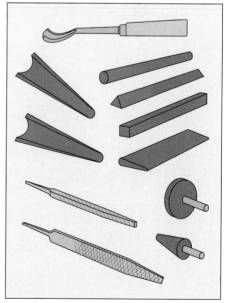

USE SLIPSTONES on curved-edge tools such as wood-carving gouges. Files and drill accessories are useful with saws, mower blades, and other equipment.

POWER SAWS

Although portable power saws can be used in a home shop to good effect, most large projects and intricate work can be done with more precision and much more easily with nonportable shop saws. *Table* and *benchtop saws* and *radial arm saws* use blades like those for a portable circular saw (see page 43). *Scroll saw* blades are similar to those for coping and saber saws. A *band saw* uses flexible loop blades somewhat like hacksaw blades. The features and basic capabilities of these four types of shop saws are discussed here.

TABLE AND BENCHTOP SAWS

A table saw is a freestanding unit on legs or a base that puts the work surface at a convenient height. A benchtop saw has a shallow base that sits on top of a bench or work table. Otherwise, the design of these saws is the same. Their flat, open work surfaces make it easy to rip long boards and cut wide panels, as well as to make other straight-line cuts.

In these saws a motor with a blade from 7½ to 12 inches in diameter is mounted below the table. A guard covers the blade edge that protrudes up through a slot in the table. The blade can be raised or lowered, and also tilted for bevel cuts. The teeth cut as they rotate downward, so work is fed into the saw with the good side positioned face up. An adjustable fence sets the width of rip cuts, and a miter gauge aligns the wood for 90-degree or angled crosscuts. A typical 8-inch blade can cut stock up to 1¾ inches thick, and a 10-inch blade will handle stock up to 3½ inches thick.

To use a table saw, set the blade height to no more than about ¼ inch above the wood to be cut. Keep the blade guard in place; it will ride over the surface of the piece being cut. Move the wood by pushing on the miter gauge, or with push sticks for rip cuts.

TABLE AND BENCHTOP SAW TECHNIQUES

Before using your saw for projects, test it for cutting accuracy. This will tell you if the blade needs adjustment and it will give you a chance to practice cutting with the saw before working on a major project. Don safety goggles and make sure that you are thoroughly familiar

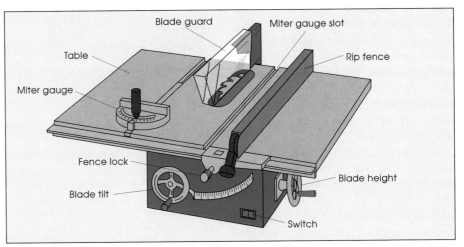

TABLE AND BENCHTOP SAWS have the same design, controls, and features. This is a typical model. Both types can make straight, angled, and beveled cuts in panels and long boards as well as in smaller pieces.

POWER SAW SAFETY

Read the saw instructions carefully and follow them exactly. Wear safety goggles and keep the work area well lighted. Do not wear long sleeves or loose fitting clothing when operating any power tool. Wear a dust mask when cutting pressure-treated wood.

Use feeder sticks to push lumber through rip cuts. Never get your fingers close to moving saw teeth. Provide extra support for pieces that are much longer, or wider, than the saw table.

With a table saw, always keep the saw guard in position when cutting wood. Use the miter gauge or push sticks to feed the work toward the blade, and never reach across a spinning blade.

With a radial arm saw, the blade has a tendency to feed itself into the work, so control the saw with a stiff arm to prevent it from coming on too fast. Never place your arm or fingers in the path of the blade.

Unplug the saw when changing blades.

Remove the blade or lock the switch in the OFF position when the saw is not in use. Stay alert.

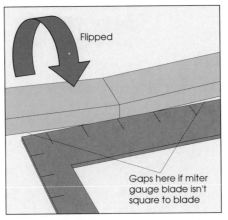

CUT A PIECE OF 1 X 4 WOOD in half. When placed against a ruler, the edges of both pieces should be in perfect alignment. If not, the miter gauge needs adjustment.

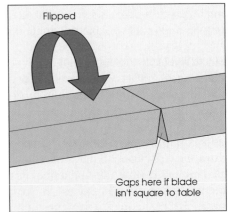

CUT A PIECE OF 1 X 4 WOOD in half. Flip one piece over and butt the ends together. The ends should mate perfectly. If not, the blade angle needs adjustment.

with the following (these items should be covered in the owner's manual): adjusting the height and angle of the blade; using the safety features, especially the blade guard; using the miter gauge; using the rip fence; and changing the blades.

Test for the squareness of the cut by cutting a 24-inch piece of 1 x 4 wood in two pieces. Set the blade angle to zero. Use the miter gauge set for a 90-degree angle as a push guide to make the cut. Test the cut by placing the two cut pieces on a flat surface. Flip one piece over and butt the ends together. The ends should mate perfectly with no gaps in between. If not, the blade angle needs adjustment. Next, place a straight edge along the edges of the two pieces. The edges of both pieces, butted together, should be in perfect alignment. If not, the miter gauge needs adjustment.

RADIAL ARM SAWS

In a radial arm saw, a motor with an 8- to 12-inch diameter blade is held in a yoke attached to a carriage on an arm above the saw table. For crosscutting, the carriage is pulled along the arm to pass the blade through work held against a fence. For rip cuts, the yoke is turned 90 degrees to set the blade parallel with the fence, and the work is pushed through. Because the saw teeth cut on their upward rotation, work is placed with the good face down. For rip cuts, work must be fed into the blade from the side at which the teeth are rotating upward.

The saw arm can be raised and lowered and swung from side to side to adjust the depth and horizontal angle of the cut. And the motor can be tilted to vary the bevel angle between vertical and horizontal. The blade can be replaced with shaping cutters, disk or drum sanders, and other accessories.

These features make a radial arm saw far more versatile than a table saw. However, the arm length limits saw travel to a maximum of 24½ inches (or less in smaller saws). That is just enough to rip a 4-foot-wide panel, but two passes are necessary to make a full-panel crosscut. The panel is turned around between the two cuts. Many *Continued*

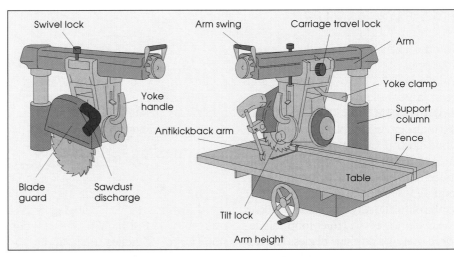

A **RADIAL ARM SAW** makes straight or angled crosscuts when the blade is pulled through the work. For rip cuts, the blade is locked in position and the work is pushed along the fence, into the upward-rotating teeth.

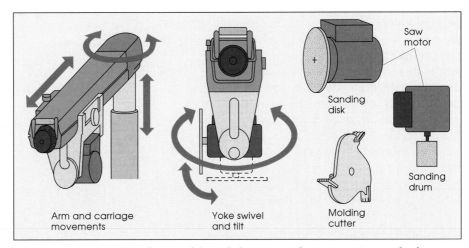

VERSATILITY is a major feature of the radial arm saw. The arm, carriage, and yoke movements can put the blade in any position, and the blade can be replaced with a variety of cutting, shaping, and finishing accessories.

WHEN RIPPING PANELS, always feed the work against the rotation of the blade and be sure to use the splinter and antikickback pawls.

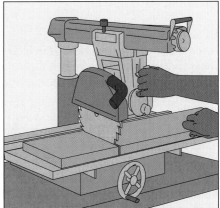

CONTROL A RADIAL ARM SAW with a stiff arm to prevent it from coming on too fast. Never place your arm or fingers in the path of the blade.

POWER SAWS *Continued*

woodworkers choose a radial arm saw for its versatility and use a portable circular saw to cut very wide pieces.

RADIAL ARM SAW TECHNIQUES

To make crosscuts, position the board, good side up, on the saw table. Place a piece of scrap plywood under the workpiece to prevent splintering. Make sure both ends are adequately supported with roller stands or sawhorses. Check the accuracy of the cut by flipping one piece over and butting the ends together (see pages 54–55).

Although the saw fence can be set farther back for a wide cut, the maximum setting will only allow you to rip a panel to 24 inches wide. Feeding a large panel into the saw can be difficult and even dangerous. It is better to rip the panel to an approximate width with a circular saw then trim it with the radial arm saw. When ripping a board, always feed the work against the rotation of the blade and use the antikickback levers for safety. For added safety enlist the aid of a helper to control the piece as you work.

Miter cuts require precise saw adjustment. It is best to set the saw, then cut the workpiece slightly longer (about ⅛-inch) than necessary. Check the angle of the cut with a protractor and bevel gauge. If the angle is correct, trim the piece to the exact size. If the angle is not right, adjust the saw accordingly, then cut again.

SCROLL SAWS

A scroll or bench jigsaw has a thin blade that moves rapidly up and down through an opening in the saw table. The blade is held in upper and lower chucks that pull it tight to keep it from bending. A hold-down adjusts to the thickness of the work being cut. Usually the hold-down has a blade guide to help reduce blade flexing. Stiffer, thicker saber blades are held only by the lower chuck and the blade guide. Blades range from about 7 teeth per inch (tpi) for very fast cutting to 20 tpi for fine work.

A scroll saw excels at cutting tight curves, intricate patterns, and veneers.

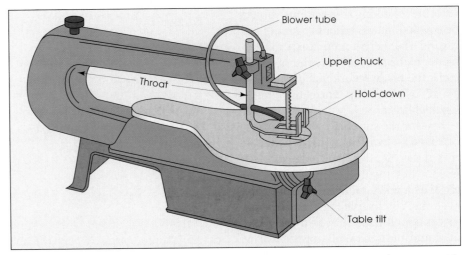

A SCROLL OR BENCH JIGSAW is the only way to cut intricate curves and patterns with precision in stock up to 2 inches thick. Blades of various widths and number of teeth can be matched to the project at hand.

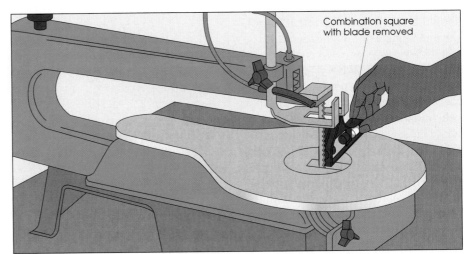

BEFORE USING A SCROLL SAW, check the alignment of the blade to the saw table with a small combination square.

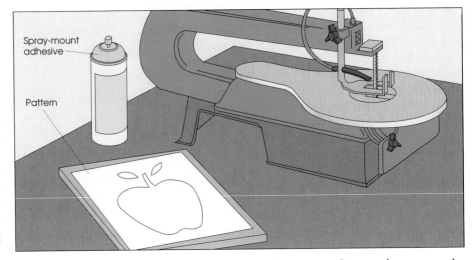

DRAW DESIGNS and complicated patterns on tracing paper and mount the paper on the wood with spray adhesive before making any cuts.

Work is guided by hand to keep the blade on a marked cut line. A small blower keeps the cutting path free of sawdust. On most models, the table can be tilted for bevel cuts. The maximum width of a workpiece is determined by the throat, which is the distance from the blade to the back post. The maximum wood thickness a scroll saw can handle is about 2 inches.

SCROLL SAW TECHNIQUES

The scroll saw can either be positioned on its own stand or on a workbench. It should be bolted down to minimize vibration. Before using the saw, check the alignment of the blade to the saw table (this is necessary only if the saw has a tilting table) with a small combination square. Position the square on the table against the blade. Loosen the table-tilt knob and realign the table to the blade. Tighten the knob after the adjustment is made and the table is level.

When designing and cutting complicated patterns, it is best to draw them on thin paper first—tracing paper is ideal for this—then mount the paper on the wood with common spray adhesive, which can be found in home centers or art supply stores. This will allow you to get the design just right before making any permanent cuts. It will also allow you to position the pattern around unsightly flaws, such as cracks or knots, in the wood.

To make an inside cut, drill a pilot hole through the area that will be cut away. Remove the blade and place the workpiece in position on the table with the pilot hole over the lower blade chuck. Push the blade through the hole and lock it in place, then make the cut and take out the waste matter.

BAND SAWS

The blade of a band saw is a continuous loop that passes around upper and lower wheels. The wheel diameter determines the throat size, and thus the size of the lumber that can be cut. In most models the table tilts for bevel cuts, and has a fence for ripping and a miter gauge for crosscutting. Like a scrollsaw, a band saw can cut curves and circles. Blade width ranges from ⅛ to ¾ inch. Narrow blades are used for curves, wide blades for straight cuts. In home workshop models, the wide blades are strong enough to cut lumber up to 6 inches thick.

BAND SAW TECHNIQUES

Cutting tight curves with a band saw can be tricky because the blade has a tendency to bind in the wood. You can avoid this by making relief cuts around the pattern. *Relief cuts* are a series of straight cuts from the waste matter at the edge of the workpiece to the outside of the pattern. As the saw cuts through the pattern, the waste matter will fall away in separate blocks. For tight curves, use more relief cuts and space them closer together.

For straight cuts, be sure to lock the table in position before turning on the saw. Use the miter gauge or adjustable fence to guide the work. Adjust the hold-down blade guide so it is as low as possible to the wood.

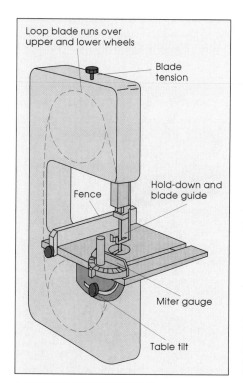

A BAND SAW CAN MAKE cuts in curves and circles like a scroll saw, and other shapes, in bigger, thicker stock, which is a significant advantage.

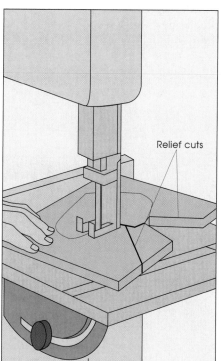

MAKE RELIEF CUTS around a pattern and the blade of the saw won't bind. Pieces of waste will fall away as you begin to cut out the pattern..

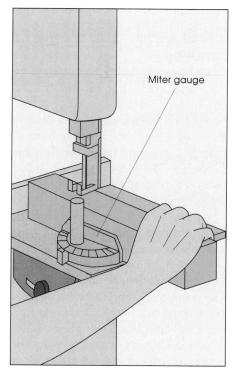

FOR STRAIGHT CUTS, be sure to lock the table in position before turning on the saw. Use the miter gauge or adjustable fence to guide the work

4 CONSTRUCTION EQUIPMENT

Big home repair and improvement jobs often call for heavy-duty or specialized equipment. Choosing the right construction tools and equipment can mean the difference between doing a job quickly and completely, or working at a disadvantage and struggling just to finish it.

Some things, such as a stepladder, are worthwhile to buy or, like sawhorses, to make. But renting is the best choice for larger and more specialized equipment. This chapter deals with some of the most useful equipment for large home projects: ladders, sawhorses, scaffolding, concrete mixers, some special-purpose power equipment, hoists, and various kinds of jacks.

LADDERS

When you need elevation to do a job, do not climb up on a household step-stool or a stack of boxes. Use a proper ladder, or for large-area work a scaffold (see pages 60–61). There are four types of ladders to choose from, the familiar *stepladder,* a fixed-length *straight ladder* or an *extension ladder,* and versatile *folding ladders.*

Whichever type you need for a job, choose a ladder that is rated Type I Industrial/Commercial or Type II Commercial and that complies with the Occupational Safety and Health Act. The rating and compliance notice must be given on one of the rails, along with warnings and basic use information. Type I ladders meet standards for the most rugged continuous use. Type II ladders are quite adequate for home use and are less expensive.

Ladders are made of wood, metal—aluminum, steel, or magnesium alloy—or a combination of fiberglass rails and metal steps or rungs. Metal and fiberglass ladders are essentially maintenance-free, and especially in large sizes are much lighter in weight than wood ladders. All are equally useful for almost all kinds of work, but wood or fiberglass are safest for electrical work, to minimize shock hazards. Valuable features are nonskid pads or pivoted shoes on the ladder feet, and nonmarring bumpers or rollers at the top. A stabilizer that bolts to the top of a straight or extension ladder makes the ladder much safer to use.

STEPLADDERS

Stepladders range from 3 to 12 feet or more in height when closed; the open work height is a bit less. A 6- or 8-foot ladder is a good household choice. It should have rugged hinges and folding spreader braces, and both horizontal and X bracing in the rear legs. The ladder should be firm when open, and the steps should flex little or not at all as you stand on them. A wooden ladder should have metal braces or tie rods under the steps. A pail shelf is extremely useful; don't consider a stepladder without one.

STRAIGHT LADDERS

A straight, fixed-length ladder is specifically meant for working on vertical surfaces and climbing to high spots. Both the rails and the rungs must be sturdy. Rungs may be round (the least comfort-

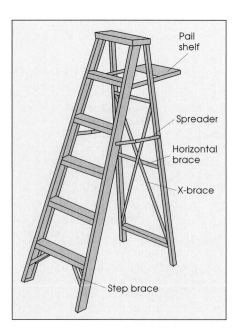

A STEPLADDER can be used for most indoor work as well as low-height outdoor jobs. Look for these features.

Pail shelf

Spreader

Horizontal brace

X-brace

Step brace

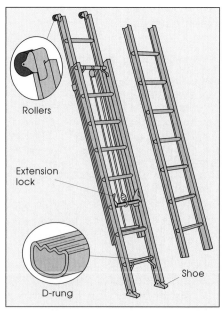

Rollers

Extension lock

D-rung

Shoe

A STRAIGHT OR EXTENSION LADDER is what you need for working 10 feet or higher outdoors.

able and safe shape), D-shaped, or flat as in a stepladder. Flat and D rungs should have ridges or some other non-slip surface.

EXTENSION LADDERS

An extension ladder is actually two straight ladders of equal length. One rides in brackets or tracks on the other and can be extended by pulling on a plastic rope that runs over control pulleys. Locks on the extension section fit over the rungs of the lower section to provide secure support. The nominal sizes of extension ladders are from 16 to 40 feet, the total length of both sections. The actual maximum working length is 3 to 5 feet less, because the sections must overlap at least that much when extended.

FOLDING LADDERS

There are two types of highly versatile folding ladders. One, a folding straight ladder, consists of three or four hinged sections that can be folded into A, inverted-U, or M shapes for various situations. The other is a kind of stepladder in which the rear legs are two extension ladder sections. It can be used normally, straight, or on stairs, as illustrated at the right. These ladders must have strong rails and rungs and, above all, rugged hinges that work freely and lock securely in each position.

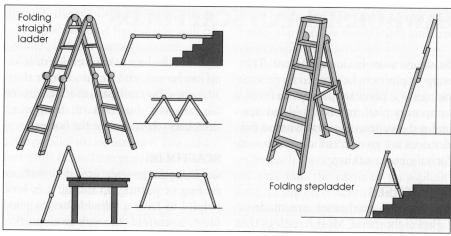

FOLDING LADDERS can be used on stairs and uneven ground or as scaffolds, as well as conventionally. The prime requirement is strong hinges that lock positively but are easy to release when desired.

CARRY A TALL LADDER this way. Bend your knees to lift or lower the ladder. Be sure the route is clear overhead.

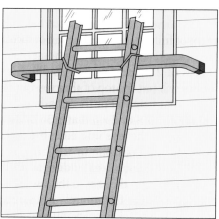

A STABILIZER bolts to the top of a ladder. It prevents side tilting and can span window openings.

WORKING WITH LADDERS—SAFETY POINTS

- Never move an unfolded or extended ladder more than a very short distance.
- Before moving a ladder, inspect the route for hazards on the ground and above. Overhead tree branches or wires could tip a tall ladder out of control, or give you a serious electrical shock.
- To carry a tall ladder in a vertical position, brace it with one rail against your shoulder and thigh as illustrated above. Crouch slightly and grasp a lower rung with one hand. Grasp an upper rung at forehead height with the other hand. Keep the ladder tight against your body as you straighten your knees to raise it slightly. Walk steadily to your destination and bend your knees to lower the feet of the ladder to the ground.
- Pull the base of a straight or extension ladder out from a wall a distance equal to one-fourth the length of the ladder—for example, 4 feet for a ladder extended to a 16-foot

working length. That will give a safe lean angle of about 75 degrees. And make sure the ladder does not lean left or right.
- The ladder feet or shoes must be on firm, level support. Put down boards on soft earth; clear away gravel, if any, to reach firm ground below.
- Use a stabilizer, illustrated above, across the top of a ladder both on flat wall surfaces and to bridge window openings.
- Whenever possible, tie off the top of a ladder to a chimney, to a 2 x 4 across the inside of a window opening, or to any other secure point. Have a helper steady the foot of the ladder as you climb, or stake a cleat across the feet to prevent their slipping.
- Let a ladder top extend at least two feet above a roof edge, and three feet or more above a tree branch. A branch may deflect a bit as you climb the ladder. Use only a tree branch that is strong and that angles up, not

down, from the trunk. That way, if the ladder should happen to slide, the top will move toward the trunk, which will stop it.
- Do not climb a ladder with tools or other equipment in your hands. Wear a tool belt with tools hanging at the sides or behind you, never in front, or use a rope and large S-hook to pull up what you need in a bucket after you have gotten to working height.
- Before starting to climb a ladder, be sure your hands and shoes are clean and dry so you will not slip.
- Keep your hips within the width of the ladder rails. Work out to either side to the extent your arms can reach, but do not stretch or lean farther sideways. Move the ladder instead.
- On a straight or extension ladder, keep your waistline below the level of the top rung. On a stepladder never stand on the very top step (the seat) or the step just below that.
- Never have two people on one ladder.

The success of any home improvement project depends on the materials used to do the job. This section provides information on selecting, buying, and using the most common types of building products. These materials and techniques are used in a wide range of repairs and improvements as well as in a number of specialized projects discussed in later chapters.

WHERE TO BUY MATERIALS

There are many sources of supply for the materials you need for working on your home. Most outlets also carry the tools and related equipment required to install or use the products they sell.

Lumberyards offer a full range of wood products in the most popular species and the most requested sizes, and related items such as fasteners. A good yard can special-order just about any wood product you need. Some yards do custom cutting and millwork, and even make doors, windows, and cabinets.

Building supply yards sell cement, sand, gravel, bricks, concrete blocks, wood and steel beams and posts, structural hardware, and a great deal more required for basic construction.

Home centers carry just about everything involved in home improvement—from concrete to wallcoverings. Home centers are like supermarkets, with row after row of products, allowing you to take your time to pick over items to find what you are looking for. Many *mass-market stores* include home centers or have departments devoted to home improvement materials, tools, hardware, and related items.

Hardware stores stock tools, ladders, various materials and finishes, and other products as well as nails, screws, hinges, and traditional hardware items. Many are essentially medium-sized home centers.

Specialty stores sell one major type of product. Examples are paint stores, glass dealers, tile, floor covering, and wallcovering stores, and plumbing suppliers.

II MATERIALS, FINISHES, AND HARDWARE

Mail order suppliers deal widely in tools, fasteners, and specialty hardware. Some are good sources for hard-to-find materials such as exotic woods and finishes.

HOW TO BUY MATERIALS

Many materials, such as lumber and plywood, are graded to ensure consistent quality, and to help match the product to the job. Other products, such as finishes and paints, have labels with information that is important when making a selection. Rating systems and directions for deciphering product information are included in discussions of specific materials. Here are some general purchasing guidelines.

• Buy the right materials for the job, to get long-lasting results.

• Look for materials that are free of damage. Edges should be continuous and free of nicks. Corners should be square. Curves should be continuous and smooth.

• You may wish to buy about 10 percent more than you think you will need. That way, if a material is damaged or you make a mistake, you will have extra on hand. Some materials vary from lot to lot; buying extra ensures having replacements that match.

• Always shop around for the best price consistent with good quality.

5 LUMBER, FASTENERS, AND TRIM

Few building products are as versatile as wood. It can be used as timbers that support a building, as joists, studs, and rafters for the framework or skeleton, and as panels, boards, moldings, and other elements that finish the structure. This chapter deals with structural and framing lumber, with fasteners (nails, screws, and adhesives) and ways of joining wood pieces together, and with trim pieces. Plywood and similar panel products are covered in Chapter 6. There is additional information about wood for flooring in Chapter 11, and about moldings in Chapter 16.

WOOD SPECIES

Tree species are divided into *softwoods* and *hardwoods*. Softwoods comprise most of the stock in lumberyards. They are less expensive and easier to work with than hardwoods. Most softwoods come from evergreen (cone bearing) trees. Hardwoods come from broadleaf, deciduous trees, such as oak and maple. They are not widely stocked, and may have to be specially ordered. Generally, hardwoods are denser and heavier than softwoods. They can be worked more precisely in making joints. Softwoods are usually used for house framing, exterior trim, decks, and porches. Some species are also used for flooring. Hardwoods are most often used for finish flooring, for specialty pieces of interior trim, and for furniture.

LUMBER AT THE MILL

At a sawmill, tree trunks are debarked, rough cut, and then finish cut into the pieces sold at lumberyards and home supply centers. Sawmills use two common methods to cut up a log, plain sawing and quarter sawing. Because the

growth rings—visible as the "end grain"—of quarter-sawn lumber are at a 45- to 90-degree angle with the surface, the wood shrinks and warps less than plain-sawn lumber, and therefore it is preferred for construction.

Just after a log is cut, as much as 50 percent of the weight of the green (undried or unseasoned) wood is moisture. In lumber for general construction use, the moisture content is reduced by either kiln or air drying to between 15

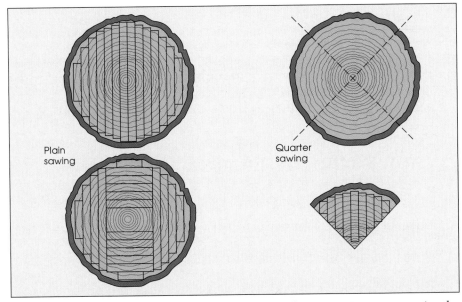

Plain sawing

Quarter sawing

IN THE SAWMILL logs may be plain sawed in either of two ways. In quarter sawing the log is cut into quarters and each is then cut into lumber. Quarter-sawn lumber is more stable because the growth rings are from 45° to 90° with the surface.

SELECTED SPECIES FOR CONSTRUCTION LUMBER

SOFTWOODS (varieties)	Idaho white; longleaf	Black cherry
Cedar (Alaska; incense;	yellow; shortleaf)	Cottonwood
Port-Orford; eastern,	Redwood	American elm
western red; northern,	Spruce (eastern;	Rock elm
southern white)	Engelmann; Sitka)	Sweet gum
Cypress	Tamarack	Hickory
Fir (balsam; Douglas; white)	Yew (Pacific)	Mahogany
Hemlock (eastern; moun-		Sugar maple
tain; West Coast)	**HARDWOODS**	Red oak
Larch (western)	White ash	White oak
Pine (jack; lodgepole;	Basswood	Poplar
Norway; ponderosa;	American beech	Black walnut
sugar; northern;	Yellow birch	Willow

and 19 percent. Wood for flooring should have only 7 to 10 percent moisture content.

LUMBER DIMENSIONS

A log is rough cut into pieces of various *nominal* (named) sizes. Planing and smoothing, called *dressing,* reduce the overall dimensions of each piece, and the wood shrinks a bit as it dries. So although the lumber is still identified by nominal size, the actual size is smaller. For example, the "two by four" that you buy was rough cut to a full 2 × 4 inches, but the finished piece you get actually measures 1½ × 3½ inches. The standardized nominal and actual widths and thicknesses of softwood lumber are listed at the right. Softwood lumber is sold in lengths of 6 through 20 feet in increments of 2 feet. The stated length of lumber is the actual dimension.

Where width does not need to be specified, lumber is often identified only by thickness—1× or 2×, for example. The following terms are also used to describe softwood lumber; the sizes mentioned are all nominal dimensions.

Boards are 1 inch thick and 6 or more inches wide. Narrower pieces are properly termed *strips,* but "board" is often used. *Planks* are 1¼ or more inches thick and 8 inches or more wide. *Dimension lumber* is at least 2 inches thick and wide. *Timbers, posts,* and *beams* measure at least 5 inches in their smallest dimension.

Hardwood thicknesses for 1 × 2 and larger boards are expressed in quarter inches of the rough cut. "Four quarter" or ¼ lumber is nominally 1 inch thick, and "eight quarter" (⅝) is nominally 2 inches thick; the actual dressed sizes are smaller. Flooring has other thickness and width differences; see the lumber dimensions box.

BUYING LUMBER

The amount of lumber you buy usually determines how you are charged for it. If all you need are, say, a few 2 × 4s, retailers often charge by the piece. But for larger orders the price is based on the total number of board feet. A board foot is a measure of volume: 144 cubic inches of wood, whatever the nominal

dimensions may be. As illustrated below, the number of board feet in one piece is:

$$(T \times W \times L) \div 12$$

and in several pieces of the same nominal size:

$$(T \times W \times L \times N) \div 12$$

where T is the thickness in inches, W is the width in inches, L is the length *in feet,* and N is the number of pieces. Boards less than 1 inch thick are figured with a nominal thickness of 1 inch.

Specialty pieces such as moldings, and some hardwoods, are commonly priced by the linear or running foot of length.

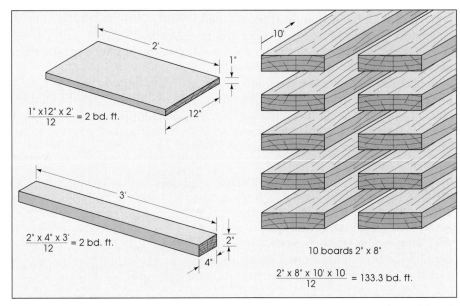

BOARD FEET are calculated from nominal thickness and width in inches and actual length in feet. The method for single pieces is at the left. For several pieces of the same size, the calculation is at the right.

DRY LUMBER DIMENSIONS

SOFTWOOD, inches		HARDWOOD, inches	
Nominal	Actual	Nominal	Actual
1 × 2	3/4 × 1 1/2	**Thickness**	
1 × 3	3/4 × 2 1/2	4/4 * (1)	3/4
1 × 4	3/4 × 3 1/2	5/4 (1 1/4)	1 5/32
1 × 6	3/4 × 5 1/2	6/4 (1 1/2)	1 13/32
1 × 8	3/4 × 7 1/4	7/4 (1 3/4)	1 19/32
1 × 10	3/4 × 9 1/4	8/4 (2)	1 13/16
1 × 12	3/4 × 11 1/4	9/4 (2 1/4)	2 3/32
2 × 2	1 1/2 × 1 1/2	10/4 (2 1/2)	2 3/8
2 × 3	1 1/2 × 2 1/2	11/4 (2 3/4)	2 9/16
2 × 4	1 1/2 × 3 1/2	12/4 (3)	2 3/4
2 × 6	1 1/2 × 5 1/2	16/4 (4)	3 3/4
2 × 8	1 1/2 × 7 1/4	*quarter-inch nominal size	
2 × 10	1 1/2 × 9 1/4	**Width**	
2 × 12	1 1/2 × 11 1/4	2–7	1/2 in. less than nominal
3 × 4	2 1/2 × 3 1/2	8–wider	3/4 in. less than nominal
4 × 4	3 1/2 × 3 1/2		
4 × 6	3 1/2 × 5 1/2	**HARDWOOD FLOORING, inches**	
6 × 6	5 1/2 × 5 1/2	**Thickness**	
8 × 8	7 1/2 × 7 1/2	3/8–5/8	1/16 in. less than nominal
		1–1 1/2	1/4 in. less than nominal
SOFTWOOD DECKING, inches		**Width**	
Thickness , 1/2 in. less than nominal		2–6	7/8 in. less than nominal
Width, 5–6, 1 in. less; 8–12, 1 3/4 in. less			

LUMBER GRADES AND QUALITY

In addition to standardized dimensions, lumber is classified according to various categories of use and grades of appearance and quality. Grading standards are established by the American Lumber Standards Committee of the Department of Commerce. Specific grading practices vary a bit among the fifteen-plus softwood lumber inspection associations, but they generally ensure products with uniform levels of quality throughout the industry. Softwood lumber is grade-stamped when it leaves the mill. However, some retailers cut long pieces into shorter standard lengths, so you may not find a grade mark on every piece you buy.

SOFTWOOD GRADES

There are distinct quality and use grades for softwood boards (1 inch thick and less) and for dimension lumber (2 × 2 inches and larger). Grade names are listed in the accompanying box. In each category the highest grades have the fewest defects. For general construction projects, No. 1 or No. 2 Common boards, and Select Structural or No. 1 Dimension lumber will provide the best combination of quality and price. Choose higher-grade boards for use wherever good appearance is a significant concern, and be prepared to pay more for them.

STRESS-RATED LUMBER

Dimension lumber graded as suitable for carrying heavy loads—for use as girders, for example—must be machine tested to determine its load-carrying capabilities. The test rating is marked "SR" or "Stress Rated." If you are doing structural work, consult with your lumber supplier for material with a proper stress rating.

HARDWOOD GRADES

The National Hardwood Lumber Association sets the rules for hardwood grading. Top-quality hardwood has a combined grade of Firsts and Seconds (FAS), or sometimes separate First and Second grades. As with soft-woods, the grades reflect the size and condition of the boards, but there are far fewer use categories because hardwoods are primarily used for finish work and other applications where appearance is important.

PRESSURE-TREATED LUMBER

A few softwood species, such as redwood and cypress, have a natural resistance to moisture, insects, and decay. Others can be protected by high-pressure impregnation with preservative chemicals. This is done by the wood producer, and the wood is specially stamped. Almost all codes require pressure-treated or equivalent lumber for outdoor structures such as decks, fences, stairs, and balconies, and wherever structural members are in contact with the earth or foundation masonry. Do-it-yourself treatment by soaking, spraying, or brushing is not sufficient

LUMBER CATEGORIES AND GRADES

SOFTWOOD BOARDS (equivalent terms)	No. 4 (Utility)	Construction
	No. 5 (Industrial)	Utility
Select	Siding	
B and Better (Supreme)	Construction	HARDWOOD
C (Choice)	Standard	Firsts and Seconds (FAS)
D (Quality)		No. 1
Finish	SOFTWOOD	No. 2
Prime	DIMENSION LUMBER	No. 3
E	Select Structural	Selects (FAS1FACE)
Common	No. 1	Common
No. 1 (Colonial)	No. 2	No. 1
No. 2 (Sterling; Premium)	No. 3	No. 2
No. 3 (Standard)	Stud	No. 3A, 3B

SOFTWOOD LUMBER STAMP

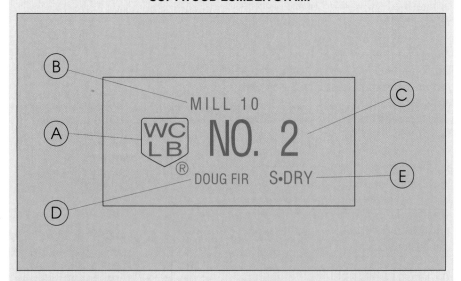

Key to stamp, above.
A. Grading agency (West Coast Lumber Inspection Bureau)
B. Mill identification
C. Grade
D. Species
E. Seasoning or moisture content

Common Abbreviations on Lumber Stamps

A: Appearance	SR: Stress rated
B&B: B and Better	KD: Kiln dried
C&Btr: C and Better	S-Dry: Air seasoned,
Const: Construction	19% max. moisture
Sel Str: Select	S-Grn: Over 19% max.
Structural	moisture
Stand: Standard	MC 15: 15% max.
Util: Utility	moisture

for such applications. The amount of preservative the lumber retains determines how it should be used. Lumber marked .25 (pounds per cubic foot) is for aboveground use; lumber with a retention level of .40 can be placed in contact with the ground. A level of .60 is required for below-ground structural use. Exposure conditions are marked LP-2, aboveground; LP-22, belowground; or FDN, all-weather.

CAUTION
The chemicals that make wood decay-resistant are poisons. Always handle preservative-treated wood as follows.
  • Wear gloves. Wash your hands thoroughly after working with treated wood.
  • Wear a mask over your nose and mouth. Avoid inhaling sawdust from treated (or untreated) lumber.
  • Wear eye protection when sawing and hammering.
  • Bury waste wood or take it to a proper disposal agency. Do not burn treated wood.
  • Do not use pressure-treated lumber for interior construction.
  • Do not use treated lumber as edging or framing for a vegetable garden.

PRESSURE-TREATED LUMBER STAMP

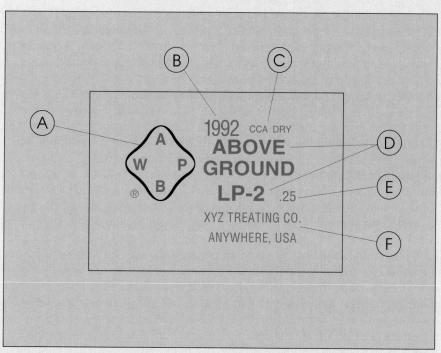

A, certifying agency (American Wood Preservers Bureau). B, year of treatment. C, preservative used. D, exposure (use) conditions. E, preservative retention level. F, treatment company and plant location.

SELECTING AND STORING LUMBER

If you need only a few pieces, a lumber dealer may allow you to pick them out. For large orders, yard personnel usually select the lumber, but you can reject any substandard lumber at the time of delivery.

Defects in lumber can range from discolorations that affect the appearance but not the strength, to warping and twists that can make a board useless. Besides such distortions of shape and dimension, lumber defects include:

Checks. Small surface separations.
Decay. Crumbly or spongy wood caused by fungi.

Knots. The base wood of branches of the tree.
Pitch pocket. A cavity that held, and may still hold, resin.
Splits. Grain separations that go all the way through the board.
Wane. Tree bark or surface curvature where bark grew.

If it is necessary to store lumber outdoors, stack it in layers as shown below. Leave about 2 inches between adjacent pieces for air circulation, and space 2x supports and 1x separators no more than 24 inches apart. Cover the stack with a waterproof tarp.

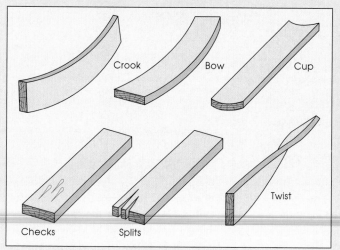

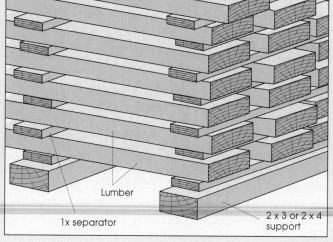

LUMBER FASTENERS

LUMBER FASTENERS

Nails and screws are the universal basic fasteners in carpentry and general building. They are quick and easy to use, and are available in great variety for a vast number of applications. In some cases they may be supplemented or replaced by specialty fasteners (page 72) or adhesives (page 73).

NAIL SHAPES AND SIZES

Nails are designed to do specific jobs. *Common nails* have heavy-duty shanks for strength and large flat heads for better holding power in general construction work. *Finishing* and *casing nails* are slender and have small heads designed to be driven below the surface of the wood and concealed; they are used for fine work, such as installing trim. Other nail shapes are similarly specialized.

Nail size can be indicated by length in inches or by pennyweight, abbreviated "d" (see box). Some types, such as dry-wall and roofing nails, are usually sized only in inches. Generally, as nail length increases, diameter also increases.

USING NAILS

To make a good fastening, nail through the thinner piece into the thicker one. About two-thirds of a nail's length should penetrate into the thicker, receiving board. To avoid splitting softwood when nailing near an end, blunt the nail by tapping the point once or twice with your hammer before starting to drive it. In hardwood, drill a small pilot hole. To conceal a nail with a small head, use a nail set as shown below. To drive a flathead nail home in a tight spot, use a flat-ended nail set. Most nails are made of steel, which can rust. For outdoor and damp-area projects, use rustproof galvanized, aluminum, or copper nails. When nailing, always wear safety goggles to protect your eyes.

NAIL SIZES AND QUANTITIES

Small quantities of nails are sold by count in boxes or other packages. In bulk quantities, nails are sold by the pound. Use the number of nails per pound listed here for common and finishing nails as a guide for ordering other types of similar size.

Length, inches	Penny-weight	Approx. No. of Nails/lb.	
		Common	Finishing
1	2d	810	1,470
1 1/4	3d	560	850
1 1/2	4d	300	630
1 3/4	5d	265	520
2	6d	170	285
2 1/4	7d	155	245
2 1/2	8d	95	195
2 3/4	9d	90	175
3	10d	65	120
3 1/4	12d	60	110
3 1/2	16d	45	90
4	20d	30	65
4 1/2	30d	25	—
5	40d	15	—
5 1/2	50d	13	—
6	60d	12	—

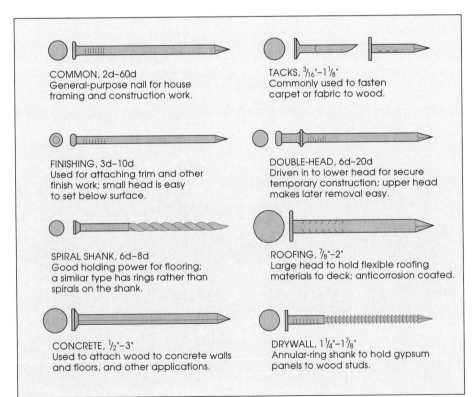

COMMON, 2d–60d
General-purpose nail for house framing and construction work.

FINISHING, 3d–10d
Used for attaching trim and other finish work; small head is easy to set below surface.

SPIRAL SHANK, 6d–8d
Good holding power for flooring; a similar type has rings rather than spirals on the shank.

CONCRETE, 1/2"–3"
Used to attach wood to concrete walls and floors, and other applications.

TACKS, 3/16"–1 1/8"
Commonly used to fasten carpet or fabric to wood.

DOUBLE-HEAD, 6d–20d
Driven in to lower head for secure temporary construction; upper head makes later removal easy.

ROOFING, 7/8"–2"
Large head to hold flexible roofing materials to deck; anticorrosion coated.

DRYWALL, 1 1/4"–1 7/8"
Annular-ring shank to hold gypsum panels to wood studs.

NAIL TYPES AND USES. These are the types of nails most widely used for home projects, their standard size ranges, and common applications. For pennyweight/inch equivalents, see the box at the top of this page.

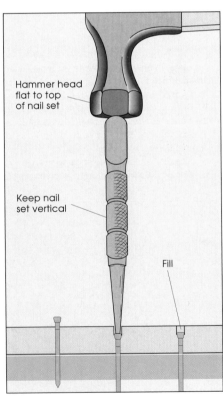

Hammer head flat to top of nail set

Keep nail set vertical

Fill

USE A NAIL SET for the last few blows to drive a finishing nail head below the surface. Fill the hole with wood putty.

SCREWS AND BOLTS

Screws and bolts have superior holding power compared to nails, and unlike nails they can be reused—removal and replacement are quick and easy.

Screws are sized by length in inches and by shank diameter, expressed as a gauge number. *Wood screws* have sharp threads that taper to a point. *Self-tapping screws* have full-length threads that cut their way through wood and metal once the tip is inserted into a small starting hole. *Drywall* and *sheet metal* screws are self-tapping screws. *Lag screws* are heavy-duty, boltlike fasteners with coarse threads and square heads that are turned with a wrench.

SCREW HEADS

Most screw heads are either flat, oval, or round. Flat heads are installed flush with or countersunk below the surface. Oval heads protrude slightly, but the lower portion of the head is in the material. Round heads sit above the surface, as do pan heads, commonly found on sheet metal screws. Most screw heads have either a straight slot or crossed slots, called a Phillips head, to accept a matching screwdriver blade. A third type of head has a square socket, and there are others for special applications.

USING WOOD SCREWS

At least two-thirds of the threaded portion of a wood screw should enter the base material. To avoid splitting the wood, drill a full-depth pilot hole. For a screw head to sit flush with or below the surface, the hole must be countersunk at the top. In hardwoods, the upper, shank portion of the hole should be larger than the lower, thread portion. The easiest way to do this is to use a combination drill and countersink bit (see page 20), available in most screw gauge sizes. Or use standard bits (see box) and a separate countersink.

BOLTS

Common bolts, also called machine bolts or cap screws, and *carriage bolts* have straight shanks with threads along about half their lengths. *Stove bolts* and smaller diameter, finer threaded *machine screws* are threaded full length. All bolts require a full-diameter hole drilled through both pieces of material being fastened; they are secured with nuts.

Bolts are sized by diameter, thread count, and length. For example, a ⅜-18 × 6 bolt is ⅜ inch in diameter with 18 threads to the inch, and is 6 inches long. Retailers commonly stock bolts from ⅛ to ¾ inch in diameter and from ½ to 12 inches in length.

Common bolts have square or hexagonal heads. Carriage bolts have round heads and square shoulders that dig into the wood and keep the bolt from turning. Stove bolts and machine screws have slotted heads of various shapes.

WASHERS AND NUTS

Washers spread the pressure of a fastener head or a nut to prevent damage to a surface. Flat washers may also be used as spacers. Lockwashers exert counterpressure against a nut to keep it secure where movement or vibration may occur. Nuts fasten the threaded ends of bolts. Square and hex nuts are most common. Jam and lock nuts have locking shoulders or inserts. Wing nuts can be spun easily by hand for quick placement or removal.

PILOT HOLES FOR SCREWS

For a shank hole, use a bit the same size or 1/64 inch larger than the shank diameter.

SCREW		THREAD HOLE SIZE inches	
Gauge No.	Shank Dia., in.	Softwood	Hardwood
1	1/16	Use	3/64
2	5/64	awl	1/16
3	3/32	point	1/16
4	7/64		5/64
5	1/8	1/16	5/64
6	9/64	1/16	3/32
7	5/32	1/16	3/32
8	5/32	1/16	7/64
9	11/64	5/64	1/8
10	3/16	5/64	1/8
12	7/32	5/64	5/32
14	15/64	7/64	5/32
16	17/64	11/64	3/16
18	19/64	3/16	15/64
20	3/8	15/64	1/4

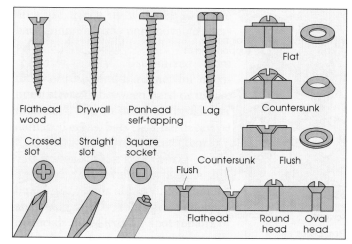

SCREWS. Screw size, threads, and head design vary with intended use. Screw heads can be driven directly against wood, or used with washers that protect the surface.

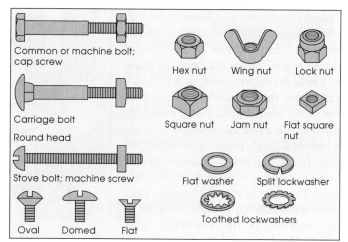

BOLTS. Bolts will accept any style nut with a matching thread size. A flat washer is needed under a nut against wood, and especially between wood and a lockwasher.

WORKING WITH LUMBER

There are many ways to join one piece of wood to another. Those shown on these two pages are quick and efficient. Others, on pages 76–77, enhance the appearance of the job and strengthen the joint. Just about any joint can be made with either hand tools or power equipment. In either case, measure and mark carefully before cutting. It is also a good idea to practice making the more difficult joints with scrap wood before using them in a project.

BUTT JOINTS

The simplest joint consists of the end of one piece butted squarely against another to form a T or an L that is nailed, screwed, or glued together. Butt joints are used extensively in rough carpentry. Framed walls are made of vertical 2 × 4 studs butted at the top and bottom to horizontal 2 × 4s called plates. The crosspieces in rough openings for windows and doors butt against studs on either side. You can fasten such joints either by toenailing or by nailing through the flat piece into the end of the butted

piece. Where nailing is not possible or a joint needs extra strength, you can use screws and metal braces called T-plates, L-plates, and corner or angle brackets, or you can glue a block in the inside corner, as shown below.

It is important to get a butt joint square, even in rough framing. Use a try square to mark one side and an edge of the butting piece so you can make a straight cut both across and down through the wood. Mark a square line across the piece that it will butt against, and then use the square to make sure that the joint is at a right angle as you fasten it. When fastening a vertical piece such as a stud, make a square butt joint at one end, then use a level to get the piece truly vertical (plumb) before fastening the other end.

MITER JOINTS

A miter joint is a butt joint with one or both pieces cut at an angle. Usually both pieces are cut at 45 degrees so they form a perfect right angle when put together, for example in installing door

and window trim, going around outside corners with molding, and making picture frames.

The best way to make the angle cut is with a miter box and back saw, or with a power miter saw. Most circular saws can be adjusted for 45-degree cuts that are adequate for rough framing, but not always good enough for finished carpentry. When using a miter box, first lock the saw precisely at the angle you want. Mark the cut line on the wood cleanly and precisely, and hold the stock securely against the back and the floor of the box. Cut just on the scrap side of the line. You can sand or plane off any slight excess if necessary. Cutting too short or even fractionally off angle will result in a loose or gaping joint.

You can fasten a miter joint by nailing from both edges. If the pieces are secured in place, as with door trim, for example, nailing is easy. If not, fasten them to a board with C-clamps or hold them in a vise while you nail. Use a square to get true right-angle alignment before fastening, and drill tiny pilot holes to guide the nails if necessary. To strengthen a miter joint, apply glue

MAKING BUTT, MITER, AND LAP JOINTS

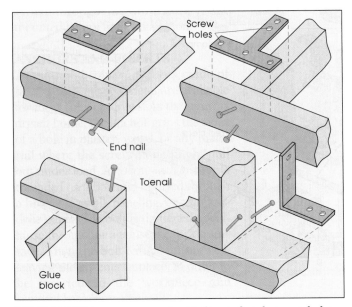

BUTT JOINTS are easy to make. Nailing is fast, but metal plates and screws or corner blocks give greater strength where needed. Drive toenails from both sides of a butted piece; see page 161.

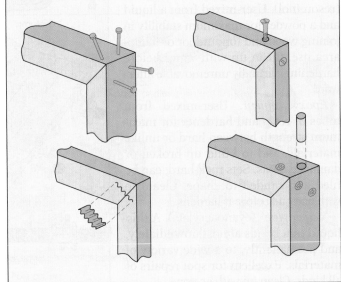

MITER JOINTS must be precisely cut for a good fit and finished appearance. Glue can be used with any of the methods shown. Other types of metal fasteners are available.

before nailing. Or use screws, metal fasteners, or wooden dowels along with glue. There are corner clamps for gluing mitered joints in stock up to 3 inches wide.

LAP JOINTS

In a lap joint one piece lies over the other, and the thickness of one or both pieces is cut down so the completed surface is flush. In a *flat lap* joint the wide sides of the boards are in contact; in an *edge lap* joint the narrow sides intersect. The boards may cross at any angle. Joints are also called *end or corner lap, cross lap,* and *T-lap* according to where they join one another.

Depending on the thicknesses of the two pieces, any lap joint may be made as a *full lap* or a *half lap.*

In a full-lap joint one board is used full thickness and the other is cut away to receive it. In a half-lap joint the thickness of both pieces is cut down—equally for pieces of the same thickness, proportionately for pieces of different thicknesses. In almost no case should a piece be reduced to less than half its thickness; otherwise the board is likely to break at the joint.

MAKING LAP JOINTS

In every lap joint you must remove thickness from one or both boards. This must be done precisely so that the two pieces will fit together snugly. With a table or radial arm saw that is a matter of setting the blade for the proper depth of cut and then making repeated passes to cut notches of the required width. If you will be cutting the pieces by hand, use the following procedure.

Call the upper, overlapping board A and the lower, overlapped board B. Lay A across B at exactly the correct angle. (If the boards are not the same thickness, B is the thicker one.) Mark A's width on B with a scratch awl or a sharp knife blade.

Next, measure down on both sides of B exactly the depth to be cut. Mark both the sides and the bottom of the notch to be cut. For a full-lap joint the depth will be the full thickness of A. For a half-lap joint with boards of equal thickness, the depth will be half the thickness. If they are different, mark B for a deeper cut than the one you will make in A. For example, if B is 2 inches thick and A is 1 inch thick, mark B for a depth of ¾ inch, and plan to remove ¼ inch from A.

Now make the cuts across the face of B with a back saw. Stay just inside the marked lines and keep the saw blade vertical as you cut down exactly to the depth mark on each side. The easiest way to do this is in a miter box. The procedure now differs for an end lap and a lap in the middle of the board.

For an end lap, clamp the board in a vise with the cut end upward and saw straight down just inside the depth line until you reach the first cut. The scrap will fall out, leaving an end notch.

For a mid-board lap, make two or three more depth cuts across the board between those already there. Then use a sharp chisel to remove the scrap wood bit by bit until the notch is a uniform depth.

If you are making a half-lap joint, lay board A into the finished notch in B. Mark B's width on A, mark A for the proper depth, then cut the notch in A just as you did in B.

Trial-fit the joint. If necessary, use a sharp chisel to make adjustments until the fit is snug and the surfaces of the two pieces lie flush with one another. Finally, fasten the joint with glue, screws, or both.   *Continued*

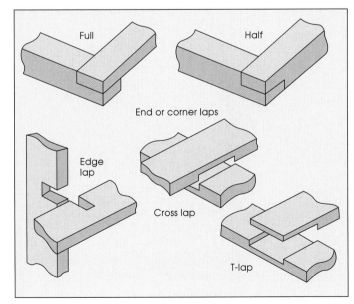

TYPES OF LAP JOINTS. Use a full lap joint when one board is twice as thick as the other, or more. Boards can intersect at any angle, for example, for X crossbracing under a workbench.

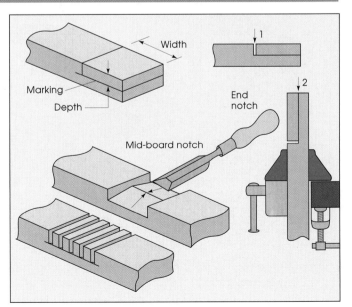

MAKING LAP JOINTS. Mark the joint width and depth precisely. Make a depth cut across face of board first, then cut in from the end, or use a chisel to clean out a mid-board notch.

WORKING WITH LUMBER
Continued

DADO AND RABBET JOINTS

A *rabbet* is a lip cut along the edge of a board. A *dado* is a square U-groove cut across the face of a board. They are used for joints in which the edge of another board fits into the lip or groove. Such joints are often used to support the ends of shelves, or to inset a back flush with the rear edges of a cabinet or bookcase. They provide a more finished appearance and a stronger structure in furniture and cabinets than do butt joints or shelf-and-cleat construction.

CUTTING RABBETS AND DADOES

The depth of a rabbet or dado is usually one-third, and no more than one-half the thickness of the board it is cut into. The width is equal to the thickness of the board that fits into it. The easiest way to cut a rabbet or dado is with a router fitted with a straight bit, or with dado blades in a table or radial arm saw. You can also use an ordinary power saw blade and make repeated passes.

With hand tools, it is fairly easy to cut a rabbet or dado across the width of a board. Cutting accurately along the length of a board is much more difficult. In either case, it helps to clamp or tack a guide strip on the board to keep the cut straight and the blade vertical. Use a back saw, and control the depth of the cut by clamping a stop block on the blade as illustrated.

To make a rabbet, mark the thickness of the insert board on the face of the board to be cut. (You may want to make the rabbet a bit wider and plane off the excess after assembling the joint. Planing is easy along the length of a board, but difficult if you are making an end rabbet.) Also mark the depth of the rabbet. Then cut down to that depth from the face of the board. Make the second cut from the edge of the board, along the depth line, to meet the first cut, just as in cutting an end lap (see page 75). Fasten the insert board in the rabbet with glue and finishing nails.

To cut a full-width or *through dado* by hand, mark the width and depth of the groove. Then cut down along each line on the face, using a guide strip against one side of the blade and a depth stop on the other side as shown. Remove the waste between the cuts with a sharp chisel. Assemble the joint with glue; nails are seldom necessary.

A *stopped dado* stops short of the front edge, giving a finished appearance. To begin, cut about an inch of the groove at the stopped end with a chisel. That will give enough room to cut the sides with a saw. Then chisel out the waste between the cuts. Notch the front corner of the insert board so that it will sit in the dado with its front edge flush with the edge of the dadoed board.

MAKING RABBET AND DADO JOINTS

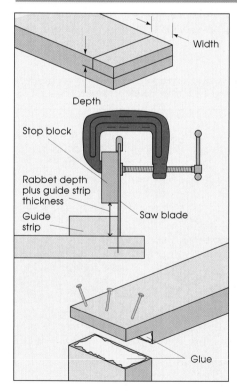

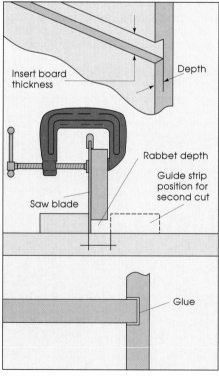

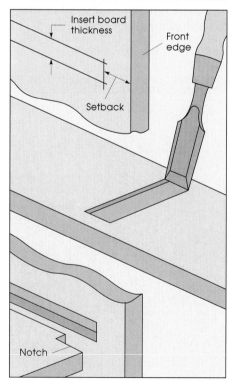

A RABBET is cut in the end or long edge of a board. Set the stop block depth so the saw will be at the bottom of the rabbet when the block rests on the guide strip.

A THROUGH DADO extends from edge to edge. Turn the board around and move the guide strip to make the second cut without changing the stop block.

A STOPPED DADO is first cut with a chisel at the stopped end, then sawed and chiseled out. A notch in the insert board brings the front edges flush.

OTHER METHODS OF JOINING WOOD

THREE SIMPLE CORNERS

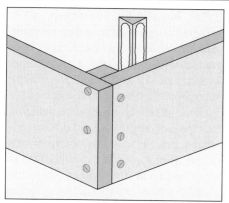

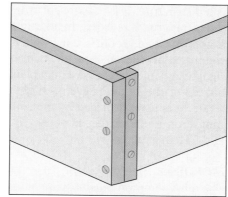

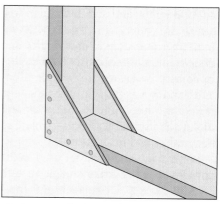

A SQUARE INSIDE BLOCK provides extra depth for nails or screws. Use glue with a triangular block.

AN OUTSIDE BLOCK leaves an unobstructed corner inside. Like an inside block it can be square or triangular.

GUSSETS of plywood make very strong joints. End-nail the butt joint, then glue and nail gussets in place.

TONGUE-AND-GROOVE JOINT

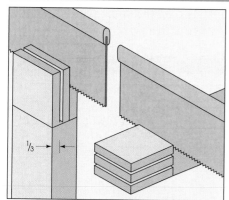

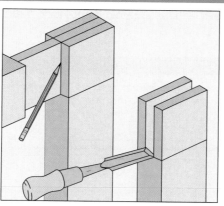

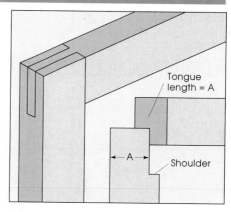

CUT A TONGUE by removing one-third of the thickness from each side. Make the end cuts first, then the face cuts.

CUT A GROOVE by marking from the tongue and cutting down from the end. Then clean out the center with a chisel.

ASSEMBLE THE JOINT with glue. For greater strength, cut a shoulder so the grooved piece will support the other one.

MORTISE-AND-TENON JOINT

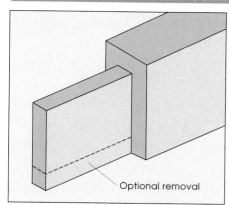

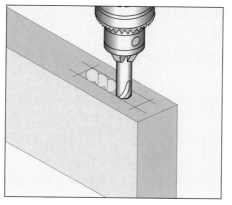

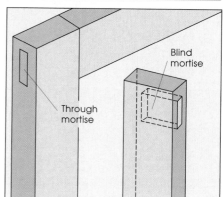

CUT A TENON like a tongue (see above), then cut away part of the top and, optionally, the bottom of the tongue.

CUT A MORTISE marked from the tenon. Drill out the center waste, then cut the sides square with a chisel; see page 23.

ASSEMBLE THE JOINT with glue. The tenon end shows in a *through mortise;* a partial-depth *blind mortise* conceals it.

TRIM

The pieces of lumber that finish edges, conceal joints, and add decoration to a house are called trim. The most common interior examples are window and door casings, baseboards, and ceiling moldings. Exterior trim includes door and window casings, cornicework—the finishing pieces under the eaves and along the edges of a roof—gable end decoration, and much more.

Some trim, such as that used at the corners of clapboard or shingled exterior walls, has a flat surface. But most trim has a profile, a shaped surface, and is usually called molding. A number of stock molding profiles and applications are illustrated below; there are more on page 210. Many exterior trim profiles are the same as interior trim, but on a larger scale.

Because trim is visible in the finished structure, it is usually cut from the better grades of wood. In addition, a great deal of wood is cut away in shaping a profile. As a result, trim is significantly more expensive than plain boards of the same or even a higher grade. It is usually priced by the running foot, and stocked in 6-, 8-, 10-, and 12-foot lengths.

MOLDING

The most common moldings are made from softwoods, although hardwood variations are available. As with other types of finish lumber, trim is graded by appearance. Clear moldings have few defects, are cut from a single length of wood, and are suitable for a natural finish or light staining. Paint-grade mold-

ings have more defects, may be composed of a number of different pieces of wood joined together, and are intended to be painted.

The installation and repair of the moldings used to trim the joints at the top and bottom of walls, such as base, cove, and bed moldings, are discussed in Chapter 16. Basic corner-making techniques are shown on the next page.

Some moldings that were designed for a particular purpose are now used in other ways. For example, *astragals* were originally mounted at the center of double doors. Today they add an interesting profile when combined with other moldings. Similarly, *glass beads* were used to hold glass in a window sash. Now they add details to other moldings. Special-purpose moldings include: *panel moldings*, used to hide joints on walls, doors, and furniture; *picture moldings*, installed on the upper part of a wall to

TRIM PROFILES AND STYLES

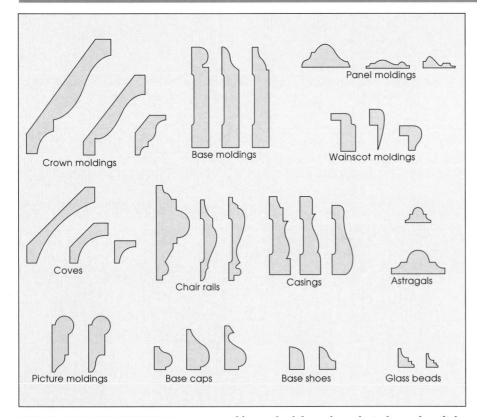

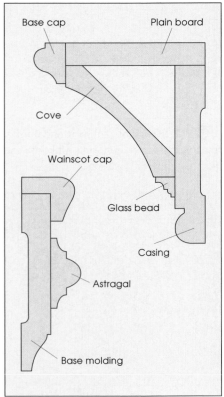

STOCK MOLDING PROFILES are reasonably standard throughout the industry, but slight variations in size or shape may make it difficult to exactly match old existing molding. One solution is to replace all of one kind of molding in a room with the closest matching new molding, and save the original pieces for repairs or alterations in other rooms.

COMPLEX MOLDINGS can be built up from stock shapes. To design distinctive trim at low cost, buy short lengths to experiment with, then order only what you need.

support hooks used to hang pictures; and *wainscot caps,* which trim the top of paneling that runs from the baseboard up to a point midway on a wall.

SPECIALTY TRIM

A few mills offer intricate running patterns such as dentils, egg and dart, and floral designs. Some are cut from wood; others are pressed-wood or die-stamped surface patterns. Other specialty trim items include medallions and wall niches. Many pieces originally made from wood are now cast from plastic resins. They are lightweight and can be cut, nailed, and painted.

WORKING WITH TRIM

Because trim is part of the finish work, it must be installed with care. You must make exact measurements and clean, precise cuts. If trim is to be painted, it saves later work to paint it before instal-

lation and then touch up as necessary. This is especially a good idea if the trim will be a different color than the adjoining surfaces.

CUTTING TRIM

Mark cut lines with a scratch awl or a knife blade, using a metal straightedge or angle to guide the line. A pencil point dulls rapidly on wood, drawing a wider, less precise line than you need.

Make sure a long straightedge or a large carpenter's square is held securely in position before marking a cut line. A guide held only by hand can easily be pushed out of alignment as you draw an awl or knife blade along it. Use clamps or masking tape, or temporarily attach small pieces of sandpaper to the underside of the marking guide with rubber cement, to prevent skidding.

When marking angles, use guides with fixed angles, such as a try square,

or adjustable guides that have a positive locking action. To mark complex lines, cut an exact-fitting template from thin cardboard, then trace the outline onto the workpiece. Mark the material on the waste side of a cut line with penciled Xs so there is no chance for error when you come to make the cut.

Use only clean, sharp tools. Trim costs too much and there is too much effort in doing finish work to risk getting ragged edges or uneven surfaces. Make a saw cut just on the waste side of a marked line, not directly on the line. The saw kerf removes some material. If that causes a piece to be fractionally short, there will be a gap that must be filled or otherwise concealed, whereas a piece that is slightly long can easily be adjusted. If a single piece of trim is not long enough for a straight run, cut two pieces for a *scarf joint* (see box, page 212) that will fall over a framing member.

MAKING CORNERS WITH TRIM

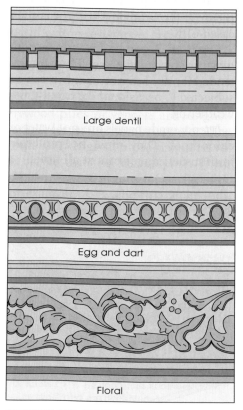

SPECIALTY TRIM with intricate detail and ornate patterns is now available in cast-plastic reproductions. Wood versions would be prohibitively expensive, if available at all.

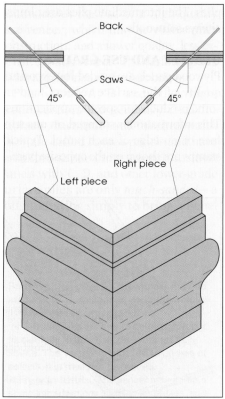

TO MAKE AN OUTSIDE CORNER, cut the lefthand piece at a 45° angle from the right in a miter box, and the righthand piece at 45° from the left. Join as shown.

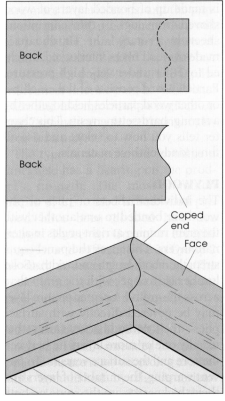

TO MAKE AN INSIDE CORNER, cope one piece to match the other. Trace the profile on the back, then cut from the back with a coping saw. See page 137 for another method.

OIL AND WAX FINISHES

When used as a final finish, oil or wax can produce the deep, lustrous glow we associate with the finest antiques made of rich woods. This kind of beauty is unattainable with any other finishing material, and there is just one secret to it: plenty of hand rubbing.

FINISHING WITH OIL

Unlike the preparation for almost all other finishes, wood that is to receive an oil finish should not be coated with a sealer. The pores must be open for the oil to penetrate. Of course the surface must be sanded absolutely smooth, and every bit of dust must be removed. This means vacuuming, wiping with an alcohol-dampened rag, and then wiping with a tack cloth. If you stain the wood first, you can use either an alcohol-based or an oil-based stain, but the real point of an oil finish is to bring out the beauty of the wood by the action of the oil alone.

Oil will darken all woods to some degree, and may cause extreme darkening with some species. It is a good idea to make a test on a scrap of the same wood, or in a concealed location on the workpiece to make sure you like the initial effect. When you judge the test, keep in mind that an oil finish will darken with age.

You can use boiled linseed oil (buy boiled oil, do not try to boil raw linseed oil—it is dangerous, and the result will not be what you need), tung oil, or any of a number of modern furniture or wood oils specially formulated for finishing. These include penetrating oils with resins, described on page 89. (Do not use a commercial oil *polish* for furniture or floors; that is a different kind of product.) If you use a commercial finishing oil, follow the directions on the container. Except for penetrating oil-resin materials, they will be essentially the same as the following steps for a traditional oil finish.

1 Dilute two parts of boiled linseed oil or tung oil with one part of turpentine. Use the mixture at room temperature. If it is cold, stand the oil container in hot water; never place it directly on a stove burner.

2 Dip a folded cotton cloth in the oil, squeeze out some of the excess, and start rubbing the oil into an area two or three feet square. Rub with a circular motion as well as back and forth, so that oil enters the wood pores from all directions. Work on this one area for ten to twenty minutes.

3 Dip the cloth in the oil again and work on an adjoining area of the surface. To avoid an excessive buildup of oil, always start in a fresh area and work back into the section you have already covered.

4 Continue this way until the surface is completely covered. Periodically wipe the oiled areas with a lintless cloth to remove any excess on the surface. The more open pored the wood is, the more excess you will find to wipe away.

5 Now go back to the first area and polish it with a hard polishing cloth. Rub briskly, with some pressure, to develop heat from friction; that is what brings out a luster.

6 Let the polished first coat of oil dry for at least two days in warm weather, longer in cold weather. Then hold your hand on the surface for three or four minutes; if you detect any oiliness, it is not yet dry. When it is dry, apply a second coat in the same way as the first.

Altogether, you should apply five to eight coats for a durable, long-lasting finish. The drying time will increase by at least a week with each coat, so the work sessions will be distributed over several months. If you are finishing cabinet doors, do both sides to prevent warping. With table leaves, apply two coats to the undersides for the same purpose.

When you are satisfied with the appearance of the surface after at least five coats, you can stop and live with the beautiful results. The final finish does not require waxing. If it gets dull or spotted, polish it with a dry, soft cloth. Apply another coat only when dry polishing does not restore the luster.

FINISHING WITH WAX

Do not apply wax directly to bare wood. It will clog the pores and be impossible to remove when it yellows (all waxes do, eventually) or gets dirty, or if you should later want to refinish the surface. Instead, sand the surface perfectly smooth, clean it with a vacuum and a tack cloth, and apply a colorless sealer. One coat of 2-pound cut white shellac (see page 96) will be a good sealer.

If you are refinishing an old surface, it must be free of dirt, grease, and old wax. Use a commercial wax remover, or wash the surface with turpentine, then wipe it off with a cloth dipped in a solution of one cup of sudsless ammonia in a gallon of water.

Use a paste furniture wax with a high percentage of carnauba wax, or for a bar top or wet-area counter, a paste automobile wax. Do not use a liquid wax or a floor wax. You can also use beeswax thinned with turpentine, but commercial waxes are more convenient. Follow the instructions on the wax container. Some types are to be applied with a damp cloth or pad, others with a dry applicator.

As a general procedure, pick up some wax on a folded cloth and rub it onto the surface with a circular motion. Cover all areas evenly with a thin coat of wax; wipe away any excess. Let the wax dry until the surface looks dull or whitish, then buff the wax with a soft cloth—or with a polishing bonnet on a power disk for better results. Build up the finish with additional coats, buffing each one thoroughly. Rebuff whenever required to restore the surface luster. If the wax gets scratched or discolored, remove it with a commercial wax stripper, clean the surface thoroughly, and apply a new finish.

CAUTION
Oil-impregnated cloths are a potential fire hazard. Do not let them sit in a discarded heap or in a closed container. Wash them immediately after use, or keep them in the container with the oil so they do not dry out.

OIL AND WAX FINISHES

SPRAYING FINISHES

Spraying is the one way to apply a finish without any brush marks. Lacquer, some enamels, thinned shellac, and alcohol- and water-based dye stains can all be sprayed. Varnish is too thick.

SPRAY GUNS

Small spray guns either have self-contained compressors or liquid pumps ("airless" sprayers). They are suitable for projects of limited size, but to get good results with paneling, cabinets, or large furniture pieces you need a spraying outfit consisting of a gun and canister, an air hose, and a separate air compressor. Such outfits are available in several price ranges, and they can be rented quite reasonably.

Spray guns are classified by type of air control and by type of liquid feed. In a *bleeder-type* gun, a stream of propellant air passes through the gun and out the nozzle continuously. In the more common *nonbleeder-type*, the propellant air flow is started or stopped by a trigger control in the handle.

In a *suction* or *siphon-fed* gun the stream of air passing through the gun creates a vacuum that pulls liquid in the canister up through a feed tube to the nozzle. In a *pressure-fed* gun, increasing air pressure in the canister forces liquid up the feed tube to the nozzle.

There are two types of nozzles: *external mix*, in which the liquid and the air are mixed just as they exit the nozzle, and *internal mix*, where mixing occurs inside the nozzle. A suction-fed spray gun can use either kind of nozzle. The external mix type is required for lacquer and other fast-drying liquids, to avoid internal clogging. An internal-mix nozzle is suitable only for paints and other heavy-bodied liquids, and must be used with a pressure-fed gun.

CAUTION
Make sure there is no open flame, such as a gas pilot light, or any spark-producing equipment in operation near the spraying area. Wear goggles, a respirator (not a dust mask), gloves, and long sleeves. Do not let spray hit your skin directly—it can penetrate!

SPRAYING A FINISH

Spray only in a well-ventilated area. Put portable workpieces inside a spray booth: a large cardboard box open only on one side, or a three-sided enclosure of hardboard, plywood, or plastic sheeting weighted at the bottom so it cannot blow around. Cover the floor with old newpapers, and provide a cover across the top of the enclosure.

Be sure the equipment is absolutely clean. Run clear thinner through a rental outfit for two or three minutes before loading the canister with the finish. Then use the following techniques to spray lacquer or other finishes.

1 Start moving the gun before you squeeze the trigger to start spraying. Keep the gun pointed perpendicular to the surface and the nozzle a constant 8 to 10 inches away. Move your entire arm as if sliding the gun on a rail. Do not twist your wrist or bend your elbow.

2 Use overlapping horizontal or vertical strokes along the long dimension of the workpiece. Make sure each row is parallel to the one preceding it.

3 At the end of each stroke, release the trigger before bringing your arm movement to a stop.

4 Spray outside corners with the gun aimed directly at the angle so the spray hits both sides. Do corners first, then spray the flat areas in between.

Lacquer is dry within a few minutes of spraying, but enamel takes somewhat longer, depending on its type. You can spray an additional coat as soon as the previous one is dry. If you made sure the surface was absolutely clean and used good technique, there should be no need to sand. Most surfaces will require two coats of enamel at most, and three of lacquer, although you may want more to achieve a higher gloss.

When you are finished, clean the entire outfit with thinner. Soak the nozzle and filter screens in thinner and scrub them with an old toothbrush.

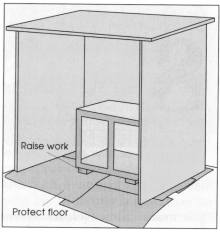

SPRAY MOVABLE OBJECTS in a booth improvised from a box, panels, or plastic sheeting. Ventilate the work area well.

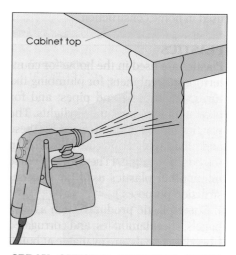

SPRAY OUTSIDE CORNERS FIRST, with the gun aimed head-on to the angle so that spray goes on each side.

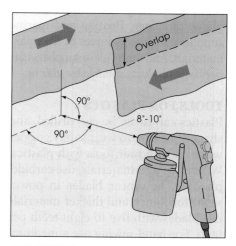

SPRAY IN STRAIGHT-LINE PASSES at a constant distance. Overlap the passes and keep the gun perpendicular to the surface.

9 HARDWARE

Hardware in a home ranges from small brads and staples to hefty joist hangers and other structural devices. This chapter deals with some basic door, cabinet, and reinforcement hardware. For other hardware, see:

Ch. 5: Nails, screws, bolts; specialized anchors; framing connectors.

Ch. 12: Metal studs.

Ch. 13: Suspended ceiling frames.

Ch. 16: Shelf and cabinet mounts.

Ch. 17: Closet fittings.

Ch. 18: Window hardware.

Ch. 19: Interior door hinges, locksets; bifold and bypass door fittings.

Ch. 22: Gutter components, fittings.

Ch. 31: Fence and gate hardware.

Ch. 33: Plumbing components.

Ch. 34: Electrical components.

Ch. 38: Security hardware.

HINGES

A variety of hinges is illustrated on the facing page. Most are some kind of metal *leaf hinge*, in which two leaves are connected by a *pin* inserted through the *knuckles* of the hinge *barrel*. The pin may be tight (fixed), or loose (removable) so the hinge can be disassembled. The leaves may be flat, as in the familiar *butt hinge* used on room doors, or bent as in *wraparound hinges* to accommodate overlay, inset (lipped), or flush cabinet doors. Hinges may fit into mortises in the door and frame edges, may be unmortised, or may fasten to the front or back surfaces of the door and the frame.

Hinges are configured for various kinds of installation: *surface,* with both leaves visible when the door is closed; *half-mortise* or *semiconcealed,* with one leaf visible; *full-mortise* or *concealed,* with only the barrel visible; and fully concealed or *invisible,* with all parts hidden from view. *Decorative hinges* come in many shapes, colors, and textures.

A *loose-joint hinge* can be separated simply by lifting the door. A *no-mortise hinge* mounts on the door and frame edges in a space only one leaf thick. A *rising hinge* moves the door upward as it swings open, for example to clear thick carpeting. A *two-way* or *double-action hinge* lets a door swing in or out; it is the familiar kitchen door hinge. *Knife* and *pivot hinges* mount on the top and bottom edges of the door. European-style or *Euro-hinges* mount in the back of the door and frame and are completely concealed when the door is closed. Long door panels and folding screens may be joined by plastic *strip hinges* or by metal *piano hinges*. A *glass-door hinge* is a U-shaped shoe that slips over the edges of a glass panel, with a screw to clamp the panel in place.

HINGE INSTALLATION

You must install hinges correctly for a door to swing properly. Be sure the pins or pivot axes align vertically when viewed from the front and from the side. Locate hinges accurately; some are supplied with templates to mark the locations. Cut or drill hinge mortises square to the door and frame edges. Make them fit the hinge leaf or cylinder exactly. Hinge mortises can be cut one leaf deep in both the frame and the door, double depth in the door when you do not wish to alter the stile or jamb, or in other ways, as shown on the opposite page. Mortising techniques are covered on pages 22–23 and 244.

Drill pilot holes for hinge screws that are truly perpendicular to the surface the hinge fits against. Otherwise screw heads will not lie flush in the countersunk holes in a mortised leaf, or flat against the surface of a visible leaf.

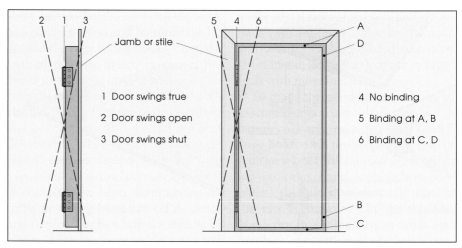

HINGE ALIGNMENT determines whether a door swings true and remains in position *(left),* and whether it is free of binding in the frame *(right).* The degree of misalignment (broken lines) is exaggerated here for clarity.

BUTT AND WRAPAROUND HINGES

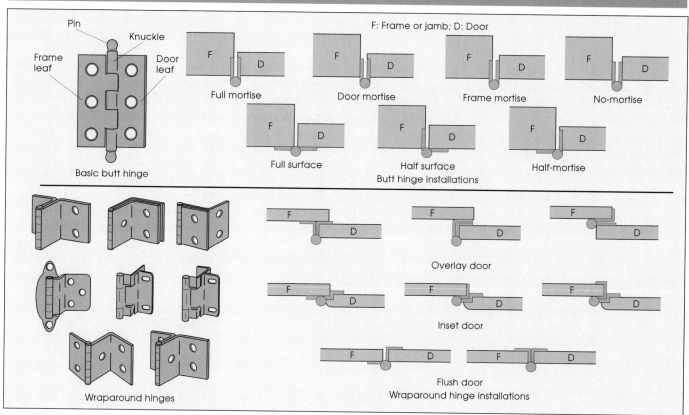

Pin
Knuckle
Frame leaf
Door leaf

F: Frame or jamb; D: Door

Basic butt hinge

Full mortise
Door mortise
Frame mortise
No-mortise

Full surface
Half surface
Half-mortise

Butt hinge installations

Wraparound hinges

Overlay door

Inset door

Flush door

Wraparound hinge installations

OTHER TYPES OF HINGES

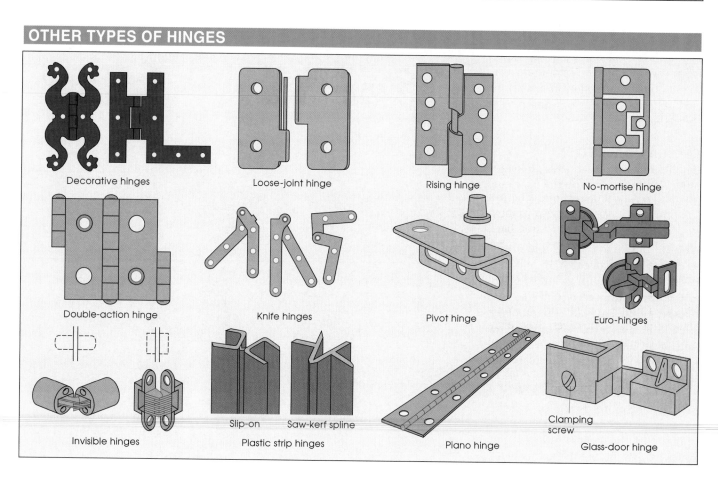

Decorative hinges

Loose-joint hinge

Rising hinge

No-mortise hinge

Double-action hinge

Knife hinges

Pivot hinge

Euro-hinges

Invisible hinges

Slip-on   Saw-kerf spline

Plastic strip hinges

Piano hinge

Clamping screw

Glass-door hinge

CATCHES, KNOBS, PULLS, AND HANDLES

Exterior doors and interior room doors generally require a full latch set or lock/latch set to open, close, and secure them (see Chapter 19). Lighter weight doors, such as screen doors and cabinet doors, and drawers, call for smaller, less complex hardware.

CATCHES

A properly selected and installed catch will hold a door securely closed, but will allow it to be opened without difficulty when desired. A variety of catches and their mounting in a number of configurations are illustrated here.

Catch mechanisms include magnets, rollers, springs, balls, and friction clamps. A special type is the safety catch, meant to prevent accidental opening, especially by young children. It often combines two kinds of action, or requires more than one operation to open it, which makes it essentially childproof. Some catches are available with or without an integral lock, often operated by a pushbutton or slide lever. Others are mounted on a common plate with a simple key-, button-, or lever-operated lock. Only the nonlocking types are shown here.

CATCH INSTALLATION

Catches consist of two parts, a tongue or strike that mounts on the door, and the catch mechanism itself, which mounts on the frame and captures the tongue. The great majority of catches require surface mounting; a few, such as the bullet or ball catch, fit into mortises. Surface-mounting catches generally have slotted screw holes so they may be adjusted to hold a door properly aligned in the frame. Mortise catches must be installed in exactly the right position; later adjustment is not easy, and in some cases is not possible.

Place a catch close to the door knob or pull, not more than 3 or 4 inches away. If it is farther away, the door may tend to rack the hinges as the free edge starts to open before the pull is strong enough to overcome the holding action of the catch. The installation of most catches is self-evident, and usually they are supplied with instructions or at least a basic diagram. Complex and mortise catches often have templates to assist you in locating them properly. As with other hardware, take pains to get things square or parallel with door and frame edges, and to drill perpendicular pilot holes for the mounting screws. Careful installation avoids having to redo or correct a job, and helps ensure years of troublefree operation.

KNOBS, PULLS, AND HANDLES

While the terms for cabinet door and drawer opening grips are not precise, they can be distinguished as follows (see illustation, next page). A *knob* is a protruding shape that is grasped between the fingers and thumb. It is usually fastened at a single point. A *pull* is most often a piece attached to the surface that is shaped so one or more fingers can be inserted into it. A special type of finger pull is a recess in the surface or a groove in the edge that the fingers can reach into. A *handle* may have a single *pendant* hanging from a stud. However, the most common type of handle has a U-shaped *bail* that stands or hangs free of the surface so that fingers can be inserted into it. It is com-

TYPES OF CATCHES AND INSTALLATION

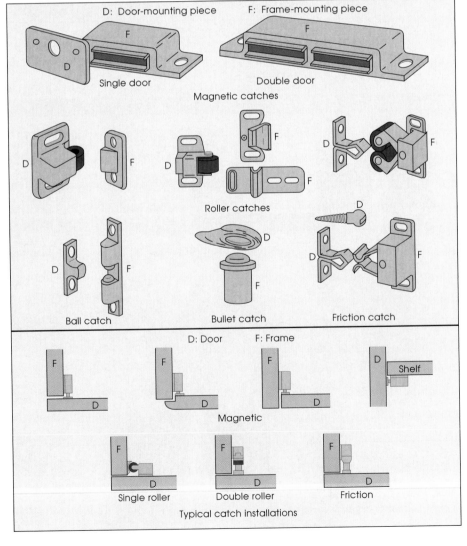

D: Door-mounting piece   F: Frame-mounting piece

Single door   Double door

Magnetic catches

Roller catches

Ball catch   Bullet catch   Friction catch

D: Door   F: Frame

Magnetic

Single roller   Double roller   Friction

Typical catch installations

monly fastened to the surface at two points. The bail may be fixed, with no moving parts, or it may hang or pivot between end posts. A hanging bail is usually mounted on a decorative plate called an *escutcheon* that protects the surface from wear as the bail hits against it with repeated use.

There is seemingly no end to the available styles, materials, colors, and finishes of all kinds of knobs, pulls, and handles. Choosing one is a matter of matching the style of the piece on which it will be mounted, and finding a design that is comfortable and convenient to use.

INSTALLATION

Installing a knob, pull, or handle usually calls only for drilling one or two holes. The holes must be accurately located to place the pull both for the best appearance and to exert the most efficient force in pulling a door or drawer open.

Generally, center a single pull in both the length and width of a cabinet door stile or a drawer front. With a pair of pulls, as on a wide drawer, locate one about 6 inches from each end, as illustrated at the right.

Drill holes from the face of the piece, with scrap wood backing up the hole to prevent splintering inside. For a door that will be seen from both sides, drill a very small pilot hole all the way through, then drill the full-size hole from the face on each side. Be sure to get all holes level or vertically aligned with the frame and with one another.

SOME TYPES OF KNOBS, PULLS, AND HANDLES

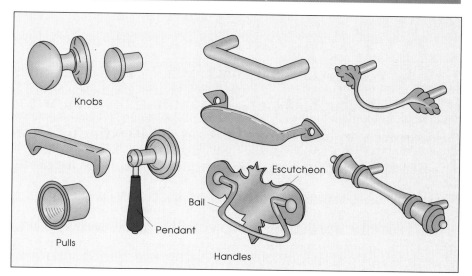

Knobs

Pulls

Pendant

Bail

Escutcheon

Handles

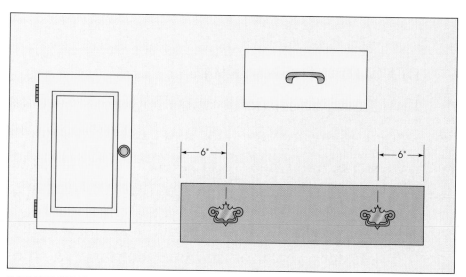

LOCATE KNOBS, PULLS, AND HANDLES for easy access and both visual and operating balance. The positions shown will provide an equal distribution of force when opening or closing a small door or a drawer.

REINFORCEMENT HARDWARE

A largely neglected item of hardware is the flat metal device called a mending plate. The true mending plate is a straight rectangle with screw holes, but the term is often extended to include the L-shaped corner plate and the T-plate. A related item is the more widely used corner brace.

The plates lie flat on the surface or they can be recessed in a surface mortise. They are used to repair splits or cracks, and to reinforce joints. An L-plate, for example, is useful to restore square alignment to the frame of a gate or a screen door. A T-plate can be used wherever one piece runs into the midpoint of another.

The use of mending plates is obvious, and simple. However, a few points are important.
• Use plates with staggered holes. In-line holes tend to cause splitting.
• Fasten plates with screws, not nails.
• Drill pilot holes; use flathead screws large enough to fill the countersink in the plate holes.
• Bridge a split or crack with a plate long enough to place screws in solid wood, well away from the damaged area.
• Where there is more than one screw hole on either side of a joint or damage line, put a screw in each hole. A single screw will act as a pivot, allowing the plate to swivel under stress.

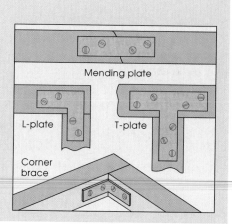

Mending plate

L-plate

T-plate

Corner brace

This section proceeds through the interior of a home, from basement to attic, covering first household repairs, then minor and major improvements.

Each chapter begins by familiarizing you with basic nomenclature and shows you how things fit together. Repair and maintenance tips—everything from drying up a wet basement to patching a ceiling to improving attic ventilation—come next. The final sections of each chapter are devoted to do-it-yourself improvement projects. Here's where you will learn how to build a new drywall partition, put up ceiling tile, paint a room, install wallcovering, and much more.

DEVELOPING D-I-Y SKILLS

If you are a novice do-it-yourselfer, interior projects offer a good way to get started. Many are small jobs that can be accomplished in an afternoon or over a weekend. And when working indoors, you aren't under pressure from weather or seasonal changes. Big indoor projects, such as finishing a basement or attic or paneling a den, can be stretched out over an entire winter, if necessary.

To master a repair or improvement process, study the appropriate instructions presented in this book, refer to product literature, then mentally rehearse your plan of attack step by step. As you envision each step, note what tools and materials you will need and how you can minimize household disruption from dust and debris.

Once you have started a project, remain flexible. Even professionals sometimes miscalculate, and as an amateur you will almost certainly encounter unforeseen circumstances from time to time. When this happens, take a break and rethink the situation. Do not continue prying, pounding, or other futile activities that could cause damage.

III INTERIOR REPAIRS AND IMPROVEMENTS

Finally, budget time at the end of a project for cleaning tools and the work site. Many interior projects create a mess that soon gets tracked to other areas of the house. Dirty tools don't perform well and could pose a safety hazard.

IMPORTANT

This section stops short of interior projects that could weaken the structure of your home, such as removing or making a large opening in a load-bearing wall (see Chapter 12). Consult with a contractor, architect, or house designer before attempting a structural change. Also, you will probably need a building permit before you can take out or modify a bearing wall, and you will almost certainly need one if you plan to transform a basement, attic, or other unfinished area into living space.

Note, too, that this section does not include information about your home's plumbing, electrical, heating, and cooling systems or about safety and security matters. These are covered in Part V, Home Operating Systems, and Part VI, Safety and Security.

10 BASEMENTS

A home's basement walls and floor act like the hull of a ship, supporting the superstructure above but also holding back thousands of pounds of earth and subterranean moisture. Although there is no danger your home will sink, if your basement is taking on water it offers little potential for expanding living space and may not even be a safe place to store things.

After showing how basements are constructed, this chapter explains how to dry up a wet basement, then goes on to get you started converting it into comfortable living space.

MASONRY BASEMENT CONSTRUCTION

Most basements are constructed of poured concrete or concrete blocks, stone, or occasionally other masonry materials. In the typical example at the right, reinforced concrete *footings* support *foundation walls* of concrete blocks, and a poured concrete *slab* forms the basement floor. *Expansion joints* around the slab's perimeter are made of asphalt, rubber, or other soft material that flexes as the floor expands and contracts.

Under the slab, compacted sand or gravel *fill* absorbs groundwater that might otherwise rise and crack the slab. A plastic *vapor-retarding barrier* helps prevent condensation from building up on the floor. Homes in cold-winter climates may have a layer of *rigid board insulation* under the slab.

Outside, a *drain field* captures water and diverts it from the foundation to a dry well or a downgrade area. It consists of coarse gravel, a *fabric filter* that prevents clogging, and *perforated drainpipe* that carries the water away.

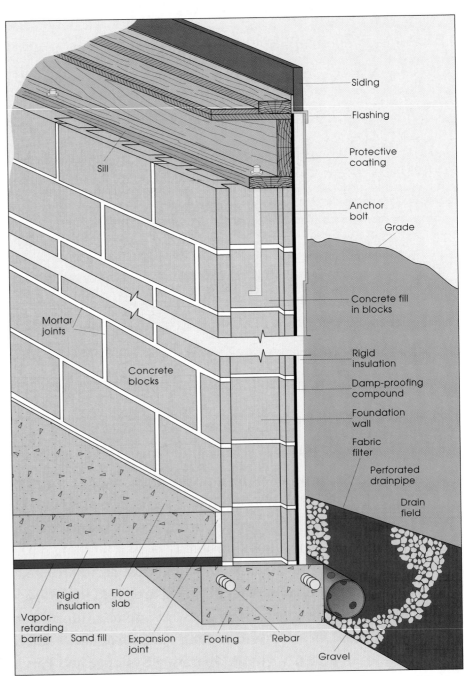

Siding

Flashing

Protective coating

Anchor bolt

Grade

Concrete fill in blocks

Rigid insulation

Damp-proofing compound

Foundation wall

Fabric filter

Perforated drainpipe

Drain field

Sill

Mortar joints

Concrete blocks

Rigid insulation

Floor slab

Vapor-retarding barrier

Sand fill

Expansion joint

Footing

Rebar

Gravel

MASONRY BASEMENTS are typically made of concrete blocks set in mortar. A footing supports the walls and floor, as well as the weight of the entire house above. A drain field around the perimeter captures water that could undermine the foundation.

Asphalt-based *damp-proofing compound* seals the exteriors of basement walls. As with floors, some basement walls are insulated, others are not. With exterior insulation, rigid panels with a protective coating are glued to the foundation walls. To learn about interior wall insulation, see pages 120–121.

At the top of a basement wall, *anchor bolts* are embedded in concrete poured into cavities in the upper courses of block. These secure the *sill* that supports the floor and wall framing above.

POURED CONCRETE BASEMENTS

Poured concrete basements resemble masonry basements except that their walls are made of solid concrete. After installing footings, the builder constructs forms and fills them with concrete, which is usually reinforced with steel rods called *rebars* (reinforcing bars). After the concrete has set, the forms are removed, the drain field is installed, and earth is backfilled against the outsides of the foundation walls. A poured concrete foundation usually costs more than masonry block walls. But because there are no mortar joints in this type of construction, it is somewhat less prone to developing cracks through which moisture can penetrate.

WOOD BASEMENTS

Basements in a few newer homes are made entirely of pressure-treated wood. After excavating, the builder installs a *gravel footing pad*, then a pressure-treated lumber *footing plate*. Walls on top of this plate are framed with 2 × 6-, 8-, or 10-inch pressure-treated *studs* and sheathed with pressure-treated plywood. A polyethylene *membrane* protects the outer surface of the plywood. Batt or blanket *insulation* between the studs keeps the basement warm. Some wood basements have concrete slab floors; others are framed with pressure-treated wood in much the same way as the aboveground floor illustrated on page 123. Wood basements are warmer than those made of masonry or concrete, and because they are flexible enough to ride out minor shifts in the earth, cracking is rarely a problem.

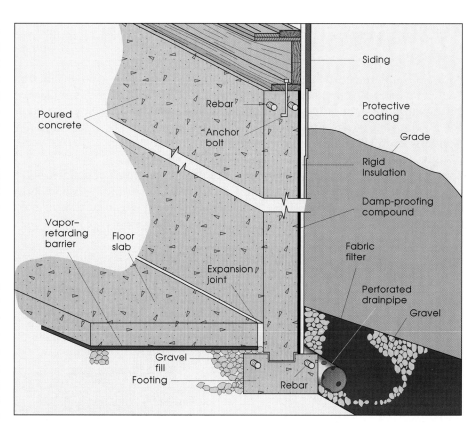

POURED CONCRETE BASEMENTS have the same elements as masonry basements, but their walls are concrete instead of block.

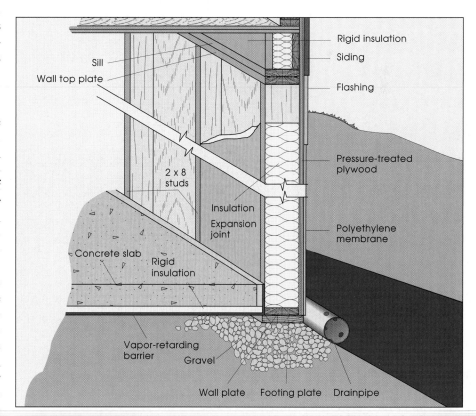

WOOD BASEMENTS are constructed of lumber and plywood that has been pressure-treated to withstand decay from moisture and insect damage.

DIAGNOSING BASEMENT PROBLEMS

Most problems unique to basements are caused by water. The first step in drying out a wet basement is to determine where the water is coming from. Is condensation the culprit? Is water seeping in from outside, or trickling through a crack in a wall or the floor? Is a high water table trying to push your basement out of the ground? As you investigate each of these possibilities, as described below, bear in mind that the problem could be the result of a combination of ills.

CONDENSATION

The prime symptoms of condensation are damp walls and pipes—especially in humid weather—rusty hardware, mold or mildew, and a musty odor. To find out for sure, tape a piece of foil to the dampest wall and check it a day or two later. If the outer face has fogged up or is beaded with droplets of water, your basement is suffering from a condensation problem.

Condensation results from excess humidity, often from an internal source such as a washing machine, unvented dryer, or basement shower. It forms where warm moist air comes in contact

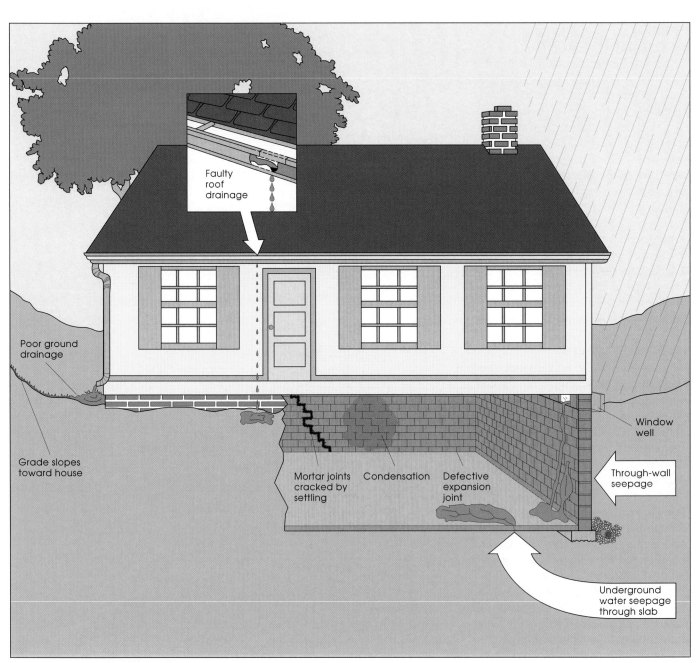

Faulty roof drainage

Poor ground drainage

Grade slopes toward house

Mortar joints cracked by settling

Condensation

Defective expansion joint

Window well

Through-wall seepage

Underground water seepage through slab

WHERE'S THE WATER COMING FROM? If your basement has a moisture problem, these are the key points to check. After identifying the source or sources of the problem, turn to pages 116–119 for solutions.

DIAGNOSING PROBLEMS

PROTECTING AGAINST RADON

Odorless, colorless, and radioactive radon gas comes from the natural decay of radium into soil and underground water. Emitted through cracks and joints in basement floors and walls, it can build up in concentrations that, over the years, can pose a serious health hazard.

Home centers sell radon testing kits, with instructions telling how to use them and an address to which you can send samples for laboratory analysis. If the analysis indicates that your home has a radon problem, the same measures that keep water out of basements can also provide a barrier against radon.

If these don't work, a waterproofing or pollution-control specialist can install a venting system that pulls radon from underneath the floor and discharges it into the air. This is not a feasible do-it-yourself job.

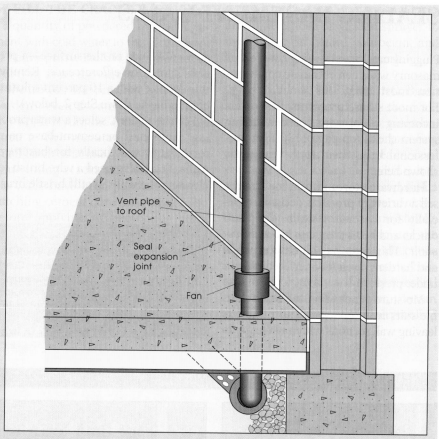

RADON VENTING uses perforated pipe under the floor to collect the gas, then directs it to a vent pipe to the roof. A fan in the vent moves the gas upward.

with a significantly cooler surface such as an exterior wall or a cold water pipe.

Cure condensation by installing a dehumidifier, improving basement ventilation, or wrapping cold-water pipes with insulation. Then apply a dampproofing compound to the walls, as shown on page 117.

SEEPAGE

If moisture is collecting on the floor or on one wall near the floor, it's probably seeping in from outside or up from under the floor. Tape a piece of foil to the wall and wait for a rainy day. If water collects *behind* the foil, you have a seepage problem.

Seepage usually occurs because water is forcing through an expansion joint or through pores and hairline cracks in the foundation. First look around outside and see if you can identify a source for the water. Perhaps a gutter is leaking or overflowing, or a

downspout (leader) lacks a splash block or ground pipe. Maybe a window well is filling up and flooding. Also check that the ground around your house is graded away from the foundation, not toward it. Repairing gutters and leaders is explained in Chapter 22; for information about solving foundation drainage problems, see Chapter 25.

Sealing basement walls, as shown on the next two pages, may stop minor seepage. If not, install a channeling system (page 118) or hire a waterproofing contractor to employ one of the strategies illustrated on page 119.

LEAKS

Often you can *see* water trickling down a basement wall or oozing up through a crack in the floor. As you look for the source of a leak, pay special attention to mortar joints between blocks or the expansion joint between the wall and the basement floor.

Most basement leaks result from poor drainage, especially roof runoff, or a grading problem, aggravated by cracks that result from the normal settling of the structure. Check for these as explained above. Most leaks can be plugged with hydraulic cement (see pages 116–117); walls that are extensively cracked need professional attention.

UNDERGROUND WATER

One of the most troublesome causes of a chronically damp basement is a spring or high water table that pushes water up through the floor under high pressure. This often shows up as a thin, almost imperceptible film. To determine if you have an underground water problem, lay a sheet of plastic on the floor and leave it there for two or three days. If moisture collects under the sheet, it is coming up from below. An underground water problem requires professional help.

INSTALLING A SUBFLOOR

If your basement floor is uneven, chilly underfoot, or both, a new subfloor can lay the way for the finish flooring of your choice. With a slab that is only slightly uneven, conserve headroom by putting down *sleepers*, installing rigid-panel insulation between them, and covering everything with plywood.

If your basement has a very uneven slab, or none at all, frame a new subfloor with *joists*, insulate with blankets or batts, and nail plywood to the joists. This system subtracts 8¼ or more inches from the headroom, depending on the finish flooring you select.

SUBFLOORING WITH SLEEPERS

1 CUT 2 × 3 OR 2 × 4 LUMBER to fit around the edges of the floor, and pieces to run between them across the narrower dimension of the floor. Use a level to find the high point of the floor and work from there. Lay sleepers 16 inches apart, wide side down in construction adhesive. Level the sleepers with thin scraps of lumber as necessary before driving concrete nails every 24 inches through them into the floor. (Always wear safety goggles when nailing or drilling into concrete.)

2 USE A UTILITY KNIFE AND STRAIGHTEDGE to cut rigid panel insulation to fit between the sleepers. Glue these to the floor. If the insulation does not have a foil vapor barrier, stretch 4-mil plastic sheeting over the entire floor and staple it to the sleepers.

3 LAY DOWN PANELS of ⅝-inch grade C-D plywood, C side up, and draw lines to show where the sleepers are located. Drive ring-shank flooring nails along these lines, spaced 8 inches apart across the panels and 6 inches apart along the edges. Stagger the ends of panels so they don't all fall on the same line of sleepers. Space panel edges ⅛ inch apart to prevent squeaking.

1. INSTALL SLEEPERS by gluing and nailing 2 × 3s or 2 × 4s to the slab. Level the sleepers with shims as necessary, working from the high spot in the floor.

2. INSULATE THE SUBFLOOR with rigid sheet material cut to fit between the sleepers. If the insulation does not have a foil or facing, staple down plastic sheeting.

3. NAIL SUBFLOOR PANELS of plywood or particleboard to the sleepers. Stagger end joints and space panels ⅛ inch apart. Mark sleeper locations so you know where to nail.

FRAMING A NEW SUBFLOOR

Begin by attaching 2 × 8 lumber to the walls at either side of the basement's narrower dimension. These will be the *end joists*. Use lag screws into existing framing, or into lead anchors inserted in holes drilled in concrete walls. Level the end joists with shims, if necessary. Then fasten 2 × 6 *floor joists* to the end joists using joist hangers. Space the floor joists 16 inches on center. Support them every 5 feet with shims, or with short legs nailed to their sides as shown at the right. Insulate with batts or blankets between the joists, add plastic sheeting if needed, then nail down plywood panels as explained above.

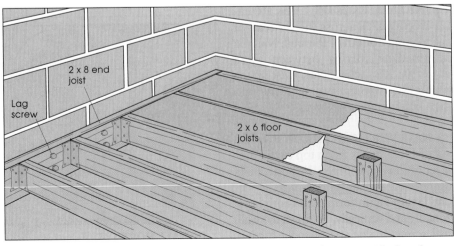

FRAME A NEW SUBFLOOR with 2 × 8s and 2 × 6s. Support the 2 × 6s with short legs as shown, or with shims. Insulate with batts or blankets stapled to the joists, foil side up.

11 FLOORS, FLOORING, AND STAIRS

Flooring materials are many and varied, but underneath all of them you'll find some type of slab-on-grade or wood framing system, as shown here. (For stairways, see pages 151–152.)

SLAB ON GRADE

Some slab-on-grade floor systems resemble shallow basements. *Footings* support low *foundation walls* and a *reinforced concrete slab*. A layer of *gravel* underneath drains water that might otherwise freeze and crack the slab. Some slabs have *rigid insulation,* either around the perimeters of their foundations or underneath. Wall framing rests upon *sills* on top of the foundation. Other slab-on-grade floor systems have no foundations.

WOOD FRAMING

Wood-framed floors begin with a *sill* atop the foundation wall that carries all of the load of your home's outside framing. The sill is commonly made up of 2 × 6s or wider boards secured to the foundation with anchor bolts.

A *girder* or main supporting beam is usually installed across the foundation, midway between opposite walls. The girder's ends commonly fit into pockets in the foundation walls. A girder may be a steel I-beam or a wood beam, either a heavy timber or pieces of 2 × 8 or 2 × 10 lumber nailed together to form a support 6 inches thick. *Continued*

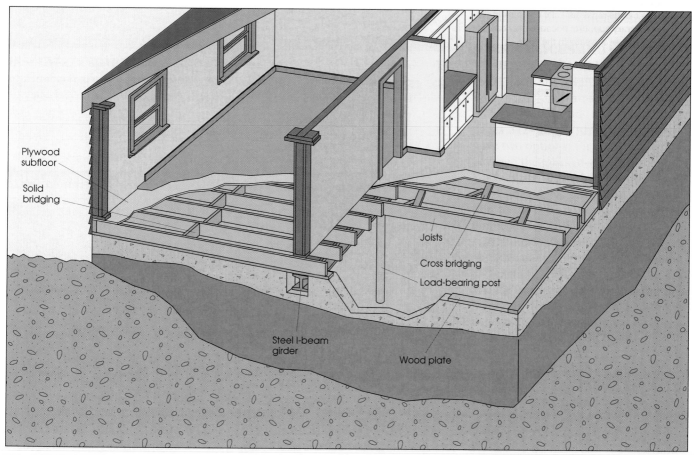

Plywood subfloor

Solid bridging

Joists

Cross bridging

Load-bearing post

Steel I-beam girder

Wood plate

WOOD-FRAME FLOOR SYSTEMS consist of joists resting on a sill atop the foundation and a steel or wood girder notched into the foundation walls. Plywood serves as subflooring; in older homes the subfloor may be boards laid at right angles or diagonally across the joists.

123

INSTALLING UNDERLAYMENT

The pages that follow show how to install resilient tile, resilient sheet flooring, carpeting, ceramic tile, and hardwood. Of these five flooring materials only hardwood can be applied directly to a subfloor; with all the others you must first put down underlayment.

Underlayment strengthens, stabilizes, and smooths out the floor system. It also raises it slightly, a factor you need to take into consideration when installing it. Follow the flooring manufacturer's recommendation for selecting the type of underlayment to use.

Plywood underlayment—¼ or ⅜ inch thick—smooths the way for new flooring without raising the level of the floor more than those fractions of an inch. If, for instance, you want to refloor a kitchen with resilient tile, use plywood. Simply nail sheets of plywood underlayment directly onto the old resilient tile and then lay tile over the entirely new surface. (One precaution: Hammer blows will dent the surface of plywood. Fill all dents with floor-leveling compound before laying resilient tiles, sheet flooring, or ceramic tiles.)

Particleboard underlayment is somewhat thicker than plywood—½ or ⅝ inch—but it costs less and does not dent easily. If you need to raise the floor level more than ⅜ inch, or simply want to save money, use particleboard.

Both plywood and particleboard are available in 4 × 8-foot sheets. Whichever you choose, nail down the panels with 8-penny (2½-inch) cement-coated box nails. Their great holding power prevents squeaking and ensures that the nails won't work their way up through finish flooring.

Before laying down the underlayment, check the subfloor for irregularities. Set any popped nails; fasten loose boards; replace warped or damaged boards. Sweep the floor and scrape it, if necessary, to remove any daubs of drywall joint compound or other particles that might be adhering to it. Pry off the shoe moldings at the bottoms of the baseboards. Work carefully if you want to reuse the moldings.

INSTALLATION

1 PLANNING THE LAYOUT. Underlayment panels should lie at right angles to the long seams in plywood or parallel-board subflooring. With diagonal-board subflooring, place underlayment with its long dimension running across the joists below. Seams between underlayment panels should not fall over seams in the subflooring. Because underlayment and plywood subfloor panels are the same size, 4 × 8 feet, cut the first underlayment panel to two-thirds width (32 inches) and three-quarter length (72 inches), to avoid coinciding seams. Make a sketch to plan the layout. Other panels in the first row must be 32 inches wide too, but full length.

2 LAYING THE FIRST SHEET. Start in one corner of the room to install the first sheet of underlayment. Look for rows of nails in the subfloor. These tell you where joists are located. Mark a line across the underlayment over each joist as a nailing guide. Extend these guidelines to succeeding panels as you lay them in place.

HOW TO INSTALL UNDERLAYMENT

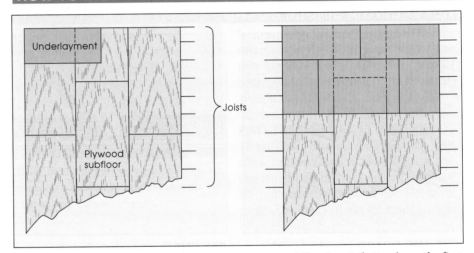

1. PLAN THE LAYOUT so underlayment runs across subflooring. *Left:* Cut down the first row of panels so seams will not fall over subfloor seams. *Right:* Remaining rows can use full- and partial-length panels, full width.

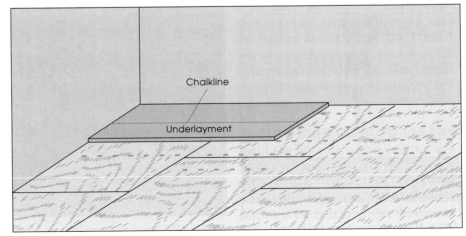

2. LAY THE FIRST SHEET of underlayment in one corner. Use the lines of nails in the subfloor to mark the joist locations on the panel surface.

3 **NAILING UNDERLAYMENT.** Nail along the guidelines, driving nails into the joists every 8 to 10 inches. Also drive nails 6 inches apart around the perimeter. Driving cement-coated nails into any surface is difficult, but particleboard can be especially frustrating. If you hit a coated nail even slightly off the mark, it will fold up. To minimize this, hold the hammer somewhat loosely near the end of the handle; its head will settle more squarely onto the head of the nail, improving your chances of a direct hit.

4 **PULLING CRIPPLED NAILS.** Regardless of how carefully you drive them, a few box nails will bend, and removing them can also be an exercise in frustration. If you try to rip out the bent nail by tugging at its head with the claw of a hammer, you'll pull the head completely off. For better results, extract the nail by gripping the shank instead of the head. Then hit the hammer's head with a plastic soft-face hammer or mallet to force the claw into the nail's relatively soft metal. (**CAUTION:** *For safety, never hit one metal hammer with another. Hardened steel striking hardened steel could dangerously fracture one hammer or the other.*) Once the claw has locked onto the nail, lean the hammer sideways and the nail will pull out more easily.

5 **STAGGERING AND SPACING UNDERLAYMENT.** Continue to nail sheets to the floor. To avoid squeaking, do not butt panels together. Place thin nails between the panels to leave some space between the edges. Remove the spacers after each sheet is nailed down. Stagger seams by starting every other row with a partial sheet. Cut panels where you encounter obstructions. Cut both plywood and particleboard with a fine-toothed blade in a circular saw. Cut from the underside to minimize chipping of the top face.

6 **FINISHING THE JOB.** Don't fret about small gaps here and there. Fill hammer dents in plywood and any space greater than ¼ inch with wood putty, but don't fill spaces smaller than that; it could cause creaks as the floor shifts slightly underfoot.

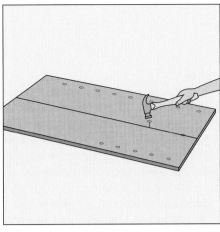

3. DRIVE 8-PENNY CEMENT-COATED BOX NAILS along the lines. Nail through into the joists every 8 to 10 inches. Nail around the perimeter, too, every 6 inches.

4. PULL BENT NAILS by striking the hammer's head with a soft-face hammer, as shown, then lean the hammer sideways. Never hit one metal hammer with another.

INSTALL UNDERLAYMENT

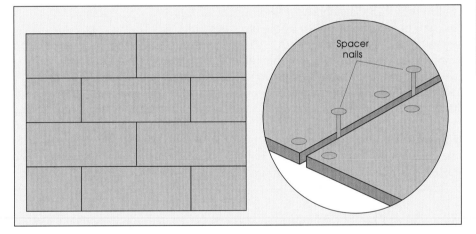

5. STAGGER SEAMS by starting every other row with a partial-length panel. Space seams as shown. Locate panel perimeter nails opposite one another along seams.

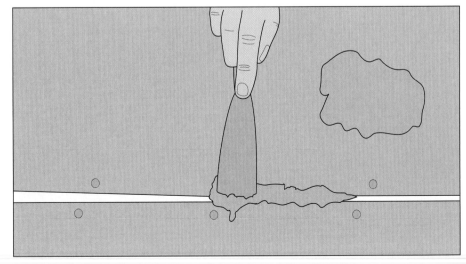

6. PUTTY HOLES OR GAPS that are greater than ¼ inch. After the wood putty dries, sand it smooth. With plywood, you also must fill dents around nail heads made by hammering.

INSTALLING RESILIENT FLOOR TILE

Resilient flooring, so called because it is flexible underfoot, comes in 9- and 12-inch square tiles and in rolls up to 12 feet wide. Of the two forms, tiles are much easier to work with.

SELECTING RESILIENT TILE

The most popular resilient tiles, called vinyl composition tiles, consist of solid vinyl or a layer of vinyl over other materials. Many such tiles come with self-stick backings.

Other resilient tiles are made of rubber and cork. These, and some vinyl and vinyl composition tiles, must be installed with a special adhesive. Use only the type of adhesive specified by the tile manufacturer. Determine also if the tiles you have in mind are suitable for the place you intend to install them. Some resilient tiles should not be used below grade on basement floors.

ESTIMATING NEEDS

To figure out how many tiles you will need, first measure the length and width of the room in feet and multiply to get the area. The number of 12-inch tiles required is equal to the area in square feet. For 9-inch tiles, multiply the area by 1.8. For example, to tile a 10 × 10-foot room, you would need 100 12-inch tiles or 100 × 1.8 = 180 9-inch tiles. Add 5 percent for cutting and mistakes.

If a fireplace or other structure protrudes into the room, measure it separately, calculate its area, and subtract the appropriate number of tiles. Divide irregularly shaped rooms into two or more rectangles, calculate the number of tiles needed for each, then combine those figures to get the total and add 5 percent.

1 PREPARING THE FLOOR. Resilient tiles can be installed on wood, concrete, or underlayment, and in some cases on top of other resilient flooring. Because resilient materials are flexible, they will assume the shape of whatever is beneath them, so the surface of the old floor must be smooth and clean.

Check a wood floor for protruding nails, loose boards, high or low spots, cracks, and gaps. Don't lay a resilient tile floor directly over plank or strip flooring; instead, install underlayment first.

Clean a concrete floor to remove oil, dirt, and grease, and seal it to provide a good moisture barrier between the concrete and the new tile. Check with your dealer for the type of cleaner and sealer to use. Chip away any high spots and fill low spots with floor-leveling compound.

Inspect old resilient flooring for loose pieces and for cracks and holes; patch damaged areas as shown on page 128. Clean the surface with a household floor wax remover. If the old floor is uneven or badly damaged, install underlayment, which is easier than removing existing flooring.

At least 48 hours before you begin, carry the cartons of tile into the room you will be tiling and open them. This lets the tiles adapt to the room's temperature and humidity.

2 ESTABLISHING A STARTING POINT. Because not all rooms are perfectly square, nor are very many room dimensions exact multiples of 9 or 12 inches, you need to determine a

HOW TO INSTALL RESILIENT FLOOR TILE

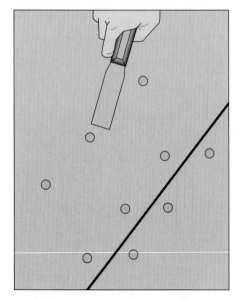

1. CHECK THE SURFACE. Pull a putty knife blade across nail heads. A click means a nail is sticking up; drive it below the surface.

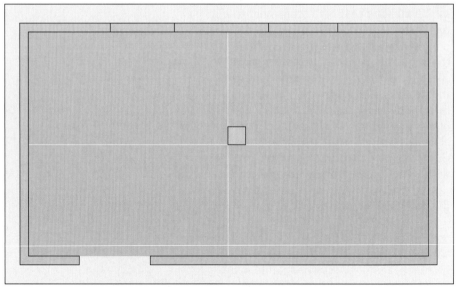

2. SNAP CHALKLINES between midpoints of opposite walls. They should intersect at a right angle; check with a tile or carpenter's square. If necessary, shift one line, but keep the orientation so that tile rows will lie perpendicular to the main doorway.

starting point in the middle of the room. Then you can plot out the tile positions so they will be arranged in even lines and a symmetrical pattern.

To do this, determine the midpoints of opposite walls, snap a chalkline between them, and repeat on the other two walls. Check to be sure that the lines intersect at a right angle in the center of the room. If not, adjust one line. Dry-lay tiles in quadrants in the field, starting where the lines intersect, then adjust the tiles so border rows will be uniform in width at opposite ends and opposite sides of the room.

3 LAYING FIELD TILES. If you will be setting tiles in adhesive, read the instructions on the container. Some adhesives can be applied with a stiff brush; with others you need an inexpensive notched trowel. Working times differ, too. Don't cover too large an area with adhesive at a time or the adhesive will be too dry before you finish.

Lay the first tiles along the chalklines. If you're using adhesive, leave the lines visible for guidance. Don't slide tiles into place; butt the edges of each tile against ones already in place, then lay it firmly in position.

4 MARKING BORDER TILES. You will have to cut tiles to fit around the room's edges and also at any obstructions. To mark these, place a loose tile on top of the last whole tile, the one nearest the border, aligning edges with each other. Now lay another tile on top of these two as a marking gauge. Extend it out to touch the wall. Draw a pencil line along the inner edge of the top tile, marking the face of the tile beneath it. You will use the exposed portion of the marked tile, not the portion underneath the marking gauge.

5 MARKING TILES AT AN OUTSIDE CORNER. Use the same technique to mark around protruding corners. First, mark from one of the walls, as you would for a border tile. Now move the tiles to the other wall, align them with the last full tile, and mark again. Mark the portion you'll be cutting away with an X.   *Continued*

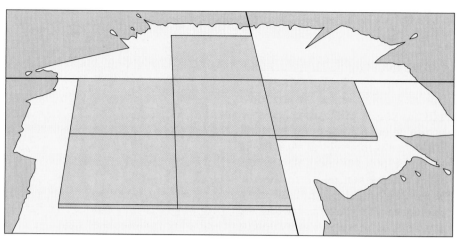

3. LAY TILES ALONG THE CHALKLINES in all directions. Some tiles have arrows stamped on the back to help you match or alternate the pattern.

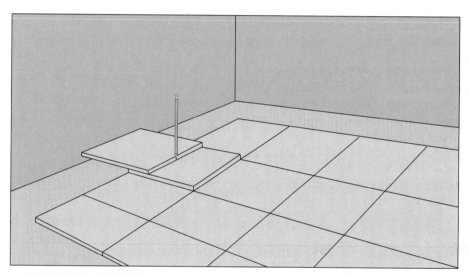

4. MARK BORDER CUTS by placing a loose tile on top of the last full tile; align their edges. Lay another tile on top of that, butted against the wall, and mark the section to be cut off.

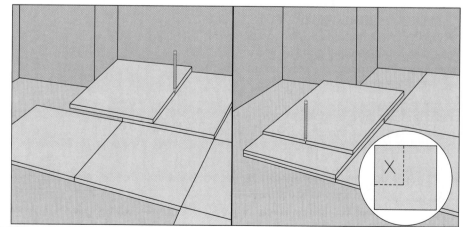

5. AT PROTRUDING CORNERS, use the same technique to mark a border tile for cutting. Mark from one side of the corner, then move the two tiles to the other side and mark again.

INSTALLING RESILIENT FLOOR TILE   *Continued*

6 CUTTING TILES. Thin press-and-stick tiles can be cut with metal snips or a utility knife. Thicker vinyl and vinyl composition tiles should be warmed before cutting. Some tile manufacturers recommend warming tiles in an oven; a propane torch also works well, because you need warm only the line you'll be cutting, not the entire tile.

Hold the underside of the tile over the flame and move it continuously up and down the line. When the tile begins to bend slightly, it is ready for cutting.

Use the underside of an extra tile as a cutting surface for all the work ahead. Lay the warmed tile on the extra tile and cut along the pencil line with a sharp utility knife.

7 PLACING CUT TILES. The tile will stay warm for a few minutes after you've cut it. This means you can push it into just about any shape you need to make it fit, but an overwarm tile can stretch if handled too much. To minimize damage, get the tile into place as soon as possible, using the edge of another tile, if necessary, to maneuver it.

8 FITTING AROUND PIPES. Use the tile-on-tile technique to mark the point where a pipe will penetrate. Cut out the hole, then slit the tile to one edge. To install the tile, warm it, fold back along the slit, and press it in place for an all-but-invisible seam.

9 MAKING IRREGULAR CUTS. Scribe irregular cuts with a compass. Move its point along the irregular edge or surface and let the pencil trace an outline on the tile you'll be cutting. Or trace the outline on a piece of cardboard and cut out a template you can use for marking a series of irregular cuts, such as around door casings.

10 ROLLING THE FLOOR. After all tiles are in place, bond them to the adhesive by rolling the floor in both directions with a floor roller, available as an inexpensive rental item. Clean the roller and the floor before starting.

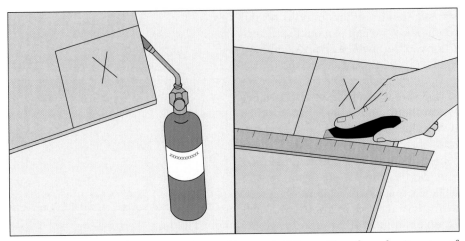

6. CUT THICK TILES by warming them with a torch. When a tile softens, lay it on top of another tile turned face down to act as a cutting board. Cut from the finished side with a straightedge and a sharp utility knife.

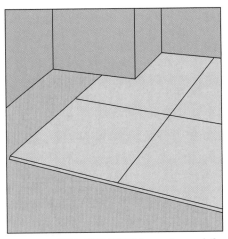

7. SLIP THE CUT TILE into place while it's still warm and pliable. Press the edges into the adhesive.

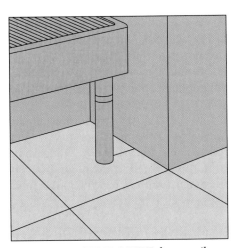

8. TO FIT AROUND A PIPE, lay one tile on another and transfer the pipe's dimensions. Cut the hole, then cut a slit to the edge.

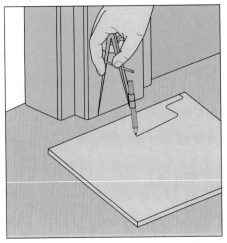

9. USE A COMPASS to scribe lines for irregular cuts, such as around door casings.

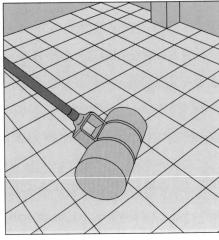

10. EMBED RESILIENT TILE in adhesive by rolling the entire floor.

INSTALLING RESILIENT SHEET FLOORING

Not all manufacturers of resilient sheet goods recommend their products for do-it-yourself installation, and wrestling with room-size materials is a job usually best left to professionals. One exception is cushioned sheet vinyl, some types of which are designed to be loose-laid and secured with adhesive only at the seams and around the edges.

Cushioned sheet vinyl can be laid over just about any smooth, sound surface, including below-grade concrete floors. Prepare the floor as you would for resilient tile (page 132), including putting down underlayment over a rough subfloor if necessary.

1 **MAKE A TEMPLATE.** In small rooms and simply shaped spaces you can just unroll the flooring and trim it to fit. For bigger rooms or those with irregularly shaped spaces, it is best to first cut a template, then transfer its outline to the vinyl. Some flooring manufacturers offer template kits. Or you can make your own template out of heavy construction paper or inexpensive building felt. You may need to tape several pieces together to get a sheet that is about 6 inches longer and wider than the floor you are covering.

2 **FIT THE TEMPLATE.** Unroll the template and carefully trim it to fit around irregularities. Finally, with a linoleum or utility knife, cut the template to the room's exact dimensions, less about ⅛ inch all around for expansion. This ensures that the vinyl will fit even a room that is out of square. After cutting the first edge, tape the template in place so it won't shift as you cut each of the other edges. When you roll up the template, roll it toward the room's longest and straightest wall. This will be your starting edge.

3 **CUT THE FLOORING.** Now unroll the vinyl, finish side up, in a space that's larger than the one you intend it for. If you must work outdoors to have enough space, sweep up any grit or stones that could dent the vinyl. Check that the edge you plan to align with the template's starting edge is straight and square. If it is not, use a square and chalkline to snap a true line. Lay the template on top of the flooring, align it with the edge or chalkline, secure the template with pieces of tape, and trace the room's outline with a pencil or felt-tip pen. Lay a straightedge along this outline and cut with a utility or linoleum knife. Some cushioned flooring can also be cut with heavy-duty scissors or with long-handled metal snips. Roll up the sheet so its starting edge will be on the outside.   *Continued*

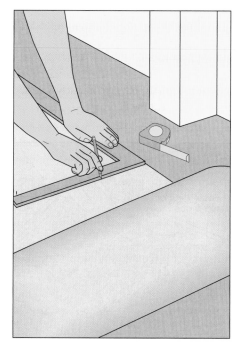

1. MAKE A FULL-SIZE TEMPLATE of the floor by cutting heavy paper to fit. In large rooms you'll probably need to tape several pieces of paper together.

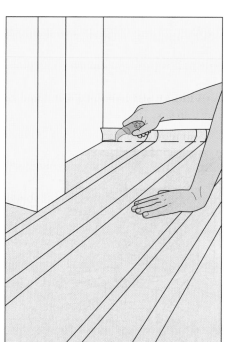

2. TRIM THE TEMPLATE to fit around obstructions and into nooks and crannies. Then cut around the perimeter of the room ⅛ inch from walls.

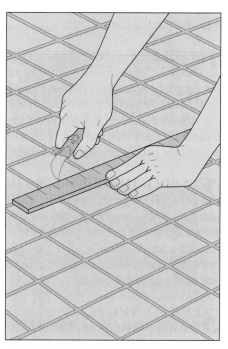

3. TRACE AROUND THE TEMPLATE onto the flooring, then cut the flooring along the lines with a knife and long straightedge. Some flooring can be cut with large scissors.

INSTALLING CARPETING

Although made from a variety of natural and synthetic fibers, in myriad densities and colors, wall-to-wall carpeting is manufactured in one of three ways.

Woven carpet, by far the most costly, is woven on looms, like tapestries. Because it is so expensive, and because some types require special installation techniques, laying woven carpet is best left to professionals.

Integral-pad carpet, also called foam-backed and cushion-backed carpet, has a layer of foam padding laminated to its backing. Integral-pad carpeting is inexpensive to moderate in price, and of course you needn't invest in separate padding. Since laying integral-pad carpet requires no special tools or skills, it's an easy do-it-yourself project.

Tufted carpet ranges from moderate to expensive in price. It is made by machines that sew pile yarn into a fabric backing. Tufted carpeting is usually installed over felt or foam padding and secured around the edges by special *tackless strips.* These have angled points that bite into the carpet backing. Techniques for installing tufted carpeting in this way are shown on pages 140–141. It is also possible to use hook-and-loop tapes (such as Velcro) on the carpet and floor.

PLANNING AN INSTALLATION
Carpet comes in rolls up to 12 feet wide. This means that if a room's narrower dimension is greater than 12 feet, you will need to seam the carpeting at one or more places. To plan seam locations, first carefully measure the room and draw it to scale on graph paper. Next, consider traffic patterns and identify the areas of a room where people seldom walk. Because seams are weak spots, locate them here, not in high-traffic areas near doorways, and never run a seam at a right angle up to or through a doorway.

As you plan seam locations, remember that carpet fibers all lean the same way, a property called "pile direction." If you make a seam with the fibers in the two pieces leaning in different directions, the seam will be very noticeable. Matching the pile direction may require buying extra carpet or making another seam or two, or both.

INSTALLING INTEGRAL-PAD CARPETING
You can lay cushion-backed carpeting over just about any clean, dry surface, using the adhesive specified by the manufacturer. If you must seam the carpet, you will also need seaming fluid, which comes in a squeeze bottle with a nozzle. Begin by marking any seam locations with chalklines on the floor. If the baseboard has a shoe molding at the floor, you'll get the best-looking results by removing the molding carefully now and replacing it to hide the carpet edges at the end of the job.

1 ROUGH-CUT carpeting by referring to your diagram and the seam lines marked on the floor. Add 2 inches for overlap at each of the room's edges. Mark the carpet with a pencil (never mark the face of a carpet with chalk). Cut along the line with a sharp carpet knife or utility knife and a straightedge. Align the edge to be seamed with the line on the floor. Position the adjoining piece so that it overlaps the first by about ¼ inch. Both pieces should overlap the baseboards by about 2 inches.

2 SPREAD ADHESIVE at the seam line. Roll back about 3 feet of carpet on both sides of the seam and apply adhesive to the floor on both sides of the chalkline. Use a trowel or spreader with notches as recommended by the adhesive manufacturer. Roll the first piece of carpeting into the adhesive, positioning its edge carefully. Press the backing into the adhesive with your hands and work out any air bubbles by pushing away from the seam.

3 APPLY SEAMING FLUID to the edge of the first piece's backing, between the pile and the pad. Work carefully so you do not get fluid on the pile. Now unroll the adjoining piece until it overlaps the first, then pull it with your fingers until the edge drops into place. Again, smooth out bulges and bubbles by pressing outward from the seam.

4 FOLD BACK CORNERS of the carpeting after the seam has set, then fold the carpet edges away from the wall. Apply adhesive to the floor and fold everything back in place. Use your hands and the cardboard core that came with the carpet to smooth it out.

5 CREASE ALONG EDGES at baseboards with a putty knife, trim the excess with a sharp carpet or utility knife, then use the putty knife again to wedge the carpet pile snug against the baseboard.

6 AT DOORWAYS, install metal *binder bars* that clamp the carpet edge and hold it to the floor with metal points on the bottom of the bar. Tuck carpeting into the bar and tamp it closed by tapping with a hammer and block of wood. At a doorway between two carpeted rooms, make a seam that runs across the width of the doorway.
Continued

CAUTION

Do not install integral-pad carpeting on stair steps. Constant up and down traffic can pull the face away from the backing and create a tripping hazard. Also, for safety reasons hire a professional to lay tufted carpet on a stairway.

REMOVING OLD CARPETING

About the only thing you can't install new carpeting over is old carpeting. Although integral-pad carpeting goes down more easily than tufted carpet, it is more difficult to remove, because when you try to pull it up the pad remains stuck to the floor. Scrape away old padding and adhesive with a garden spade, broad knife, or other sharp-edged tool.

Tufted carpeting comes up easily. Simply grasp it near the edge, pull toward the baseboard, and lift the backing free of the points on the tackless strips (see page 140). If the new carpet is about the same thickness as the old one, you can reuse the tackless strips, and maybe the padding as well.

INSTALL CARPETING

HOW TO INSTALL INTEGRAL-PAD CARPETING

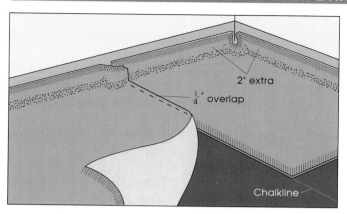

1. MARK SEAM LOCATIONS on the floor with a chalkline. Cut one piece of carpeting to align with this line and overlap baseboards by 2 inches. Cut a second piece, also wider at the edges, and position it to overlap the first by ¼ inch.

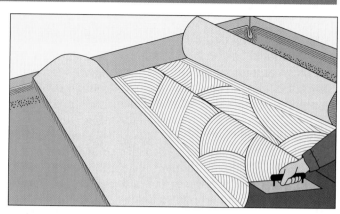

2. ROLL BACK BOTH PIECES from the seam line and spread adhesive in the area between them. Then carefully roll the first piece into the adhesive, making sure its edge falls in place along the chalkline. Smooth it down.

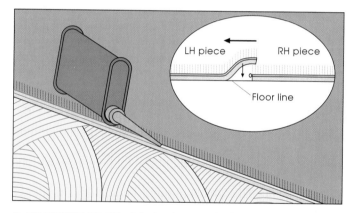

3. COAT THE EDGE of the backing on the first piece of carpeting with seaming fluid, taking care not to smear fluid on the pile. *Inset:* Lay the second piece over the first and carefully slide it away from the seam until its edge falls squarely against the edge of the first.

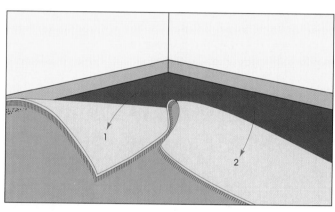

4. FOLD CORNERS in on themselves, then fold back the entire carpet toward the seam to expose flooring that has not been coated with adhesive. Apply adhesive there, then fold the carpet and corners back in place and smooth them into the adhesive.

5. TRIM EDGES. First crease them against the baseboard with a putty knife, then slice off the excess with a carpet knife or utility knife. Press the carpet into the adhesive with the putty knife. Then replace the shoe molding, if any.

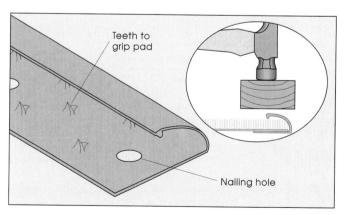

6. CLAMP EXPOSED CARPET EDGES at doorways, archways, and other locations with C-shaped metal binder bars. Slip a bar over the carpet and secure it by tapping along its length with a hammer and block of wood.

INSTALL CARPETING

INSTALLING CARPETING Continued

TUFTED CARPETING

The traditional method of installing tufted carpeting is to hook it over the points of tackless strips nailed or glued around the perimeter of the room and pull it taut, like an artist's canvas. To do this you'll need to rent two tools: a *knee kicker* for hooking the carpet to the strips along two sides of the room and a *power stretcher,* to pull the carpet taut and hook it to the strips on the opposite sides of the room. If you must make seams, also rent a *seaming iron* to activate the adhesive on special seaming tape and a *row-running knife* for making precise seam cuts.

Plan the installation and seam locations on graph paper. Besides carpeting, padding, and tools you will need tackless strips with points just long enough to pierce the backing of the carpet.

1 INSTALL TACKLESS STRIPS. One type of tackless strip comes with partially driven nails that you hammer into wood or concrete. Another type can be cemented to nonnailable surfaces such as ceramic tile. Remove the shoe molding from the baseboard and install the strips all around the room. Use a scrap of wood to space the strips from the baseboard a distance equal to two-thirds the thickness of the carpet. Cut the strips with a saw or heavy-duty snips and position them so the pins point toward the wall. Make butt joints at corners. At doorways, plan to use binder bars (see pages 138–139).

CAUTION: Wear heavy work gloves when handling tackless strips.

2 INSTALL PADDING. Rough-cut padding with heavy scissors to a size large enough to overlap the tackless strips. Spread out the padding, waffle-textured side up, and staple or cement it to the floor within the space bounded by the strips. Space staples 6 inches apart along the edges and throughout the field. Butt the edges of the padding strips together and join the seams with duct tape. After the padding is fastened down, trim it with a sharp knife, leaving a ¼- to ⅛-inch gap between the edges of the padding and the tackless strips. This space provides room for the padding to expand after the carpet is laid.

3 CUT CARPETING. Unroll the carpet in a clean, dry area and transfer measurements from your graph paper plan, adding 3 inches for overlap at all sides. *Cut-pile* carpeting has individual strands of yarn and should be cut from the back; *loop-pile* carpet has loops of yarn and should be cut from the face. To mark cutoff lines, measure and cut notches at each side, then mark a line between the notches. Make the cuts with a straightedge and a carpet knife

HOW TO INSTALL TUFTED CARPETING

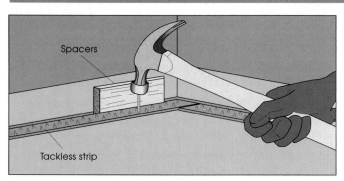

1. INSTALL TACKLESS STRIPS around the room's edges. Space them a uniform distance from the baseboard, two-thirds of the carpet thickness. Pin points should angle toward the wall.

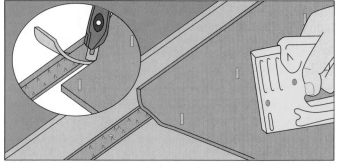

2. STAPLE OR GLUE PADDING waffle-side up overlapping the tackless strips, then trim with a utility knife. Leave a ¼- to ⅛-inch expansion gap between the pad and strips.

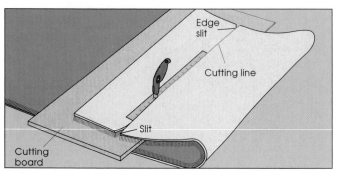

3. MARK A CUTTING LINE between slits made in the edges. Cut loop-pile carpet from the face, cut-pile carpet from the back. Use a cutting board, a straightedge, and a carpet or row-running knife.

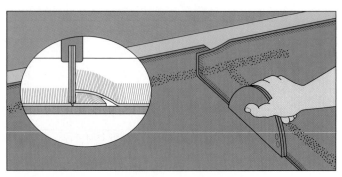

4. CUT SEAMS by overlapping pieces 1 inch. The pile on top should lean into the seam; use its edge as a guide for the row-running knife. A runner on the knife separates fibers so the blade cuts only the backing.

or a row-running knife. Use a strip of plywood or hardboard to protect the carpet under the cut line.

4 CUT SEAMS. To ensure tight seams, overlap two pieces by about 1 inch. Put the side with pile leaning into the seam on top. Use the upper-layer edge as a guide to cut through the lower layer. Again, put a protective board under the cut. Discard the cut strip from the lower layer and the edges should butt evenly.

5 TAPE SEAMS. Cut seaming tape to the length of the seam. Roll back one carpet edge and slide half the width of the tape under the other edge, adhesive side up. Fold back that carpet edge and activate the adhesive with a hot seaming iron. Hold it directly on the tape for about 30 seconds, then slowly draw it along the tape, pressing both edges of the carpet into the tape as you go. Lightly separate the pile with your fingers to see if the edges butt evenly; adjust as necessary. Weight the seam with heavy, flat objects or roll it with a rolling pin.

6 KICK-HOOK THE CARPET. Dig the knee kicker's teeth into the carpet at one corner, about 6 inches from the side wall and 1 inch from the tackless strip directly in front of the kicker. Bump the cushioned end with your knee to hook the carpet backing onto the tackless strip. Next, kick carpet over the strip on the adjacent corner wall, again about 6 inches from the corner. Now switch to the stretcher.

7 STRETCH THE CARPET. Pad the stretcher's tailstock with a scrap of carpet and brace it against the baseboard at one of the points you have just kick-hooked. Extend the stretcher across the room to a spot about 6 inches from the opposite wall. Dig the stretcher's points into the carpet here and gently lower the lever. You'll quickly learn just how much to stretch the carpeting taut without straining it. When the tension is right, use the side of a hammer head to press the carpet down and roll it onto the hooks of the tackless strip.

Return to the kick-hooked corner and shift the stretcher so it is at the second kick-hooked spot on the adjacent wall. Stretch the carpet to the opposite corner and roll it onto the tackless strip there. This completes operations 1–4 in the last drawing below.

8 KICK AND STRETCH. Kick-hook the carpet onto the strip along one wall, then the adjacent wall—steps 5 and 6 in the sequence drawing. Then stretch and hook to the opposite walls, steps 7 and 8. When the carpet is stretched and hooked perfectly flat, trim and tuck the edges and flatten binder bars over exposed edges, as explained previously.

INSTALL CARPETING

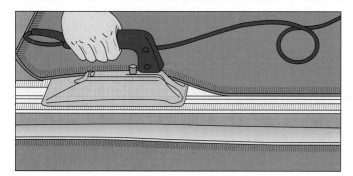

5. CENTER SEAMING TAPE adhesive side up under the seam. Melt the adhesive with a seaming iron, then immediately press the carpet edges into the tape. Adjust the seam if necessary, and weight or roll it.

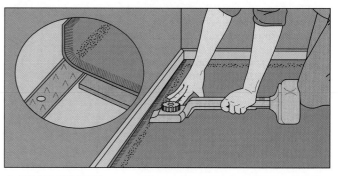

6. HOOK CARPET over tackless strips with a knee kicker. Dig the kicker's teeth into the carpet backing and kick its cushioned end with your knee. Begin by hooking the carpet at both walls in one corner.

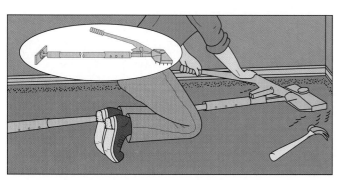

7. STRETCH CARPET by hooking the stretcher into the carpet 6 inches from the opposite wall. Lower the handle to pull the carpet taut, then roll it onto the tackless strip with the side of a hammer head.

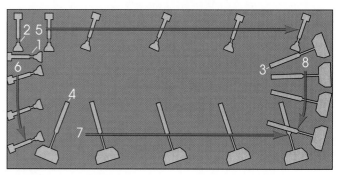

8. KICK AND STRETCH the carpet in this sequence. Use the kicker for steps 1, 2, 5, 6, the stretcher for steps 3, 4, 7, 8 along opposite walls. If the carpet wrinkles, unhook it from the tackless strips and try again.

INSTALLING A CERAMIC TILE FLOOR

Ceramic and other hard-surface floor tile has a well-earned reputation for durability, but the success of any installation depends largely on what lies underneath. Unlike resilient and wood flooring, hard-surface tiles have absolutely no "give" to them. This means that the floor over which you install them must be as rigid as the tiles themselves. Any movement will break the mortar grout between tiles and may even crack the tiles.

Concrete makes an excellent subsurface for ceramic tile. You can also tile over vinyl tiles and sheet goods, except cushioned vinyl. Do not tile over a hardwood floor, because the surface may warp. For underlayment, use only cement board (see page 164) or ⅝-inch exterior grade plywood, not particleboard.

The surface must be even as well as rigid. Any high or low spots will also crack the grout, so sand or fill the subfloor as necessary before tiling.

SELECTING TILES

Floor tiles differ from wall tiles in that they're thicker and less glossy. (High-gloss glazing would be slippery underfoot.) Some floor tiles, called quarry tiles, have no glaze at all; these usually should be sealed after you install them.

Although tiles come in fairly standard sizes, those made by one manufacturer are not necessarily interchangeable with those made by another, so stick with one maker. *Loose tiles* are sold by the carton, each containing enough tiles to cover a given area, generally 5 or 8 square feet. *Mosaic tiles* are smaller and commonly come in sheets from 6 × 12 inches to 12 × 24 inches. Back-mounted mosaics are on a plastic mesh that keeps them evenly spaced and helps them adhere to the floor. Face-mounted mosaics have a paper covering over the finished side. You lay these in adhesive, then dampen and pull away the paper after the adhesive has set, before grouting.

Whether loose or in sheets, *field tiles* make up the bulk of an installation. Specialty tiles include *cove bases* that serve as ceramic baseboards, *inside* and *outside corners*, which enable bases to change direction, and marble *saddles* that serve as sills at door thresholds. There are other shapes, too. Because you don't need very many of them, specialty tiles are sold by the piece.

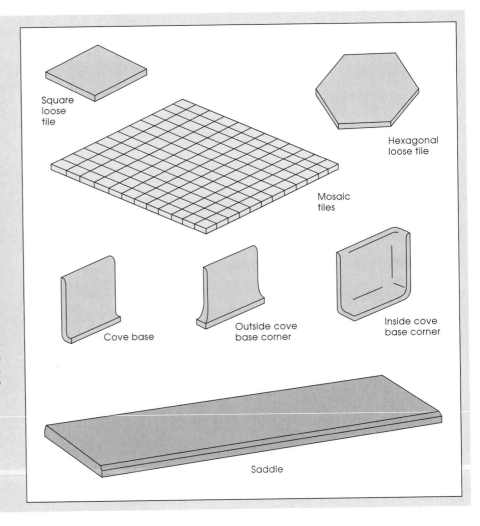

TILE SHAPES AND SIZES

Floor tiles come in a variety of configurations. Loose tiles are typically 4 1/4-, 6-, or 8-inch squares, hexagons, or oblongs. Mosaic pieces usually measure 1 or 2 inches across their long dimension and are bonded to plastic mesh. Cove base tiles serve as ceramic baseboards. Order a marble saddle cut with a length equal to the width of your doorway opening minus 1/4 inch.

The great majority of tiles are manufactured with spacing lugs on the edges for grout lines of uniform width. If not, use tile spacers (see next page). Tiles on backing sheets or mesh are usually spaced for grouting, but occasionally one or more tiles will be out of alignment. If that is the case, pull them free and replace them with a dab of adhesive on the back after the entire sheet has been put in place.

Custom tiles may vary considerably from standard sizes and thicknesses, especially if they are handmade. It is best to do a good deal of sorting according to size and thickness before starting to lay such tiles.

Square loose tile

Hexagonal loose tile

Mosaic tiles

Cove base

Outside cove base corner

Inside cove base corner

Saddle

TOOLS FOR TILING

Tiling tools include a notched trowel for adhesive work, a rubber float for grouting, a tile cutter for making straight cuts, nippers for curved cuts, and plastic or wood spacers you temporarily insert between tiles to maintain even grout joints. You will also need some sponges to clean up after grouting, and some old bath towels or similar cloths for dry-wiping the surface at the very end.

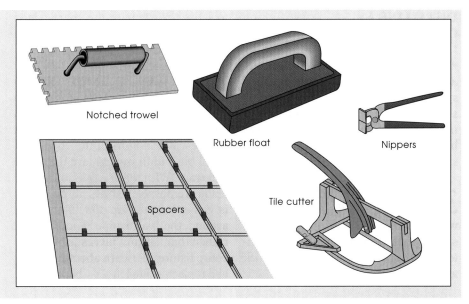

Notched trowel

Rubber float

Nippers

Spacers

Tile cutter

TILING TOOLS AND SUPPLIES

At the time you purchase your tiles you should also pick up a few other items. You'll need *adhesive* to attach the tiles to the floor. Different surfaces call for different adhesives, so be certain your supplier knows exactly what surface you'll be tiling over. The dealer should also advise you about *grout,* the thin mortar that goes between tiles. Grout comes either as a powder that you mix with water or as a premixed compound. Whichever you choose, make sure it's a type designed for floors, not walls. If your tiles do not have self-spacing lugs on the edges you will need plastic *spacers* to keep the seams a uniform width.

Besides these supplies, you'll several specialized tiling tools. Among the tools to buy from the supplier are a *notched trowel* for spreading adhesive and a *rubber float* for applying grout. Plan to rent a *tile cutter* for making straight cuts and *nippers* for irregular cuts. To save money, first set all the field tiles, then rent the cutter and nippers for trimming around the edges.

1 PLOT A STARTING POINT. Establish where you will begin tiling. Keep the overall pattern appearance in mind. In a bathroom, the most conspicuous section of the floor is generally along the base of the tub, so plan your installation to cut as few tiles here as possible. Place tiles up against the tub at each end. Be sure to leave grouting space between the tiles and the tub. Mark where the outer edges lie, then snap a chalkline between these two points. All your tiles will be positioned in relation to this line.

In other rooms, try another reference point, such as the most frequently used doorway. Draw a line across the center of the entrance, then, using a square, snap a chalkline at a 90-degree angle to that line.   *Continued*

PLANNING A TILE INSTALLATION

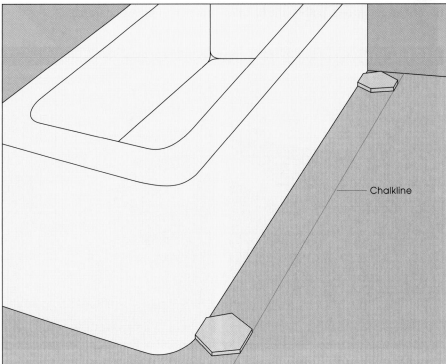

Chalkline

1. PLAN YOUR INSTALLATION for a minimum of cutting at the room's most conspicuous point—along the tub edge in a bathroom. Snap a chalkline one tile width away and extend it the length of the room.

SANDING SEQUENCE

In order to achieve a smooth, even finish on your floor, it is essential to sand with the wood grain. Sanding against or across the grain can create scratches that are difficult to erase. Start sanding at the center of the room and work out to the walls. One reason for adopting this technique is that the center of the room gets the most traffic and therefore has the most wear. If you start in the center and overlap passes, the floor will get the most attention where it really needs it. To start at the same position each time, draw a chalk line across the room designating the center line of the sanding pattern.

A parquet floor presents a challenge because the boards are positioned in a pattern at right angles to each other. If you attempt to sand parallel to a wall, you will always be sanding against some of the grain. Here it is best to adopt a diagonal approach and sand at a 45-degree angle to the parquet squares; the first pass should go in one direction and the second pass should go at a 90-degree angle across the first. The final pass will be in line with the parquet seams. This pass will go against the grain of some of the boards, so use fine-grit sandpaper and move in line with the length, not the width, of the room.

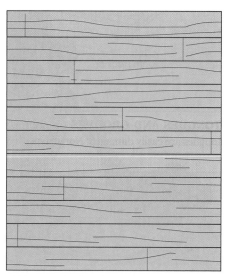

SAND STRIP FLOORING with the grain of the wood. Start at the center and work toward the walls.

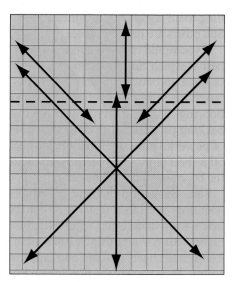

PARQUET FLOORING has boards positioned at right angles, so use a sanding pattern with diagonal passes.

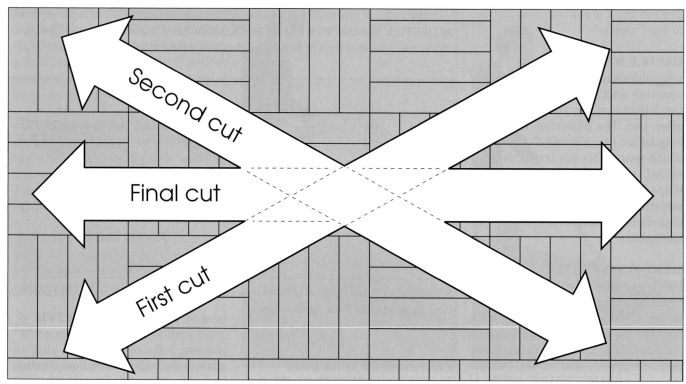

Second cut

Final cut

First cut

FINISH SANDING EITHER SURFACE with fine-grit paper. Move the grit paper parallel to the floor squares. Touch up any missed or rough spots by hand-sanding with a paper wrapped around a sanding block.

STAIRS

Constructing an interior staircase is one of the trickiest jobs a carpenter ever has to undertake, which may explain why many stairways come prefabricated from millwork factories. The elements of a staircase are shown at right.

Stairs consist of a *stringer* on each side notched to support the *treads* you step on. Vertical *risers* separate the treads. In a very simple staircase, such as one to a basement, there may be no risers, simply open spaces between the treads. More sophisticated, closed-riser staircases include risers dadoed into the edges of treads.

Stairways with walls on either side need only *handrails* attached to one or both walls. If, however, the stairs are open on one side, the handrail becomes part of a more complex assembly known as a *balustrade*. A balustrade starts with a *newel post* at the bottom. Its handrail is supported by *balusters*, usually two per step. If the stairway includes a landing, there will be a *landing newel* here. A *half newel* anchors the balustrade to a wall.

Building a complete interior staircase is a task for only a very experienced carpenter. However, building simple, open-riser stairs, such as those to a deck, is a feasible do-it-yourself project (see Chapter 30), as are the stairway repairs shown here and on page 153.

TIGHTENING A HANDRAIL

Loose handrails are annoying and also pose a safety hazard. If you have a wobbly rail, examine the joints where the individual balusters meet the handrail. If these seem loose, you can tighten them by driving a wood screw at an angle so it penetrates through the baluster into the handrail. First drill a pilot hole, then countersink the hole so the screw head will be hidden below the surface of the wood. Driving the screw in should pull the rail and baluster securely together.

Other techniques for securing a loose rail include inserting wedges in gaps between the rail and the baluster, and installing filler blocks. These techniques are described on the following pages.

TIGHTENING A BALUSTRADE

Settling can cause an entire balustrade to loosen. Fixing the problem entails examining each baluster to see if it's loose. Tighten a baluster with glue and wooden shims. Cut a thin shim from a piece of hardwood and coat it with glue. Use a small mallet and a wooden block to drive the shim into the gap between the rail and baluster top. When the glue is dry, use a knife to trim the shim so it is flush with the baluster. You can also fix

Continued

STAIRWAY COMPONENTS

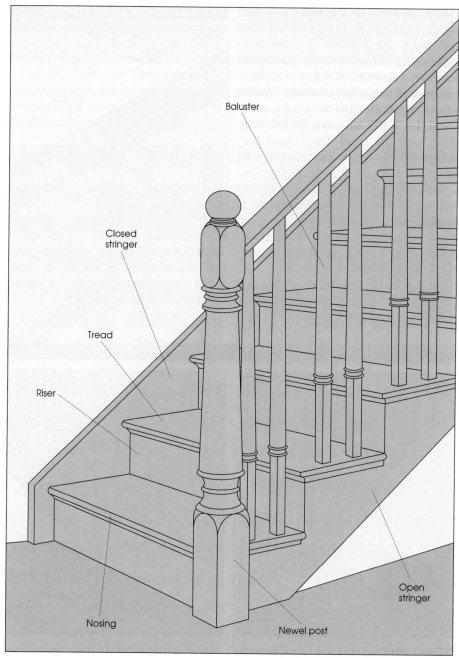

Baluster

Closed stringer

Tread

Riser

Nosing

Newel post

Open stringer

STAIRWAYS ARE CONSTRUCTED of a number of different elements: stringers, treads and risers, newel posts, and balustrades. These parts fit together like a fine cabinet. Styles vary greatly, but methods of construction do not.

STAIRS

FRAMING A PARTITION
Continued

FRAMING DOOR OPENINGS
To install the studs and header for a doorway, begin by cutting the jack studs to length—¼ inch shorter than the height of the door. When they are set on top of the sole plate there will be 1¼ inches above the door for the thickness of the top jamb and space for leveling. Face-nail the jack studs to the king studs. For a single-width door, cut two 2 × 4s to fit between the king studs, atop the jack studs. Fit pieces of ½- or ⅜-inch plywood between them to make the header thickness equal to the width of the studs. End-nail through the king studs into the header. A wider opening needs a more substantial header made of 2 × 6s spaced out to the proper thickness. Finally, nail short cripple studs between the header and top plate. Center a single cripple stud over a door opening up to 32 inches wide; space cripples 16 inches on center over wider openings. Cut away the sole plate in the door opening after the partition has been erected and secured in position. Protect the flooring when making this cut. (To learn about installing doors, see Chapter 19.)

TURNING CORNERS
When the end-wall framing is open, you need to install an additional stud at the inside corner, with the partition to pro-vide an edge to attach the end-wall dry-wall panels. To do that, fasten nailers to the end stud of the partition so the new stud can be fastened to them, as illus-trated below. If the two walls also form an outside corner on the opposite side, install a second stud in either of the two ways shown in the illustration.

Where two walls make a T intersec-tion, attach studs for inside corners on both sides where the partition butts against the end wall. In any corner con-struction, a full-length stud can serve as a nailer instead of scrap blocks.

INSTALLING FIRE-STOPS
Although not an essential feature in in-terior partitions, fire-stops add rigidity

PARTITION FRAMING DETAILS

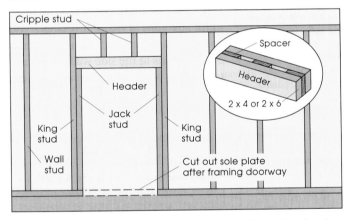

FRAME A DOOR OPENING with king and jack studs, a header, and cripple studs. Buy the door first and determine what size rough opening it requires. Detail shows header construction.

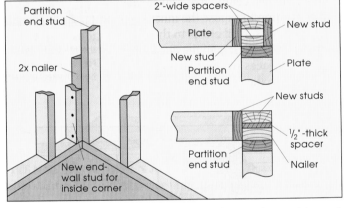

TURN INSIDE CORNERS by nailing blocking to the partition end stud, then nailing a new end-wall stud to the blocking. Inside/out-side corners can be framed in either way shown at the right.

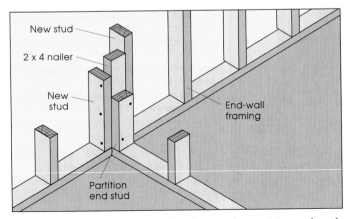

AT T INTERSECTIONS install nailers on the partition end stud, then add a stud for an inside corner on each side. Nailers can be short blocks or a full-length stud.

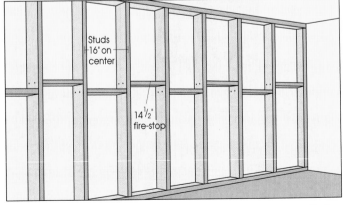

IF FIRE-STOPS ARE REQUIRED, install 2 × 4s horizontally be-tween studs. Stagger the height so you can nail through the studs in-to the ends of the stops.

to a wall. Cut 2 × 4s to fit between the studs and nail through the studs into their ends. Install the stops at points about halfway up the wall, alternating their heights for easy end nailing. Where joist spacing is 16 inches on center, the stops will be 14½ inches long.

FRAMING WITH METAL STUDS

Metal framing is more fire resistant than wood, and in some locations cheaper. Also, metal framing goes together much faster.

The U-shaped components consist of steel studs and lighter-gauge metal track used as top and sole plates. You screw lengths of track to the floor and ceiling, cut studs to length, and space them at 16- or 24-inch intervals. A stud is inserted between the plates with its width facing outward, then given a quarter turn to snap-lock it into place edgewise. Precut openings in the studs allow pipes and wiring to be run through the walls. The framework seems insubstantial until you tie everything together with ⅝-inch-thick drywall and special self-tapping drywall screws.

Because they are not prone to warping, metal-framed walls usually are straighter and more uniform than partitions built with wood 2 × 4s. But because metal studs have less compressive strength, you should not use them in a wall that must support cabinets or heavy shelving.

Metal and wood studs have the same dimensions. This means you could use metal components for the plates and some studs, and wood 2 × 4s as studs at points where greater strength is needed, such as around the opening for a heavy door. Here's how to work with metal framing.

1 **CUT STUDS AND TRACK.** Use metal shears or snips to cut metal framing components. Cut the sides of the channel first, then bend back the wide face and cut across it. Protect your hands with work gloves. Lay out floor and ceiling lines and screw the track into position as floor and top plates.

2 **FIT STUDS INTO TRACKS.** For an easy fit, cut the studs ¼ inch shorter than the height of the wall. Slip each one into the tracks sideways and twist to seat it. You needn't worry about exact spacing at this point. After all the framing is in place, you can go back and tap the studs into position and get each one plumb.

3 **ATTACH DRYWALL.** Drive drywall screws through gypsum board into metal framing with a drill/driver or, better yet, a drywall screw gun, which has a clutch that stops the bit when the screw head is just below the surface. (For more about installing drywall, see pages 164–167.) The screws secure the framing as well as the drywall.

METAL STUD FRAMING

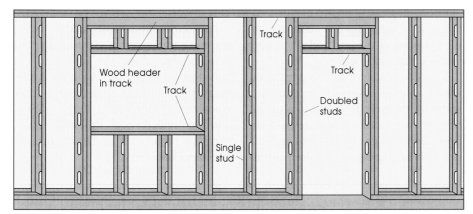

METAL FRAMING COMPONENTS use U-shaped tracks for top and bottom plates and to span openings. Metal studs, with cutouts for electrical and plumbing lines, snap into the tracks. Double up metal studs around openings, just as you would with wood studs.

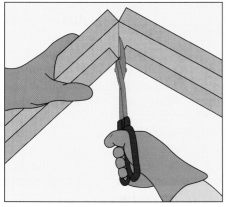

1. USE METAL SHEARS to cut metal framing. Snip through the sides of the channel, bend, and cut across the face.

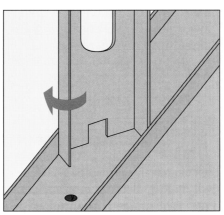

2. FIT EACH STUD into the track at an angle, then twist until the track grips it. When all are in place, adjust spacing and plumb.

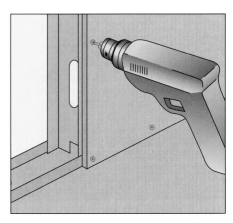

3. DRIVE SCREWS through drywall to tie the metal framing together and complete the wall. Use a power screwdriver.

FRAMING A PARTITION

INSTALLING PLANK PANELING

Putting up solid-wood planks, either new lumber or recycled barn boards, requires a few more carpentry skills and a lot more nails than installing sheet goods. Planks are more versatile, however. You can nail them up vertically, horizontally, even diagonally. And because planks are thicker than sheet paneling—typically ¾ inch, compared to ³⁄₁₆, ¼, or ⁵⁄₁₆ inch—codes may permit you to nail them directly to studs.

SELECTING PLANKS

Planks come in a wide variety of hardwood and softwood species, with several different edge and surface treatments. Some are square-cut ordinary lumber. Others fit together with tongue-and-groove or lapped edges. Widths range from 2 to 12 inches, and you can intersperse differing widths for design variety. Some planks are milled to have a shaped profile, or surface, on one face. Others are saw kerfed or rough sawn for a rustic look.

PREPARING FOR PLANK PANELING

If you are planning to install planks horizontally, you can nail them directly to studs or furring, or through drywall or plaster into the studs. For vertical plank paneling install horizontal nailing blocks between studs or furring strips spaced 24 to 36 inches vertically.

As with sheet paneling, planks should be acclimated to a room's moisture conditions by storing them in the room, stacked with wood spacers across the pile to promote air circulation.

You can completely prefinish planks with stain and sealer before installing, then go back and touch up saw cuts and minor blemishes afterward. If you prefer to finish tongue-and-groove or lapped paneling after it's on the wall, stain or seal the edges beforehand. Otherwise, normal shrinkage could exposed unfinished wood later on.

INSTALLING MOLDINGS

Unless the existing baseboards, casings, and other trim in the room you will be paneling are at least as thick as the planks and have square edges, you will need to replace them with square-edge stock. You'll find it easier to do this first, then cut the planks to fit up against the new molding. Remove the old trim and install replacements, as shown in Chapter 16. In some cases the planks themselves can serve as molding.

PUTTING UP THE PLANKS

With vertical tongue-and-groove paneling, start at an inside corner and place the grooved edge into the corner. Hold a level against the tongue to see if the plank is plumb. If it is not, measure carefully and rip along the grooved edge as required to get the board plumb. Check each successive board for plumb and adjust it before nailing. The last plank on each wall will also need to be ripped to fit.

For horizontal installation of tongue-and-groove planks, start at the bottom of the wall and work up. Place the tongue edges pointing up and check

SELECTING PLANKS

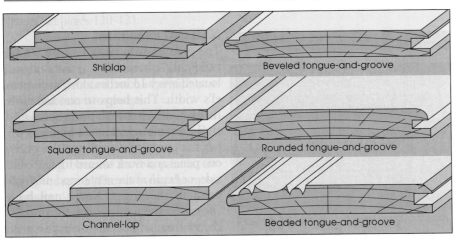

Shiplap

Beveled tongue-and-groove

Square tongue-and-groove

Rounded tongue-and-groove

Channel-lap

Beaded tongue-and-groove

PLANK STYLES range from plain square-edge boards (*not shown*) through a variety of tongue-and-groove and lapped-edge profiles. These examples are among the most widely used. Many other patterns and surface textures are available in widths from 2 to 12 inches.

PREPARING WALLS

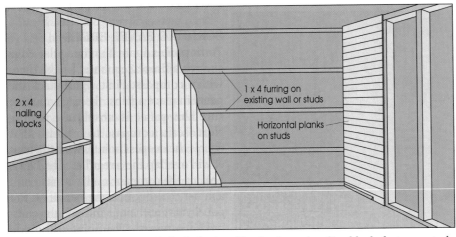

2 x 4 nailing blocks

1 x 4 furring on existing wall or studs

Horizontal planks on studs

PREPARE WALLS for vertical planks by installing horizontal nailing blocks between studs or putting up horizontal furring, spaced no more than 36 inches apart. Horizontal planks can be nailed directly to studs or to vertical furring over an existing wall surface.

that each board is level before nailing it. To join boards, miter the ends for an overlapping scarf joint. Locate joints over studs or furring strips and stagger them from course to course. Use these same procedures to install square- or lapped-edge planks, but use a different nailing technique, explained below.

NAILING PLANK PANELING

Tongue-and-groove planks can be blind-nailed through their tongues so that the groove of the next board covers the nails. Use 6-penny finishing nails and a nail set to drive them flush with the surface of the tongue. Lapped-edge and other types of boards must be face-nailed through the surface and the nail heads countersunk with a nail set. After staining and sealing the paneling, cover the nail heads with colored putty. Face-nail with 8-penny finishing nails. In corners you will need to face-nail the last course or two of tongue-and-groove paneling, since the tongues won't be easily accessible for blind nailing.

ADJUST ELECTRICAL OUTLETS

Electrical boxes must be made deeper so that the switch or outlet will be flush with the finished wall surface. Do this with extender collars, available at most hardware stores. Turn off the electricity and remove the faceplate from the outlet. Next, remove the switch or receptacle mounting screws, fit a collar into the box, and adjust it to the proper depth. Finally, remount the device, secure the extender with the longer screws that come with it, and replace the faceplate.

HOW TO INSTALL PLANK PANELING

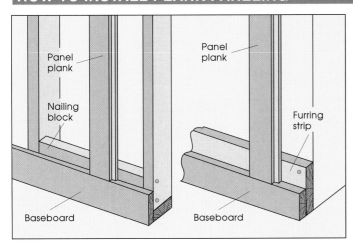

INSTALL MOLDINGS before putting up planks. Here both baseboard and paneling are backed by a nailing block between open studs *(left)* and a furring strip over a closed wall *(right)*. The same methods are used for ceiling trim.

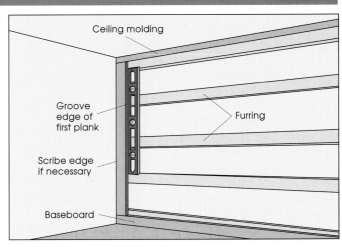

INSTALL THE FIRST PLANK at an inside corner, with its groove against the wall. Hold a level against the tongue and adjust the plank until it is plumb. If necessary, rip the grooved edge for a tight fit in the corner when the plank is plumb.

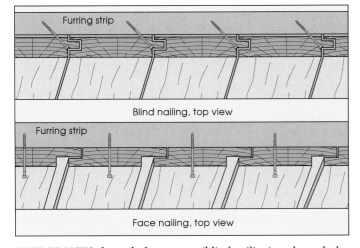

NAIL PLANKS through the tongues (blind nailing) or through the surface (face nailing); drill pilot holes to avoid splitting, if necessary. Use a nail set to countersink the nails. With face nailing, cover the nail heads with putty colored to match the paneling.

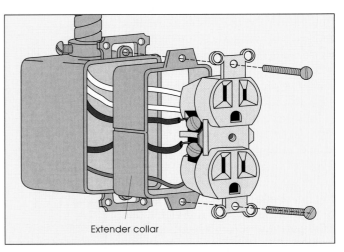

EXTENDER COLLARS will put electrical switches and receptacles flush with the surface of the finished wall. Shut off the power and unscrew the device, then insert the collar and reinstall the device with longer screws.

INSTALLING CERAMIC TILE

Covering a wall with ceramic tile is a two-stage process. First you cement the tiles to the wall, trimming them at edges and to fit around obstacles; then, after the adhesive has set, you fill the spaces between tiles with mortarlike *grout*. Tiling walls calls for the same tools and many of the same techniques used for laying floor tiles (see pages 142–145).

HOW MUCH TILE ?

Field tiles, which comprise the bulk of a tile installation, are sold by the carton. Each carton will cover a given number of square feet, so simply multiply the width times the height of each wall you will be tiling and take that number to the tile dealer. In a shower, tile should extend at least six inches above the showerhead; other bathroom walls are typically tiled about halfway up. In a kitchen, bring tile up to align with the bottoms of wall cabinets. Add 10 percent to the total square footage to allow for waste and leave you with a few left-over tiles for future repairs.

Trim tiles finish off the edges of a tile installation and are sold by the piece or linear foot. You can use *bullnose tiles,* which are the same size as field tiles but have one or two rounded edges. Or you can use *cap tiles,* which are longer and narrower than field tiles. Those with two rounded edges go at the left and right top corners of the wall, with single rounds in between. There are many other specialty tiles, such as the cove bases shown on page 142. You can also buy matching or contrasting towel bars, soap dishes, and other ceramic fixtures.

Besides the tiles, you will need adhesive, grout, and grout sealer. For a shower or other wet-use location, order Type I tile adhesive; elsewhere use Type II. One gallon of adhesive covers about 50 square feet. Grout comes premixed or in a powder that you mix with water. The premixed type is easier to work with. Grout is available in a wide variety of colors to match tiles. Coverage varies, so check the manufacturer's specifications to determine how much you will need for the job.

Specialized tools for tile work include the notched trowel, rubber float, nippers, and tile cutter shown on page 143.

PREPARING WALLS

You can install ceramic tile over any drywall or plaster surface that is sound, firm, and even. Remove any wallcovering or old ceramic tile. Scrub dirt and grease off painted walls, scrape any peeling sections, and sand glossy finishes. Patch holes and cracks in drywall or plaster and seal with primer.

Do not use ordinary drywall as a backing for tile in a shower or other wet location. Instead use special moisture-resistant drywall or, better yet, *cement board* (see page 164), which is very resistant to water and also provides the rigidity that is essential to a successful tile installation. It is put up in the same way as drywall, but with special corrosion-resistant screws.

HOW TO INSTALL CERAMIC TILE

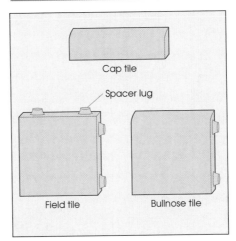

WALL TILES include field tiles, which cover most of the area, and cap or bullnose tiles, used at the edges. Spacer lugs on the tiles maintain uniform grout lines.

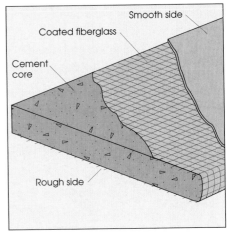

CEMENT BOARD is an excellent tile backer for showers and other wet locations because it is both rigid and water resistant. For walls, install it smooth side out.

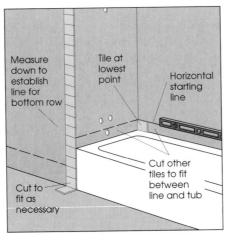

DRAW A LEVEL STARTING LINE one tile plus ¼ inch above the tub edge; work down to mark a line for a row at the floor. Without a tub, work from the lowest point of the floor.

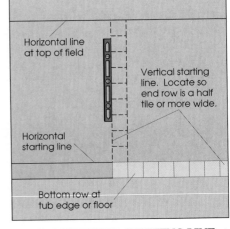

DRAW A VERTICAL STARTING LINE at the midpoint of the wall; adjust it to get at least a half-tile width at each end. Also mark a level line for the top edge of the top row.

LAYING OUT A TILING PROJECT

The key to a good-looking tile wall is to plot horizontal and vertical starting lines that don't leave you with less than half a tile width along any edge. In a bathroom, check the top of the tub with a level. If it is within ⅛ inch of being level, draw horizontal lines ¼ inch above the tub edge and plan to begin with a full row of tiles along this line. (The gap below will be filled with caulk, which flexes to absorb the movement of the tub as it is filled and emptied.)

If the tub is more than ⅛ inch out of level, find the lowest point, set a full field tile here on top of a ¼-inch shim, and mark the wall at the top of the tile. Using a level, extend this line around the tub. All other tiles below this line must be cut to fit. If you will be tiling an adjacent wall, bring the horizontal line around the corner and use it as a reference point to determine whether you will need to cut a tile at the floor. If you will be tiling the floor, include the floor-tile thickness in your calculations.

To establish a vertical starting line, find the midpoint of the wall and lay out tiles from there to one corner. If your tiles do not have spacing lugs on the edges, use plastic spacers to allow for grouting. If the end tile will have to be cut to less than half its width, shift the vertical line left or right a bit.

Finally, measure up from the horizontal starting lines and draw a second horizontal line where the topmost field tiles, not the cap tiles, will be located.

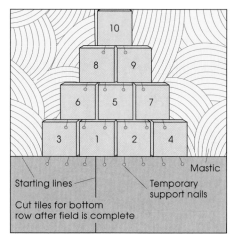

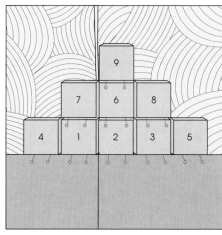

A RUNNING BOND has the first tile centered over the vertical starting line. Stagger the next course of tiles so the grout lines will be centered over the first-course tiles.

A JACK-ON-JACK BOND begins with a tile on each side of the starting line. Do not stagger the next course. Set tiles horizontally, then vertically, then horizontally again.

SETTING THE FIRST TILES

The first tiles must be precisely aligned with your horizontal and vertical starting lines. Begin by spreading adhesive onto a 3-foot-square wall area with the straight edge of a mastic spreader, then turn the spreader over and go back over the adhesive with the notched edge.

Now carefully position the first tile at the intersection of the starting lines. For a *running bond*, with staggered vertical grout lines from course to course, this first tile should straddle the vertical line. For a *jack-on-jack* installation with continuous grout lines both vertically and horizontally, align one edge of the first tile with the vertical line. Set the tile with a slight twisting motion; do not slide it. If the tile begins to slip, partially drive nails along the horizontal starting line to support the bottom row of tiles.

Next, set tiles to the left and right of the first tile. Insert plastic spacers between the tiles if needed. After setting three to five tiles along the bottom row, set three atop these. Continue working out and up, pyramid fashion, until you have covered the wall with all the tiles that do not need to be cut. Then go back and embed the tiles by holding a rubber grouting float against them and tapping it with a mallet.

MAKING STRAIGHT CUTS

Do not spread mastic for the ends or bottom row until you have cut tiles to fit. Measure carefully, being sure to allow for grout spacing, insert a tile into a tile cutter, and score across it only once. Press down on the cutter's lever to snap the tile into two pieces. Smooth any rough edges with an ordinary wood file or a Surform® file.   *Continued*

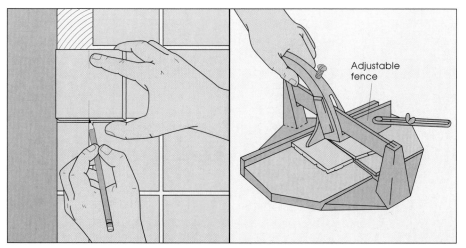

AT CORNERS, mark tile cuts as shown, then adjust the fence on a tile cutter and run the cutting wheel across the tile to score it. Going over the cut line more than once causes uneven breaks and dulls the cutting wheel. Push down on the handle to break the tile along the scored line. Smooth rough edges with a file if necessary.

INSTALLING CERAMIC TILE
Continued

MAKING CURVED CUTS

Use tile nippers to make irregular cuts around faucets, shower heads, and other protrusions. Hold the tile glazed side up and chew away at it with the nippers in small bites. Don't worry about making these cuts perfectly even; caulking will fill any gaps, and escutcheons around plumbing fittings will cover the caulk. You can also bore holes through the back sides of tiles with an electric drill and a carbide-tipped hole saw.

TURNING CORNERS

Use bullnose tiles to finish outside corners. If the adjacent wall will also be tiled, the bullnoses should project far enough to cover the unfinished edges of the field tiles around the corner. At inside corners, use cove tiles or ordinary field tiles. In all cases, leave room for a grout joint; do not butt corner tiles tightly against one another.

INSTALLING CAP TILES

Finish off the wall edges with cap tiles. To keep adhesive off the untiled wall surface, lightly butter the back side of each cap tile with adhesive, draw the shorter notched edge of the spreader across the adhesive, and carefully press the tile into place.

INSTALLING FIXTURES

Set ceramic fixtures, such as soap dishes, after all the tiles are in place but before grouting. Do not use ordinary tile

FINISHING TILE INSTALLATION

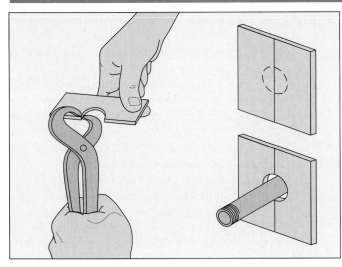

MAKE CURVED CUTS with tile nippers, starting at the edge and taking small bites. To fit around a pipe, cut a tile in two and nip semicircular cuts from each piece.

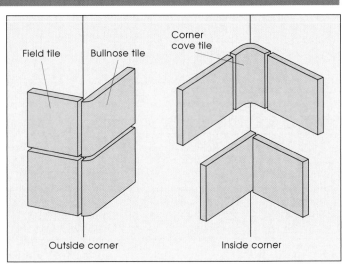

TURN OUTSIDE CORNERS with bullnose tiles on one wall. These should cover the edges of field tiles on the other wall. Turn inside corners with cove tiles, or with field tiles separated by grout.

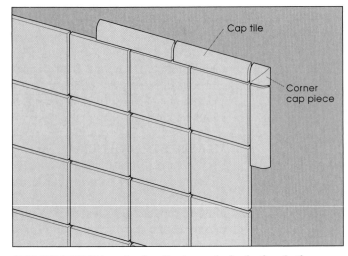

SET CAP TILES last. Apply adhesive to the back of each tile, not to the wall. Maintain proper grout spacing and stagger joints with the field-tile grouting. Use corner cap pieces where appropriate.

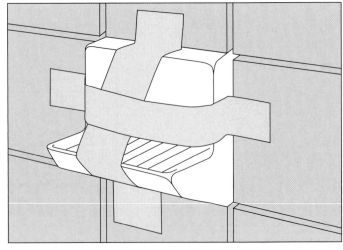

INSTALL FIXTURES with epoxy or fixture-setting cement, not ordinary tile adhesive. Press the fixture into place and secure it with duct tape for several days.

FINISHING UP WITH CAULK

The final step in a ceramic tile installation is to caulk wherever the tile adjoins the edge of a tub, door, window frame, or other nonceramic surface. Do not use grout at these points, because expansion and contraction will eventually crack it. Select a good quality, silicone-based caulk in a color that matches or harmonizes with the grout.

Caulk comes in squeeze tubes, like toothpaste, and in cartridges that load into an inexpensive caulking gun. With either, first slice off the tip of the tube at a 45-degree angle. The trick here is to create an opening that is the same size as the width of the crevice you will be filling. Look carefully at the tapered tip; many are marked in fractions of an inch—typically ⅛, ¼, and ⁵⁄₁₆. Slice through the tip with a utility knife at the point that matches the width of the joint you will be filling. Then poke a nail into the opening to puncture the seal between the nozzle and the tube or cartridge contents. If you will be caulking crevices with several different widths, start with the smallest, caulk all gaps that are that size, then cut the tip for the next wider opening.

Before caulking a joint, run the tip of a nail or screwdriver along it to remove any loose grout or other debris. Next, moisten a cloth with denatured alcohol and run it along the edges of the joint. Then place the tip of the caulking tube at a 45-degree angle at one end of the crack and slowly draw it toward you, squeezing the tube or the trigger of the gun as you go. (With a gun you will first need to engage its plunger so it pushes against the bottom of the cartridge as you squeeze the trigger.) After the first few passes you will find yourself able to gauge just how fast you need to move the tube or gun.

At the end of each pass, lift the nozzle off the joint with a twisting motion. If you are using a gun, disengage the plunger by turning it 90 degrees and pulling it back. Wipe off any caulking that remains on the tip. Finally, moisten the tip of your finger with alcohol and draw it along the joint to smooth the caulk and further force it into the opening.

To caulk around a tub, first fill it with water. Adding several hundred pounds of water will cause the tub to settle slightly. After you fill the gaps around its edges and let the water out, the tub will rise and compress the caulk for a tight seal.

When you finish caulking, seal the tip of the tube by sticking a flat-head nail into it.

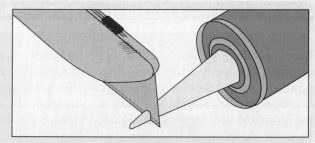

Cut the tip opening to match the joint width.

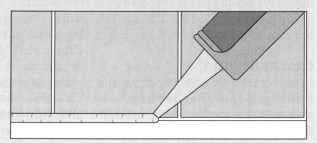

Hold tube/cartridge at an angle when squeezing out caulk.

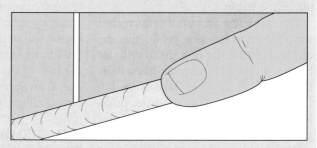

Smooth caulk with a moistened fingertip.

---

adhesive to affix this kind of fixture. Instead, use with epoxy putty or a special fixture cement; your tile dealer can supply the proper material. First scrape off any tile adhesive from the area you have planned for the fixture. Apply cement to the back of the fixture as recommended by the adhesive manufacturer and press the fixture firmly into place. Secure it to the wall with duct tape for the recommended curing time.

GROUTING WALL TILE

Grouting wall tile calls for the same procedures used to grout floor tile (see page 144), with one additional step. After the grout has thoroughly cured for 20 to 30 days, apply silicone sealer to every joint line with an artist's brush or old toothbrush. The sealer prevents mildew in the joint lines. Floor grouting should not be sealed.

INSTALLING PREGROUTED TILE

Although not available in nearly as many colors and sizes as ordinary wall tiles, sheets of tile held together by flexible grouting greatly speed up the installation process. You lay out the walls and spread adhesive as you would for individual tiles. Then you tack wood cleats along the starting lines to hold the sheets in position temporarily, and press the sheets to the wall.

To fit around plumbing fittings, remove individual tiles at those points in the sheets. Set the sheets on the wall, then cut the removed tiles to shape with nippers and fit them in place. Do the same with tiles at edges and corners, using a tile cutter.

Finally, fill the joints between the sheets with silicone caulking, as explained in the box above.

Temporary cleat

Work up from a support cleat to install pregrouted sheets. Protect the tub with a drop cloth and a thick layer of newspapers to stand on.

14 INTERIOR PAINTING

Nothing transforms a room quite so easily and quickly as a fresh coat of paint—which probably explains why interior painting is the most popular do-it-yourself activity. Master the fundamentals in this chapter and you'll get professional results every time.

SELECTING INTERIOR PAINTS

Interior paints fall into two overall categories. *Latex paint* is water based, which means you can wipe up smears and spatters with a damp rag and clean painting tools with soap and water. *Alkyd paint,* sometimes called oil paint, has a nonpetroleum solvent base and must be cleaned up with turpentine or almost odorless mineral spirits, also called paint thinner.

Latex paints dry much faster than alkyd paints and are all but odorless. Alkyd paints are slightly more durable and cover somewhat better than latex, but some communities prohibit their use because of disposal problems. Most professional as well as amateur painters choose latex paint because you can apply two coats in a single day.

Latex and alkyd paints come in lusters that range from *flat* to *high gloss.* Intermediate designations include *satin, semigloss,* and *eggshell.* Flat paints work well on interior walls and ceilings because they provide better coverage with less glare and cost less than other finishes. But flat paint is less durable and less washable than semigloss and high-gloss paints, so use the shinier coatings on woodwork and on walls that must be wiped down periodically, such as those in kitchens and baths.

CHOOSING COLORS

Paint store personnel can custom-tint just about any hue you desire, but take your time in making a selection. Because colors change under different lighting conditions, a shade that looks just right in the store may turn into something quite different in your home. Try out colors by collecting paint chips and comparing them at different times of day. When you've narrowed your selection to one or two possibilities, buy small quantities of these and paint 4-foot-square sections of a wall with them. Large areas of color can become far more intense than they appear on paint chips, and custom-tinted paints usually can't be returned.

SPECIALTY PAINTS

For most interior painting projects you'll need only flat paint for walls and ceilings, and semi- or high-gloss paint for trim. However, manufacturers also offer a variety of specialty paints. *Ceiling paint* consists of flat, white, glare-resistant latex or alkyd. It costs less than wall paint. *Dripless paint* is also formulated for ceilings. It costs more than wall paint. *Textured paint* brings textural interest to walls and ceiling surfaces (more about this on page 183). *Acoustic paint* can be used on ceiling tiles without impairing their sound-absorbing qualities. *One-coat paints* have more pigment for extra covering ability. They cost more, too. *Metal paints* are self-priming and adhere well to radiators, register grilles, and other metallic items. *Primers* are thinned paints that seal surfaces and provide a good bond for the finish coat.

DO YOU NEED TO PRIME FIRST?

In most situations the answer is no, with three exceptions: Prime unfinished wood, drywall, or plaster; prime latex-painted surfaces that will be painted with alkyd; and prime before a significant color change. Primers are always white, but can be tinted for more hiding power. Use only the primer specified on the label of the finish paint.

SELECTING BRUSHES

Quality brushes give quality results and last much longer than bargain-bin specials. Generally, the more and longer the bristles, the better the brush. Good bristles vary slightly in length and are "flagged," like the split ends of hair, for smoother paint application. The bristles should taper to a chisel-like edge so you can get paint into tight spots.

Formerly, the best brushes had natural, animal-hair bristles, but today's synthetic-bristle brushes work just as well, and they are the only choice for latex paint; natural bristles soak up water and make it all but impossible to flow latex on evenly.

For most interior painting projects you can get by with two or three brushes. Use a 3-inch *wall brush* for cutting in around the edges of walls and ceilings and a 2-inch flat-end *trim brush* for painting woodwork. If you will be painting windows or woodwork with lots of corners, add a 1½-inch angled *sash brush.*

Some painters like *foam brushes;* others feel bristle brushes offer better control. Because foam brushes are inexpensive you can throw them away after use, which eliminates having to clean them.

SELECTING ROLLERS AND PADS

Rollers coat open spaces in half the time it would take to paint the same areas with a brush. They also give walls and ceilings a bit of texture. The main items you'll need are a *roller frame,* a *roller cover,* and a *paint tray* that hooks onto the shelf of a stepladder. If you'll be painting a ceiling or tall walls, an *extension pole* will save trips up and down the ladder.

Roller covers are hollow tubes covered with lamb's wool, mohair, or synthetic materials. Wall rollers commonly are 9 inches long; specialty rollers are shorter. They slip over a roller frame from one end. For water-based paints, select a synthetic cover with a plastic or phenolic-impregnated cardboard tube. Wool or mohair covers with cardboard tubes work well with solvent-based paints. Roller naps range from $3/16$ inch for very smooth surfaces to 1 inch for heavily textured surfaces such as stucco, plaster, or concrete blocks. A ⅜-inch nap does a good job on most interior surfaces.

Specialty rollers include 3-inch-long *trim rollers* for plain-surface trim, and doughnut and cone-shaped *corner rollers* for more sculptured moldings, and for cutting in where two planes intersect. Good wall and trim brushes can do all the jobs these specialty rollers perform, in just about the same time.

Paint pads, which slip or clamp into a handle, are made of the same materials as rollers. They paint faster than a brush, slower than a roller, and leave a smoother finish than either.

SELECTING OTHER TOOLS

Besides paint, brushes, and roller equipment, you'll need a paint scraper, a putty knife, taping knife, spackling compound, and sandpaper for preparation. You'll also need a *stepladder,* a *clamp light,* razor-blade and hook-blade *scrapers, masking tape,* and plastic, paper, or canvas *drop cloths.*

To prepare glossy painted surfaces get a small can of *deglosser,* a liquid that will provide "tooth" for the new paint to adhere to. Also get *goggles, rubber gloves,* a *respirator* or paper *face mask,* and a *painter's hat.*

TOOLS FOR INTERIOR PAINTING PROJECTS

YOUR PAINTING EQUIPMENT should include good-quality brushes, rollers and roller accessories, a stepladder, and a number of other items. Common preparation tools are not shown. Most such equipment will last for years if you clean it thoroughly after each project.

HOW MUCH PAINT DO YOU NEED?

A gallon of paint typically covers about 400 to 450 square feet, but coverage varies somewhat, so check the label. To estimate the number of square feet you will be painting, measure the total footage around the perimeter of the room and multiply by the ceiling height in feet. Do not subtract for windows, doors, or other openings unless they add up to more than 100 square feet. If you will be painting the ceiling, add its area in square feet to the wall area. Divide the total number of square feet by the coverage listed on the paint label. Round up to the next gallon so you will have paint left over for touch-ups. Finally, don't skimp on the quality of the paint you buy. Cheap paints have less pigment per quantity of vehicle and so do not cover as well as name brands. Poor coverage means you might have to invest additional money and effort in a second or third coat.

PREPARING A ROOM FOR PAINTING

The success of any painting project depends largely upon the preparation that precedes it. Begin by patching any holes, cracks, or other blemishes; patching techniques are explained on pages 156–159 and 181. Prime all patches and bare spots and new plaster or drywall. If a wall or ceiling has brownish water marks, seal these with shellac, alkyd primer, or alkyd paint, even if you will be using latex for the finish coat.

Remove lightweight furniture, pictures, and other items from the room. Move heavy furniture pieces into the center of the room and cover them with plastic drop cloths. If you will be painting the ceiling, cover each piece individually so you can move them easily to make room for your ladder. Protect floors with canvas drop cloths, not slippery plastic sheeting. Even canvas over plastic is unsafe underfoot. Now you are ready to begin preparation of the surfaces to be painted.

1 SCRAPE AND SAND. Using a strong work light, carefully inspect all wall, ceiling, and woodwork surfaces. Hold the light at a low angle to the surface to throw any surface defects into clear relief. Chip away loose paint and varnish with a razor blade scraper and sand rough spots and old paint runs with 150-grit sandpaper. Wipe painted woodwork and semigloss walls with liquid deglosser. The deglosser will dissolve the shiny surface of the old paint and create tooth that the new paint can adhere to. If the woodwork is covered with varnish that is badly deteriorated, strip it now. After repainting the walls, refinish the woodwork. Techniques for stripping and refinishing woodwork are covered in Chapter 7.

2 MASK AREAS NOT TO BE PAINTED. Even if you plan to paint the switch and receptacle plates, remove them and paint them separately so they don't stick to the wall. Cover all the exposed switches and receptacles with masking tape, along with anything else you don't want to get paint on.

Kitchen foil molds easily over irregular shapes such as knobs and latches, but never use it on electrical devices!

3 PROTECT WOODWORK. Use wide masking tape to keep spatters off woodwork. Press the wall edge of the tape down firmly with a putty knife to seal it. For a wide molding or baseboard, use masking tape at the edges.

PREPARATION

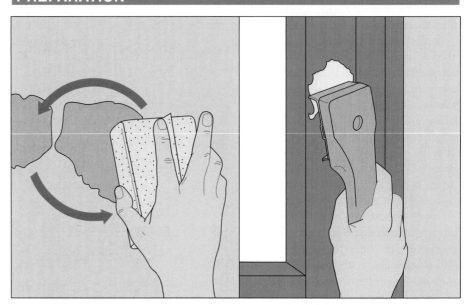

1. SCRAPE AND SAND all irregularities. Use a scraper to remove loose paint or varnish, and take care not to gouge the surface. Fill dents and holes with spackling compound. Sand walls in a circular motion with fine-grit paper. Spot-prime bare areas and all patches.

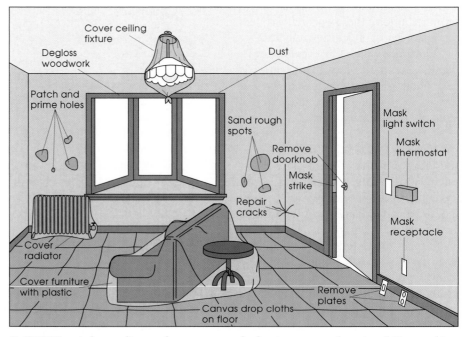

2. COVER switches, radiators, thermostats, and other items not to be painted. Use masking tape, foil, plastic, or newspaper, but never put foil over switches or electrical outlets. Remove doorknobs, electrical plates, and similar items.

If you will be painting the ceiling but not the walls, or if you want to keep paint off a fireplace, drape lightweight plastic sheeting over the areas to be protected. Hold it in place with masking tape.

Vacuum-clean all edges where masking tape must adhere, so it will not peel loose before the job is done. When everything is masked, finish with a top-to-bottom cleaning. Dust or vacuum-clean all surfaces that will be painted. Vacuum up all debris so you won't be stirring dust into the air. Finally, scrub the ceiling, walls, and woodwork with household detergent, rinse well, and let them dry before you begin painting.

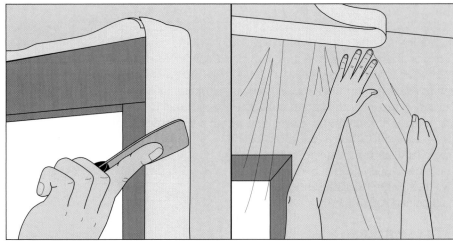

3. MASK AND DRAPE all woodwork and any walls that will not be painted. Use wide masking tape on woodwork edges, sealing its inside edge with a putty knife. Drape walls with plastic as shown.

CUTTING IN

Start with the ceiling and paint a room from the top down. For best results, methodically complete surfaces one at a time, first "cutting in" around the edges with a brush, as shown here, then rolling paint onto open expanses, as shown on the following pages.

Don't be tempted to save effort by cutting in the edge of a ceiling and the top of a wall in the same operation. By the time you've finished the ceiling, the border at the top of the walls will be dry, and applying wet paint over dry leaves lap marks. For the same reason, work in small sections, cutting in a few feet out from a corner along each edge of a ceiling, filling in with the roller, then resuming with the brush. The secret to avoiding overlap marks is to always keep a "wet edge." Here's how to handle a brush.

1 LOAD THE BRUSH. Dip no more than one-third of the brush's bristles into the paint, lift them free, and without wetting them again gently tap the bristles against the rim of the can. Dipping deeper overloads the brush; wiping the bristles against the rim removes too much paint. The objective is to load the brush to just short of the point where it will drip on the way to the wall or ceiling.

2 APPLY PAINT. Hold the brush as you would a pencil and gently flow paint onto the surface. If the adjacent surface will be the same color, apply the paint in four or five short strokes that are perpendicular to the edge. If colors will change here, use the technique shown below. Don't worry about brush marks just yet. Instead, concentrate on distributing the paint evenly.

3 SMOOTH THE STROKES. Now work the brush in one long, smooth stroke parallel to the edge. This last stroke smooths out brush marks (more of a problem with alkyds than with latex) and ensures even coverage over the area.

4 USE BEADING TECHNIQUE WHERE TWO COLORS MEET. If the ceiling and walls will be different colors, spare yourself the bother of masking by cutting in with a technique called "beading." Do this with a 2-inch flat sash brush, not the wall brush shown in steps 1 to 3. Lightly load the brush and draw its broad edge in a line that is about 1/16 inch from the edge. Press hard enough to bend the bristles slightly and paint will flow out just up to the edge of the adjacent surface.

1. DIP ONE-THIRD of a brush's bristles into the paint. Remove excess by tapping, not wiping, the bristles against the can's rim. You'll soon learn how much the brush can hold.

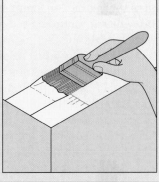

2. APPLY PAINT with short brush strokes at right angles to the adjacent surface. A 3-inch tapered wall brush makes short work of most cutting-in jobs.

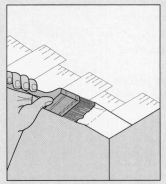

3. SMOOTH OUT the perpendicular strokes with a long stroke parallel to the edge of the adjacent surface. This will result in a border that is 3 inches wide or more.

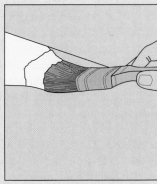

4. USE BEADING at color junctures. Move a 2-inch sash brush in a smooth line about 1/16 inch from the adjacent surface. Light pressure will cause the paint to bead out.

PAINTING CEILINGS AND WALLS

Cutting in with a brush (see box on preceding page) establishes a border of wet paint that you can work toward. Then switch to the roller to paint the adjacent large area. Procedures for painting ceilings and walls differ somewhat. Let's look first at the basic techniques of loading and handling a roller. Then we'll examine the differences between ceiling and wall work.

ROLLER BASICS

You must precondition a new roller. To do that, wet it with water if you will be using latex paint, or solvent if you will be using alkyd paint. Squeeze out the excess. To simplify cleanup, line the roller pan with heavy-duty aluminum foil or use inexpensive disposable pan liners, available at paint suppliers. Throw them away at the end of the day.

1 LOAD THE ROLLER. Begin by filling the paint tray's reservoir about two-thirds full with paint and dip the roller into it. Lift the roller out and roll it back and forth on the tray's ramp. This evenly distributes paint around the roller's circumference. The nap should be saturated with paint, but not dripping. You may need to dip and roll a dry roller several times before it fills up. After that, one dip should be enough.

2 LAY ON THE PAINT. Start at a point about 3 feet from the border you have cut in and roll diagonally toward it. When you reach the border, roll diagonally away from it at a different angle. Three or four zigzag strokes like these will distribute paint evenly across the entire area. Roll slowly to minimize spattering.

3 SMOOTH OUT THE PAINT. Now go back over the diagonal strokes with parallel back-and-forth strokes. Apply moderate pressure. Too heavy or too light a hand will cause the roller to skid. Watch for bare or thin spots, and repeat strokes if necessary. Ceilings and walls require somewhat different initial and final strokes.

PAINTING A CEILING

Because a ceiling is usually the largest expanse in a room, you may have to work quickly to maintain the wet edges that are critical for lap-free results. This is especially true with latex, which typically dries to the touch in about 45 minutes. While you must use a ladder to cut in the edges with a brush, an extension handle greatly speeds up the major part of ceiling work because you can cover a large area from the floor without repeatedly having to stop, take down the

ROLLER BASICS

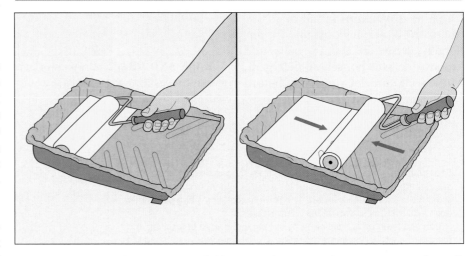

1. LOAD A ROLLER by immersing it halfway into the paint in the tray reservoir. Then roll it up and down the textured ramp until paint is evenly distributed over the entire roller.

2. LAY ON PAINT with diagonal passes. Aim first toward the cut-in wet edge. Reverse direction and roll diagonally away from the wet edge. Repeat this pattern.

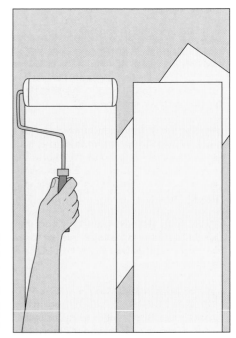

3. SMOOTH OUT THE PAINT with crosswise horizontal and vertical strokes. Strive for even coverage throughout an area of about 2 or 3 square feet.

paint tray, move the ladder, and put the tray back up.

Make the first strokes in a W pattern, first pushing the roller away from you, working from the dry ceiling to the wet edge you cut in, then pulling the roller back toward you. Smooth out the paint as explained above. Here you need to take special care with the final strokes, rolling them all in one direction. Because ceilings are viewed from an angle, irregular strokes up there will be much more noticeable than on walls.

PAINTING WALLS

With walls, make the first stroke upward, toward the wet edge at the ceiling. Then make diagonal strokes down, up, and down again to form a large M. Starting on an upstroke minimizes dripping. Fill in the M's open spaces with crosswise strokes, as explained for the Ws in painting ceilings. With flat paint you needn't worry about lap marks or strokes that are not perfectly straight. These will disappear when the paint dries. If you are using a gloss or semigloss paint, take pains to straighten out these final strokes.

Because wall work goes quickly, you can often cut in all of a wall's top, side, and bottom edges at once, then roll on paint in 2- or 3-foot-square sections. Finish one wall completely before applying any paint to the next one.

GIVE YOURSELF A BREAK

Painting can be tiring, so take a breather every so often. Don't stop in the middle of a wall or ceiling, however, or you'll lose the wet edge and create lap marks when you resume painting.

For breaks of half an hour or so, simply lay the roller and the brush's bristles on the paint tray's ramp. Do not leave the brush standing in paint. This could deform the bristles.

For longer breaks, wrap brushes and the roller in aluminum foil, plastic wrap, or sandwich bags. Cover the tray tightly with foil or plastic and reseal the paint can.

If you're stopping overnight, pour any paint left in the tray into the can. Store wrapped brushes and the roller in the freezer. Defrost them the next day and they will be ready for immediate use.

PAINTING CEILINGS

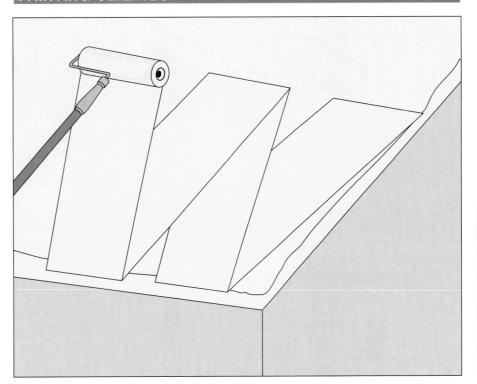

PAINT A CEILING by starting in a corner with diagonals that form a W. Fill it in with paint, then smooth out the paint with uniform strokes that all run in the same direction.

PAINTING WALLS

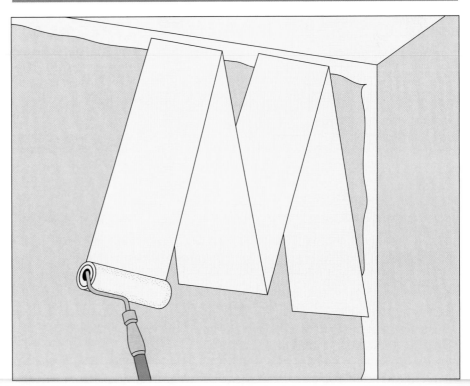

BEGIN TO PAINT WALLS with an M-shaped pattern. Final wall strokes needn't be uniform or run in the same direction. Just be sure you haven't missed any spots.

PAINTING WOODWORK

Compared to the speed with which you can roll paint onto ceilings and walls, painting a room's windows, doors, baseboards, and other trim is slow going. However, you do not have to do these areas at the same time that you paint the large flat areas; you can deal with them one by one as you have time.

Start at the top and work downward. This minimizes the possibility of dripping onto previously painted surfaces.

Also, instead of using masking tape, master the knack of painting freehand. Anyone with a steady hand and good sash brush can do it. Use a 2-inch flat-end sash brush for flat trim, and an angled sash brush for window sash. Keep a putty knife and a water- or solvent-dampened rag handy so you can quickly wipe away any mistakes that happen during the process. (To learn about painting cabinets, see page 216.)

PAINTING WINDOWS

Remove the sash locks and lifts, then paint from the glass outward. Use a 1½-inch angled sash brush. Dip about ½ inch into the paint, then tap the bristles against the can's rim to remove excess.

1 PAINT SASHES. Begin in a corner and lightly draw the brush along the edge by the glass, overlapping the glass about ⅟₁₆ inch for a tight seal. If paint smears farther onto the glass, wipe it off right away with a clean rag wrapped around the blade of a putty knife, or

PAINTING WINDOWS

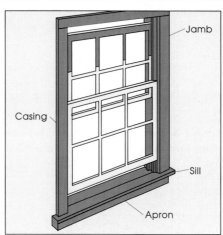

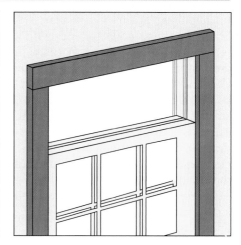

1. START WITH THE SASHES and paint around all the panes, working out from the center. Begin painting a double-hung window with the sashes arranged as shown.

2. REARRANGE THE SASHES as shown, paint the upper part of the top sash, then the casing, sill, and apron. Don't paint the jambs until the sashes are dry.

3. PAINT THE JAMBS of double-hung windows in two sessions. Lower the top sash and paint the upper jambs. After they dry, raise both sashes and paint the lower jambs.

PAINTING DOORS AND BASEBOARDS

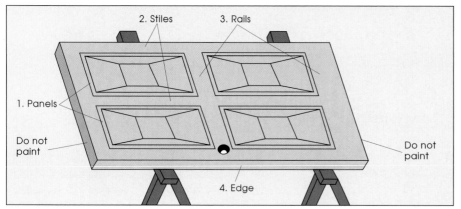

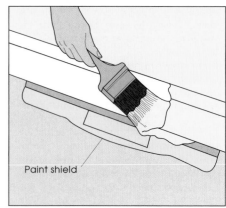

PAINT A PANEL DOOR in the sequence shown here. Work from top to bottom and paint each element before going on to the next. Use long, smooth brush strokes along the grain of the wood on the stiles and rails. Do not paint the top or bottom edges.

PAINT BASEBOARDS LAST. Cut in the top edge first. Protect the floor with a paint shield, thin cardboard, or masking tape.

wait until the paint dries and remove it with a razor blade scraper. When using a scraper, cut a line through the paint on the glass, about 1/16 inch from the wood, then scrape up to this line.

With double-hung windows you will need to move the sashes in order to paint their top and bottom edges. Open casement windows to paint the sashes. Leave all sashes open until the paint dries.

2 PAINT CASINGS. With a casement window, paint the *jambs, casing, sill,* and *apron* in one operation, working from the top down. Switch to a 2- or 3-inch-wide flat sash brush if you want to pick up speed on the frames. With a double-hung window, paint only the frame, sill, and apron. Do not attempt to paint the jambs at this time.

3 PAINT JAMBS. When the sashes of double-hung windows are dry to the touch, you can paint the jambs. First lower both sashes all the way and paint the upper jambs. Use interior color paint for the inner (lower sash) jamb channels, and exterior color paint for the outer channels. After they are dry to the touch, raise both sashes and paint the lower jambs. Do not paint any metal parts. If the sashes stick after painting, lubricate the jambs with silicone spray or spray furniture wax.

PAINTING DOORS

To paint a door, either open it wide and steady it with a wedge underneath, or remove it from its hinges (see box, page 241) and lay it across a pair of sawhorses. Remove the knobs, strikes, and other surface hardware before painting. For a door left in place, paint the casing and jambs first, then the door itself.

A roller makes short work of flush doors. With panel doors, paint the *panels* first, then the horizontal *rails,* vertical *stiles,* and vertical *edges.* Do not paint the top and bottom edges. If the door has never been painted, coat these edges with clear sealer to prevent warping.

Paint a door quickly, completing an entire side in one operation so you don't end up with lap marks. For speed, alternate between a narrow sash or trim brush and a 3-inch wall brush.

PAINTING BASEBOARDS

Baseboards should also be painted from the top down. First cut in the top edge, using the beading technique explained on page 195. Then paint the baseboard and shoe molding. Use a paint shield to keep paint off the floor, or hold a piece of thin cardboard against the baseboard or shoe molding and slide it along as you paint. Clean the shield or switch to fresh cardboard, as needed.

CLEANING BRUSHES, ROLLERS

To clean a brush, first remove as much paint as possible by working it back and forth across newspaper. If you have been working with alkyd paint, immerse the brush's bristles in a small jar of solvent or mineral spirits and apply pressure on the handle to bend them back and forth. After the solvent clouds up, change it and repeat the process.

Finally, wash the brush with dish detergent and warm water to remove all solvent; store as explained below.

To clean latex paint from a brush, simply wash it under running water, bending the bristles back and forth in the palm of your hand to work out all traces of paint.

Clean a roller or pad used with alkyd paint by pouring solvent into the paint tray and rolling the roller back and forth in the solvent, then up and down the ramp. Repeat until all paint is gone from the roller's nap, then wash with warm water and detergent, rinse, and squeeze out as much moisture as you can. Wash a roller used with latex under the faucet.

Hang brushes and stand rollers on end until they are dry, then wrap them in plastic or paper toweling secured with a rubber band.

PAINTING WOODWORK

CLEANING UP

Attend to leftover paint and your brushes, roller covers, and other painting equipment immediately after you finish a painting project.

If you have been working from several cans of paint, consolidate them into one can. The fuller a can is, the longer it will keep. Leave empty cans open and throw them away after the paint has dried. To seal a paint can, wipe out the groove in the rim with a piece of scrap cloth or paper towel. Set the lid in place, drape a cloth over the can, and tap around the edges with a hammer. The cloth will absorb any paint remaining in the rim that may squirt out when you force the lid into it.

To clean brushes and roller covers, follow the instructions given in the text above and illustrated at the right.

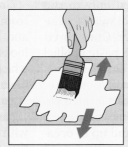

CLEAN BRUSHES AND ROLLERS by first working them across newspaper. Then use solvent (for alkyd) or water (for latex) to remove the remainder of the paint.

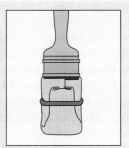

SHAPE THE BRISTLES of brushes, let them dry, then wrap in plastic or paper towel secured with a rubber band. Store brushes by hanging them from holes in their handles.

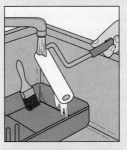

WASH LATEX PAINT FROM TOOLS by running warm water over them. Clean out the tray first and use it as a basin for scrubbing brushes and roller covers.

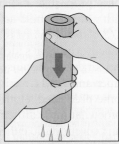

SQUEEZE WATER FROM a roller cover after washing, stand it on end to dry, and wrap it in plastic. Some painters simply discard inexpensive covers at the end of a job.

REPAIRING WALLCOVERINGS

Blisters, loose seams, tears, and holes in wallcovering are easily fixed. You'll need a single-edge razor blade, some wallcovering adhesive and an artist's brush for applying it, straight pins, a seam roller, and—for patching—a piece of wallcovering, a straightedge, and masking tape. Use leftover wallcovering for a patch, or cut a section from an inconspicuous spot, such as in a closet.

FLATTENING BLISTERS

Air or excess adhesive trapped behind wallcovering can cause it to bubble. First try pricking a blister with a pin and gently squeezing out the trapped air. If this doesn't work, slit the bubble in a cross and peel back the four flaps. If there is a lump of adhesive beneath, scrape it away. Apply fresh adhesive, stick the flaps to the wall, and roll them.

REPAIRING LOOSE SEAMS

Stick down loose wallcovering at a seam by lifting it slightly, daubing adhesive underneath with an artist's brush, and pressing the material into the adhesive. Roll the seam and temporarily secure it with pins pushed through the covering into the wall. With an overlapped seam in vinyl wallcovering use vinyl-to-vinyl adhesive.

PATCHING HOLES AND TEARS

In old-fashioned, all-paper wallcoverings, patch small damaged areas that are no more than 3 inches across by tearing a roughly circular patch from a scrap of the same material and pasting it in place. Tearing leaves a feathered edge around the patch so it will lie smoothly, with no white edges to give it away. First trim off any ragged edges around the damaged spot on the wall. Now hold the scrap face up with one hand and begin tearing with the other, pulling the patch toward you. Tear slowly, rotating the paper as you go. The object is to end up with a rough circle with an intact design on the printed side and feathered edges behind. Coat the back of the patch with adhesive, line up the pattern with the wall, press the patch into place and roll it.

DOUBLE CUTTING A PATCH

Repair holes that are bigger than 3 inches or in wallcoverings that can't be torn, such as vinyls and foils, by double cutting a patch. Begin by using a utility knife and straightedge to cut a patch that is about 2 inches wider and 2 inches longer than the damaged area. Lay this against the wall and match it up with the pattern around the hole. Secure the patch with masking tape or pins, whichever will damage the wallcovering least. Then, with the knife and straightedge, cut a rectangle that is slightly larger than the hole, slicing through both the patch and the existing wallcovering underneath. Remove the patch material you taped or pinned to the wall and then the cutout rectangle of existing wallcovering. Scrape away any adhesive and glue the patch into the rectangular opening on the wall. It will fit and match perfectly.

REPAIRING COVERINGS

REPAIRING BLISTERS AND SEAMS

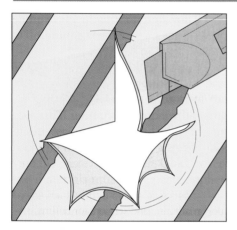

SLIT BLISTERS with crosswise cuts and peel back the flaps. Scrape off any adhesive underneath, daub paste into the blister, then press the flaps flat.

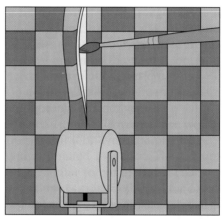

LIFT A LOOSE SEAM just enough to work adhesive underneath, then roll it flat. If the seam begins to curl, tack it with straight pins until the adhesive dries.

PATCHING HOLES

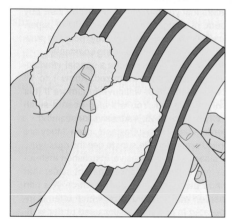

TEAR A PATCH from a scrap of all-paper wallcovering to get feathered edges on the back. Apply paste, align the patch with the wallcovering pattern, and stick it in place.

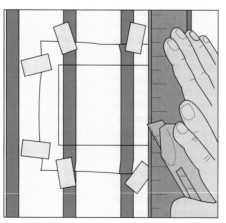

DOUBLE CUT a patch by fastening scrap material over the hole and cutting through both layers. Peel off the damaged wallcovering, paste the patch into place, and roll it.

STRIPPING WALLCOVERING

How you go about removing old wall-covering depends in part on what the covering is made of and in part on what's underneath it. Strippable materials, usually vinyls, are the easiest of all. You simply work a corner loose with a knife and peel the covering off the wall.

If this doesn't work and your walls are built of gypsum board, your only choice is to dry strip the wallcovering, as explained below. Wallcovering on plaster walls can be removed by slitting or scoring or perforating the surface and soaking it. Or use a rented steamer. Do not use water or steam to strip covering from drywall; moisture will soften the gypsum board's paper face.

1 DRY STRIPPING. Use a slitter to dry strip wallcovering from gypsum board walls. First hold the slitter perpendicular to the wall and make a series of horizontal slits spaced 8 to 10 inches apart. Don't press too hard or you may cut into the drywall. Next, insert the slitter blade into a slit at an angle and loosen a section of wallcovering, then pull it free with your fingers.

2 SLITTING AND SOAKING. With plaster walls, water or liquid paper remover accelerates the stripping process. After slitting or scoring through the covering, wet it with mist from a plant sprayer. Soak the paper thorough-ly and spray water into the slits so it can work its way behind the covering. Wait about 10 minutes, then scrape off the wallcovering with the slitter or a wide-bladed knife. If water doesn't work, try a liquid paper remover, following the directions on the can.

3 STEAMING. Use steam to remove stubborn wallcoverings from plaster. You can rent a steamer. It consists of a boiler connected by hose to a perforated plate that you hold against the wall. Steam is forced through the pores of the paper, softening the paste behind. After you've steamed a 6-foot section of the wall, scrape off the covering with a knife. If the wallcovering resists steaming, slit or score through the surface and steam a second time.

THREE WAYS TO REMOVE WALLCOVERING

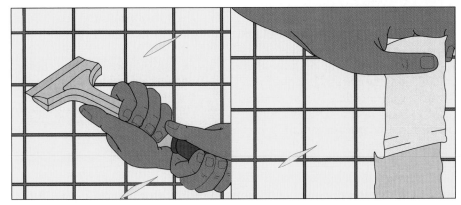

1. DRY STRIP wallcovering applied to gypsum board. With a slitter, make horizontal cuts spaced 8 to 10 inches apart horizontally and vertically. Work the slitter into a slit at an angle and gently loosen the covering. Peel the paper upward.

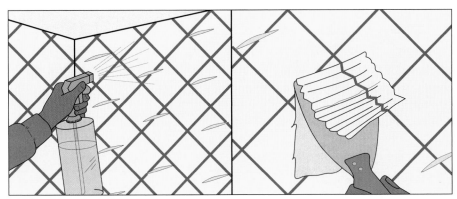

2. SLIT AND SOAK coverings on plaster walls. First slit the wallcovering as shown, or score through with a serrated scraper. Then spray with water or liquid paper remover. After about 10 minutes, try scraping off the covering with a wide knife. If necessary, wet again.

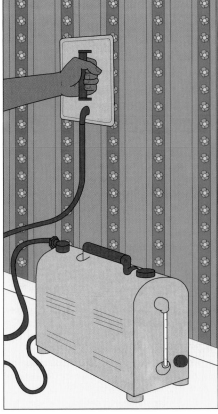

3. STEAM WALLCOVERINGS that resist slitting/scoring and soaking. Hold the steam plate against the wall until moisture darkens the material around it. After steaming a 6-foot-long section, work it loose with a broadknife and peel the strip from the wall.

PREPARING SURFACES FOR WALLCOVERING

If you neglect to prepare walls and ceilings properly for a wallcovering project, any holes, cracks, or other defects in the original surface will soon show through, and the covering may not adhere well.

First, remove all nails, picture hooks, and other accessories. Turn off the power and remove switch and wall outlet cover plates. Fill nail holes and patch any cracks, dents, or gouges with spackling compound. Lightly sand all repairs and any rough spots or paint runs. If you plan to paint the ceiling, woodwork, or any walls that won't be covered, now is the time to do so; it's all but impossible to remove paint spatters from some wallcovering materials. From here on, procedures differ somewhat, depending on whether the walls are unpainted, painted, or papered.

PREPARING UNPAINTED SURFACES

Unpainted plaster or gypsum board surfaces and any patches must be primed so that they won't absorb adhesive. Use an alkyd-base primer-sealer formulated especially for wallcovering work. These not only seal the surface but serve as size, which increases the slip time you have to maneuver the wallcovering. Latex wallcovering primer costs less, but it doesn't seal bare surfaces well. Apply the primer with a roller and brush, just as you would any paint. Wait at least two weeks before sealing and covering new plaster.

PREPARING PAINTED SURFACES

Scrub painted walls and ceilings with household detergent; rinse thoroughly and let them dry, then coat with a latex-base wallcovering primer. This sizes the wall and also facilitates removing the wallcovering when it's time to redecorate. Dull glossy finishes with sandpaper or liquid deglosser before priming.

PREPARING PAPERED SURFACES

Strip old wallcoverings if at all possible. Hanging one covering over another could loosen the original layer and pull it off the wall or ceiling. If you can't remove the old material without gouging the surface underneath, you must prepare the existing paper carefully.

Begin by flattening blisters, repairing loose seams, and patching any holes or tears. Glue down any curled edges with wallcovering adhesive. The old covering must be securely attached to the surface at all points.

If the existing wallcovering has overlapping seams, sand them smooth so they don't show through the new covering. Finally, thoroughly seal the surface with alkyd-base wallcovering primer. This will keep moisture from the paste or adhesive for the new covering from soaking through the old one and destroying the paste that holds it in place.

PREPARING PANELED SURFACES

Fill all grooves in paneling with wood putty or drywall joint compound and sand the entire surface smooth. Seal hardboard and particleboard paneling with alkyd primer-sealer. Plywood paneling must be sealed and covered with lining paper so water in the paste won't raise the wood grain and let it show through the wallcovering.

WARNING

Shut off electrical power to the room before you begin hanging wallcovering. Working with water and wet paste around open switches and receptacles poses a serious shock hazard. Cover switches and receptacles with masking tape.

HANGING LINING PAPER

Lining paper helps smooth out rough and plywood-paneled walls and is a must with grass cloth, foils, and some fabrics. Also, if you plan to hang a lightweight covering over a dark pattern, lining paper will keep the old pattern from showing through. However, it is better to strip the old paper if at all possible.

To ensure a good bond, hang lining paper with the same adhesive you will use for the finish covering. Use the same techniques, too, with these exceptions:

Hang lining paper horizontally on walls and at right angles to the final covering for ceilings so that no seams in the two layers will coincide.

Do not lap the seams between strips of lining paper. Instead, butt them as best you can, or leave a gap of no more than ⅛ inch between them and at all edges. It's difficult to get a perfect seam with lining paper, and any overlap ridges would show through the final covering.

Let lining paper dry for 48 hours before hanging the top covering.

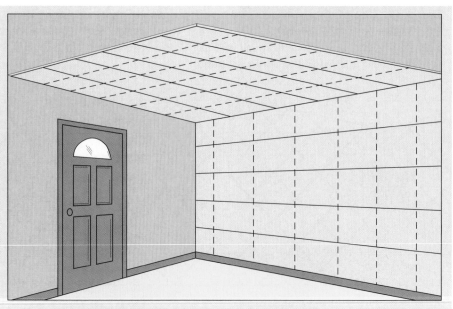

The butt seams of lining paper (solid lines) should run at right angles to the seams of the finish material (broken lines) that will cover the walls and ceiling.

HANGING WALLCOVERING

Take your time at the beginning of a wallcovering project. The first strip you hang serves as the keystone for all that follow. If you intend to cover the ceiling, do that first; see page 209.

PLANNING THE LAYOUT

Because you'll have to cut the last strip to width, its pattern will probably not match up exactly with the first. Locate this mismatch at the least conspicuous point; the room's darkest corner is best. If at a corner, measure along the first wall the width of a roll of wallcovering, minus ½ inch. (If the starting point is not in a corner, measure a full roll width.) Draw a vertical pencil line here.

Now, use a width of covering to mark where each seam will fall around the entire room. At each corner the wallcovering must overlap at least ½ inch onto the adjacent wall. Seams that fall close to the edges of a window, door, or fireplace are difficult to fit. If necessary, move the starting line to shift the seams.

CUTTING AND MATCHING

Next, measure the height of the wall and add 4 inches for trimming. Unroll a strip of covering, pattern side up, on the worktable and cut it to length. To match patterns, unroll a second strip next to the one you've just cut, line them up, and cut the second strip to length.

WETTING AND BOOKING STRIPS

With prepasted coverings, loosely roll the first strip, pattern side in, and submerge it in a water tray on the floor. Let it soak for the time specified on the label. Grasp two corners and slowly pull the strip out of the water. Let excess water drain into the tray, then stretch it out on the table, adhesive side up.

After half of the wet strip is on the table, loosely fold the end to the center, pasted side to pasted side. Align the edges, but do not press the surfaces together and do not crease the fold. Slide the folded end off the table and fold the second half in the same way. Finally, fold one of the folded halves on top of the other. This *booking* makes handling the strip easy. (To learn about handling nonprepasted coverings, see page 207.)

PREPARING TO HANG WALLCOVERING

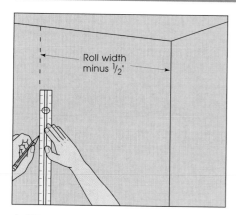

1. MARK A VERTICAL STARTING LINE. Measure as shown if you start at a corner. The first strip will align with this line.

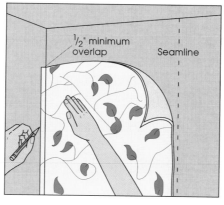

2. PLOT WHERE SEAMS WILL FALL all around the room. Seams must overlap at corners by a minimum of ½ inch.

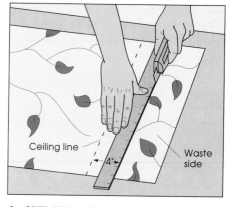

3. CUT THE FIRST STRIP to the wall height plus 4 inches. Plan the top end cut to avoid a partial pattern at the ceiling.

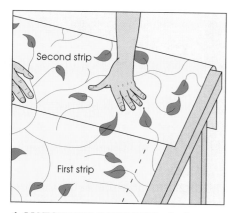

4. MATCH THE PATTERNS of adjoining strips before cutting. You can match and cut several strips, then wet and book them.

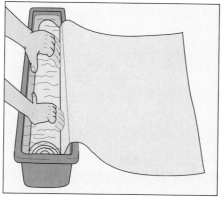

5. ACTIVATE PREPASTED PAPERS by loosely rerolling a strip paste side out and immersing it in water.

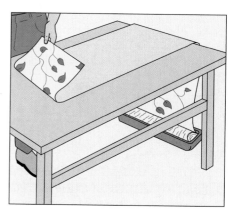

6. BOOK A STRIP by folding its pasted surfaces in on themselves, then folding once again. Fold gently. Do not crease.

HANGING THE FIRST STRIP

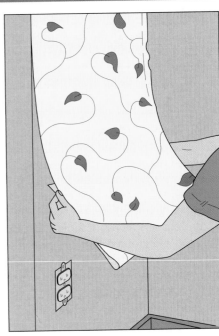

1. GRASP THE TOP CORNERS of the booked strip, open the first fold, and align it with the starting line on the wall. The strip should overlap 2 inches onto the ceiling; another 2 inches will overlap the baseboard.

2. SMOOTH THE TOP HALF. Brush at the ceiling line, then into the corner, then out and downward. It is crucial to work out all air bubbles under every strip. Slit the covering at the ceiling line in the corner.

3. PEEL THE BOTTOM HALF LOOSE, align it with the starting line, and smooth as above. Then smooth the entire strip again, working from the center out. Cover electrical boxes and trim them later (see page 208).

HANGING SUBSEQUENT STRIPS

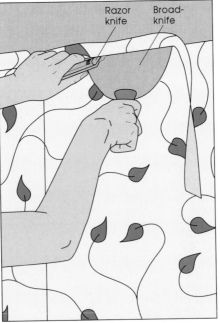

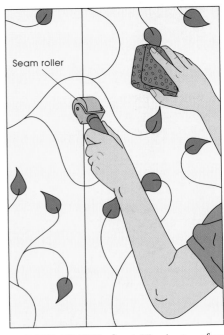

1. POSITION THE NEXT STRIP by lightly holding it on the wall and matching patterns. Then tightly butt the edges, forming a seam that projects about 1/16 inch from the wall. This will shrink flat as the adhesive dries.

2. TRIM AT THE CEILING and baseboard with a utility knife; use a broad-bladed joint knife as a straightedge. If you have covered the ceiling, trim with scissors instead, to avoid puncturing the ceiling covering.

3. ROLL SEAMS about 15 minutes after hanging each strip. Begin at the center and lightly roll upward and downward. Wipe adhesive from the roller and seam with a damp sponge, then sponge the wallcovering clean.

TURNING CORNERS

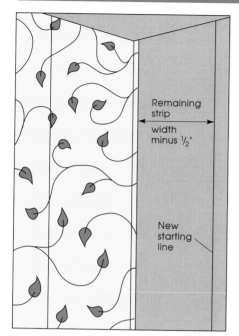

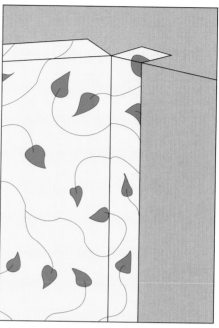

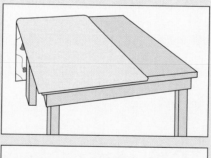

1. AT INSIDE CORNERS, measure from the last strip to the corner, add ½ inch, and cut a strip that wide. Hang this strip, wrapping it around the corner. Then measure to mark a new vertical starting line as shown.

2. HANG THE REMAINDER of the corner strip, aligning it with the new starting line and overlapping the turned edge back at the corner. If the wallcovering is vinyl, use vinyl-to-vinyl adhesive for this seam.

3. AT OUTSIDE CORNERS, check whether the corner is plumb. If so, wrap fully around the corner and continue. If not, wrap around the corner ½ inch, mark a new starting line, and proceed as for an inside corner.

PASTING WALLCOVERINGS

Most wallcoverings now come prepasted. If you've selected one that's not, you'll need to follow a slightly different procedure than the one shown on page 205.

Premixed paste comes in ready-to-use liquid form. Mix powdered paste according to directions on the package.

Apply paste to the back of the wallcovering with a paste brush or a paint roller. Try to completely coat the covering without smearing paste onto the table. To do this, paste the strip in quadrants. Align it with the corners and edges of the table as shown at the right, in the following sequence:

1. Square one corner of the strip with one side and end of the table, slide the strip so its end and edge extend about 1/4 inch past the table edges, and apply an even layer of paste.

2. Slide the wallcovering to the other side of the table and paste the second quadrant.

3. Book the half-strip pasted side to pasted side, drape the folded section over the edge of the table, and paste quadrants three and four, aligning the strip first along one side of the table, then the other. Fold the second half over on itself, set the book aside, and paste the next strip. Let the paste cure for the time specified on the package before hanging each strip.

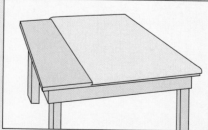

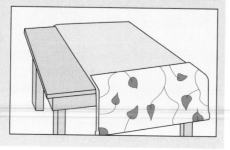

WORK CLEAN

Wallcovering paste, whether applied at the factory or at home, is inherently messy stuff—and after paste dries it's impossible to remove from the surface of some covering materials. The box at left shows how to keep paste off your worktable. Here are some other habits worth cultivating.

Wash your hands frequently. Some professional workers dust their hands with talcum powder to minimize smudges on the wallcovering.

Sponge off each strip with clean water immediately after hanging. Use a damp, but not dripping sponge, and do not let water run along seams, where it could weaken the adhesive underneath. Change the rinse water after you've hung two or three strips.

Keep your worktable spotlessly clean, checking it carefully before you cut and wet or paste each strip.

Keep tools clean, too. Wipe off scissors blades and handles, the cutting knife's blade and handle, the paste brush or roller handle, and the roller and handle of the seam-rolling tool.

Never lay wet wallcovering on newspaper. The oily newspaper ink can smudge clean surfaces easily and may react with the inks used on wallcoverings.

HANGING AROUND OPENINGS

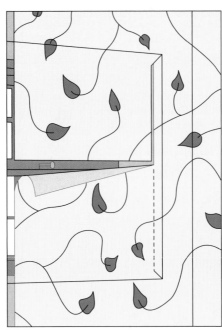

AT DOORS AND WINDOWS, hang a full strip that overlaps the casing. Cut away all but about 2 inches of the excess with scissors, then carefully trim around the casing with a sharp knife.

AT A RECESS, hang covering over the opening. With scissors, cut horizontally in the middle to within 1 inch of the edge, then cut vertically to within 1 inch of the top and bottom. Snip diagonal cuts to the corners.

FINISH A RECESS by pasting down and trimming the flaps you've cut. Then cut a piece as wide as the recess is deep and long enough to overlap ½ inch at the top and bottom. Paste in place; repeat on the other side.

COVERING SWITCHES AND RECEPTACLES

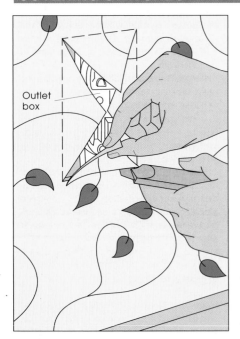

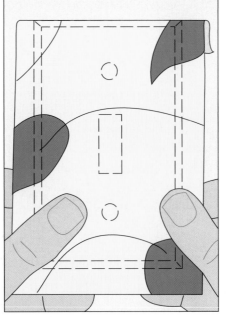

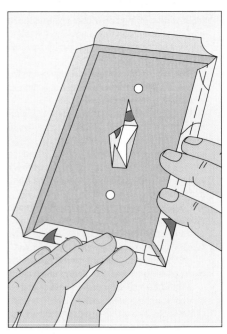

CUT OPENINGS for electrical devices. First, double check that the power has been turned off before starting to cut. Make diagonal slices from the corners of the box and trim off the flaps.

FOLD COVERING over the top of a switch or receptacle plate, matching it to the pattern on the wall along the top edge. Adjust for a close match at the sides, then fold the side and bottom edges around the plate.

CEMENT THE FOLDED COVERING to the entire surface of the plate with adhesive. Turn the plate over, trim the edges of the covering, and snip diagonal cuts as shown. Paste the edges to the back of the plate.

COVERING CEILINGS

Ceiling work is challenging because you usually must work with strips so long that it is difficult to handle them. If you decide to cover a ceiling, choose a pattern that does not have an obvious direction. Cover the ceiling first, then the walls. Techniques are the same as for walls, with the following exceptions.

MARKING A STARTING LINE

Plan to run strips across the ceiling's narrow dimension. Begin at the most conspicuous wall–ceiling edge running in that direction. Subtract 1 inch from the wallcovering width, then measure and mark this distance from the starting wall at several points. Use a straightedge to connect these marks with a pencil line across the ceiling.

BOOKING CEILING STRIPS

Cut strips to length, adding 4 inches for trimming. After pasting the strips, fold them accordion-style, pasted side to pasted side. Take care not to crease the paper or smear paste on the pattern. Accordion-folded strips are more manageable than the triple folds used for wall work.

INSTALLING THE STRIPS

Work on a rented scaffold or on stout planks between two stepladders. As a helper feeds the wallcovering from a booked strip, align it with the starting line and smooth it in place with a brush. Lap the strip about 2 inches onto the walls at the ends, 1 inch onto the wall at the side. Cut notches to fit into corners. Lay subsequent strips with butted seams, as in covering a wall. Trim the last strip to width plus 1 inch for overlapping onto the wall alongside.

SMOOTHING CEILING COVERING

After the entire ceiling is covered, smooth it with a clean, dry paint roller on an extension handle. Work across the width of the strips, then finish with lengthwise strokes. If the covering begins to pull loose, smooth again and secure with pins until the adhesive dries.

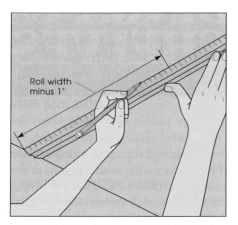

ESTABLISH A STARTING LINE by measuring the width of the covering, less 1 inch, from one of the room's shorter walls.

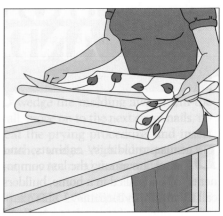

BOOK CEILING STRIPS with accordion folds. Fold pasted surface to pasted surface. Align the ends and do not crease the folds.

ALIGN THE FIRST STRIP with the starting line and smooth it in place. Notch the corners. A helper can unfold the book and check that the strip is straight. Put up successive strips in the same way, with butt seams. Overlap the final strip 1 inch onto the side wall.

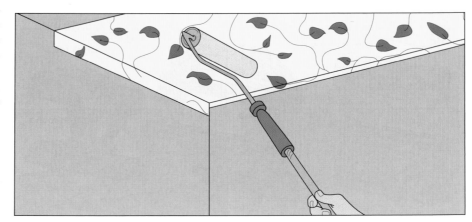

SMOOTH EACH STRIP with a short-nap paint roller. Flatten seams with a seam roller. If you're covering only the ceiling, trim edges with a broadknife and a utility knife. If the walls will be covered, don't trim; the wall strips will overlap the turned-down ceiling edge.

ORGANIZING CLOSETS FOR MORE SPACE

The standard arrangement of a single rod with a shelf above does not make good use of space in a clothes closet. To get nearly 50 percent more hanging space, put a tier of two rods for short clothes on one side of a center tower of shelves or drawers, and a single rod for longer apparel at the standard height of 62 inches on the other side.

You could remodel a closet this way in about a weekend, using plywood or an unfinished shelf unit and standard closet hardware. With a prefabricated closet organizer kit, you can achieve the same results in much less time.

INSTALLING AN ORGANIZER KIT

Closet organizer kits made of enameled steel, plastic-coated wire, plywood, or particleboard adjust to suit various closet widths. Assembly procedures vary, but you can put together most prefab closet organizers with just a few simple tools. Here's a typical installation.

1 **MARK SHELF LOCATIONS** on the closet walls. Measure up from the floor and draw a level line for each shelf. Drill holes and install the shelf clips along these lines, spacing them as specified by the manufacturer.

2 **FIT SHELF SUPPORTS** or, with some systems, the shelves themselves into the clips. One or more shelves may need to be cut to length. Deal with them in Step 4.

3 **ATTACH UPRIGHTS** to the front edges of the shelves or shelf supports. Check these with a level to ensure that they are plumb; adjust if necessary.

HOW TO INSTALL A CLOSET ORGANIZER KIT

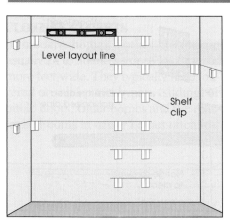

1. DRAW LEVEL LINES on the walls. Install the shelf clips along these lines. Space clips as per kit instructions.

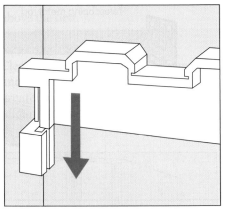

2. ATTACH SUPPORTS or shelves to the clips. Wait to install any shelves that must be cut until after the uprights are in place.

3. FASTEN UPRIGHTS to the front edges of the supports or shelves. Check that the shelves are level and the uprights are plumb.

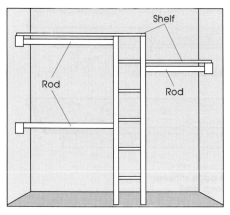

4. CUT THE SIDE SHELVES and rods to fit between the center unit and the end walls. Cut steel or wire shelving with a hacksaw.

BUILDING A CLOSET ORGANIZER

Follow the drawing at the right. Adjust widths to fit your closet. Locate hanging rods 12 or more inches from the back wall and 1 3/4 inches below shelves so hanger hooks will clear. The vertical dimensions can vary, but allow a minimum of 3 inches space beneath hanging clothes. Make the tier of shelves 20 to 24 inches deep. The top and bottom shelves can be fixed, the others adjustable.

Use plywood or particleboard. Assemble and paint the tier of shelves before installing it. Finish wooden rods with polyurethane.

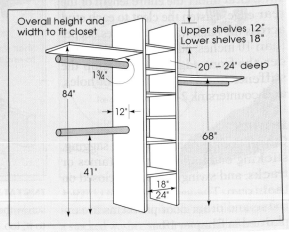

4 **CUT SHELVES AND CLOTHES RODS** to length with a hacksaw. Install mounting brackets on the side walls and fit the shelves and rods into place. In some systems the rods are integral with the side shelves.

ORGANIZING A WALK-IN CLOSET

Closet organizer kits can greatly increase the capacity of walk-in closets. In a narrow closet, install one along the closet's wall. If the closet is 6 feet wide or more, there is room for organizers on both side walls. And if the closet is more than 5½ feet deep, you can put storage units along the rear wall as well.

CREATE A DRESSING ROOM

A small walk-in closet can be turned into an efficient dressing room. Place an organizer along one side and shelving on the other side. A full-length mirror opposite the door will aid in grooming and make the space seem larger. You may need to install a new fixture for better lighting (see Chapter 34).

ORGANIZING SPECIALTY CLOSETS

Tailor linen closets, coat closets, utility closets, pantries, and other specialty storage for the items they must hold. Here are some things to keep in mind.

Linen closets. Pull-out drawers, baskets, or trays make sheets, towels, and other linens easier to get at. Compartments with doors for bathroom tissue, soap, and similar items help, too.

Utility closets. Mops, brooms, buckets, vacuum cleaners, and other odd-shaped items need both horizontal and vertical spaces. Hang awkward items such as dust pans. Build shelving with particleboard or plywood, or assemble inexpensive steel utility shelving.

Pantries. Keep pantry shelving shallow—the depth of two cans or jars or a cereal box. Space shelf heights to accommodate standard can and package dimensions. U-shaped shelving inside and shelves on the door make everything visible and easy to get at. For a deeper pantry, consider buying shelving units with slide-out wire racks, baskets, or trays. They are available at home centers and storage specialty shops.

WALK-IN CLOSET

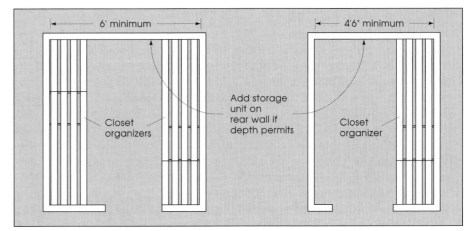

INSTALL ORGANIZERS along one, two, or three walls, depending on how large the closet is. The dimensions shown here are minimums.

DRESSING ROOM

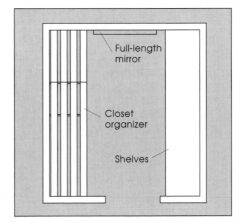

ADD A MIRROR and good lighting to convert a closet into a dressing room. Here an organizer unit and shelving provide space.

SPECIALTY CLOSETS

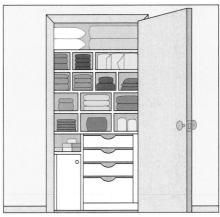

LINEN CLOSETS need compartments sized for folded items. Here, bedding is up top, with towels and linens below.

CLEANING CLOSET shelves can be tailored to hold an assortment of containers. Provide vertical storage for tall objects.

A PANTRY with shallow shelves lets you locate items quickly. Door racks work well, but stronger hinges may be needed.

BUILDING A NEW CLOSET

Reorganizing existing closets greatly improves their capacity, but when storage space is seriously lacking, building a new closet or closets may be the only answer.

If that is the case at your house, begin by deciding where best to locate the new storage space. Sometimes small closets in adjacent rooms can be combined into a single larger closet that serves just one of the rooms—but then you will need to make up for the storage shortfall somewhere else. Often, rather than taking up floor space in main living areas it is better to create a big new closet in the basement or attic. Keeping out-of-season clothes, suitcases, and other occasionally used items there can take the pressure off existing closets.

PREFAB CLOSETS

Prefabricated closets made of wood, metal, or particleboard offer two advantages over conventional built-in closets: They typically occupy less floor space, and most can be assembled in an hour or so, much less time than it takes to construct partitions and install doors. Also, because prefab closets are modular you can line up several of them along a wall and perhaps fit a desk or vanity between two of them. Prefabs may cost more than drywall partitions, but you can relocate them easily as your needs change, and even take them with you when you move.

PLANNING A NEW CLOSET

If a new closet is what you need, plan carefully. Measure the room or area where you want to locate the closet and draw a plan to scale on graph paper.

For a clothes closet, allow 28 to 30 inches interior depth (minimum 24 inches). Pantry, utility, and linen closets can be 12 to 18 inches deep. If the closet will house a washer and dryer, typical interior dimensions are 36 inches deep and 2½ or 5 feet wide, depending on whether the laundry equipment will be stacked or installed side by side. As dis-

HOW TO BUILD A NEW CLOSET

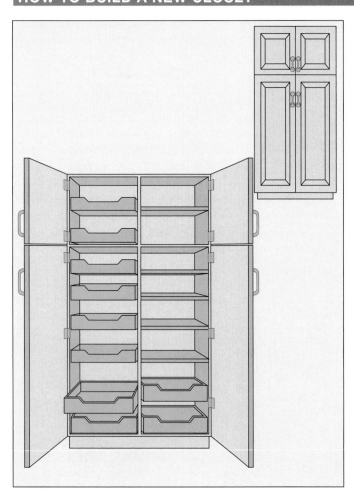

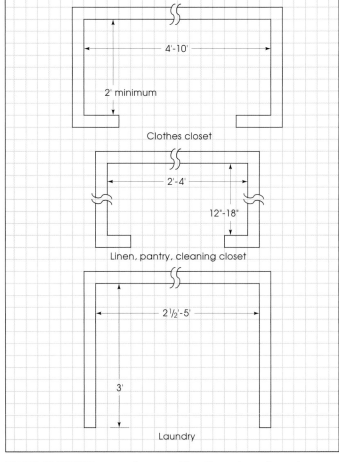

PREFAB CLOSETS provide storage quickly. This configuration can serve as a pantry or linen closet; many others are available. Prefab closets come knocked down, for on-site assembly.

PLAN CLOSETS on graph paper. The dimensions shown here are for finished interiors (wall surface to wall surface) and are suggested minimums; more space is almost always preferable.

cussed on page 222, carefully check both the manufacturer's specifications and local codes regarding materials, size, ventilation, and wiring and plumbing requirements for any room that will house a major appliance.

Walk-in closets must be at least 4½ feet wide, which provides hanging space along one wall and a 2-foot-wide corridor. If you want to hang clothes along both walls, make the minimum width 6 feet.

FRAMING A NEW CLOSET

Frame a closet as you would any other interior partition (see pages 160–163). To conserve space, use 2 × 3s instead of 2 × 4s for studs and plates. Make the header with 2 × 4s set on edge. Install the dry-

wall inside the closet first. It's easier to maneuver panels through the open wall framing than through the doorway.

FINISHING A NEW CLOSET

After taping and painting the drywall, install hinged, bifold, or bypass doors (see pages 247–248), then fit out the interior with shelves and a rod or with a closet organizer, as explained on the preceding pages.

The simplest way to install a rod is to attach end brackets to cleats or studs in the end walls. You can also use end cleats with holes in them. For rods up to 1½ inches in diameter, use 1 × 4 boards for cleats if there is to be no shelf above, or 1 × 6 boards if there will be a shelf. Cut the cleats at least long

enough to fasten to a stud on either side of the hole, and to reach the back wall if they will support a shelf. Drill holes for the rod midway from top to bottom in the cleats. The hole centers must be at least 12 inches from the back wall when the cleats are mounted.

Cut the rod ⅛ to ¼ inch shorter than the wall-to-wall distance it will span. Slip both cleats onto the rod before screwing the first one in place. Make sure the first cleat is level from front to back when you attach it. Then use a level on the rod to mark the proper height for the other cleat. Make sure the second cleat is also level from front to back as you screw it to the studs. This is necessary to ensure that a shelf resting on the cleats will be level.

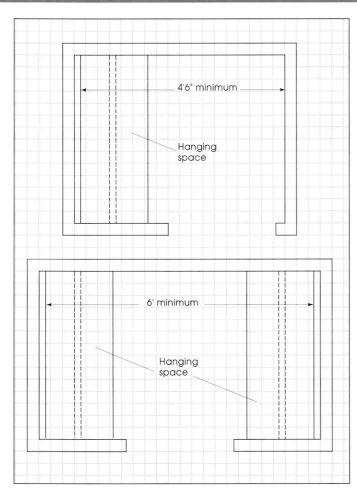

WALK-IN CLOSETS must be at least 4½ feet wide. If you want space to hang clothes on both sides, you will need 6 feet or more interior width in order to have uncrowded access.

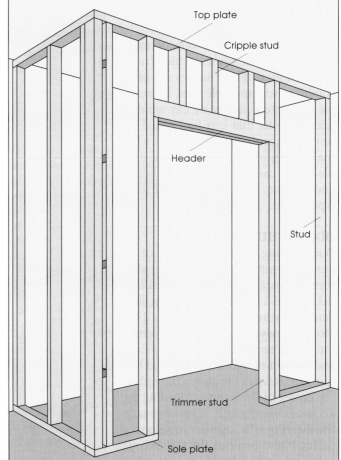

FRAME A CLOSET as shown here and explained in Chapter 12. Use 2 × 3s for studs and plates. Span door openings up to 8 feet wide with a 2 × 4 header—it is nonload-bearing.

REPAIRING CRANKED AND SLIDING WINDOWS

When a casement, awning, or jalousie window malfunctions, the problem usually lies with its hinges, the extension arm and track, or the operator mechanism. When a sliding window jams, the track may be bent or dirty, or rollers may need to be adjusted or replaced.

LUBRICATING HINGED WINDOWS

When a window is balky, first check its moving parts. Are the hinges dirty, bent, rusty, or encrusted with paint? If so, clean, straighten, and lubricate them. With casement windows, check the extension arm to see if it slides smoothly in its track on the sash. If the arm binds, clean a metal track with solvent and a wire brush. (Solvents may dam-age plastic components. Clean them with hot water and detergent, and a brush with nonmetal bristles.) If the lip of the track is bent, straighten it with pliers, then spray with a silicone lubricant. Also lubricate the latch and operator, working them back and forth to loosen them.

Often, lubrication will also free up an awning window. Pay special attention to the pivots at the sash, between the scissor arms, and at the operator.

In a jalousie window, lubricate the operator and the pivot points at both ends of each louver. If the operator seems to work all right but the window jams, you probably will need professional help, because the levers that move the panes are behind a metal jamb and the entire window must be taken out to get at them.

LUBRICATING AND REPLACING OPERATORS

To gain access to the gears in an operator, open the window wide. There is an open section in the outer edge of the stop into which the extension or scissor arms fold. It provides access to the mechanism. If the crank's worm gear and the gear at the pivot end of the extension arm are rusty or caked with dried grease, clean them. Lubricate metal gears with silicone. Do not lubricate plastic gears.

If a gear is stripped or too worn to mesh properly, you must replace the operator. This is a simple job once you have located an exact match. Be sure to get a lefthand or righthand operator, as required: different operators open the sash to the left or to the right as viewed from inside.

HOW TO SERVICE CRANKED WINDOWS

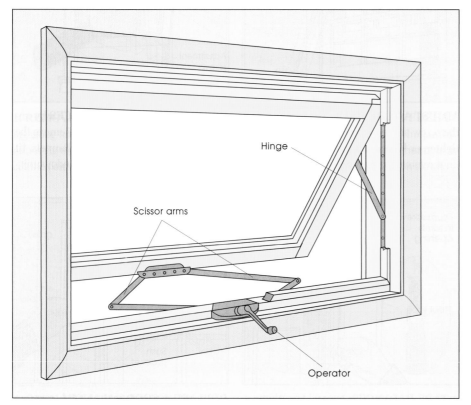

LUBRICATE AWNING WINDOWS at the labeled points after cleaning away any accumulated dirt or paint. Dry silicone spray lubricant lasts longer than grease or oil and does not attract dirt, which can build up and affect proper operation.

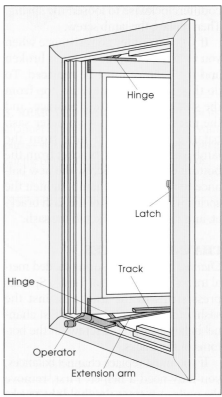

LUBRICATE CASEMENT WINDOW hinge and scissor arm pivots, and the operator gears with dry silicone spray.

To install a replacement, first detach the extension arm or scissor arms from the sash track. You will find a notch in the lip of the track, usually at the mid-point and sometimes marked with an arrow. Open the window until the extension arm pivot is at this point, depress the arm, and it will pop free. In an awning window, the scissor arms hook into a bracket on the sash and can be lifted or pried free.

Next, remove the screws that hold the operator to the sill or inside stop. Some operators have visible screws; in others the screws are covered by the inside stop, which must be removed for access. Pull the operator free and install the new one in its place.

TIGHTENING UP A LOOSE WINDOW

A hinged window that does not latch snugly against its stops lets in drafts and wastes energy. In some cases you can tighten up the window with a card-board or thin metal shim under the latch or between the operator and the lower stop. If not, install weather stripping between the sash and stops; see pages 236–237.

REPAIRING SLIDING WINDOWS

The movable sashes of most sliding windows can be removed for servicing: Center the sash, lift up until its bottom edge clears the track, and swing it free. With some windows you can remove screws to take out the fixed sash as well. If a sliding window binds, first clean the track and lubricate it with silicone spray. Straighten a bent track with pliers or by tapping it with a hammer and block of wood. If after a few passes the sash still sticks, remove the sash, clean its grooves, and lubricate them.

Large sliding windows and sliding patio doors roll on grooved, self-lubricating nylon wheels known as *sheaves*. The height of some sheaves can be adjusted with screws at the bottom edges of the sash, to slightly raise a lower sash edge or drop an upper edge that rubs against the track. If a sheave is damaged, lift out the sash, remove the sheave assembly, and replace it.

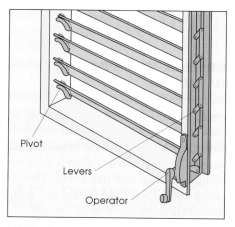

LUBRICATE JALOUSIE WINDOWS at all accessible pivot points and at the operator. A window specialist is needed to repair the levers hidden behind the side jamb.

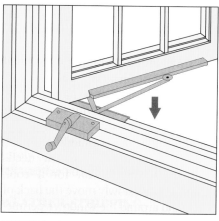

DISENGAGE THE EXTENSION ARM of a casement window by opening the sash until the arm end is at the notch in the track. Press down and the end will drop out.

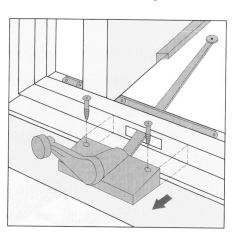

REMOVE AN OPERATOR by loosening the screws that hold it to the sill or stop. You may need to remove the bottom stop to get at the mounting screws.

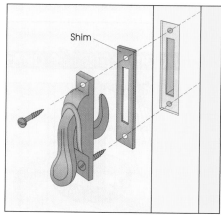

TIGHTEN A LOOSE WINDOW by removing the latch or operator and placing a metal or cardboard shim between it and the sash. Or install weather stripping.

HOW TO SERVICE SLIDING WINDOWS

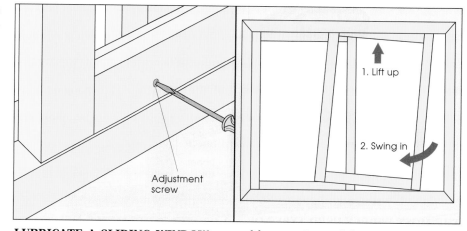

LUBRICATE A SLIDING WINDOW top and bottom. Some sliding windows roll on wheels. Turning an adjustment screw moves the wheels up or down. To remove a sliding sash, center it, lift up, and swing the bottom edge inward, free of the track.

19 INTERIOR DOORS

Interior doors can be classified by their construction—panel or flush—or by their mode of operation: swinging, folding, or sliding.

PANEL DOOR CONSTRUCTION

Traditionally styled doors, known as *panel doors*, have horizontal top and bottom *rails* and vertical *stiles* that frame one or more *panels*. Most also have a third *lock rail* just below the center of the door. There may also be vertical *mullions* between panels. In a swinging door the stiles are identified as the *hinge stile* and the *latch stile*, according to the hardware attached to them.

Panel door variations include *louvered doors*, which have shutterlike slats instead of panels, and *sash doors*, with glass for the panels.

FLUSH DOOR CONSTRUCTION

A *flush door* has a framework of rails and stiles covered on both sides with thin *face panels* of plywood, hardboard, plastic laminate, or metal. Most flush doors have a smooth, unbroken surface, but some are embellished with moldings to look like panel doors.

In a *solid-core* flush door the rails and stiles frame solid material, either wood blocks bonded together or thick particleboard. A *hollow-core* door has lattice framing of wood strips, cardboard, or other lightweight material inside the stile and rail frame to add rigidity to the face panels. Solid-core and hollow-core doors look identical, but you can easily distinguish between them by the difference in weight, or simply by rapping with your knuckles.

SWINGING DOORS

Panel or flush *swinging doors* most often move on hinges attached to the stile and the *hinge jamb* at one side and usually have a *latch bolt* that fits into a *strike* on the opposite jamb. When

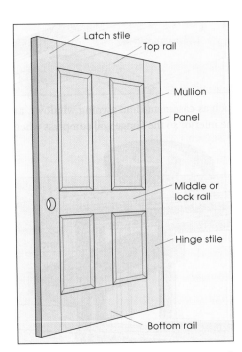

PANEL DOORS have one or more wood panels framed by rails and stiles. Some versions have louvers or glass in place of solid panels of wood or other material.

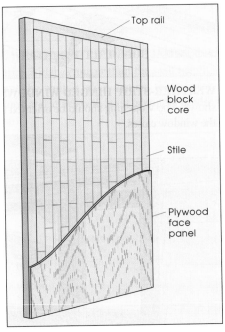

SOLID-CORE FLUSH DOORS have edge framing around a core of dense wood or particleboard. Thin plywood or other facing material covers everything.

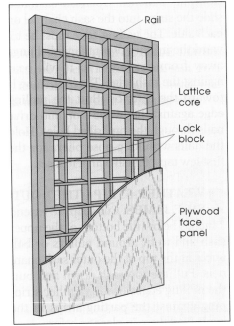

HOLLOW-CORE FLUSH DOORS have a latticework core of lightweight material. They cost and weigh less than solid-core doors and transmit sound more freely.

closed, the door rests against *stops* on the side jambs and the *head jamb*. A *double-acting door* swings in both directions. It has pivot hinges top and bottom, no latch, and no stops. As with window openings, *casing* around the perimeter of a doorway conceals gaps between the jambs and the wall surface. Some doorways have a *saddle* at the floor, which makes a transition between the finish flooring or floor coverings of adjoining rooms.

FOLDING DOORS

The most common style of folding door is a *bifold door*, which consists of two narrow panel or hollow-core flush doors hinged together. Top and bottom *pivots* fit into *jamb brackets* at the outside corners of one door panel. As the doors open, a *guide* at the top corner of the other door panel slides along a *guide track* attached to the head jamb. In four-panel installations, consisting of two bifold sets, *aligners* located near the bottoms of the center panels mesh when the doors are closed. There may also be spring *snuggers* in the tracks that keep the doors from rattling when they are closed. Some bifold doors have wood jambs, and casings that frame the opening. Other installations simply fit the door into an opening without casings or other trim.

SLIDING DOORS

A sliding door may be just a single door that moves sideways. Or it may be a set of *bypass doors*—two or more flush or panel doors that slide past each other. *Hangers* at the top of each door roll on wheels along a top-mounted *track*. *Floor guides* keep the bottoms of the doors in alignment. Some bypass doors have wood jambs and casings; others do not.

A single-unit *pocket door* slides into the wall through a *split jamb* and split studs. Pocket doors weighing up to 125 pounds are suspended from hangers that roll along an overhead track, like bypass doors. In old houses, heavy pocket doors ride on pulleylike wheels called *sheaves* that roll on a track on the floor. A rubber *bumper* at the end of the wall pocket stops the door when it is fully open.

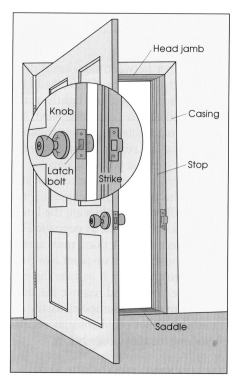

SWINGING DOORS operate on hinges or top and bottom pivots. Hinged doors rest against stops when closed. A latch engages with a strike on one jamb.

BIFOLD DOORS have hinged panels. One panel is mounted on pivots at the top and bottom; the other has a guide that moves along a track.

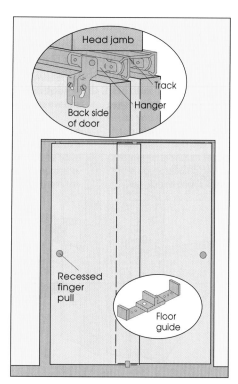

BYPASS DOORS are suspended from hangers that roll along a double track. Floor guides keep the bottoms of the doors from colliding with each other.

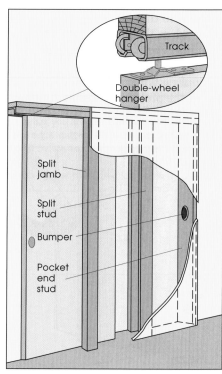

POCKET DOORS slide into a wall through a split jamb. They are suspended on wheeled hangers that move in a track attached to the head jamb.

INTERIOR DOORS

INSTALLING A FIREPLACE KIT

Installing a prefabricated fireplace kit requires next to no masonry work. It does, however, require some carpentry skill. A prefab fireplace consists of an insulated firebox, usually a heat-circulating type, that can sit directly on a combustible floor. A kit also contains sections of insulated or double-wall flue pipe and elbows, and other installation accessories. Along with the hardware, manufacturers supply extensive do-it-yourself installation instructions. Check your local building code before starting, and follow the instructions that come with your fireplace to the letter. An improper installation is a serious violation and may void your fire insurance coverage. Here's how a typical installation is done.

CHOOSE A LOCATION
You can put a prefab fireplace in a corner or along a wall, use it as a room divider, or recess it into an exterior wall. The intended location largely determines the model you need to buy.

PLAN A CHASE
In choosing a location, consider how you want to route flue pipe from the firebox to the roof. You can enclose only the fireplace and leave the chimney exposed. Or you can conceal both the chimney and the fireplace in a chase constructed inside or outside the house. With a freestanding fireplace you needn't construct any enclosure.

SELECT A FIREPLACE
Most situations call for a standard 36- or 42-inch-wide firebox with three solid sides, but you can purchase models with two or more glass sides—to serve adjoining rooms, for example.

Make sure that the fireplace you purchase is UL-approved. Check its acceptability with the local fire department, as well as the building department. Many building codes now stipulate that new fireplaces have a fresh-air intake. Most prefab units have knockouts for air intakes, a gas starter or logs, and a fan.

HOW TO INSTALL A PREFAB FIREPLACE

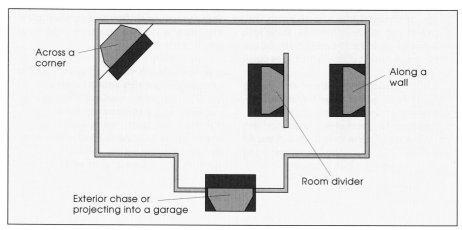

LOCATE A FIREPLACE in a corner, along an inside or outside wall, freestanding or in a room divider, or recessed into an exterior wall and chase.

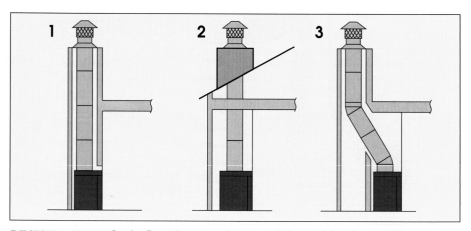

DESIGN A CHASE for the flue. Shown are three possibilities: (1) fireplace and flue in an exterior chase; (2) straight rise in an interior chase; (3) offset in an exterior or interior chase.

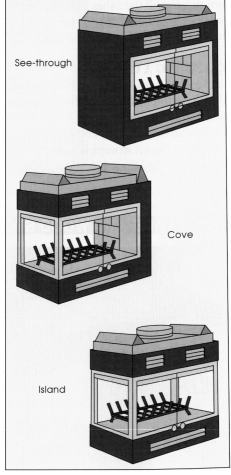

FIREPLACE STYLES can suit a wide variety of situations. These configurations have glass on two, three, and four sides.

FRAME CHIMNEY OPENINGS

Set the fireplace in place and check that the distances from the edges of the fireplace opening to combustible walls are no less than the manufacturer's specified minimum; typically they are 14 to 18 inches. Level the firebox and screw it to the floor.

If the flue will rise straight from the firebox through the ceiling and roof, drop a plumb bob from the ceiling and center it in the firebox flue outlet. Frame openings in the ceiling and roof to provide at least 2 inches clearance on all sides of the insulated flue—that is, outside flue diameter plus 4 inches. If you plan to offset the flue, assemble the sections and elbows to determine where the overhead openings should be made.

INSTALL FIRESTOP SPACERS

Wherever the chimney penetrates a floor or ceiling there must be a firestop spacer to maintain the required 2-inch distance between the chimney and combustible materials and to block air flow around the outside of the chimney pipe. In an attic, nail the firestop spacer to the tops of the joists. In living spaces, nail spacers to the bottom edges of the joists. At the roof, a chimney flashing serves as a firestop spacer. Install this as you would a vent flashing (see page 279).

ASSEMBLE CHIMNEY SECTIONS

Starting at the firebox, fit sections of insulated or heatproof flue pipe together, installing elbows as needed. Lock the sections securely together according to the instructions. Then pull firmly on the joint to test it. Chimney sections come in a variety of standard lengths and cannot be cut.

TOP OFF THE CHIMNEY

Terminate a chimney by slipping a section down through the roof flashing and locking it to the section below. This final section must rise a minimum of 3 feet above the roof. If it is 10 feet or closer to the roof peak, it must also extend 2 feet above the peak. Slip a collar around the chimney and flashing and caulk around it. Fit the top of the chimney with a terminal cap, which keeps debris out of the chimney and arrests any sparks that might rise from the fire.
Continued

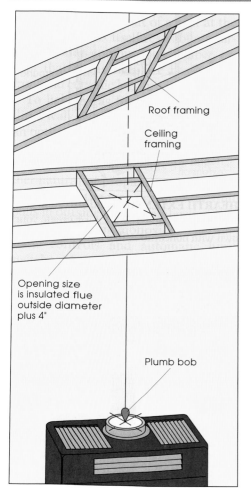

LOCATE OPENINGS where the flue will pass through the ceiling and roof. Frame to provide 2 inches clearance on all sides.

Roof framing

Ceiling framing

Opening size is insulated flue outside diameter plus 4"

Plumb bob

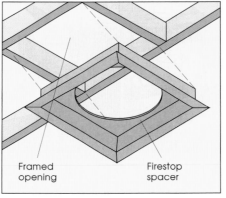

Framed opening

Firestop spacer

FIRESTOP SPACERS maintain a 2-inch clearance between the flue and framing members. Install one wherever the flue penetrates a ceiling or floor.

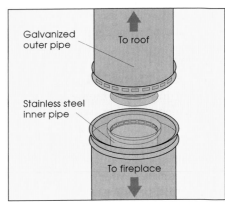

Galvanized outer pipe

To roof

Stainless steel inner pipe

To fireplace

SNAP CHIMNEY SECTIONS together. Test each joint by pulling up on the flue to ensure that the sections are locked together. Most systems do not require screws.

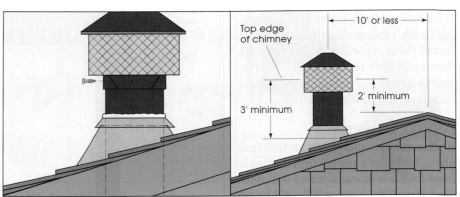

Top edge of chimney

10' or less

3' minimum

2' minimum

ATTACH THE CHIMNEY CAP after installing the flashing. The chimney top must be at least 3 feet above the roof. If it is within 10 feet of the roof peak, it must rise 2 feet higher than the peak.

This section takes you outside the house to deal with all the exterior factors that require attention. It begins with the roof, then goes on to exterior walls, and the outside elements of windows, doors, and foundations. Subsequent chapters cover garage doors and automatic door openers, house painting, and walks, patios, decks, porches, fences, and garden and retaining walls.

Weather is the implacable foe of any home's exterior, so much of this section is devoted to maintenance and repair procedures that ward off or undo damage inflicted by nature. Sealing up small chinks in your home's armor will help prevent bigger problems later on.

INSPECTING THE EXTERIOR

Because exterior elements do not get day-in/day-out scrutiny, you should systematically inspect your home from top to bottom twice a year, in early spring and early fall. Look for lifted or damaged roofing, sagging gutters, gaps in siding, peeling paint, cracked concrete or mortar joints, and the other conditions explained on the pages that follow. Make a list of areas that need attention, then refer to the appropriate chapter in this section for repair procedures.

DO IT YOURSELF OR HIRE A PRO?

Many large projects—replacing a roof or siding, for example, or cutting an opening that will bridge rafters or wall studs—are best accomplished by contractors with the skills and expertise to get the work done quickly and properly. In some instances, product warranties and building codes mandate hiring a professional. The discussion throughout this section identifies tasks best assigned to a contractor. Page 516 tells you how to engage a contractor and gives more information on zoning, codes, and permits.

IV EXTERIOR REPAIRS AND IMPROVEMENTS

Despite its emphasis on repair and maintenance, this section also presents dozens of improvements, from installing a garage door opener to building a spacious deck, that a homeowner can confidently execute. Many exterior improvement items now come in kit form, with step-by-step, do-it-yourself instructions.

IMPORTANT

Before beginning any procedure that requires climbing a ladder, review the ladder safety tips presented on page 59. If heights make you nervous, stay off ladders altogether.

Many projects call for lifting stones, blocks, bundles of shingles, and other heavy materials. Do not strain yourself. For moderate loads, enlist a helper and lift with leg, not back, muscles. If you begin to tire, take a break. Fatigue can cause accidents. For large loads, or to lift materials to a roof or scaffold, use a hoist or pulley, as explained on pages 62–63.

Finally, check building codes and zoning ordinances before undertaking a major improvement such as a patio, deck, wall, or fence. To learn what code and zoning provisions typically require, see page 516.

REPAIRING ROLL ROOFING

Because roll roofing is commonly installed on flat or slightly pitched roofs, such as shed roofs, it is more prone to leaking but easier to repair than shingles on more steeply pitched roofs. Here is how to deal with the most common problems encountered with roll roofing.

REPAIRING A BLISTER

Air or water trapped under roll roofing causes blisters that can break open and cause a leak. Cut a blister with a utility knife and flatten it. If water oozes out, moisture has condensed under the roofing, or possibly has seeped there from nearby flashing. Air blisters usually occur because roofing cement was unevenly applied or has dried out.

Raise the cut edges and let the blister dry thoroughly. Then work roofing cement underneath, press the roofing edges into it, and drive roofing nails along each side of the incision. Finally, cut a patch from matching roll roofing that is at least 2 inches wider than the blistered area in all directions. Spread roofing cement over the area the patch will cover, put the patch in place and nail all around its perimeter, then coat the nail heads and the edges of the patch with more cement. Check patches annually for cracked cement.

PATCHING ROLL ROOFING

Extensively blistered, buckling, or cracked sections of roll roofing should be cut out, replaced with sound material, and covered with a patch.

Mark off a rectangle around the damaged section and use a utility knife and straightedge to slice along the lines. Remove layers of roofing until you reach sound material—down to the sheathing, if necessary.

Scrape away all old roofing cement, cut new roofing to fit the cutout area, and cement it in place. Install as many layers as you have removed, with cement under each layer. When the replacement area is as thick as the roofing around it, nail around the perimeter on both sides of the seams. Finally, cover the cutout area with a patch that is several inches larger in all directions. Cement and nail this in place and coat the edges and nail heads with roofing cement. If your roof has a gravel topping, coat the entire patch with a thick layer of roofing cement and sprinkle gravel into it.

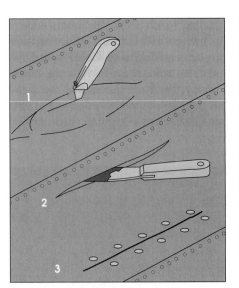

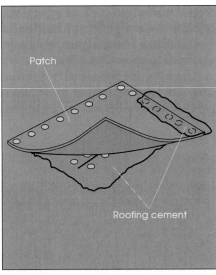

SLICE THROUGH A BLISTER to release air or water inside. Work roofing cement underneath and drive roofing nails along the edges of the cut.

CEMENT A PATCH over the repaired blister. Drive roofing nails around the perimeter, and coat the nail heads and edges with more roofing cement.

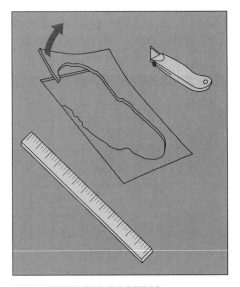

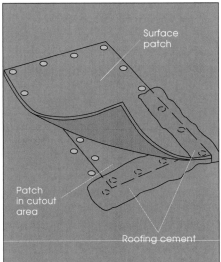

TO PATCH ROLL ROOFING, cut a rectangle around the damaged area and remove one or more layers as necessary. Cut new roofing to fit into the rectangle.

CEMENT THE INNER PATCH and nail its edges, then cover it with a surface patch secured in the same way. Cover the edges and nail heads with roofing cement.

> **CAUTION**
>
> Moving around on a flat or low-pitched roof is less hazardous than clambering up a steep slope, but roll roofing is easily damaged, so walk on it as seldom as possible. Provide a board to lay your tools on, to protect the surface, and consider laying down plywood or hardboard panels that will distribute your weight over a broad surface area.

REPAIRING METAL AND TILE ROOFING

Metal and tile roofs can last several decades with minimal maintenance. Major repairs should be made by a knowledgeable roofing contractor or, in the case of tile, a mason familiar with how tile roofs go together and are sealed with mortar. You can, however, repair small cracks in either material with roofing cement. Also, you can refasten metal roofing that has been lifted by wind and ice.

REFASTENING SHEET METAL ROOFING

Replace popped nails with longer, spiral roofing nails or, better yet, with screws. All fasteners should have neoprene washers so that water can't leak in around the head. If old fasteners are secure but do not have washers, spot the heads with clear silicone caulk. Drive screws or nails through the ridges, not the valleys, of the panels. Drive them just deep enough to compress their washers. Do not dimple the ridge and create a pocket where water could collect.

SOLDERING METAL ROOFING

Steel, copper, zinc alloy, and terne roofing can be repaired by soldering a patch over a damaged or corroded area. Patch only with the same material—copper over copper, for example, or steel over steel. Electrolytic reaction between dissimilar materials can cause corrosion.

To fasten the patch, use spool or bar solder, and rosin soldering flux with copper, acid flux with steel, zinc alloy, and terne roofing. With emery cloth, clean a 1-inch border all around on the underside of the patch and corresponding strips on the roof. Apply flux to the cleaned borders of the patch, heat them with a propane torch and flow on a thin layer of solder; this is called *tinning*. Do the same with the prepared spots on the roof. Then position the patch solder side down on the roof, weight it down, and heat the borders to cause the two tinned solder coatings to fuse. This technique is called *sweat soldering* or simply *sweating*. Finally, apply flux to the seam and add a bead of solder all around the edges of the patch.

PATCHING ALUMINUM ROOFING

Aluminum can be soldered with aluminum solder and a special flux. However, aluminum soldering is tricky. It is easier to make a repair by applying a *cold patch* of fiberglass or polyester mesh and roofing cement. Scour the damaged area with a wire brush and cut two mesh patches. Coat the aluminum with roofing cement, press one patch into it, apply more cement and add the second patch. Cover the repair with a final application of cement and a piece of aluminum or foil-surfaced roofing material. Seal the edges with clear caulking. You can make a cold patch on any metal roof, but the repair will not last as long as a soldered patch.

ROOF COATINGS

When an old roof loses its luster and begins to dry out and crack, you can temporarily prolong its life with an acrylic-, asphalt-, or aluminum-formulation *roof coating*, also known as *roof paint*. After thoroughly cleaning the roof and repairing any damaged areas, you simply roll on two thin coats according to the manufacturer's instructions.

White acrylic coatings add reflectivity to asphalt, slate, metal, and tile roofing and can be tinted to match or change the color of the roof. Asphalt coatings are black and intended for asphalt or metal roofs. Aluminum roof coating brings reflectivity to asphalt and metal. You can also buy clear sealant for asphalt shingles.

Most roof coatings wear off after a few seasons and recoating is not advised, so after you have coated a roof, plan to replace it before long.

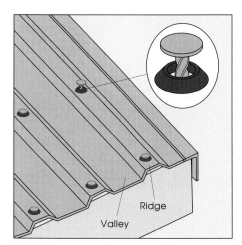

REFASTEN SHEET METAL with spiral roofing nails or screws driven through ridges, not valleys. Prefit the fasteners with neoprene washers.

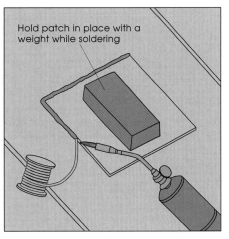

PATCH METAL ROOFS other than aluminum by sweat soldering a patch of the same material to the roof surface. The technique is explained in the text.

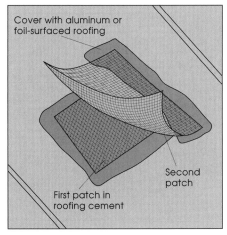

START A COLD PATCH on a metal roof with two layers of fiberglass or polyester mesh and roofing cement. Finish as described in the text.

INSTALLING NEW SHINGLES

In most instances, reroofing an entire home is not advisable for a do-it-yourselfer (see box below). You might, however, decide to reshingle a simple sloped roof such as one over a porch, outbuilding, or vacation cabin. Here are the procedures for applying asphalt shingles over existing asphalt shingles.

DETERMINING THE ROOF PITCH

The degree of slope or *pitch* of a roof has a bearing on the material you choose as a covering. The pitch is expressed by the number of inches (or feet) of vertical *rise* for every 12 inches (or feet) of horizontal *run*. Make measurements on a rafter in the attic or on the roof edge or rake board at an exterior gable end. Use a level to measure a horizontal run of 12 inches, and from that point measure vertically to the rafter or roof edge. A roof that rises 4 inches for a 12-inch run has a pitch of 4:12, or 4 in 12. On slopes that are less than 2:12, install roll roofing (see pages 286–287), not shingles.

ORDERING MATERIALS

Shingles are sold by the *square*, enough material to cover 100 square feet. (They are packaged in bundles for easy handling, often three bundles per square.) To calculate how many squares you will need, measure the length and width of each roof surface to be reshingled and multiply these dimensions to compute the area. Add 10 percent to account for places along eaves, ridges, and hips where double layers of shingles will be installed and round the result up to the next 100 square feet.

INSTALLING ASPHALT SHINGLES

Fiberglass-reinforced asphalt shingles offer the easiest, quickest, and least expensive way to cover existing roofing.

Each shingle is 3 feet wide by 1 foot high and has two or three 5-inch-long tabs that are exposed to simulate the look of individual shingles.

To prepare a roof for reshingling, nail down all curled edges and replace any deteriorated or missing shingles. Use the existing shingles as a guide for aligning the new ones. Install new metal or vinyl drip edge flashing over the old roofing at all eaves and rakes.

1 LAY A STARTER COURSE. Make shingles for the starter course by cutting the tabs off standard shingles to get solid strips that just cover the exposure of the old first course. Score the backs with a utility knife and straightedge, then snap along the scored line. Nail each starter shingle with four 1½-inch roofing nails along the top edge.

2 LAY THE FIRST COURSE. Next, install a layer of shingles with tabs overlapping the starter course. Trim the end of the first shingle so the seams

---

SHOULD YOU DO ROOFING WORK?

In most cases the answer to this question is no. Steep roofs pose a safety hazard for amateur roofers and require scaffolds and other specialized equipment. Installing wood shingles and shakes is best handled by roofers who specialize in these materials. Similarly, if valley and chimney flashings must be replaced, the work should be done by a professional.

Many building codes prohibit the extra weight of more than three layers of roofing material, and some houses can support only two. This means that a roof that has been shingled two or three times must be stripped to the sheathing. Removing old shingles is messy work and disposing of them poses another problem, especially if the old shingles contain asbestos.

Finally, the manufacturer's warranty may not cover materials installed by a do-it-yourselfer. A reputable roofing contractor will make repairs and replacements throughout the warranty period.

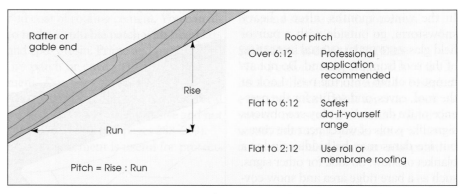

Roof pitch	
Over 6:12	Professional application recommended
Flat to 6:12	Safest do-it-yourself range
Flat to 2:12	Use roll or membrane roofing

DETERMINE THE PITCH OF A ROOF by measuring the inches of vertical rise at the end of a level 12-inch run.

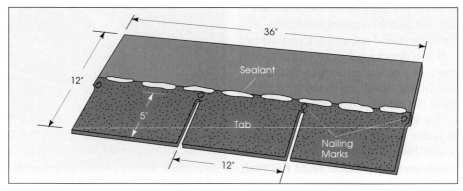

STANDARD ASPHALT SHINGLES have these dimensions, with two or three tabs. Nail position marks are common.

between shingles in this course do not align with those in the starter course. Edges should lightly touch. Trim the top edges of this course to fit against the bottom edges of the old course above it. Nail as marked in the coverage area, usually one at each end and one above each tab division.

3 LAY SUBSEQUENT COURSES. To minimize color discrepancies between bundles, lay shingles from left to right or right to left, but not directly up the roof. Use the old shingles as guides to keep the tabs staggered from one course to the next.

4 INSTALL RIDGE AND HIP SHINGLES. When you reach the ridge or a hip, remove the old shingles over the angle and replace them with special hip and ridge shingles or with sections of a standard shingle cut apart at the tabs. This will give you three 12- × 12-inch pieces from a standard shingle. Start at the end of the ridge that is opposite the prevailing wind, or at the bottom of a hip. Nail the shingles to each roof slope, lapping them for a 5-inch exposure. At the end of the ridge or the top of a hip, cut the last shingle to size, secure it with exposed nails, and seal the nail heads with roofing cement.

CAUTION

If you choose to install roofing yourself, be sure to heed these safety precautions:

• Wear rubber-soled shoes for secure footing, and do not reroof in wet weather. Moisture makes roofs slippery and dangerous.

• Install shingles on clear days when it is warm but not hot. Temperature extremes turn shingles brittle or soft.

• Lift only easy loads; better yet, use a pulley or hoist (see page 63). Shingles are heavy and awkward to carry up a ladder.

• Secure ladders top and bottom (see page 59) and keep the roof surface clear of debris.

• Place shingles and tools where they won't slide off the roof. Put a safety line or safety cleat at the bottom edge of the roof.

• Keep people away from the work area.

HOW TO INSTALL ASPHALT SHINGLES

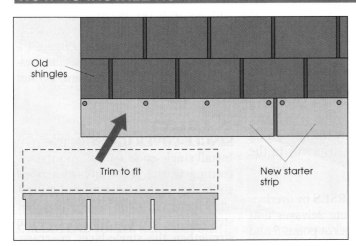

1. LAY A STARTER COURSE along each eave. Trim off the tabs to get shingles that completely cover the exposure in the first course of the old roof. Nail only along the top edge as shown.

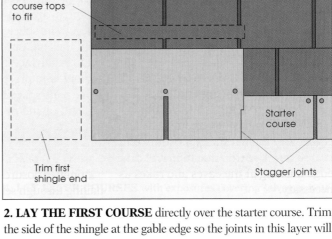

2. LAY THE FIRST COURSE directly over the starter course. Trim the side of the shingle at the gable edge so the joints in this layer will be staggered over those between the shingles below.

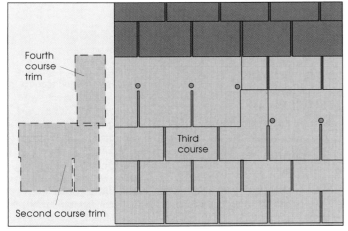

3. LAY UP SUBSEQUENT COURSES in horizontal rows. Trim the first shingle in various courses as necessary to stagger joints. Start the third course with a full shingle.

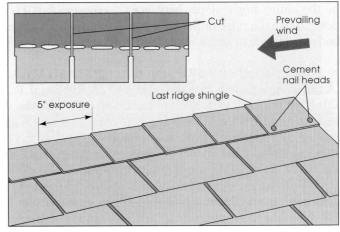

4. AT THE RIDGE AND HIPS, replace the old shingles with hip and ridge shingles or sections cut from a straight shingle. Lap them for 5-inch exposure, oriented as shown.

INSTALLING SHINGLES

23 EXTERIOR WALLS

The exterior walls of your home define the character and appearance of the house and protect both the structure and the living space within. Keeping these walls in good condition is extremely important. This chapter shows you how to maintain exterior walls, and how to install new siding if you decide to remodel or to build an addition.

EXTERIOR WALL CONSTRUCTION

Almost all twentieth-century houses in the United States have walls constructed of wood *framing* that is covered on the outside by *siding* attached to *sheathing,* and on the inside by gypsum panels (drywall) or lath and plaster. A new method of construction using structural foam panels, and older methods of solid masonry construction are far less common than wood framing.

Virtually all houses are built with *platform framing,* in which the walls of each story are built on the platform of the joists and subfloor for that level (see Chapter 11 for floor framing). As explained in Chapter 12, wall framing consists of vertical studs that run between horizontal sole and top plates, with headers spanning door and window openings. Other methods of framing are found primarily in pre-twentieth-century houses.

WALL SHEATHING

Whatever the method of construction, exterior wall framing is covered with structural sheathing—panels of plywood, oriented-strand board, or some kind of fiberboard. The sheathing covers the open framework and provides continuous bracing between the members. Nonstructural panels such as rigid-foam plastic panels can be used as sheathing in conjunction either with diagonal braces throughout the frame, or with single sheets of structural sheathing for bracing at the corners.

Non-weather-resistant sheathings require a surface barrier that stops water but is permeable to air circulation to allow humidity changes in the sheathing. Modern, highly energy efficient construction may include a vapor-permeable air barrier over the sheathing to reduce air infiltration while allowing humidity adjustments.

SIDING

Siding is the outer layer of an exterior wall, the protective and decorative skin. The siding and any necessary finish

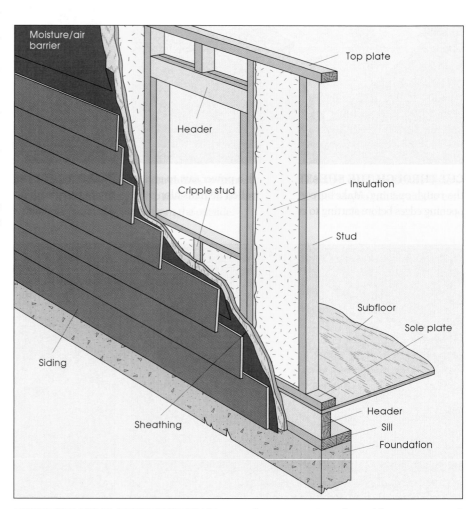

EXTERIOR WALL CONSTRUCTION in most houses consists of wood framing covered with sheathing and siding applied over a moisture/air barrier. Siding materials include wood, plastic, metal, and masonry. Insulation in framing cavities is essential.

coat—paint, stain, or water repellent—must be carefully maintained, and repaired or replaced when necessary. As long as they are in good condition, the exterior walls are protected from most of the things that could cause deterioration.

Wood is by far the most widely used siding material. Traditional wood siding consists of overlapping beveled or tapered horizontal boards called clapboards, but there are other kinds of horizontal strip siding. Wood sidings also include vertical boards with various kinds of joints; shingles and shakes; and panels of plywood or wood-fiber materials with plain or shaped surfaces. Vinyl and aluminum sidings are made to look like traditional clapboards or like vertical board siding. Mineral fiber shingles are also used as siding. All of these sidings are nailed directly to the exterior wall sheathing.

Solid masonry construction is rare today. Brick or stone siding is usually a veneer, a single-thickness layer laid up in front of a sheathed wood-frame wall. The veneer is secured with metal ties that are nailed to the sheathing and inserted into the mortar joints of the siding. Cement or cementlike stuccos are used for joint-free masonry siding. They are applied to metal mesh (lath) nailed to the sheathing.

OTHER WALL FEATURES

Inside the wall framing, insulation prevents the loss of interior heat during cold weather and keeps out exterior heat during hot weather. A vapor-retarding barrier over the insulation slows the movement of airborne moisture into the wall, where it can condense, causing mildew and rot and reducing the effectiveness of the insulation. For more on insulation and vapor retarders see pages 312–313 and Chapter 21.

In highly energy efficient homes, exterior wall construction may involve deeper framing for extra interior insulation, exterior insulation under the siding, gaskets and caulks to reduce air/moisture infiltration, and many other measures. The interior surfaces of walls in most homes are gypsum board (drywall), although various other materials may be used (see Chapter 12).

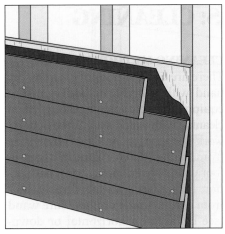

TRADITIONAL CLAPBOARDS are overlapping beveled boards. Nails go through one board and sheathing into wall studs.

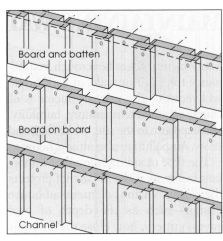

BASIC VERTICAL BOARD SIDING uses flat-surface boards. Similar joints may be used with large panels.

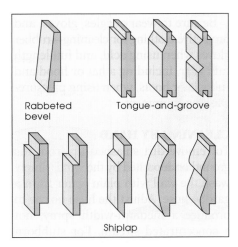

OTHER SIDING JOINTS are used with plain or shaped-surface boards. Some can be applied horizontally or vertically.

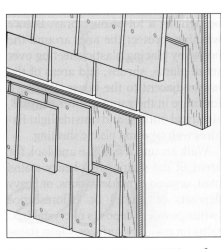

WOOD SHINGLES AND SHAKES are fastened with nails; joints must be staggered, as in roof shingling.

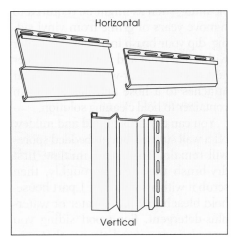

VINYL AND ALUMINUM SIDING comes in single and double strips and panels for horizontal and vertical installation.

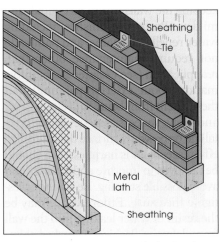

MASONRY SIDINGS include brick or stone veneer *(top)* and cement finishes such as stucco *(bottom)*.

REPAIRING WOOD LAP SIDING, SHINGLES, AND SHAKES

It is inexpensive and almost always more effective to replace a split or damaged shingle, shake, or piece of lap siding entirely rather than to try patching or gluing it.

REPLACING SIDING

Pry under the edge of a damaged piece of lap siding to raise it a bit. Then tap it down to leave the nail heads exposed and pull the nails. Next, drive wedges under the damaged board to raise it and cut through the face with a back saw. Protect the siding below and above with scrap wood. Split off the exposed portion and use a keyhole saw to cut through the remaining overlapped portion. Work that piece out with a chisel. Use a hacksaw blade to cut any nails in the course above that are holding it, and then pull the shanks or cut them off flush at the sheathing. Finally, cut a new piece to length, slip it into position, and nail it as the original piece was nailed.

REPLACING A SHINGLE OR SHAKE

Split a damaged shingle or shake with a hammer and wood chisel and pull out the pieces. Pull the exposed nails and use a hacksaw blade to cut through any nails under the course above that held the damaged shingle. Tap against a wood block to drive a new shingle up into place. If it does not go all the way, measure the difference at the butt, remove it, and cut that much off the tapered top end. Replace it, and drive nails angled upward just under the edge of the shingle above. Use a nail set for the final blows to avoid damaging the upper shingle edge.

PRY UP DAMAGED SIDING to raise the exposed nails, tap it down, and pull them. Protect good siding with scrap wood.

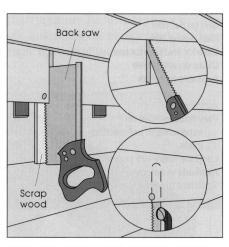

CUT OUT THE DAMAGED SECTION as shown. Use a keyhole saw and a hacksaw blade to finish the removal as necessary.

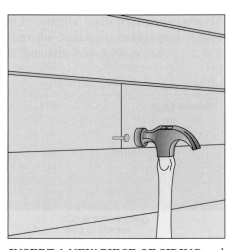

INSERT A NEW PIECE OF SIDING and nail it in place. Fill nail heads and finish to match the surrounding siding.

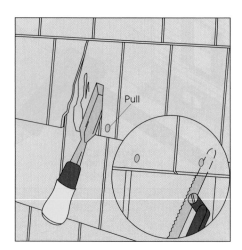

SPLIT A DAMAGED SHINGLE and pull out the pieces. Then pull the exposed nails and cut off the concealed nails.

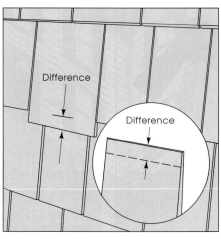

POSITION A NEW SHINGLE, measure the difference in length, and remove that much from the tapered top end.

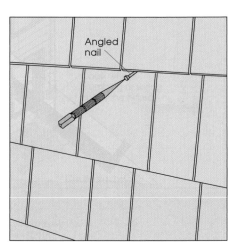

ANGLE-NAIL THE CUT SHINGLE at the top. Drive the nails up under the shingle above. Use a nail set to avoid damage.

REPAIRING PLYWOOD AND HARDBOARD PANEL SIDING

Plywood siding may blister when the glue between surface and core layers fails. Both plywood and hardboard siding are susceptible to dents or gouges, and panels may buckle from expansion or localized swelling.

BLISTER REPAIR

With a knife, make one or two slits the full length of the blister, parallel to the grain. Mask around the slits and lift the veneer enough to insert a gap-filling adhesive such as construction adhesive.

Press the veneer flat, staple securely, and wipe off any squeezed-out adhesive. Carefully remove the staples after one week and touch up the finish.

DENTS AND GOUGES

Use a high-quality polyester-base auto body repair putty to fill in dents and gouges. Remove all loose, splintered wood and mask off the area around the damage. Apply the filler with a putty knife and texture it with a comb, brush, or other tool to match the siding. Touch

up with stain or paint, minimizing overlap with the existing finish.

BUCKLING

Expanded material that has buckled may not fit or may split when forced back into its original position. For buckling along an edge between fasteners, try adding fasteners, working from each end toward the center of the buckled area. Use rustproof screws or ring-shank nails. For buckling in mid-panel where there is access from behind, add blocking between the wall studs and drive screws from the face, as for edge buckling. If these methods do not work, the only cure is to remove and replace the panel, and refinish it as required.

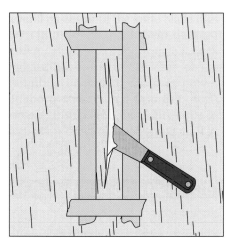

SLIT A PLYWOOD BLISTER and work construction adhesive under it. Mask the area against smeared adhesive.

STAPLE THE BLISTER FLAT and wipe away excess adhesive. Carefully remove staples after a week and touch up as necessary.

FILL A DENT OR GOUGE with polyester-base auto body filler after removing all loose fibers and chips.

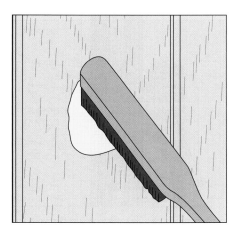

TEXTURE THE SURFACE before the filler hardens. When it has cured, stain or paint the filled area to match the panel.

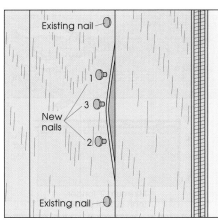

ADD FASTENERS TO CLOSE AN EDGE BUCKLE. Work alternately from the ends to the center of the buckle.

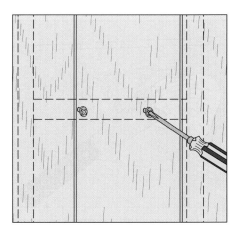

FASTEN A MID-PANEL BUCKLE with screws if blocking can be added; if not, remove and replace the panel.

SELECTING NEW SIDING

Choosing siding for your home requires careful thought. Siding should be suitable both to the design of the house and to your own taste. It should also be suitable to the climate and other physical conditions where the house is located.

The type of siding used on similar houses in good condition in your area is a good guide to making a satisfactory choice. But perhaps your home is unique and you want it to have a distinctive appearance. Or perhaps there is a design problem that can be resolved with siding rather than more extensive alterations. In such cases it would be wise to pay a consultation fee to an architect or designer. In addition to guidance regarding style and physical suitability, a professional may provide valuable information about local regulations, sources of supply, and other factors that will affect the job.

COSTS

Your choice of a siding must take into account both the cost of the materials and the "life cycle" cost, which includes durability and maintenance. Of course, you can make a major saving by doing the installation yourself, as explained in the following pages.

In general, vinyl, hardboard, and plywood are low-cost sidings; metal, wood boards, and stucco are medium cost; and wood shingles and masonry (brick and stone veneer) are the most expensive. Vinyl and metal sidings are prefinished and so require virtually no maintenance. Masonry and stucco sidings require little maintenance other than attention to cracks and caulking. Wood shingles require little attention if the species is properly chosen for the climate and the shingles are properly installed. Painted or stained wood board and panel sidings require periodic renewal of the finish (see Chapter 27) and annual attention to caulking.

VINYL AND METAL SIDING

Sidings of vinyl and metal—aluminum and steel—are popular because they are maintenance-free and are easily installed over existing siding or directly on sheathing. Metal has the greatest fire resistance of all kinds of siding; vinyl has essentially none.

Because metal siding is stronger and more rigid, it can bridge uneven spots on a wall that would require shimming under vinyl siding to avoid a wavy appearance. However, metal siding can be dented by objects falling or hitting against it. And it may vibrate noisily in high wind, or drum in a heavy rain. In some communities metal siding must be grounded as an electrical safety measure—an important point to check in your area. Vinyl siding does not dent and does not require grounding.

Both vinyl and metal sidings come in single- and double-course strips that look like various kinds of wood siding, and in panels of various widths, either plain or with surface detail. They are prefinished in many colors. Dark colors will fade more, and vinyl faster than metal. Most siding styles include a wide range of trim for historic or traditional detailing.

WOOD SIDING

There are three major categories of wood sidings: board siding, unmilled (flat surface) or milled in a wide variety of profiles; panels, including plywood and hardboard; and shingles and shakes.

Redwood, cedar, and various pine, spruce, and fir woods are used for siding, and most are graded for quality. Premium grades are clear (knot-free) and have fewer other characteristics that might be visually objectionable or might affect performance. The best, heartwood grades of cedar and redwood are very weather, insect, and decay resistant. Properly maintained, with periodic renewal of the finish, if any, wood siding will last a lifetime.

Wood board siding is relatively easy to install, requiring basic carpentry skills and tools, and accurate measuring and cutting. Wood shingles and shakes—thick, hand-split shingles—are no more difficult but are more time consuming to install and, if better grades and species are used, very costly.

However, they offer excellent protection, design versatility, easy tie-in and repair, and they give a wall a unique texture. Weather-resistant species such as Western Red Cedar can be left untreated and will last for decades, which helps offset the high initial cost.

Wood panel siding is available in 4 × 8-, 4 × 9-, and 4 × 10-foot sheets of plywood and hardboard (pressed wood fibers). Installation goes quickly because each panel covers so much area. If you use rated structural siding panels (see page 80), there is no need for sheathing or wall bracing; you can fasten the panels directly to properly prepared framing. Panels imitate various wood siding patterns. Although they can be installed horizontally if design and framing account for the vertical joints, they are usually installed vertically. Horizontal joints, unavoidable on walls over 10 feet tall, are dealt with in a variety of ways (see page 310).

STUCCO AND RELATED FINISHES

Traditional stucco is a multilayer finish of cement mortar. It can be applied directly to clean masonry, or to metal lath over sheathing or old framing. The surface can be smooth or highly textured. Stucco is as hard as concrete, extremely durable, and requires virtually no maintenance. It is commonly left unpainted; if painted, the finish will have to be renewed periodically.

BRICK AND STONE VENEER

The visual appeal of brick and stone makes them extremely popular, but because this kind of siding is quite expensive it is often used only on the street side of a house, or just around an entry area.

Both brick and stone are available in a great variety of colors and textures and can be installed in many designs. Putting up a veneer wall is a good deal of work, but is a feasible do-it-yourself project; wall-building techniques are covered in Chapter 32. When constructed as siding, a single-layer masonry wall must be built on a concrete foundation. Metal ties fastened to the sheathing (see page 293) and spaced 24 inches apart must be inserted in the mortar joints at every fifth course.

INSTALLING WOOD SHINGLES AND SHAKES

Use No. 1 grade, rejointed and rebutted (R&R) shingles or shakes, which have been machine-trimmed to size and shape. Shingles are 16, 18, or 24 inches long; shakes, more rustic looking, are 18 and 24 inches long. Both can be installed for either *single-course* or *double-course* exposure. Double-coursing uses an underlayer of lower-grade shingles.

Apply shingles over 15-pound building felt stapled to sheathing, with extra strips 6 inches wide around door and window casings and 18 inches wide bent around corners. Plan course exposure—the amount of shingle left uncovered in each course—so that a course aligns with the tops of windows or a door. Mark the course spacing on a story pole to use as a ruler in marking the walls.

Install corner trim, if any, and flash inside corners. Mark a level line 1 inch below the bottom edge of the sheathing and install a double-layer starter row for single-coursing, or a three-layer row for double-coursing. Stagger joints between layers. Use only the type and size of fastener, and the fastener material, specified by the shingle or shake manu-facturer. The wrong material could cause staining. 4d nails are commonly used for single-course shingles, 6d nails for shakes and all double-coursing. Staples may also be approved by some manufacturers.

Now install succeeding courses. With shakes, staple a layer of 30-pound felt under each course. To mark the butt line for each course, snap a level chalkline between marks transferred from your story pole, or tack up a straight board. In double-coursing, extend the finish layer butts ½ inch below the underlayer butts on each course. For overlapped inside or outside corners, work on both walls to complete the corner for each course. Cut the top course shingles to fit against the soffit or other eave or roof trim.

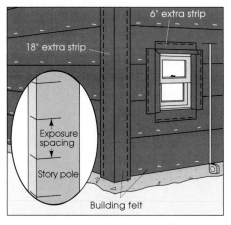

PLAN EXPOSURE so course ends at a window or door top. Minimum exposure is 4 inches; maximum depends on shingle length.

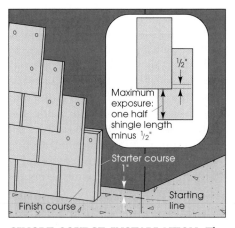

SINGLE-COURSE INSTALLATION. The starter course seals the joints behind the first finish course. Locate fasteners as shown.

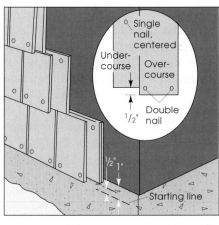

DOUBLE-COURSE INSTALLATION. The starter course is a double layer. Finish layer butts extend ½ inch lower in each course.

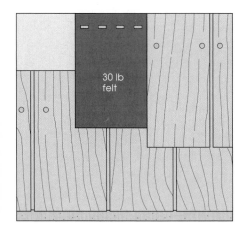

STAPLE 30-POUND BUILDING FELT between courses of shakes. Their irregular surfaces require this extra moisture barrier.

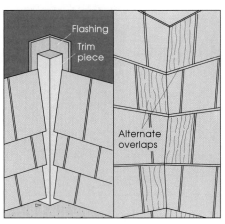

MAKE INSIDE CORNERS with a trim piece three shingles thick, or with alternate-course overlaps. Flash all inside corners.

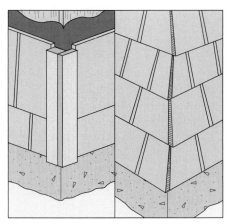

MAKE OUTSIDE CORNERS by butting shingles against trim boards, or trim alternate courses for an interwoven corner.

INSTALLING LAP SIDING

Whether you plan to install vinyl, metal, or wood horizontal lap siding, start by calculating the total area to be covered (length × width of each wall) and subtract the total area of all windows and doors. Add 10 percent for cutting waste. Take that figure to your supplier, who will calculate how much you need of the kind of siding you have chosen. Get the longest lengths available, and plan optimal use. Have as few joints as possible near highly visible areas such as the front entry. For vinyl or metal siding, also record the sizes and number of all window and door openings. You and the supplier will need these measurements to calculate what trim pieces you need, and in what quantity.

PREPARATION

Install siding over sheathing covered with 15-pound building felt. Staple extra strips 6 inches wide around all door and window casings, and bend 18-inch-wide strips around or into corners.

Install flashing over windows and doors if needed (see pages 322–323).

To mark the spacing of the courses, establish a level base line. For metal, vinyl, and fixed-depth wood siding, sim-ply measure courses up from that line. For wood siding with a variable overlap, such as clapboards, measure from the line to the top of a window or door casing and divide that into equal-size courses, allowing a minimum of 1 inch overlap between courses. Mark the course spacings on a story pole, transfer the marks to the underlayment on the sheathing, and snap level chalklines between them.

VINYL AND METAL SIDING

These sidings, which go up quickly and easily, have similar components and installation techniques. Components are nailed through the center of the slots on their nailing flanges wherever there is a stud. Leave a space about the thickness of a playing card under each nail head to allow for expansion.

First install a level starter strip along the bottom of each wall, and install either undersill or soffit trim at the tops of the walls. Next nail up inside and outside corner posts; be sure to get them plumb. Add J-channel around windows, doors, and all other openings. Put the channel over flashing across the tops of these openings.

Cut a strip of siding to length, snap its bottom edge over the starter strip, and slip one end into a corner post; then nail through the slots in the flange. The next course will hook over the edge of the nailing flange, and so on, up the wall. At joints between strips in a course, cut off the nailing flange at the end of one piece to allow the exposures of the strips to overlap 1 inch. Nail a backer plate behind each joint in aluminum siding. Stagger joints at least 4 feet between courses. Notch strips as necessary to fit around openings and into the trim. In the last course, cut off the top of the strip so it can slip into the trim there, then snap the bottom edge into place.

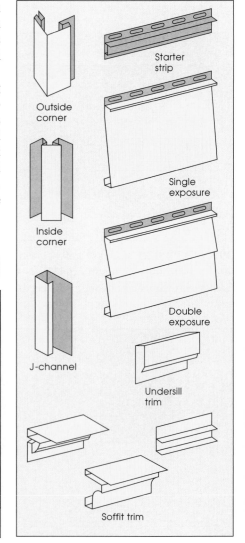

METAL AND VINYL SIDING COMPONENTS are similar. Strips have single- or double-exposure profiles.

PREPARING FOR LAP SIDING INSTALLATION

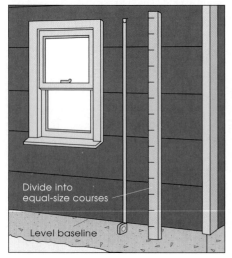

Divide into equal-size courses

Level baseline

MAKE A STORY POLE marked with the course spacing. Use this method for siding with a variable overlap.

Chalkline

MARK THE COURSES ON THE WALL. Transfer marks from the story pole and snap chalklines between them.

WOOD LAP SIDING

The major techniques for installing wood lap siding are shown below. Before installation, after the material has been at the site for a few days, prime all sides, edges, and end cuts of the siding boards and the trim. This will limit moisture absorption and consequent expansion and contraction, which could open joints and lead to further problems. Be sure the primer will be compatible with the final coat.

Install inside and outside corner trim if any, and flashing, as needed. Then nail a level base course all along the bottom. With bevel (clapboard) siding, first nail a strip of ³⁄₈-inch-thick lath along the bottom edge to give the first course the proper slant.

Nail up succeeding courses. Use your chalklines as a guide, but also check each course with a level. Place nails as illustrated for various kinds of siding, spacing them to go into studs behind the sheathing. For clear or unfinished siding, use ring-shank stainless steel or high tensile strength aluminum nails. Hot-dipped galvanized nails (with blunted tips to minimize splitting) are fine for nails to be set, filled, and painted over. Use casing nails for blind-nailing, siding or box nails for face-nailing. Avoid nailing through the upper portion of the course below, and predrill for nailing at board ends. Cut ends for gable courses as shown. Caulk the ends of boards that butt against any trim.

HARDBOARD AND PLYWOOD SIDINGS

Plywood and hardboard lap sidings are installed somewhat differently than board lap sidings. The specifications for underlayment, spacing, nailing (nails are driven through both courses, and are not set), caulking, and other factors are not the same, and they have a significant effect on siding performance and life expectancy. Be sure to get detailed installation information from your supplier, the siding manufacturer, or the American Hardboard Association.

INSTALLING WOOD LAP SIDING

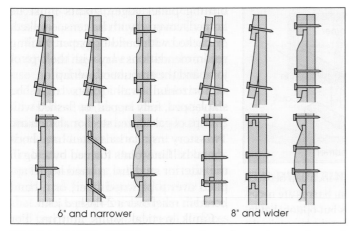

6" and narrower   8" and wider

PLACE SIDING NAILS as shown here for various styles and widths of siding. Drive nails into studs behind the sheathing. Use 8d nails for ³⁄₄-inch siding, 6d nails for thinner boards.

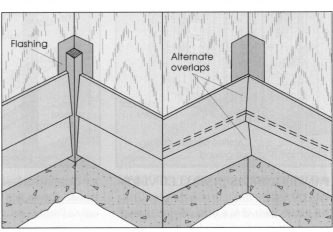

Flashing

Alternate overlaps

INSIDE CORNERS are easy with square-cut boards butting against a trim piece. For an overlap corner, work on both walls at the same time and cut each end to match the siding profile it butts against.

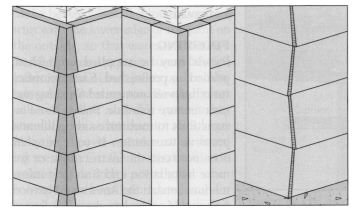

OUTSIDE CORNERS are easiest to make with metal end caps or by butting square-cut ends against trim. Alternate-overlap corners are more work but give the siding a wraparound appearance.

Cut template to gable angle

Bevel gauge

Level

AT GABLE ENDS cut each board to a slant. Use a bevel, or scribe the angle on a scrap piece to use as a template for marking boards. Measure the length of each board across the bottom edge for cutting.

REPAIRING WINDOWS AND SCREENS

Replacing a single-glazed window pane is an easy do-it-yourself job, as is repairing or replacing screening. Replacing double or triple glazing or thermal insulating glass is a professional-level task and may require an entire new sash.

REGLAZING A WOOD SASH

Besides new glass, which you can buy cut to fit at a glass or hardware store or a home center, you will need *glazing compound,* often called putty, linseed oil, and a box of *glazier's points* to secure the glass in place.

1 REMOVE THE OLD GLASS. If the glass is cracked, tape it so you can remove it in large pieces. If it has shattered, pick out loose shards with pliers and then pry out the old glazing compound. Use a putty knife or an old chisel, and if necessary soften the old compound with a heat gun or propane torch (protect the paint on the sash). Pull out the glazier's points as you uncover them.

Measure the height and width of the frame at the corners and the middle, and purchase a new pane that is ⅛ inch smaller in each direction.

2 PREPARE THE SASH. Carefully scrape the sash rabbets clean, then paint them with linseed oil to seal the wood so it will not absorb oil from the glazing compound. Wait 20 minutes, then apply a thin bed of new glazing compound to the rabbets.

3 FIT THE GLASS IN PLACE, centering it to get equal space all around. Press the edges lightly to compress the compound. Place glazier's points on the glass and press them into the wood with a putty knife. Space the points 4 to 6 inches apart.

4 SEAL WITH GLAZING COMPOUND. Roll glazing compound between your palms to form a ⅜-inch-diameter rope, and press the rope into place around the edges of the glass. Smooth the compound by drawing a putty knife along the edge, with the blade at a 30- to 40-degree angle to the glass. If compound sticks to the knife, wipe the blade with linseed oil. Let the compound dry for a week, then paint it, overlapping onto the glass by about ¹⁄₁₆ inch for a tight seal. Do not break this seal when you scrape the glass clean.

REGLAZING METAL SASHES

Some metal sashes hold the glass in rabbeted grooves with special spring clips (see illustration, next page). After removing the old glass and compound, sand the rabbets in the sash clean and prime them to prevent rust. Then clip the glass in place and seal it with a glazing compound made especially for steel windows.

Combination windows and doors typically have aluminum or steel sashes that can be dismantled for reglazing. Remove the screws or clips at the corners, pull apart the frame, and remove the broken glass and the vinyl or rubber gasket that seals the edges. You may be able to reuse the gasket, but it is best to get a new one when you buy the glass. Fit the gasket onto the glass edges, fit the pane into the frame, and reassemble the corners.

> **CAUTION**
> • Wear work gloves to handle glass and metal screening.
> • Wear safety goggles.
> • Dispose of broken glass safely.

1. REMOVE THE BROKEN GLASS, old glazing compound, and glazier's points. Protect your hands with gloves.

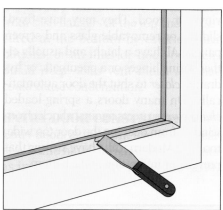

2. PREPARE THE SASH. Scrape the sash rabbets to bare wood and prime with linseed oil. Apply a thin bed of glazing compound.

3. FIT THE GLASS IN PLACE. Press it into the compound and secure it with glazier's points every 4 to 6 inches.

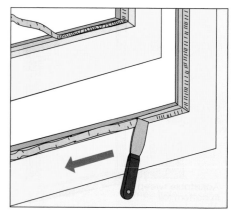

4. SEAL WITH GLAZING COMPOUND. Press a rope of compound into place. Smooth it to a bevel with a putty knife.

MENDING SCREENS

To repair a very small hole in fiberglass, plastic, or metal screening, simply daub the spot with clear silicone glue. This may require several applications; allow the glue to dry between applications.

Mend a larger hole with a piece of identical screening material. Use scissors to cut a plastic or fiberglass patch slightly larger than the damaged area. Affix this to the screen with clear silicone glue.

Use snips to cut metal screening. First cut the hole into a square shape, then cut a patch that is about 2 inches larger overall. Unravel a half-inch of the mesh on all sides of the patch and bend the strands 90 degrees. Fit the ends through holes around the cutout and fold them flat on the other side.

REPLACING METAL-FRAME SCREENING

Plastic, aluminum, or rubber splines are wedged into a groove around the edges of a metal frame to lock screening in place. Pry up the ends of the splines with a screwdriver, peel them out, and pull the old screening free.

Purchase new screening, a roll of splining, and an inexpensive *spline roller*. Cut a piece of screening the same size as the frame's outside dimensions. Center the piece over the frame, then use the convex wheel on the spline roller to force the screening into the groove along one of the frame's shorter sides. Next, cut a length of splining, lay it on top of the groove, and use the concave wheel to press it into place. Pull the screening taut and repeat this process on the opposite side. Then do the same on the two longer sides. Trim off excess screening with a utility knife.

REPLACING WOOD-FRAME SCREENING

Carefully pry off the molding around the edges of the screening and remove the nails or staples holding the screening to the frame.

Place the frame on a flat surface with a ¾-inch-thick wood strip under each end rail. Clamp the stiles at their midpoints to bow the frame downward. Staple screening to the top rail, pull it taut, and staple to the bottom rail. Remove the clamps and staple the screening to one stile, then the other. Replace the molding and trim off excess screening with a utility knife.

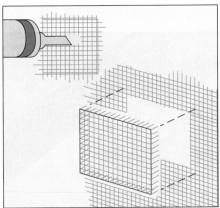

METAL SASHES with permanently assembled frames use spring clips and a metal-compatible glazing compound *(left)* to hold glass in place. Frames that can be disassembled use gaskets that fit over the edges of the glass *(right)*.

MEND SCREENS by sealing punctures with clear cement, or by cementing or weaving a patch in place.

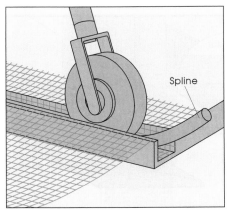

SECURE SCREENING IN A METAL FRAME with splines in the sash channels. Use a spline roller.

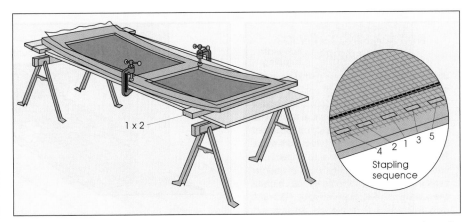

BOW A WOOD FRAME with wood strips and C clamps. Staple screening to one end, working from the center outward, then to the other end. Release the clamps so the frame will straighten out and pull the screening taut. Then staple the sides in the same sequence.

REPLACING A PATIO DOOR

A modern replacement patio door system has multiple glazing, low-E coatings (see page 230), tight-fitting seals, and thermal breaks between interior and exterior surfaces of its aluminum frame. It offers a way to greatly upgrade a home's energy efficiency, and two people can install one in a weekend or less.

First decide what kind of door you want. Sliding doors have a movable *vent panel* and one or more fixed panels. Patio French doors have one or two hinged panels that usually swing inward. There are also sliding doors that are styled to look like French doors.

Before ordering a new patio door system, pry off the interior casing around the existing door and measure the rough opening that the existing door is fastened to: header above, rough sill below, and trimmer studs on each side. Order a replacement unit to fit. With most sliding doors you can install the vent panel to slide to left or right, as you prefer. With French doors you must specify whether they should swing out or in when you order the unit.

Door systems are supplied with specific installation instructions. The following typical steps give an overview of installing a relatively inexpensive unit.

Some more expensive units are shipped with the frame assembled and doors held firmly in place. The entire unit is set in the opening, and secured when it is plumb and square.

1 ASSEMBLE THE FRAME. Lay out the frame components on a flat surface. Attach the side jambs to the head jamb and the sill. With some units you also install the fixed sash at this time.

2 REMOVE THE OLD DOOR. Lift out the old vent sash and pry off all remaining trim. Remove the nails or screws that hold the fixed sash in place and lift it out. Then remove the screws and nails that hold the frame in the rough opening and pry it free.

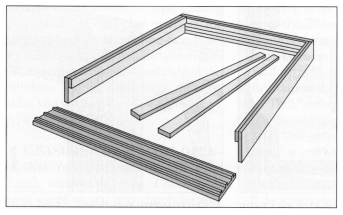

1. ASSEMBLE THE FRAME on a flat surface. Connect the side jambs to the head jamb and the sill to the side jambs. With some systems you also install the fixed sash when you put the frame together.

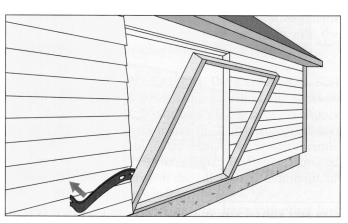

2. REMOVE THE OLD DOOR. Take off all the trim and remove the panels. In a sliding door, lift the movable panel out, then unmount the fixed panel. Finally, unfasten the frame and pry it free.

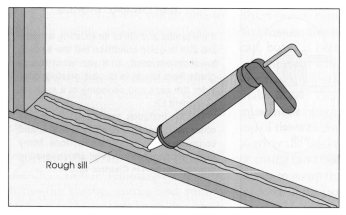

Rough sill

3. PREPARE THE OPENING. Clean the framing, scraping away all old caulking and pulling nails or driving them below the surface. Then get the rough sill level and lay down two beads of caulking.

4. FIT THE FRAME into the opening, bottom first. This is a two-person job. Set the sill onto the caulking; do not slide it. Raise the unit by the side jambs and get the mounting flanges against the framing.

3 PREPARE THE OPENING. Remove all old shims, nails, and caulking in the opening. The opening must be plumb and square, and the rough sill must be absolutely level for the doors to operate properly. Level it with shims, if necessary, then apply parallel beads of silicone or latex caulking to the sill across the width of the opening.

4 FIT THE FRAME INTO PLACE. You will need a helper to keep the frame from twisting out of shape. First slip the sill into position, then lift the side jambs to tip the unit into place.

5 SQUARE THE FRAME. Center the frame in the opening and screw the sill to the floor. Hold a level against first the edge, then the face of each side jamb and plumb it both ways by inserting shims between the jamb and stud. Check whether the frame is square by making diagonal measurements between opposite corners; they must be exactly equal. If not, reshim the jambs. Unequal measurements mean the frame is out of square, which will cause a door to bind. Do not shim the head jamb.

6 FASTEN THE FRAME. When the frame is absolutely square, drive galvanized fasteners through the holes in the mounting flange around the frame. Some systems call for nails, others for screws. Once the frame is secure, cut off any protruding shims.

7 INSTALL THE DOORS. Hang French doors according to the instructions supplied with the unit. With sliding doors, install the fixed panel as directed. Then fit the sliding panel into the top track, lift it up, and engage it with the bottom track.

8 COMPLETE THE INSTALLATION. If a sliding door does not move smoothly, raise or lower it by turning the adjustment screw located near the leading edge. Caulk and install trim around the exterior. From inside, fill the gaps between the frame, studs, and header with fiberglass or aerosol foam insulation. Then reinstall the casing on the interior.

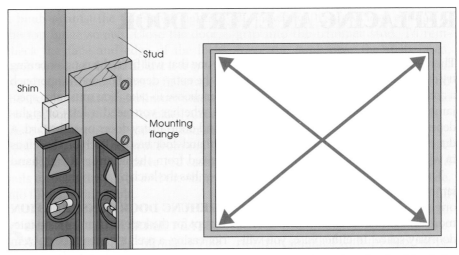

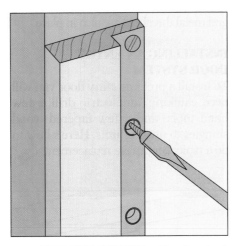

5. SQUARE THE FRAME with shims between the side jambs and studs. Check both the side and face edges of each jamb with a level. Then measure the diagonals: if they are equal, the frame is square; if not, adjust.

6. FASTEN THE FRAME with galvanized nails or screws, as specified in the instructions. Do not bow a frame member.

7. INSTALL THE DOORS. Secure the fixed panel first, then mount the sliding or hinged door in the frame.

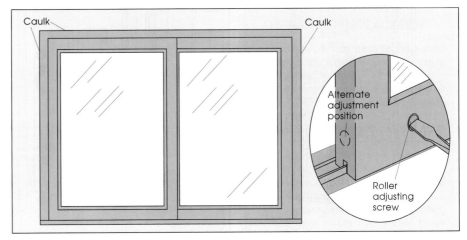

8. COMPLETE THE INSTALLATION by checking the door movement and making adjustments as required. Then install and caulk the exterior trim, insulate around the frame, and replace the interior casing moldings.

REPLACING A PATIO DOOR

26 GARAGE DOORS AND OPENERS

Garages are constructed in the same way as houses, and many are an integral part of the house, separated by only a fire-resistant wall and a passage door that is weather-stripped to keep cold air and fumes out of living areas. This chapter focuses on what is unique to a garage: the door through which cars enter and exit from the garage, and openers—the mechanisms that move the door up and down.

GARAGE DOOR CONSTRUCTION

Old garages commonly had two doors hinged on opposite edges and opening outward to either side. Most modern garages have doors that open upward, of either sectional or swing-up design.

A *sectional garage door* consists of four or five horizontal panels hinged together. *Roller hinges* at the sides of the door move along *tracks* mounted to the side jambs and to the garage ceiling. A *lock* at the center of the door operates a pair of *bars* that slide into strike openings in the jamb tracks. Some locks have a cable-and-spring system instead of bars. A sectional door is counterbalanced by one of the systems shown on the next page.

A *swing-up garage door* has a single panel with a pair of rollers at the top corners. As the bottom of the door is pulled out and up, the rollers glide along tracks attached to the garage ceiling. Springs connected to brackets at the edges of the door and on the jambs counterbalance the door. A swing-up door has the same kind of lock arrangements found on sectional doors.

Older doors are commonly made of wood. Newer garage doors are of steel, aluminum, or fiberglass construction. The panels of *noninsulated doors,* meant for unheated garages, usually have a heavy-gauge steel frame covered on the outside with preprimed and painted sheet metal. *Insulated doors* typically consist of wood stiles and rails, a thick polystyrene core, and steel, aluminum, or fiberglass facings inside and out. Good quality insulated sectional doors also have gaskets along the interlocking edges of the sections.

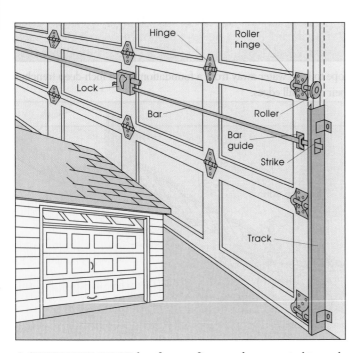

A SECTIONAL DOOR has four or five panels connected to each other with hinges. Rollers at the edge hinges fit into a track. A lock at the center moves bars that engage strikes in the tracks.

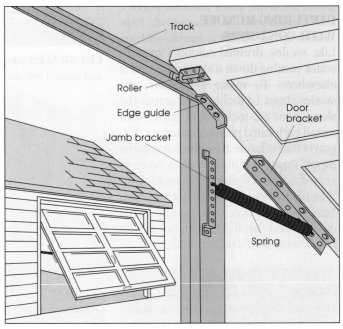

A SWING-UP DOOR is a single panel that moves on rollers along an overhead track. Springs at the sides assist in raising the door and slow its descent.

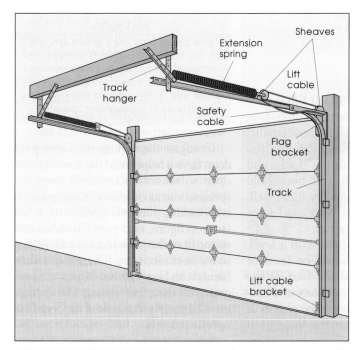

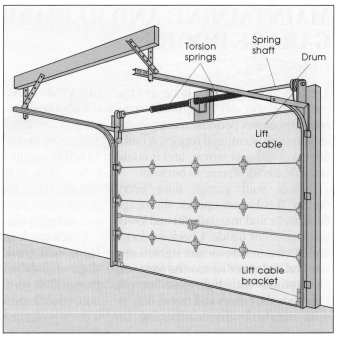

EXTENSION SPRING LIFTS use a pair of springs above the ceiling tracks connected to the door via cables and a system of pulley-like sheaves. A safety cable through each spring restrains the spring if it should break.

A TORSION SPRING LIFT uses energy from a pair of tightly wound springs that rotate a bar with drums at each end. The lift cables roll up around the drums to raise the door. As it is lowered the springs are rewound to full tension.

LIFTING MECHANISMS

Sectional doors are counterbalanced with either extension springs or torsion springs. *Extension springs* are located above each top track, with one end of each spring attached to the *track hanger* and the other to a *sheave. Lift cables* fastened to brackets at the bottom edge of the door pass up over sheaves at the top of the jambs, loop around the sheaves at the springs, and return to fasten to *flag brackets* on the jambs. As the door is lifted, the springs contract to provide an assist. Cable safety restraints strung through the springs prevent injury should a spring break.

A *torsion spring* lifting mechanism mounts on the door's head jamb. A pair of springs rotate a *spring shaft* that spans the opening. As the door is lifted, tension from the springs wraps the lift cables around drums at the ends of the shaft.

GARAGE DOOR OPENERS

Today's electric garage door openers may not only pull doors up and down; some can also operate selected lights inside or outside the house for convenience and safety.

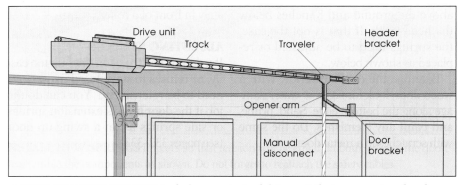

A GARAGE DOOR OPENER includes a motorized drive unit that moves a traveler along a track. The traveler attaches to a bracket near the top of the door. A safety mechanism reverses the descent if anything blocks the opening.

The heart of an opener is its *drive unit,* which hangs from the garage ceiling about 11 feet from the doorway. A signal from a hand-held or car-mounted remote control, or from a switch inside or outside the garage or house activates the drive unit and turns on a light, which can also be operated with a pull switch. A *sensitivity selector* adjusts the pressure needed to activate the opener's *safety reverse,* which automatically reverses the drive unit should the door encounter resistance on its way down.

The drive unit draws a *traveler* connected to a *door bracket* along a *track* that extends from the drive unit to a *header bracket* mounted over the top of the door opening. Pulling on a *manual disconnect* cord disengages the traveler so you can operate the door by hand if necessary.

Most openers move the traveler along the track with a *chain drive;* others have a plastic tape in place of a chain. Another type, a *screw drive* opener, turns a threaded rod inside the track.

INSTALLING A GARAGE DOOR

Replacing an old garage door with a new sectional unit can be accomplished by a couple of do-it-yourselfers in a day or so. Like door openers, sectional doors are sold in kits that include predrilled panels, tracks, hinges, lifting mechanisms, and all other necessary hardware, along with complete installation instructions. You first assemble the panels in the opening, then install the tracks and lift mechanisms.

PRELIMINARIES

When you unpack your door kit, check the contents against the parts list to make sure nothing is missing; be sure that the instructions are there, too. Familiarize yourself with the names of the parts and examine the door sections. They usually are numbered: #1 goes at the bottom; #2 is next (it is predrilled for the lock, if you are installing one); one or more #3 sections follow; and #4 goes at the top. Assemble the tools called for, then go to work. The following steps are typical.

1 PREPARE THE OPENING. If the old door has an *extension spring* lift mechanism, dismantle it (see pages 334–335). CAUTION: *If there is a torsion spring lift, have a specialist unwind the springs—do not attempt it yourself.* Then lower the door—this is a two-person job; the door is heavy—and take it apart. If it is a sectional door, start at the top. Unscrew the hinges and lift each section out of the vertical tracks. Finally, remove the tracks and pry off the old stop molding.

Check the opening measurements to be sure that the new door will fit properly, with the clearances for the side tracks and headroom above the top tracks specified by the manufacturer. Also use a level and framing square to ensure that the back jambs at the sides of the opening and header across the top are plumb, level, and square.

Some sectional door kits include vinyl stop molding that helps weatherstrip the door. Install this as directed. If the door does not come with stops, nail 1 × 3 furring strips to the jambs according to the instructions.

2 ASSEMBLE THE BOTTOM SECTION. Set section #1 on edge, upside down. Install weather stripping along the bottom edge, and loosely bolt cable brackets to the bottom corners. Attach the ends of lift cables to these brackets and set the section into the door opening, right side up.

3 LEVEL THE BOTTOM SECTION. Center the bottom section in the opening so that it overlaps the back jambs equally on either side. Place a level on top of the section and adjust the corner brackets until it is level. Tighten bolts on the brackets. To temporarily hold the section in place, partially drive a 16-penny nail into the rear of the jamb at each end, then clinch the nail by bending it at a 90-degree angle. Use clinched nails to keep each section in place during installation until the door is secured in the tracks.

4 INSTALL THE REMAINING SECTIONS. Set the second section on top of the first, center it, and clinch nails at either side. Do the same with the other sections. Then attach roller hinges at the ends of each joint between sections and intermediate hinges midspan along each joint. Follow the numbers on the hinges. Also attach roller brackets in the holes near the upper corners of the top panel. Use an electric drill/driver to speed up installing the dozens of sheet metal screws into predrilled holes. If the door is 15 feet or more wide, the instructions may also call for fastening a truss across the top of the uppermost section.

After all the hinges are in place, insert rollers into the roller hinges, into the roller brackets on the top panel, and into the cable brackets at the bottom corners. If the door will have a lock, install it in section #2 now. Also screw a lift handle or a bracket for a pull rope to the inside of the bottom section and tie the rope to it.

5 INSTALL THE TWO VERTICAL TRACKS. Preassemble the vertical tracks by fastening mounting brackets to them. If the door will have a lock, bolt the strike for each side to its track at this time.

Set each track in position over the rollers and rotate it so that the mounting brackets are against the back jambs. The tops of the tracks should be at equal distance from the top of the door opening. Check to be sure there is a ⅝- to ⅞-inch space between the edge of the door and the track over the full length of each track. Temporarily nail the brackets in place, then drill pilot holes and drive lag screws to secure them.

6 MOUNT THE FLAG BRACKET ASSEMBLIES. Lay out the flag brackets, horizontal support angles, and curved horizontal tracks on the garage floor and bolt them together. Fit these assemblies over the top hinge rollers, supporting the rear of the horizontal track on a stepladder, and check with a level to be sure the flag brackets are plumb. Temporarily nail the flag brackets to the jambs, drill pilot holes, and secure the brackets with lag screws.

7 HANG THE TWO HORIZONTAL TRACKS. Level each track and measure the distance from the track to the nearest overhead joist. Cut a piece of perforated angle iron to length, bolt it to the rear of the track, then secure it to an exposed joist or to an angle iron attached to joists through a finished ceiling, according to the instructions.

8 CHECK DOOR CLEARANCE AND ALIGNMENT. Remove the clinched nails that were driven to hold the door sections in place, then raise the door to a height of 4 feet. Prop it open with 2 × 4s or chock the door with locking pliers or C-clamps fastened to each side track. Because the door is heavy and not yet counterbalanced, you will need two people for this operation.

Level the bottom of the door and measure the clearance between the sides and the vertical and horizontal tracks. This should be ⅝ to ⅞ inch. If it is not, lower the door and adjust the track brackets or hangers to provide the proper clearance.

After you are satisfied that the tracks are properly aligned, install diagonal braces at each hanger so that the alignment will not shift. Recheck all bolts and screws to ensure that they are snug.

INSTALL THE LIFT MECHANISM

Mount the extension springs, sheaves, and lift and safety cables that help move the door, as shown on page 335. If the door you have purchased has a torsion spring lift, assemble and install its mechanism according to directions from the manufacturer, then hire a professional to tension it.

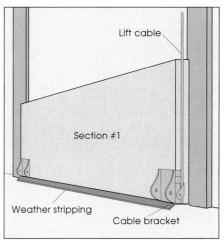

1. PREPARE THE OPENING. Remove the old door and lift, then check these measurements against the new door's specifications.

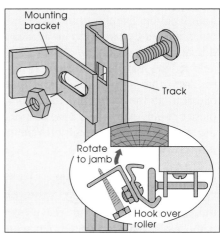

2. ASSEMBLE THE BOTTOM SECTION. Attach weather stripping, brackets, and lift cables, then set in place.

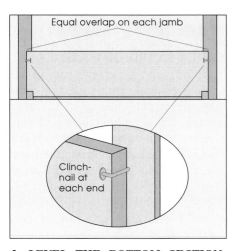

3. LEVEL THE BOTTOM SECTION. Adjust and tighten the corner brackets. Then clinch-nail the section in position.

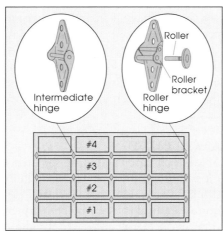

4. INSTALL THE REMAINING SECTIONS. Clinch-nail them, then attach the hinges and insert the rollers.

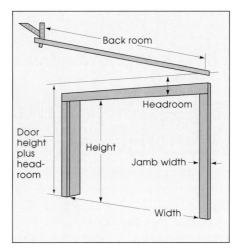

5. INSTALL THE VERTICAL TRACKS. Bolt on the brackets; put in position as shown. Secure with lag screws.

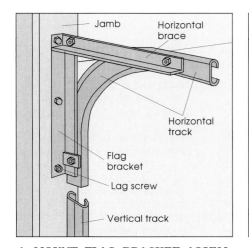

6. MOUNT FLAG BRACKET ASSEMBLIES. Fit each assembly on top of the vertical track; lag-screw to the back jambs.

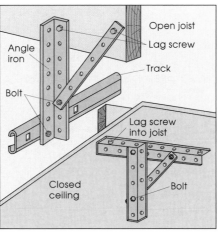

7. HANG THE HORIZONTAL TRACKS. Bolt angle irons to the tracks and secure as shown.

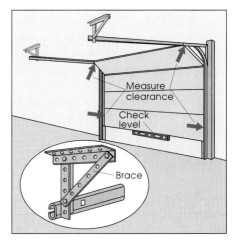

8. CHECK CLEARANCES AND ALIGNMENT. When they are correct, add diagonal braces to the track hangers.

INSTALLING A DOOR

27 EXTERIOR PAINTING

Exterior painting has three major features: it is easy, necessary, and valuable. Nothing can so quickly and simply make a major change in the appearance of your home. More fundamentally, keeping the exterior finish in good condition is basic and essential maintenance. From a financial standpoint, a good-looking exterior adds significantly to the value of a home. The amount you may invest in paint, brushes, and other supplies will be only a fraction of the increased value. For these reasons, exterior painting is one of the most satisfying home-improvement projects you can tackle.

CHOOSING THE COATING

When you decide to paint your home, the first step is selecting the proper paint. While color is a matter of personal taste, the kind of paint to use may be dictated by the type of surface to be painted.

Most exterior surfaces can be painted with either latex (water-based) or alkyd (oil-based) paint. Both kinds are available in versions to produce a flat, semigloss, or gloss finish. For specific applications, there are several specialty products. These include oil-based concrete "floor" paints, oil- or water-based exterior stains, and metallic and bituminous paints.

LATEX PAINTS

Vinyl-acrylic water-based latex paints are the best choice for exterior use because they can be applied to almost any surface, they bond and clean up easily, and they dry quickly, so a second coat can be applied in just a few hours. They have superior color quality, which is maintained by a resistance to fading from exposure to the ultraviolet rays in sunlight. In addition, latex paints "breathe" well to allow moisture to evaporate. This means they can be applied over slightly damp surfaces without trapping the moisture, which could otherwise cause problems with the paint finish or the underlying material.

The only serious disadvantages are that latex paints hold up poorly to vigorous cleaning, such as scrubbing, and they stain more readily than do oil-based paints.

ALKYD PAINTS

Alkyd or oil-based paints are somewhat more difficult to work with than latex paints because thinning and cleanup require a natural solvent such as turpentine, or a petroleum-based product. They also tend to lock in moisture. In addition, an alkyd finish is more rigid than latex paints, which can cause it to chip or crack on surfaces such as masonry that expand and contract significantly with weather and temperature changes. They also may fade more over time than latex paints.

Alkyds do offer a great deal of protection against the elements, especially when used on such items as wood trim and metal railings or grillwork—their most common exterior applications.

OTHER EXTERIOR FINISHES

Concrete paint, sometimes called floor or deck enamel, can be used on most masonry surfaces and on some woods as well. It is an oil-based enamel that penetrates the surface and provides a protective barrier against dirt and staining. It is most often used on garage floors, driveways, walkways, and patios.

Stains for exterior use are usually intended for use on wood siding or shingles. There are both "natural" stains—which are essentially clear sealers—and pigmented stains with either a latex base or an oil base. Solid-color pigmented stains are close in effect to paints, because they cover the surface with an

SELECTING AN EXTERIOR PAINT

PAINT TYPE	DRYING TIME*	APPLICATIONS
Alkyd	24	Trim, pipes, ironwork, foundation masonry, wood
Latex	4	Wood and metal siding, masonry, stucco, composition shingles, trim
Concrete	8–24	Patios, workroom floors, garage floors, masonry
Metallic	8	Metal surfaces, decorative metalwork
Bituminous	10–24	Gutters, pipes, exterior tanks

*Hours between coats. Touch-dry time is typically half as long.

opaque color; however, they do not conceal the texture of the wood as paints generally do. Transparent pigmented stains add some color to the surface but allow the texture, the grain pattern, and to some degree the natural color of the wood to be seen.

Metallic paints, with particles of aluminum or other metals, are high-gloss products that bond well with metal surfaces such as porch roofs or pipes. They are durable and are applied in the same way as alkyds. (Many nonmetallic paints can be applied to metal surfaces that are painted with an appropriate primer.)

Bituminous paints are durable, utilitarian coverings for pipes and other functional metal surfaces such as the insides of gutters. Usually black, this type of paint is considered to be an industrial product and is used more for protection than appearance.

PRIMING

Exterior surfaces on which the existing paint is stable and that are free of dirt or stains do not usually need a preparatory coat of primer. However, that is not the case with surfaces such as masonry or wood that has not been painted before, and metal or vinyl siding with a deteriorated finish. All of these require a primer coat for the best results.

To select a primer, follow the recommendations of the siding manufacturer or those on the label of the paint you have chosen for the finish coat. In some cases, a thinned coat of the same paint is called for. Usually, however, it is best to use a separate primer. If there is no specific recommendation, choose one that matches the type of finish coat: latex for latex, alkyd for alkyd.

SAFETY OUTSIDE

Exterior painting is generally safer than interior work with regard to unrestricted ventilation. However, you still need to protect your eyes with goggles, and your hair and skin with a hat, gloves, and appropriate clothing. Be sure to wear nonslip shoes. If you will be working on a ladder or scaffold, read pages 58–61 carefully.

EXTERIOR PAINT COVERAGE

Paint coverage is figured in square feet per gallon. To determine the square footage of the area you must cover, multiply the height of each wall by its width. Do not subtract window, door, or vent openings unless the wall has multiple large picture windows or glass doors; the difference is usually minimal.

On average, a gallon of exterior latex or alkyd paint applied with a brush will cover 400 square feet of prepainted wood or stucco surface; 200–300 square feet of shakes or rough wood; and 100–150 square feet of unfinished masonry. Most stains will cover 250–350 square feet of relatively smooth wood and 150–250 of rough wood. For application with a spray gun, coverage with any finish is about half as much.

These figures are only general guidelines; check the label of the paint you are using for more specific coverage data. More expensive, top-quality paints have the best coverage because they have the greatest percentage of pigment per gallon of liquid. Cheap paints often require two coats for a good appearance, making them less of a bargain.

To ensure uniformity, buy enough for the entire job at one time. Get 5 to 10 percent extra to avoid interrupting your work, and to have paint for touch-up when needed.

TROUBLESHOOTING EXTERIOR PAINT PROBLEMS

PROBLEM	APPEARANCE	CAUSE	TREATMENT
Blisters, bubbles	Unsightly raised areas pulling away from surface	Surface moisture in wood under blister, or soft paint trapped under sun-dried skin	Cut open blister; remove source of moisture; ventilate and dry area. Sand, repaint out of direct sun.
Wrinkles	Downward puckers	First coat too thick	Sand; repaint with a thinner coat.
Alligatoring	Patterned checking and cracking of surface	Improper surface preparation or primer	Scrape off loose flakes; fill severely textured areas. Sand smooth, repaint.
Peeling	Pieces and strips curling, falling off surface	Contaminant under paint	Peel and scrape away all loose paint. Sand. Repaint wood with latex; apply sealer to masonry, then repaint.
Bleeding	Knots or grain imperfections showing through surface finish	Resin in knots or grain pockets	Sand, seal with 2 lb-cut shellac (see page 96), repaint.
Chalking	Surface looks powdery, chalky	Paint deterioration with age	Scrub or pressure-wash thoroughly (see pages 294–296), then repaint.
Staining	Rust runs or spots	Nails or fasteners corroding, leaching	Sand stained areas; countersink fasteners; fill and sand. Repaint.
Efflorescence	White deposits or irregular lifting and peeling	Compounds leaching out of mortar, masonry	Scrub with dilute muriatic acid solution, neutralize, rinse thoroughly (see pages 295, 342). Apply masonry sealer, then repaint.

PREPARATION FOR PAINTING

Before applying a coat of paint, you absolutely must prepare the surface properly. Paint applied over a well-prepared surface may quite possibly hold up for a decade; paint on a poorly prepared surface is likely to require renewal or repair in as little as two years.

WASHING THE SURFACE

Different surfaces require different cleansing techniques, but just about any surface can be washed by hand or with a rented power washer. Washing equipment and techniques are covered in detail on pages 294–296. Whether you use hand or power methods, be sure to wear goggles to protect your eyes from splashes and spray, even with plain water. Gloves, a hat, and waterproof clothing are primarily a matter of comfort—staying dry—when using plain water. They are essential protection if you are using water with anything added to it, or are using a commercial cleaning solution.

Chalkiness on the surface of paint can usually be removed by scrubbing with a brush and a mild detergent solution, then rinsing. Eliminate mildew and efflorescence as explained on page 294. When you use a dilute acid solution (as for efflorescence), a water rinse is sufficient if you are just cleaning the surface. But if you plan to repaint, neutralize the acid by rinsing the surface with a solution of one cup of nonsudsing ammonia per gallon of water, then rinse with plain water.

To remove oil and grease from concrete or masonry, first soak up the excess with sawdust, old rags, or other absorbent material (dispose of it safely). Then scrub the area with a solution of trisodium phosphate (TSP), about one cup of crystals dissolved in each gallon of hot water. Use a wire or stiff bristle brush, and wear goggles and rubber gloves. Finish by rinsing thoroughly with plain water.

REMOVING PAINT

In some cases you may need to strip deteriorated paint. If the paint is over ten years old, it probably contains lead and perhaps other toxic metals. It should be removed with a bonding chemical stripper, one that combines with the dangerous substances. Check with your paint supplier for a recommended product.

In other cases, use heat to soften the paint so you can scrape it off, or use a power sander. If you choose heat stripping, a flat electric heat plate is the safest tool for exterior use (see box).

Although a disk sander is best (you can rent one), a belt sander (see page 46) can help in removing old paint or breaking the gloss of existing paint so a new coat will adhere properly. For paint removal, start with a coarse grit belt, then go back over the area with a medium grit. Use medium grit to break surface gloss. Sand along the length of siding or trim, not across the width. To remove paint from metalwork, use abrasive disks or other accessories in an electric drill (see page 42). Wear safety goggles, gloves, and a respirator when using any of these tools.

For more information about chemical and physical methods of removing paint, see pages 90–91. Remember that wherever paint removal exposes bare wood or metal, you must paint the surface with a compatible primer before applying a finish coat.

CAULKING, GLAZING, FILLING

Before painting, replace any dried-out or missing caulking in joints and glazing compound in windows (see pages 297 and 316). Nail down any loose boards. Set all new or popped nail heads, and fill and spot-prime them.

> **CAUTION**
> The blast from a propane torch or an electric heat gun can easily drive superheated air and glowing particles of paint into cracks between strips of siding or around trim, where they could ignite accumulated dust and exposed wood. Whatever heat source you use, keep a fire extinguisher or garden hose at hand, and watch where scraped-off globs of hot paint will fall. Wear goggles, gloves, and a respirator, not just a dust mask.

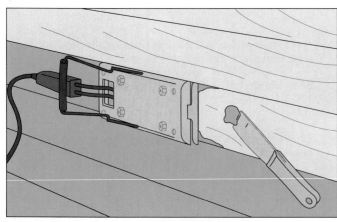

REMOVING PAINT WITH HEAT is safest with an electric plate rather than a torch or heat gun. Move it slowly, close to the surface, following right after with a paint scraper.

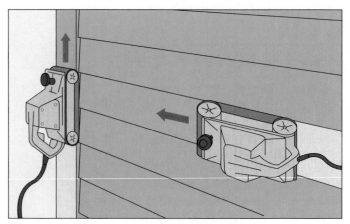

USE A SANDER to remove loose or badly deteriorated paint, or to break the surface gloss of paint in better condition. Sand along the length of each piece, not across the width.

PAINTING SIDING

Of the many exterior surface materials, the three common types of siding—aluminum, vinyl, and wood strips—are the easiest to paint. This is because they are, by and large, straight and smooth.

Aluminum and vinyl siding are installed prepainted. Although the color is an integral part of the siding, with time and weathering the surface can deteriorate to the point that it needs to be refinished. Wood strip siding—clapboards and other styles (see Chapter 23)—is usually painted immediately after installation and will need to be repainted sooner than aluminum or vinyl siding.

After cleaning and preparation (see facing page), recheck that all soffits, corners, fascias, gutters, and other attachments are securely fastened.

PAINTING PROCEDURES

The painting process is the same for all types of siding. (Painting trim and other materials is covered on the following pages.) First, plan your work (see box). Second, assemble the equipment and materials you will need. Third, spread drop cloths to protect porches, sidewalks, shrubbery, and other things below the section you will be painting. Finally, apply paint to the siding in two steps as follows.

1 PAINT THE BOTTOM EDGES. Using a three- or four-inch brush, paint along the bottom edge of each course of siding within reach.

2 PAINT THE FACES. Working horizontally, from the top down, paint the faces of the courses that have been edge-painted. Check for missed spots before moving lower or shifting the position of your ladder.

You can paint siding entirely with a brush. This is the best method, because it allows you to work the paint into the surface. However, if you need to do the job quickly, paint siding edges with a brush and use a roller or paint pad the same width as a course of siding on the faces. For an even, untextured surface, use a roller or pad with a smooth nap.

You can also paint siding with a spray gun. This is the fastest method, but it gives inferior results because it deposits a thinner layer of paint. It is also messier and requires about twice as much paint. If you choose to spray paint on, work in overlapping passes, following the length of the siding. For large smooth areas, paint first in overlapping vertical passes, then with horizontal passes from the top down. For more information about spray guns and their use, see page 99.

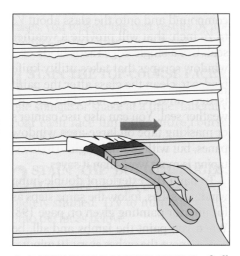

1. PAINT THE BOTTOM EDGES of all siding courses within reach first. Use a wide brush for efficiency.

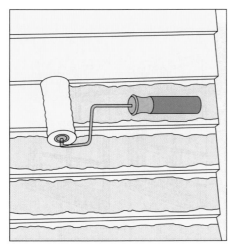

2. PAINT THE FACES of the courses from the top down. A roller or a paint pad is the least work, but a brush will do the best job.

(see page 99)

PLANNING THE JOB

Before opening a single can of paint, plan the sequence in which you will work. The best time of year is in the spring or fall, when leaves are not at full growth, but after March winds or before those of October–November.

Plan to work in dry weather, when the temperature is below 90°F. It is important to let overnight moisture or dew dry off a surface before applying paint, and not to apply paint in direct sun. Follow the sun around the house so you are always working on a shaded side that has been warmed and dried. In general, the sequence is: south-facing wall first in the morning, west wall a bit later, north wall at noon, and east wall in the afternoon. If the night will be cold, end work for the day so paint has at least two hours to set before the temperature drops below 40°F.

Work horizontally, from the top down.

Cover sections between trim pieces, such as from a corner to a window or doorway, at one time, to minimize overlap marks. On each wall, paint the siding first, the trim (including window sash) and gutters next, then railings, porches, decks, and foundations.

PAINT CAN BASICS

1. **OPEN THE LID** of a paint can with an opener designed specifically for the purpose. You can get one at paint dealers. A screwdriver will create edge dents through which air can get into the closed can.
2. **POUR OFF ABOUT ONE-THIRD OF THE PAINT** from an open can, then stir the remainder slowly, avoiding air bubbles and splashing. Most paint stores supply wooden stirrers. When the paint is thoroughly mixed, pour the first portion back in and stir well.
3. **BOX THE PAINT** to ensure uniform color. Open and stir enough cans to cover one side of the house, then pour a quantity from each can into a larger container, mix, and pour back into the original cans. Repeat this "boxing" three or four times until the contents of all the cans are well intermixed, then refill the cans and put the lids on tightly.
4. **POUR OFF A WORKING AMOUNT.** A can about two-thirds full is easier to use and move than one that is full to the brim. If there are any signs of lumps or foreign matter in the paint, strain it through cheesecloth or fine-mesh nylon.
5. **SEAL CANS COMPLETELY.** Wipe the channel in the rim with a cloth to clean out all excess paint. Then replace the lid and tap on a piece of scrap wood with a hammer to seat it securely all around.

PAINTING SIDING

BUILDING A CONCRETE WALK

Building a concrete walk is quite feasible if you take it step by step. Preparing the site and building forms are covered on these two pages. Pouring the concrete and finishing the surface and edges are covered on pages 358–359.

MARK THE SITE

The walk area will have to be excavated several inches deep, but first drive stakes at each end of the planned run and stretch strings as straight guide lines between them to mark the sides of the slab. A walk should be 3 to 5 feet wide. Use the 3–4–5 triangle method to lay out any 90-degree angles (see page 370). Lay out curves with lengths of garden hose or rope. With a spade, cut a straight line into the earth 6 inches outside each guide line to establish the edges of the trench; you need the extra width for the forms. Then temporarily remove the strings, but not the stakes.

DIG THE TRENCH

A proper subbase is essential for a sidewalk. Cracks and settling in a walk are most often due to a soft or poorly com-

pacted base or to frost heaves. The underlying soil should be well drained, free of roots, uniform, and hard. Remove loose topsoil to get to firm ground. Only in a dry, warm climate can a walk be laid directly on the excavated ground. In a cold climate, a 4-inch base of compacted gravel is needed. The walk itself should be 4 inches thick (6 inches thick where cars will drive over it), with 2 inches above grade. Dig a trench with the necessary depth between the edge lines you cut with a spade. Make the bottom level from side to side and tamp it down well. Check the depth by measuring from a board laid across the edges of the trench. Wait to add gravel until after the forms are in place.

BUILD ONE SIDE FORM

Getting the forms level, parallel, and at just the right height will be easier if you have a helper. When attaching forms to stakes, use a power screwdriver if you have one. Nailing is likely to loosen or move the stakes. Using screws makes it easy to make adjustments and disassemble the forms. Build a 2 × 4 form

along one side first. For a true 4-inch slab, the 3½-inch boards must be set ½ inch above the subbase.

Stretch the guide string between the end stakes on the first side. Lay a 2 × 4 on edge in the trench with its inner face touching the string. Drive a 1 × 2 stake against the outside face of this board near one end. Hold the 2 × 4 at the desired height and screw or nail through the stake into it. If nailing, leave the nail head protruding so later you can take the forms apart easily. Hold a sledgehammer against the inside of the form to absorb the force of nailing. Drive stakes deep enough before attaching a form board so their tops will be just below the tops of the forms.

Next, drive a stake near the other end of the form board, making sure its inner face is aligned with the guide string. Set the form at the desired height, generally following the grade, then fasten the stake to it. Butt the end of the next form board against the first, and stake and fasten it in the same way. Continue with more form boards until you reach the end of the walk. Check the height all along the form, then drive additional stakes every 4 feet and fasten them to the form boards.

PREPARING THE SITE AND BUILDING THE FORMS

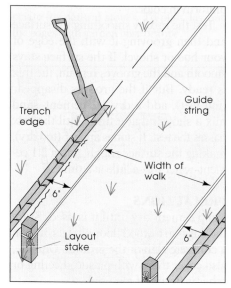

LAY OUT THE WIDTH of the walk with strings stretched between end stakes. Cut trench lines 6 inches outside each string.

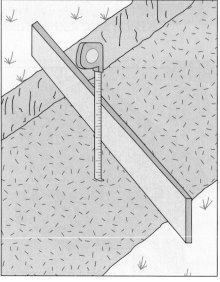

MEASURE TRENCH DEPTH from the bottom edge of a board laid across the sides of the trench.

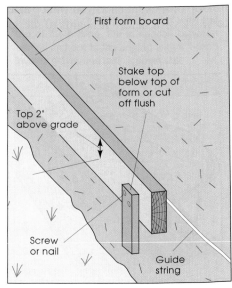

SET THE FIRST FORM BOARD against the guide string. Fasten it to a stake on the outside, top edge 2 inches above grade.

BUILD THE SECOND FORM

Stretch the guide string between the layout stakes for the other side. Drive stakes 1½ inches (the thickness of the form boards) outside the guide line, directly opposite the end stakes of each board in the first form. Remove the guide string. Rest a straight board on top of the first form at the first end stake, get it level across the width of the trench, and mark its bottom edge position on the new stake. If the walk will slope enough for good drainage from end to end, you can use this mark. Otherwise, measure down from the level mark for the required pitch from one side to the other: ¼ inch for each 1 foot of width. Use the same procedure to mark the end stakes for all the form boards in the same way. Then set the form boards in place, align their top edges with the proper marks on the stakes, and fasten them in place. Drive and fasten intermediate stakes as with the first form. Cut off any protruding stakes flush with the tops of the forms.

Once the sides are in place, fasten stop boards across both ends as needed and stake them for support. If an end will butt against masonry, make an expansion joint there. Now add a gravel base in the trench if needed, tamp it well, and cover it with 4-mil plastic sheeting to retard curing time.

LAY REINFORCEMENT

A concrete walk on soft ground needs wire mesh reinforcement to help the slab resist cracking and to hold it together if it does crack from heavy loads, ground shifts, or freezing. Use 6 × 6 10/10 wire fabric for reinforcement—10-gauge steel wire welded into a mesh of 6-inch squares. It comes in 5- and 6-foot-wide rolls and can be cut with wire or bolt cutters or with a hacksaw. Wear heavy work gloves when you work with it. Leave a 2-inch space between the mesh and the forms at all edges and at any expansion joints. During the concrete pour you will raise the mesh to the center of the slab.

PROVIDE EXPANSION JOINTS

Expansion joints prevent buckling when concrete expands with temperature changes. A walk should have an expansion joint every 15 feet or so, laid out so the spacing is consistent with the control grooves (see page 359). An expansion joint is also required wherever the walk abuts other masonry, such as a building foundation or a public sidewalk.

An expansion joint consists of a ½-inch-thick strip of asphalt-impregnated fiber between two sections of concrete; it is as deep as the slab is thick. Expansion joint filler is available in rolls so you can cut strips any length you need. Mark the joint positions on the side forms and precut strips to width. Just before you pour each section, mound some wet concrete on each side of a strip to hold it in place.

CURVED FORMS

To shape a curve, drive stakes 3 inches apart along the line of the curve. In place of rigid form boards, attach a strip or two of 1/4-inch plywood or hardboard to the insides of the stakes. The strip should be the same depth as the form. Attach cleats to the ends of the straight forms so you can fasten the curved piece flush with the form faces.

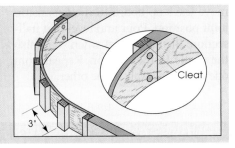

BUILDING A WALK

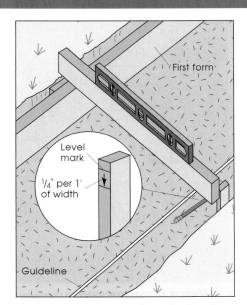

MARK LEVEL LINES from the first form to stakes for the second, then mark the drop for side-to-side drainage slope, if any.

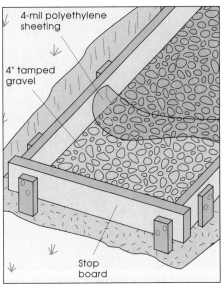

PLACE STOP BOARDS across the form ends if needed. Then pour a gravel base, tamp it well, and cover with polyethylene.

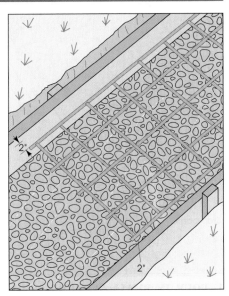

PLACE REINFORCING MESH over the base, 2 inches from the edges. Raise it to the center of the slab during the pour.

LAYING BRICKS IN SAND

In this type of patio, bricks sit on a firm bed of sand. There is a permanent edging on all sides, and sand fills the spaces between the tightly set bricks. The bricks will move a bit with changes in the weather but will remain stable. Be sure to use only SW (severe weather) grade bricks.

Setting bricks on a sand bed is the simplest way of building a patio. It takes time but requires few skills and tools, and without the pressure of rapidly curing concrete, you can work entirely at your own pace. It is also the most forgiving approach. During construction most mistakes are easily corrected because the bricks are not held in place with mortar. Over its life the patio's flexibility lets it expand and contract, rise and fall, without damage. And sections can be removed to allow design changes or planting at any later date.

Inevitably some bricks sink a bit, but they can easily be lifted out so new sand can be added and the bricks set level once again. Should a brick break or get badly stained, it can be replaced. Weed seeds will find their way into the cracks and grow into unwanted sprouts. You will have to pull them by hand or use a herbicide periodically.

PLAN PATTERN AND SIZE

Unless the dimensions of the patio area are strictly predetermined, size the patio to use whole bricks. This saves cutting (and work) and usually looks better. There are many brick patterns you can use, such as those shown on the next page. The simplest are the jack-on-jack and running patterns; more complex are the basket weave, herringbone, and related patterns. Rather than just measuring the dimensions of one brick and multiplying to calculate patio dimensions, lay out a row and column of bricks in your chosen pattern on a flat surface such as a garage floor and take measurements directly. Place the bricks touching one another.

When you know the size, lay out the boundaries of the patio with corner stakes and string. Use the 3–4–5 triangle method to get 90-degree corners (see page 370). Don't forget to allow for an edging. Mark the ground beneath the strings with sand or lime.

INSTALL EDGING

Install permanent brick, concrete, or wood edging along the borders as shown on page 353. Set the edging top at grade level or 1 to 2 inches above, as you prefer. For a large patio, wait to install the edging along two connecting edges until most of the brick has been set. Then you can check the dimensions and position the final edging accurately to accommodate full bricks.

PREPARE THE SETTING BED

Excavate the entire area within the edging to a depth of 2 inches plus one brick thickness below the top of the edging. Stretch a mason's line across the tops of the edging and measure down to check depth throughout the area. If your patio is large, install temporary guide boards that divide it into manageable sections about 8 feet wide. Set them the same height as the edging.

Lay down landscape fabric, available at nurseries and gardening centers, or 4-mil plastic sheeting that you have punctured every 5 inches to permit drainage. Pour a strip of sand about 30 inches wide along one end of a work section, to within about 2 inches of the top of the edging. Moisten the sand well with a fine spray of water to help it settle. Then accurately level (screed) the sand so it is just one brick thickness below the edging. Use a strikeoff that rests on the edging and on the section guide board or on the opposite edging. Tamp the sand down, add more and dampen it, and screed again. The sand bed must

---

HOW TO LAY BRICKS IN SAND

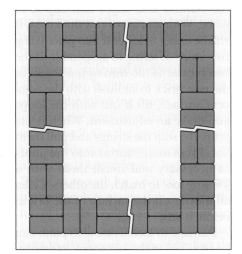

LAY OUT TRIAL COURSES to measure the patio dimensions accurately. Then install edging around the entire area.

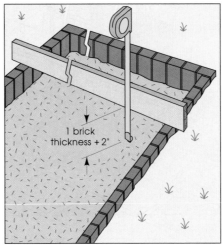

EXCAVATE THE EDGED AREA to a consistent measured depth of one brick thickness plus 2 inches for the sand bed.

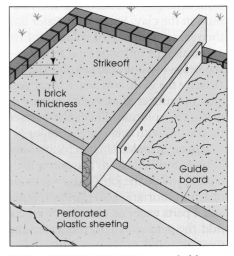

LAY A FIRM SAND BED in workable sections. Use a strikeoff as shown to make it level, one brick deep.

be firm and thick enough so that the top face of a brick will lie flush with the top of the edging.

SET THE BRICKS

Begin at one corner and lay bricks tightly against one another in your chosen pattern, one course at a time. If your pattern requires half-bricks, cut a good supply before beginning; see page 353.

When you have completed a section about 2 feet wide, brace a board against the open end of the bricks with sand or stakes. Then firmly tap down the bricks with a hand sledge on a wide, thick board. This ensures that all bricks are well seated. Stretch a mason's line from edging to edging to check for an even surface before proceeding. Build each section in the same way. If you must walk or kneel on a completed section, lay down plywood or a wide board to prevent the bricks from shifting under your weight.

When all the bricks are in place, spread sand over the surface and sweep it back and forth in all directions to push it into the joints. Spray the patio with a hose and let it dry. Repeat the process until all joints are filled to the top. The sand will settle as the patio is used, so you will have to repeat the joint-filling over the next several weeks.

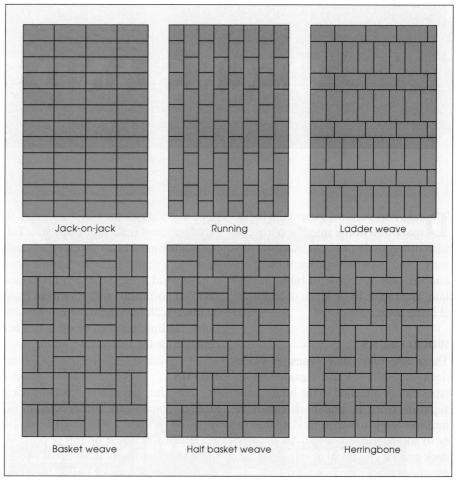

Jack-on-jack   Running   Ladder weave

Basket weave   Half basket weave   Herringbone

POPULAR PATTERNS FOR BRICK PATIOS. These are basic patterns; all except the running and herringbone patterns use full-length bricks. Many others, including diagonal and curved lines, are possible but generally require more work and brick cutting.

LAY BRICKS ON THE SAND between the edging and a guide board. Place them touching the edging and each other.

SET THE BRICKS by tapping them with a hammer and board. Set a board across the open end to keep them aligned.

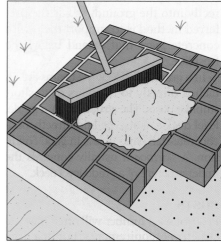

SWEEP SAND in all directions over the surface to fill the joints; wet, and let dry. Repeat until all joints are full.

BUILDING A DECK: POSTS AND BEAMS

Posts for an elevated deck must be installed plumb and all cut off at the same level. Beams must be securely attached to the posts, and level.

INSTALLING POSTS

Set a post a bit taller than needed (see below) in the base anchor on one pier and drive in one fastener. Place a level against one side, get the post plumb, and attach a temporary brace from a stake in the ground to the midpoint of the post to hold it plumb. Do the same on an adjacent side. Then drive fasteners in the other anchor base holes. Install all other posts in the same way.

Mark post height by measuring down from a level line stretched from the top of the ledger (previously installed; see page 373). If the joists will rest on the beams, and the beams on top of the posts, measure down the joist depth plus the beam depth. (If the beams are to be fastened to the sides of the posts, or the joists are to hang flush with the tops of the beams, the distance will differ; measure accordingly.) Mark each post and cut the top off with a circular saw. Once beams and headers are in place, brace the posts as needed; see pages 382–386.

INSTALLING BEAMS

For beams, use the size of lumber specified by the building code for the span between posts. Generally, for a divided beam (attached to post sides) use lumber one size larger than for a built-up beam (resting on post tops); 2 × 12s instead of 2 × 10s, for example. Beam length is full deck width, or deck width minus stringer thickness at both ends if the joists will hang flush with the beams. Sight along each piece to determine the crowned (outward curving) edge. Assemble and install beams with the crown upward.

Attach divided beams to the sides of posts with through-bolts. Or cut shoulders for the pieces to rest on and secure them with bolts or lag screws. Be sure to get them level.

Nail built-up beams together using at least three 12d or 16d nails, 32 inches on center, driven at an angle from both sides, in staggered locations. Include full-depth plywood filler pieces (flitch plates) to bring the beam to the thickness of the post. Wear safety goggles when nailing.

Attach beams on top of posts with divided post cap hardware so you can adjust to beam width. Use 12d nails. Insert shims to level the beam if necessary.

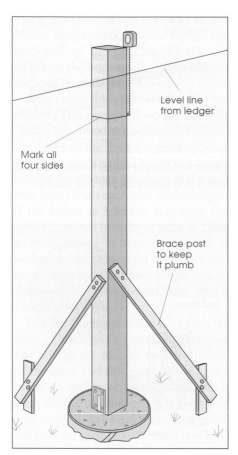

INSTALL POSTS IN BASE ANCHORS and brace them plumb. Then measure and mark each one to be cut to height.

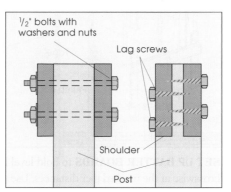

ATTACH DIVIDED BEAMS to the sides of posts with through-bolts, or with lag screws if they rest on shoulders.

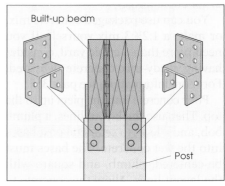

ATTACH BEAMS ON TOP OF POSTS with divided post caps, which can be adjusted to any beam thickness.

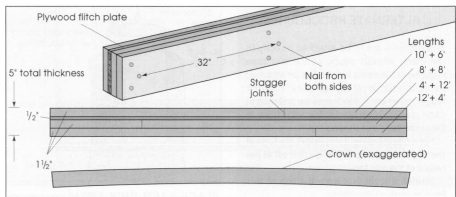

ASSEMBLE AND INSTALL BEAMS with the crowned edge upward. Use plywood flitch plates to increase thickness. Stagger joints and nail positions; nail from both sides.

FLOOR FRAMING: HEADERS AND JOISTS

Joists run at right angles to the beams. The outermost joists are called *stringers*. *Headers* run across the ends of the joists. The header attached to the house is the *ledger*. All are installed crown edge up.

LEDGER

Install the ledger before laying out the pier positions. Use the same size lumber as the joists; make its length equal to the deck width minus the thickness of the two stringers, which go outside it. Mark joist spacing on the ledger before installing it.

Fasten the ledger to the house with bolts or lag screws through the siding and into the house framing or into expansion anchors in a masonry wall. Be sure the ledger is level, and allow for the thickness of the decking above it. Use spacers or flashing to prevent rot.

STRINGERS

For long stringers, splice two pieces at a beam. Nail one piece into the end of the ledger with 12d nails. If the beam is at the same level as the ledger, for suspended joists, also nail the stringer into the end of the beam. Butt the second stringer piece against the first and nail it into both beam ends. Then install all-purpose anchors at all inside corners.

For joists supported on top of the beam, nail the first stringer piece into the ledger, make sure it is at a right angle to the ledger (triangulation method, page 371), then fasten it in place with a rafter tie-down at the beam and an all-purpose anchor at the ledger corner. Butt the second length of stringer against the first and splice them together with a metal or wood tie-plate on the inside. To get the entire stringer straight, tack wood spacers of equal thickness on the face at each end and stretch a string between them. Measure the distance from the string to the stringer at several points and adjust until all measurements are equal. Then install rafter tie-downs to the beams.

HEADER

For supported (above-beam) joists, install a doubled header, end-nailing with the stringers as shown below. Then install corner anchors.

JOISTS

Mark the joist spacing on the beams and header as on the ledger. For joists that will be overlap-spliced at a beam, shift the marked positions one joist thickness on the header. Attach joist hangers at the marked positions. Make sure they are plumb and nail just one side of each hanger now; nail the other side after the joist is in place and adjusted for final position.

Cut joists to length. Insert a joist in a hanger, get its top edge flush with the top of the ledger, beam, or header, and nail the hanger in place. Then nail through the hanger into the joist. At splices, nail the overlapped ends together. With supported joists, check the distance to the stringer for constant spacing as you install rafter tie-downs to the beams.

JOIST SPACING

The center-to-center spacing of joists depends on the decking thickness and its direction across the joists:

DECKING nominal thickness	JOIST SPACING for decking at Rt. angle	Diagonal
1"	12"	8"
5/4"	16"	12"
2"	24"	16"

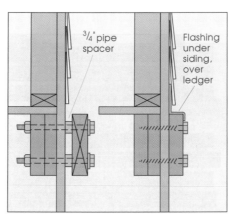

FASTEN THE LEDGER to the house framing with bolts or lag screws. Use spacers or flashing for water protection.

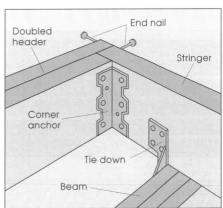

FASTEN A DOUBLED HEADER with end nails and corner anchors to stringers supported on a beam.

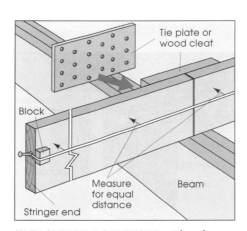

END-SPLICE A STRINGER with a cleat or tie plate on the inside. Use blocks and string to get the stringer straight.

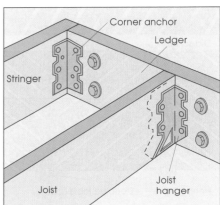

NAIL JOISTS IN HANGERS with their top edges flush with the ledger or header. Maintain proper spacing.

FLOOR FRAMING

MIXING MORTAR

Mortar is the bonding material between masonry units. It is a mix of cement, washed sand, and clean water (salty sand and salty or particle-filled water cannot be used). Lime is usually added to make mortar for laying brick or concrete block more workable and to increase its bonding power. For those materials, buy mortar cement, which includes lime (you add sand), or prepackaged dry mortar mix, which includes both lime and sand. For mortaring stones, use plain Portland cement, sand, and water; lime can cause staining.

TOOLS

You will need tools to mix and place mortar, as well as tools to lay out walls and cut or shape the bricks, blocks, or stones.

Mortar can be mixed in a power mixer, but for most home projects hand mixing will do very well. Use a heavy-duty hoe—one with two holes in its blade works best—and mix in a mortar pan or a metal wheelbarrow.

To place mortar, you need a mason's trowel and a mortarboard—a sheet of metal or exterior-grade plywood about 2 feet square—to hold a supply of mortar as you work. To fill and finish joints you will use a pointing trowel, a joint filler, and a jointer or raking tool to give joints a final contour.

To lay out and guide wall construction you will need: a carpenter's or framing square; a 50-foot measuring tape; a chalkline; a 4-foot mason's level with wood or brass-bound edges (aluminum will corrode in contact with lime mortar) or a shorter level and a long wood straightedge; mason's line (braided cord), and blocks. You can make a story pole to check the height of each course, and for stone walls a tapered batter board (see box, page 395).

For cutting brick use a small sledgehammer and a brick chisel (a brick set); for chipping mortar, use a cold chisel. Electric drills or (better) power hammer drills equipped with carbide-tipped masonry bits have all but replaced using a star drill and hammer to drill holes in masonry. Stone is cut with a stone chisel and a small sledgehammer. Important safety equipment includes safety goggles, which you must wear whenever cutting or shaping masonry; heavy work gloves to protect your hands from abrasions and the corrosive effects of cement and lime; and knee pads.

MORTAR PROPORTIONS

A good mortar mix for outdoor free-standing brick or block walls is 1 part masonry cement to 6 parts sand; for stone walls use 1 part plain cement to 4 parts sand. For retaining walls make a stronger mortar of 1 part cement and 3½ parts sand.

The amount of water required depends on how moist the sand is, but is no more than 5 to 6 gallons, added slowly, for each 1-cubic-foot bag of cement. However, you may not use a full bag of cement in a batch, because you should make only as much mortar as you can use in one to two hours. Try a half-bag mix for the first batch, to see how long it lasts. For every cubic foot of sand in the mix you will get 1 cubic foot of mortar, because the cement and water compact into the air spaces in the mixture. Do not work with mortar if the temperature is below 35°F.

MIXING MORTAR

Measure ingredients by the shovelful or pailful. If you use a power mixer, dry-mix the sand and cement for at least 1 minute, then mix for at least 3 minutes after adding water. Hand-mixing is the same as for concrete (see page 355). Layer the dry cement and sand in a mortar pan or wheelbarrow and add half of the water to a hole at one end of the mixture. Work the ingredients back and forth with a hoe into the water until all of it is absorbed and the mix has no lumps in it.

Add more water, if needed, only a little at a time, mixing well each time. Mortar that is too wet will be difficult to work with and will run out of the joints; mortar that is too dry will not form a strong bond. For bricks, mortar should have a soft, doughlike consistency; ridges should stand up distinctly and stay up when you form them with a trowel. For blocks and stone, mortar needs to be a bit stiffer.

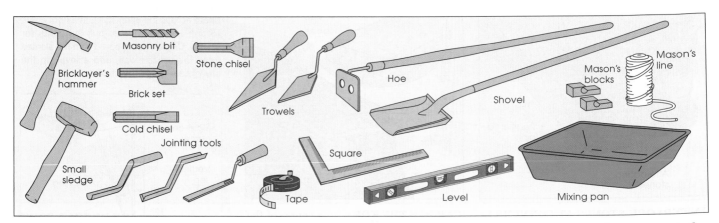

TOOLS FOR MASONRY WALL WORK include a hoe and shovel for mixing mortar, and trowels and various special-purpose tools for placing and finishing the mortar. Other tools shown are used to guide wall construction and to cut and shape bricks, blocks, and stones.

WORKING WITH MORTAR

Whether you are laying bricks or masonry blocks, the techniques you should use for placing and finishing mortar are the same.

USING A TROWEL AND MORTARBOARD

Dampen the mortarboard surface well and load several trowelsful of mortar into the center. Place the board next to the spot where you will work. Leave the bulk of the mortar in the mixing pan or wheelbarrow, out of the direct sun; cover it with plastic on a hot, dry day.

To take mortar off the board, slice down through the mass along one edge and scoop up the cut-off portion on the flat upper surface of the trowel. Each time you take mortar from the board, slice down along a different edge of the mass there. Wipe excess mortar from the trowel back into the bulk before taking up a new load. Rinse the trowels and board clean between batches.

THROWING A MORTAR LINE

A mortar line is a long, shallow bed of mortar in which a course of bricks or blocks is seated. To "throw" a line on a footing or a previously laid course, scoop up a load of mortar from the board and hold the trowel with its point touching the starting point of the line. In one smooth movement, turn the trowel over and draw it along the line, distributing the mortar over a distance of 24 to 36 inches. Use the flat bottom of the trowel to spread the mortar out a bit thicker than the final joint depth, and one brick or block wide; then draw the point of the trowel along the mortar line to create a shallow furrow down the center.

SETTING MASONRY UNITS

Before a properly dampened brick or block is placed on a bed of mortar, one end (and sometimes a side) must be buttered with mortar to bond to the adjoining unit. Scoop some mortar onto the trowel, pick up the masonry piece, and throw the mortar onto the end; then press it in place with the blade of the trowel. Set the piece in place with its buttered end against the end of the preceding piece. Tap it with the heel of the trowel handle to drive it against the adjoining brick or block and to level and align it on the mortar bed. Get both joints to proper thickness, then scrape or strike off all excess wet mortar with the trowel and return the rest to the mortarboard.

Lay succeeding pieces the same way until you reach the end of the mortar line, then continue that line or throw a line on top of the bricks you have just laid. With blocks, butter the top edges to bed the next course. When placing pieces in the second face of a brick wall, butter both the end and the side that must bond to the piece already in place.

FINISHING JOINTS

Let mortar set one to two hours, until it is firm to thumb pressure but not hard, before finishing, or tooling, the joints. Choose a tool to suit the desired joint contour. Slide it along the joint to shape and smooth the mortar, compacting it for a strong, water-shedding bond. Do vertical joints first, then horizontals. Later, when the mortar is almost dry, clean the surface of the bricks or blocks with a stiff brush.

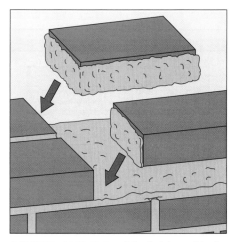

TO PICK UP MORTAR, cut down through the pile on the mortarboard, then scoop it up on the upper side of the trowel.

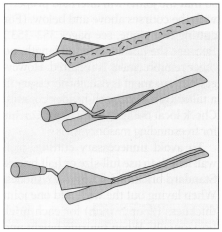

THROW A LINE OF MORTAR in three steps: distribute it lengthwise, spread it to width and depth, and make a center furrow.

BUTTER ONE END of the bricks or blocks used for one face. Butter an end and the inner side for those in the second face.

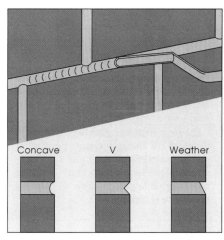

Concave   V   Weather

TOOL THE JOINTS to make the mortar less porous. Use one of these three shapes to shed water and resist weathering.

STONE AND BRICK RETAINING WALLS

Stone—commonly granite, limestone, or slate—is the traditional material for dry or wet retaining walls. SW (severe weather) grade brick, available in several sizes and colors, can also be used. A dry-laid stone retaining wall should be no more than 3 feet high; mortared walls can be higher. Use the construction techniques explained earlier in this chapter along with the following information.

Dry-laid stone. Cut the earth behind so the entire wall can slant backward 2 inches for every foot of height. Lay the base course on 6 inches of gravel in a trench 12 inches deep. As you build upward, put landscape fabric against the back of the wall with 2 to 3 inches of gravel behind it. Cap the wall with large flat stones for good water runoff.

Mortared stone. Build on a concrete footing on gravel. Provide weep holes every 4 feet. Make the back face vertical, but slope the front face about 1 inch per foot from base to top. Include bonding stones through the wall thickness at least every third course, spaced 3 to 4 feet apart. Fill all interior joints completely with mortar, and lay a ¾-inch bed for each course.

Pour 4 to 6 inches of gravel against fiberglass screening placed over the rear face, up to the last 6 inches. Mortar the capping-course joints flush with the surface; rake the face joints.

Brick. Build at least two bricks wide on a concrete footing on gravel. With plain bricks, include headers in every other course and reinforcing mesh every third course. If you use bricks with holes in the core, for mortar to key into, lay them in a bond with headers at frequent intervals. Or lay a running bond with rebars running through the aligned, mortar-filled holes about every 18 inches (plan ahead when pouring the footing and insert the rebars at the proper intervals). In all brick walls, cut a brick short every 36 inches in the second course and insert a 1-inch plastic pipe in the joint as a weep hole. Finish top-course joints flush with the top surface or add a concrete or stone cap. Rake face joints to a contoured or weather joint profile (see page 397).

(see page 397).

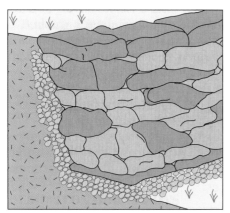

A DRY-LAID RETAINING WALL should slope backward. Gravel and fiberglass screening behind help provide drainage.

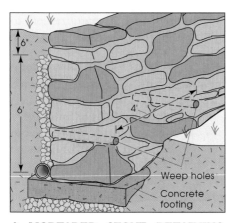

A MORTARED STONE RETAINING WALL has a sloping face and vertical back. A weep hole is needed about every 4 feet.

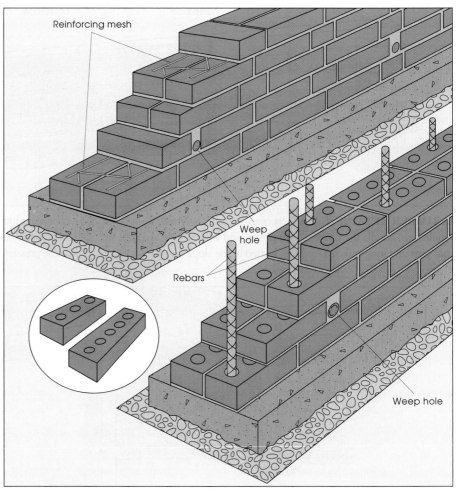

BRICK RETAINING WALLS can be built with plain bricks with headers and reinforcement, or with core-hole bricks with or without rebars. If rebars are not used, include headers and reinforcement. All brick walls need weep holes at 36-inch intervals in the second course.

BLOCK AND CONCRETE RETAINING WALLS

There are two types of concrete block and poured concrete retaining walls, *gravity* and *cantilever*. To build a block wall, use the techniques explained earlier in this chapter. For a poured concrete wall, use the techniques described in Chapter 28.

Gravity wall. The front face is vertical; the back slants outward from the top to a base equal to or wider than the height. When the base rests on solid, well-tamped earth below the frost line, this construction does not require a footing. The weight of the earth on the wedge shape helps to stabilize the wall. This design requires a good deal of excavation, but it is easy to build and it can hold a great load of earth in place, which makes it a good choice on steeply sloping ground.

Cantilever wall. Both faces are vertical. A wall up to 5 feet high is 8 inches thick, a higher wall 12 inches thick. It is centered on a footing that is two-thirds as wide as the height and 2 to 4 inches thicker than the wall. The footing distributes the weight of the narrow wall mass over a greater area, for stability. It should have a bottom key if the wall is 6 feet or higher. Where excavation is difficult, use a *toed wall* with an extended front footing and little back footing.

REINFORCEMENT AND FOOTINGS

Reinforce a footing with ½-inch rebars across the width and along the length, and with others bent at 90 degrees to extend up into the wall every 24 to 32 inches. To splice two rebars, overlap them 30 bar diameters (e.g., 15 inches for ½-inch rebar) and twist steel wire around them. In a gravity block wall, fill all block cores with a free-pouring mix of concrete. In a cantilever block wall, place two rebars in beam or lintel blocks every other course, and space vertical rebars to pass between the joints of these blocks. Fill cores and channels that carry rebars with mortar or concrete, and all other cores in the top three courses as well.

Pour footings in cleanly cut trenches, without forms, but build strong forms to hold the weight of the concrete for a poured wall. Use ¾-inch plywood with 2 × 4 stiffeners at least every 24 inches. Run horizontal stiffeners first, then nail vertical stiffeners across them. Brace the vertical stiffeners with 2 × 4 triangles secured by stakes in the earth. Assemble forms with screws or dual-headed nails so they can be taken apart easily after the concrete has set. To make weep holes, drill holes in the form and insert lengths of plastic pipe. Cut the pipe off flush after the forms are removed. (In a block wall, cut blocks or use half blocks to build around weep holes.) Keep concrete moist while it cures. Wait five days or more before backfilling with gravel and dirt behind a block or poured wall.

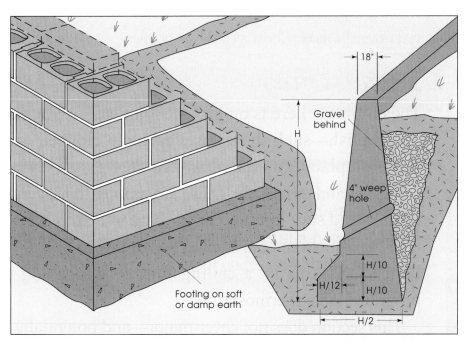

GRAVITY RETAINING WALLS can be constructed of concrete blocks with filled cores *(left)* or of poured concrete *(right)*. The broad base serves as an integral footing on hard-packed earth. Weep holes should have screening over the rear opening.

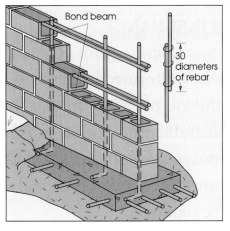

A CANTILEVER BLOCK WALL requires vertical rebars tied into the footing, and filled beam blocks with rebars every other course.

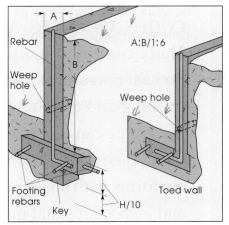

A POURED-CONCRETE CANTILEVER WALL can have a keyed or a toed footing. The wall rebars must tie into the footing.

TOOLS FOR PLUMBING PROJECTS

A good many plumbing maintenance chores can be accomplished with common household tools. A couple of medium-size screwdrivers, an adjustable wrench or two, groove-joint pliers, and a small hacksaw will take you a long way. With this modest beginning, you can repair or install most faucets, open fixture traps, or even replace a toilet.

In addition, the following plumbing tools and the supplies also shown in the accompanying illustration will make basic jobs easier and will extend the range of projects you can tackle. It usually pays to buy these items—in most cases, a basic plumber's hand tool costs less than the price of a service call. If you need something more complex, most specialty tools can be rented for a few dollars a day.

Plunger. The first and best plumbing tool you can own is a good plunger. Choose one with a fold-out funnel-like cup that conforms to toilet outlets.

Drain auger. With all the cosmetics, toothpaste, hair, and grease sent into today's plumbing lines, a hand-held drain auger to ream out clogs will serve you well. Choose one that has its cable coiled in a plastic or metal housing. The larger cranking arc required by these models will provide the torque you need to deal with stubborn clogs.

Closet auger. A closet auger works only on toilets, but when a toilet backs up, nothing works better. In many cases, nothing else works at all.

Faucet handle puller. A good many faucets go unrepaired simply because the handles won't budge. A handle puller (see page 413) can free handles that seem fused to their faucet stems without ruining them.

Basin wrench. A basin wrench allows you to reach faucet nuts located up behind sink and lavatory basins. It is the ideal tool for cramped cabinet spaces where you often must work blind.

Deep-set socket wrench. You need this wrench to disassemble faucets set behind plaster or tiled walls. Turn it with a rod or screwdriver inserted through the holes at one end.

Pipe wrenches. When threaded fittings must be uncoupled or reconnected, you will need pipe wrenches—especially if the connection is old. Purchase wrenches in pairs, one to turn the fitting, the other to hold the pipe against turning at the same time. The 10- or 12-inch size is ideal for home use.

Tubing cutter. To cut copper pipe and riser tubing cleanly and squarely, use a tubing cutter. A hacksaw will leave a rough burr that will frustrate your efforts to use compression fittings.

Faucet seat wrench. This is a tool you will want for compression faucets. Replacing the seat—the part the washer presses against to stop water flow—is the best way to add years of life to an old faucet.

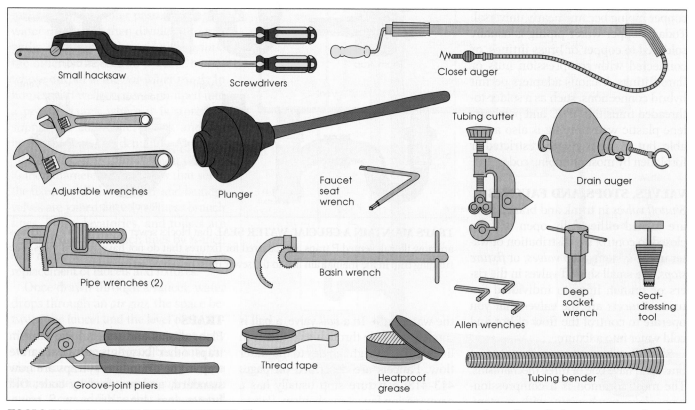

TOOLS FOR HOME PLUMBING PROJECTS. These common household and plumbing tools and supplies will allow you to complete the repair and replacement procedures explained in this chapter, and many other tasks as well. These items are worth buying as needed; larger, more specialized plumbing tools can be rented.

DEALING WITH DRAIN PROBLEMS

The only drains in a home that are not prone to clogging are those of the laundry and kitchen, and then only if the kitchen is equipped with an automatic dishwasher. Dishwashers and clothes washers scour their own lines with hot water in high-volume purges. That is a valuable clue to preventing clogs in the other drains in your home.

About every two weeks, heat two to three gallons of water to boiling and carefully pour it down a sink, shower, or tub drain as fast as safety permits. This large quantity of very hot water will work wonders in dissolving grease and soap, two prime causes of clogging. Even the hottest water from a faucet cannot compete with this treatment.

SLOW BATHROOM DRAINS

If water drains out of your bathtub slowly, there is probably a blockage in the stopper components. Pull the pop-up plug from the drain outlet in the floor of the tub. Also remove the two screws in the overflow plate and pull the trip lever out by its control handle. Chances are you will find a long tail of soapy hair clinging to the plug end or, more likely, to the spiral of the trip lever. Remove the hair, feed the lever in through the overflow opening, and replace the screws in the plate. Then insert the pop-up plug in the drain.

In a lavatory basin, twist the pop-up plug a quarter turn and pull up. If the plug does not come free, you probably must undo a lift-lever nut below the basin and pull the lever out of the back of the plug. Clean away any foreign matter and replace the plug.

If your tub does not have a pop-up stopper, remove the overflow plate and pull out the operating lever, called a *trip-waste*. Clean the plunger on the end of the lever and run a drain auger in through the overflow opening to remove any blockage in the line. In a shower stall, remove the cover screen from the drain outlet. Some screens snap-fit into the drain; others are secured by a center screw. Clean the screen and the drain. Use a fish wire or an auger in the drain.

CHEMICAL VS. MECHANICAL MEASURES

Chemical drain cleaners are not effective for toilet clogs, but they can cope with some of the most common blockages in tub, lavatory, and shower traps, and they sometimes can remove a blockage in the trap of a kitchen sink. However, most kitchen drain blockages are accumulations of grease, soap, coffee grounds, and other materials in the horizontal line just beyond the trap. Chemical cleaners are not very effective against that kind of blockage. The most powerful drain cleaners contain acids or strong alkalis that are dangerous to handle and can be destructive to plumbing. If you try a chemical cleaner, wear rubber gloves and be careful not to splash the cleaner. If you must open a trap or drain afterward, be very careful to avoid contact with the chemical-laden water.

For almost all drain blockages, mechanical methods are a better approach. First try a plunger. If that does not work, remove the cleanout plug in a fixture trap or disconnect a removable trap and clean it, or run an auger cable into the line beyond. If a fixed trap or the line beyond is blocked, run an auger cable in through the drain opening or the cleanout. These procedures are explained on this page and the next.

USING A PLUNGER

Pumping a plunger up and down over a drain opening builds up pressure that often will break a clog free. When using a plunger, maintain some water in the fixture. The greater weight and density of water exerts more pressure than air when forced against a clog. Make vigorous plunges on both the downstrokes and upstrokes. To make sure the pressure is not lost through adjoining passages, always plug the other drain openings in a two- or three-bowl sink, or the overflow opening of a tub or lavatory basin. A wet rag does a good job, but you may need a helper to hold it in place. Once a blockage has been forced free, flush the line with plenty of very hot water. *Continued*

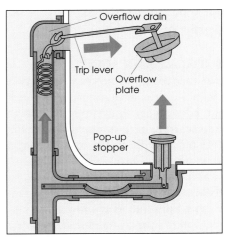

CLEAN TUB DRAINS by removing the pop-up stopper, if any, and the trip lever.

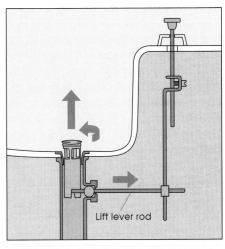

REMOVE A LAVATORY STOPPER by twisting it and lifting. Release the lift lever rod if necessary.

USE A PLUNGER with water in the fixture. Remove the stopper and block the overflow opening to concentrate the force.

DEALING WITH DRAIN PROBLEMS *Continued*

USING A DRAIN AUGER

Whether you go in through a drain or a cleanout, or remove a trap to get at a drain line, a perceptive touch is important when using a drain auger, for the resistance of the cable can tell you a great deal.

Start by loosening the setscrew on the cable and pushing as much cable into the drain line as it will take. When you feel resistance, tighten the setscrew and crank the cable in a clockwise rotation while pushing it forward. As the cable is driven into the clog, loosen the setscrew, pull more cable from its housing, reset the screw, and crank again. Repeat this process a foot or two at a time until the cable reaches the larger, vertical stack. At that point, you will feel less resistance on the crank. You may also hear or feel the head flopping inside the stack. Turn the crank to retrieve the cable, wiping it clean as you go. Replace the trap or cleanout plug, and flush with plenty of hot water.

USING A CLOSET AUGER

Use a closet auger to clear a toilet blockage that resists a plunger. Pull the auger cable back into its tube and insert the curved end of the tube into the outlet in the toilet bowl. Push the cable out, into the trap as you crank the handle. Do this at least three times; once each to left, right, and center.

USING A SEWER MACHINE

A blockage in your sewer service line may require renting a large power auger, often called a *sewer machine*. It can deal with tree roots, large objects, and dense materials that a hand-driven auger could never touch. However, the job can be tricky. You will find right off that the brass cleanout plug in the stack, line, or main trap will not wrench free. In most cases, you will need to chisel it out and buy a replacement plug. Get a plastic plug for easier access next time.

When you use the machine, do not try to cut through a sewer blockage nonstop. A sewer machine's motor is often more powerful than its cable is strong. It is easy to hit a snag of tree roots and break the cable well inside the waste pipe, so proceed cautiously. Listen to the motor as you feed cable into the line. When the motor begins to bog down, stop the machine immediately and retrieve the cable. With luck, you will pull a matting of fine tree roots back with the cable. Clean the head, run it in again, and repeat the process until you no longer retrieve roots. If you find clay on the auger head, call a plumber. Soil in a sewer line usually indicates a collapsed pipe.

CLEANING DRAINS

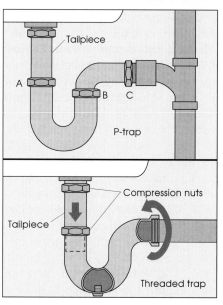

REMOVING TRAPS. Undo nuts at *A* and *B* or *C*. Threaded trap *(bottom)*: Undo the nuts, push the tailpiece down, and turn the trap.

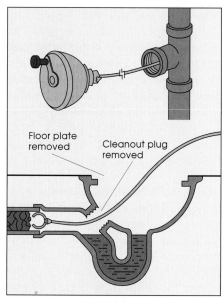

INSERT A DRAIN AUGER into a drain line with the trap removed. Work through the cleanout in a floor drain.

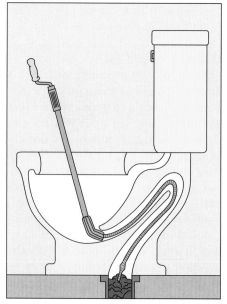

A CLOSET AUGER CABLE is just long enough to reach through the integral trap in a toilet. Turn the handle to operate the auger.

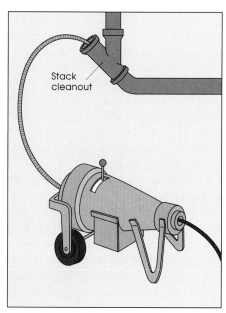

RUN A SEWER MACHINE CABLE into the main drain through a cleanout in the house trap or in the main stack.

REPAIRING COMPRESSION FAUCETS

A compression faucet is the most common kind of fixture valve. It has a washer that must be replaced every so often. Separate stems control hot and cold water flow into the fixture. Compression faucets are sturdy, familiar, and—best of all—easy and cheap to repair.

TROUBLE SPOTS

Compression faucets can develop four problems. The most common and easiest to correct is a worn *seat washer* that causes the faucet to drip. If allowed to drip too long, the second problem can occur: Water seeping past the washer will cut a channel across the brass *faucet seat*. When that happens, any replacement washer you install will soon be destroyed by the rough surface of the seat.

The third problem develops with the *stem packing*. If the packing is loose or brittle, water can leak around the stem when the faucet is turned on. The fourth problem is a worn *spout seal* that can produce a leak at the base of the faucet. It is a problem common to other faucet designs, too.

GAINING ACCESS

Work on just one faucet stem at a time. Turn the water off at the stop in the fixture riser, or at the valve at the meter or pressure tank; then open the faucet. When the water in the line has drained out, close the drain so no small parts can fall into it.

To gain access to the working parts, remove the screw from the top of the handle. You may have to pry up the "Hot" or "Cold" index or decorative cap on the handle to uncover it.

Now lift the handle from the faucet stem. If it is stuck, pry under it carefully with a screwdriver or tap it upward gently. If that doesn't work, use a handle puller, as shown below. Insert the peg of the puller into the screw hole and slide the side arms under the handle. Turn the puller handle in a clockwise direction and the side arms will pull the faucet handle free.

With the handle removed, undo the escutcheon nut and lift off the bonnet, if there is one. Open the valve stem slightly and use an adjustable wrench to undo the bonnet nut or packing nut. Then you can turn the stem out of its threaded port. Inspect the seat washer at the bottom end of the stem. If it is cracked, brittle, or badly worn, replace it. *Continued*

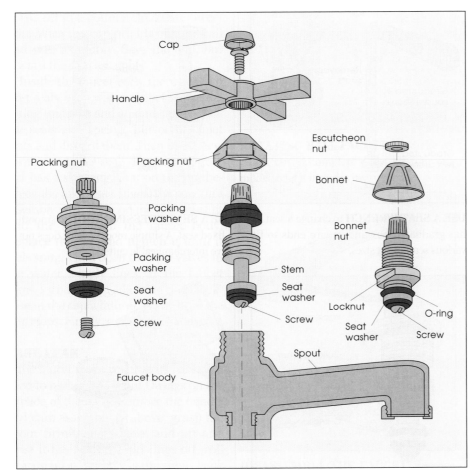

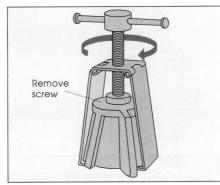

A HANDLE PULLER is especially helpful in removing deep-skirted faucet handles that are stuck on their stems.

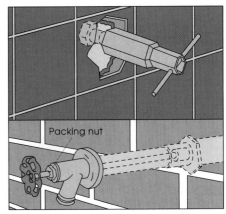

FOR BURIED FAUCETS *(top)* use a deep socket wrench. *(Bottom):* Undo the packing nut to remove the long stem of a frostproof exterior faucet.

COMPRESSION FAUCETS have various stem designs and packing washers and/or O-rings. The major types of faucets are shown here. All have a seat washer at the end of the stem, which closes against the seat to cut off the flow of water.

COMPRESSION FAUCETS

REPAIRING TOILETS

The typical American residential toilet is a mechanically simple and remarkably troublefree fixture. When problems arise, they almost always have to do with the water flow. Fortunately, almost all repairs are both simple and inexpensive to make.

TOILET OPERATION

A quantity of water is held in a toilet bowl by an integral trap. This water forms a seal against sewer gases and dilutes waste material when the toilet is used. A tank on top of the bowl holds a supply of water for flushing the toilet. When the flush lever is tripped, the stopper ball or flapper ball is lifted from the flush valve and the water can escape.

The water from the tank rushes into the bowl through a series of small openings in the rim, which scour the bowl, and through a larger opening behind the outlet in the bowl. The increased volume of water forces a flow through the trap that siphons out the water and waste material in the bowl. When the bowl water reaches a low level, the siphon action breaks and the trap begins to retain clean water.

When the tank is nearly empty, the stopper or flapper ball drops, closing the flush valve, and water again fills the tank through an opened fill valve or ballcock assembly. Water also flows through a refill tube and overflow pipe into the toilet to fill the trap and bring water in the bowl to its normal level. When the water in the tank reaches a preset level, the fill valve closes and the toilet is ready for another flush.

The fill valve may have either a compression-type plunger with a washer and seat, or a diaphragm mechanism. The valve may be operated by a float ball that rides on the falling and rising water level, or by a plastic float cup that slides down and up the ballcock shaft as the tank empties and fills.

TROUBLESHOOTING

As the only mechanical parts in a toilet are the fill valve, the flush valve, and the flush lever—all remarkably simple devices—troubleshooting to identify problems is not difficult.

Fill valve. If the water does not shut off completely, makes a hissing sound, or sprays under the tank lid, the problem is in the fill valve. First, turn the valve adjusting screw or bend the float arm to lower the float ball and cause earlier shutoff. If that does not work, turn the water off, open the valve, and replace the washers and valve seat or the diaphragm seals, depending on the type of valve. Get exact replacements. As a last resort, replace the entire ballcock/valve assembly. Codes require an antisiphon model that prevents contaminating backflow.

Flush valve. If the toilet fills, shuts off, and comes on again a few minutes later; if a trickle of water enters the bowl continuously; or if you have to wiggle the handle to make the tank fill properly, the problem is at the flush valve. You may need to adjust the stopper ball guides, replace the stopper or flapper ball, or clean or replace the flush valve seat.

Flush lever. If the flush lever breaks or seizes up, replace it. The only secret to doing this is that handle shanks have lefthand threads, so turn the retaining nut on the inside of the tank *clockwise* to remove it.

Procedures for making the adjustments and repairs that will correct these problems are shown on the facing page.

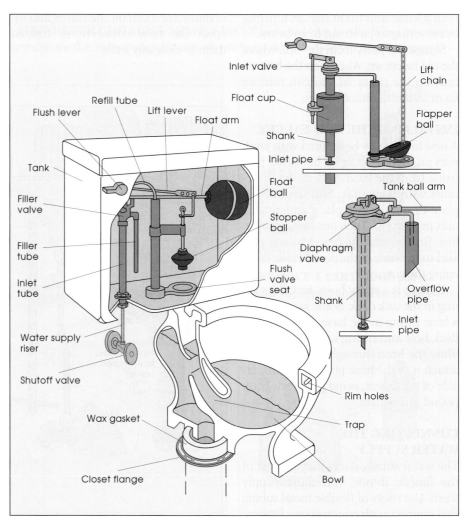

TOILET OPERATING PARTS are all housed in the tank; water flow clears and refills bowl. *(Insets):* Diaphragm-valve and float-cup ballcocks fill the tank from the bottom of the shaft. A flapper ball is an alternate way of closing the flush valve.

TOILET REPAIR PROCEDURES

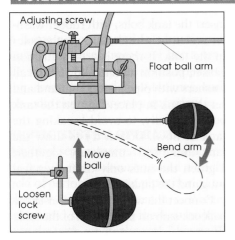

CHANGE THE INLET VALVE SHUTOFF POINT by turning the adjusting screw or changing the float ball level.

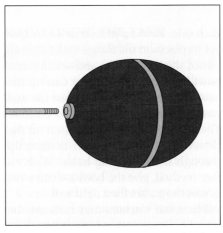

REPLACE THE FLOAT BALL if it lies more than half submerged in the tank water. It screws onto its arm.

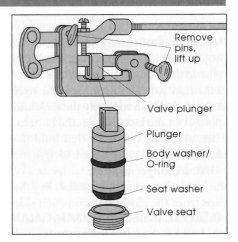

OPEN A COMPRESSION FILL VALVE by uncoupling the float arm linkage. Replace the washers or seat as needed.

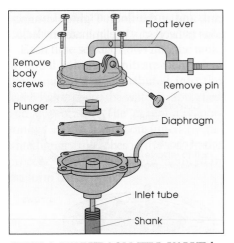

OPEN A DIAPHRAGM FILL VALVE by uncoupling the float lever and removing body screws. Replace the diaphragm.

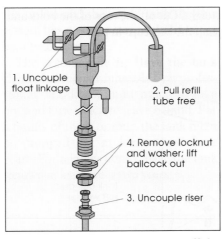

TO REMOVE A BALLCOCK turn off the water and empty the tank, then follow these steps. Reverse to install the replacement.

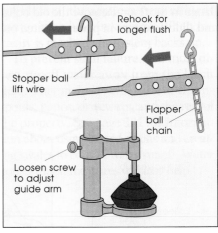

FOR A LONGER FLUSH, rehook the flapper chain or stopper lift wire. Adjust the guide so the lift wire moves freely.

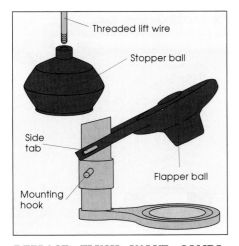

REPLACE FLUSH VALVE COMPONENTS by unscrewing a stopper ball from its lift wire or unhooking flapper side tabs.

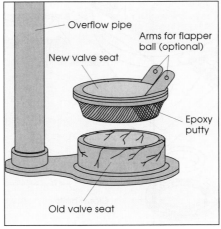

REPLACE A FLUSH VALVE SEAT that leaks or cannot be cleaned. Fasten the new seat into the old one with epoxy putty.

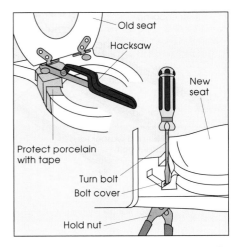

UNSCREW OR SAW THROUGH OLD BOLTS to replace a toilet seat. New models have concealed, noncorroding plastic bolts.

34 ELECTRICAL REPAIRS AND IMPROVEMENTS

This chapter provides a brief explanation of the electrical system in your home and shows you how to make some of the most common repairs and improvements. All are easy to do.

BASIC PRINCIPLES

Electricity is the flow of electrons along a conductor. The force that moves electrons is measured in *volts;* the rate at which they move is measured in *amperes,* or amps. The amount of power an electrical device must have to operate is rated in *watts.* In simple terms:

Watts = Volts × Amps

Electricity must have a complete path or *circuit* from its source, through a device, and back to the source. Interrupting the circuit, as with a switch, stops the flow. A cross-connection to an incorrect path can create a *short circuit* that can activate a protective device such as a fuse or a circuit breaker. Without such protection, a short circuit can burn out a fixture or motor, or cause a fire.

An electrical circuit is a loop. When a lamp or appliance is turned on, *alternating current* (a.c.) electricity flows both ways in the loop, changing direction 60 times a second (60 cycles, or 60 Hertz).

ELECTRICAL SERVICE

Electricity is distributed at a high voltage from a power station to a neighborhood of consumers. Local transformers reduce the voltage to two or more 120-volt phases. The electricity is then supplied to a home, usually by three wires. Two wires, commonly called the *hot* wires, each carry 120 volts. The third wire provides a return path to the transformer.

In many municipal systems, the supply or *service* wires come to the house underground. In other systems, especially in suburban and rural areas, they travel overhead. In either case, the supply circuit passes through a *service entrance* with a *meter* and goes to the *service panel,* which most homeowners call the main breaker box or main fuse panel.

THE SERVICE PANEL

Power enters the service panel through a main circuit breaker or fuse block, which can be used to cut off the entire system. In the panel, the power is distributed to individual circuits. The flow to each circuit passes through a protective circuit breaker or fuse and then along wires to the outlets and fixtures on that circuit.

The panel has a second source of protection, a large copper *grounding conductor* that provides an electrical path to the soil outside the home. If current should leave its established path, the grounding conductor will feed it safely into the soil. In older wiring systems, often only the panel is grounded. In modern systems, every circuit has a grounding wire that is connected in the panel to the grounding conductor, for protection throughout the system.

CIRCUIT WIRING

The cables that connect household circuits have a plastic, composition, or metal outer jacket. Inside there are two or three solid copper wires each encased in colored thermoplastic insulation, and often a smaller grounding wire. In a two-wire cable the insulated wires are white and black; in a three-

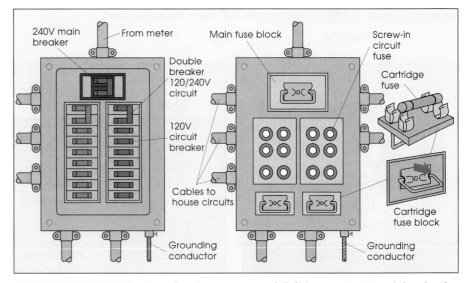

SERVICE PANELS. The circuit breaker service panel *(left)* has a main 240-volt breaker for complete shutoff, and doubled breakers for 240-volt appliance circuits. Single breakers protect 120-volt circuits. The fuse-type service panel *(right)* uses cartridge fuses in the 240-volt main and appliance blocks, and screw-in fuses in 120-volt circuits.

ELECTRICAL REPAIRS

wire cable they are white, black, and red. The grounding wire may be bare or have green insulation.

Black and red wires are connected to the "hot" side of a circuit and always carry electricity. Switches and circuit breakers or fuses are connected to hot wires. White wires are connected to the other side of a circuit and must provide a path to the panel that is unbroken by switches or other devices. Because they are connected to grounding terminals in the service panel, white wires are often called "neutral"; however, they carry electricity whenever any device in their circuit is operating. In switch loops in lighting circuits, white wires are also hot. They must be marked with pieces of black tape at each end, as a warning sign.

The amount of current that can flow through a circuit depends on the diameter, or *gauge*, of the copper wires. In household 120-volt circuits, 14-gauge copper wires can carry up to 15 amps, 12-gauge wires can carry up to 20 amps, and 10-gauge and larger (lower gauge number) wires can carry higher amperages. 240-volt circuits may carry a total of 30 or more amps.

CIRCUIT PROTECTION
An electrical *fuse* has a metal link that melts, breaking the circuit, when excessive current flow raises its temperature beyond a certain point. A *plug fuse* is a screw-in device with a window to show the condition of the metal link. Main service fuses and those in 240-volt circuits are usually *cartridge fuses,* mounted in a holder that must be pulled from the panel to gain access to them.

A *circuit breaker* is a heat-sensitive switch that automatically trips when excessive current demand causes a temperature rise. After the problem has been corrected, the lever can be returned to the ON position, or in some models to a reset position and then on.

A *ground-fault interrupt* (GFI) *breaker* will trip the instant it senses a circuit imbalance (see page 435). A screw-in, plug-type breaker, which can replace a fuse, has a pop-out button; pushing it in resets the breaker.

A circuit breaker or fuse is rated by the maximum amperage it will carry, which must match the current-carrying capacity of the wires in a circuit. If it has a higher rating, it can allow excessive current flow, which could overheat the wires or a fixture dangerously.

A demand for too much power, an *overcurrent*, occurs when too many devices are connected to a circuit or when a failed device or loose wire causes a short circuit. It also may occur when high-wattage fixtures and appliance motors are turned on, because they momentarily need much more electricity to start than they draw when operating.

If a circuit is near capacity, a start-up overcurrent can blow a fuse, even though there is no practical danger to the system. Circuit breakers are built to withstand these momentary surges; standard fuses are not. If you have a circuit that often blows a fuse when an appliance is turned on, try using a time-delay or "slow blow" fuse, which can cope with brief surge demands. If the problem continues, call a licensed electrician, who can identify the source of the problem.

WARNING
When you open a service panel to operate a breaker or change a fuse, stand on a dry, nonconductive surface, such as a rubber mat or a wooden board. Use only one hand. Keep the other in your pocket so you cannot accidentally touch something that would complete a circuit through you to ground, in case there is a current leakage.

Before making any of the repairs described on the following pages, always turn off the power to the circuit at the service panel. Then check the circuit with a voltage tester at the point where you intend to work, to be sure the power is off.

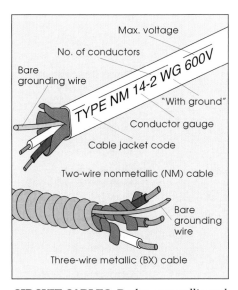

CIRCUIT CABLES. Both nonmetallic and metallic jacket cables may have two or three conductors of the same gauge, with or without a grounding wire.

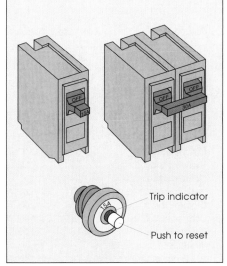

CIRCUIT BREAKERS. Breaker capacity is marked on the handle or the body. Breakers for 240-volt circuits are double width, with a joined handle.

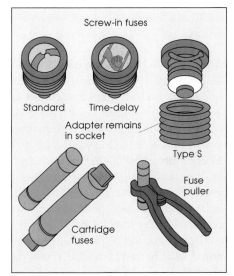

FUSES. Capacity is marked on the body and may also be color coded. Use a fuse puller or insulated pliers to remove and replace a cartridge fuse.

MAPPING CIRCUITS AND ASSESSING NEEDS

To work with your electrical system, you need to know which existing circuits are full and which offer room for expansion. You also need to evaluate whether your service panel provides an adequate number of circuits.

MAPPING CIRCUITS

To identify which receptacles and fixtures are on each circuit, you will need only a pencil, paper, and a voltage tester (see next page) or a small lamp.

Make a rough drawing of your home's floor plan and mark each permanent electrical feature. Then turn off the first 120-volt breaker or fuse in the panel and plug your tester or lamp into each outlet. Also operate each wall switch that controls a mounted fixture. On your map, write the circuit breaker or fuse number next to the symbol for every dead outlet or fixture that you find.

Now turn on the breaker, turn off the next one, and repeat the process. Do the same to map each of the other circuits. When you are finished, total up the number of openings on each circuit.

To determine if a circuit is at or near capacity, assign each outlet a value of 1.5 amps. At that rate, a 15-amp circuit will accommodate 10 outlets, a 20-amp circuit 13 outlets. Kitchen, laundry, and bath circuits should not extend to other rooms.

ASSESSING ELECTRICAL NEEDS

The electrical systems in many older homes are now strained to their limits, and some are unsafe by today's code standards. Receptacles in certain locations must now have ground-fault protection (see page 435). In new wiring, every receptacle and appliance must have a ground connection. (Existing old wiring is exempt from this code stipulation, but ought to be upgraded for safety.)

To get some idea of whether your system meets current standards, use the chart at the right for comparison. It lists circuit specifications for a contemporary home. If you need to upgrade your system, check with local code officials before making any changes or additions.

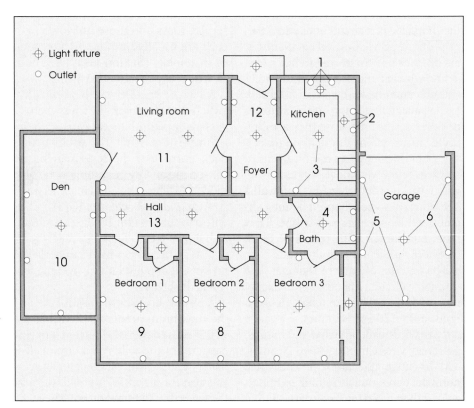

TO MAP YOUR CIRCUITS, identify each outlet by its breaker number. Calculate circuit loads on the basis of 1.5 amps per outlet. Put a list of the circuit functions (e.g., 1, 2: Kitchen counters; 3: Kitchen counters, ceiling; etc.) inside the service panel door.

CIRCUIT SPECIFICATIONS FOR ADEQUATE WIRING

FUNCTION	BREAKER AMPERAGE	CABLE	OUTLETS PER CIRCUIT	RECEPTACLE TYPE, RATING
General lighting	15	14/2 W/G	10	Duplex/Direct-connect fixtures, 120V
Kitchen lighting	15	14/2 W/G	10	Direct-connect, 120V
Kitchen outlets	20	12/2 W/G	4	Duplex/GFI,[†] 120V
Dishwasher*	20	12/2 W/G	1	Duplex/GFI,[†] 120V
Refrigerator*	20	12/2 W/G	1	Duplex, 120V
Freezer*	20	12/2 W/G	1	Duplex, 120V
Electric range*	50	8/3 W/G	1	50 amp, 240V
Microwave oven**	20	12/2 W/G	1	Duplex/GFI,[†] 120V
Clothes washer and iron	20	12/2 W/G	1[††]	Duplex, 120V
Clothes dryer*	30	10/3 W/G	1	30 amp, 240V
Bathroom outlets	15	14/2 W/G	10	GFI,[†] 120V
Whirlpool tub*	15	14/2 W/G	1	Direct-connect, 120V
Whirlpool tub w/heater*	20	12/2 W/G	1	Direct-connect, 120V
Computer**	15	14/2 W/G	1	Duplex w/isolated ground, 120V

* Dedicated (single outlet) circuit
** Dedicated circuit recommended
† Ground-fault interrupt receptacle or breaker
†† Outlets confined to laundry area

TOOLS AND BASIC TECHNIQUES

You can handle the work explained in this chapter with the tools shown at the right. The first items to get are a multipurpose tool to strip insulation, cut wire, and crimp wire connectors; a 120/240-volt voltage tester; and a continuity tester. You will also need assorted twist connectors, electrician's tape, a utility knife, Allen wrenches, and screwdrivers and pliers with handles specifically insulated for electrical work.

To run cable through finished walls and ceilings, use a flexible steel fish tape. Feed the tape through an opening into the space behind. When it reaches the desired location, fasten a cable to it and pull both back to the starting point.

STRIPPING AND FASTENING WIRES

Cut wires to length with a multipurpose tool or electrician's pliers. To fasten a wire, first strip insulation from the end. Insert the wire end in the multipurpose tool notch marked with the wire gauge, close the jaws and rotate them a bit, then pull the insulation off with the closed tool. If you do not know the wire gauge, start with a large-gauge notch, to avoid cutting into the wire itself.

To fasten a wire to a screw terminal, strip ⅝ inch at the end and bend the end into a hook. Slip it around the screw with the opening to the right. Tightening the screw will wrap the wire clockwise, closing the hook. The end should not protrude from under the screw head.

Use twist connectors such as Wire Nuts™ to fasten fixture leads and cable wires together. Strip about ½ inch from the wire ends and twist them together clockwise. Then screw on a twist connector. For additional security, wrap electrician's tape from the cap onto the wires.

MAKING ELECTRICAL TESTS

A voltage tester lights up when power runs through it. Use it to identify hot devices and wires with the circuit turned on. To check a receptacle, insert the probes in the two blade slots. If the tester lights, the receptacle is hot. In a
Continued

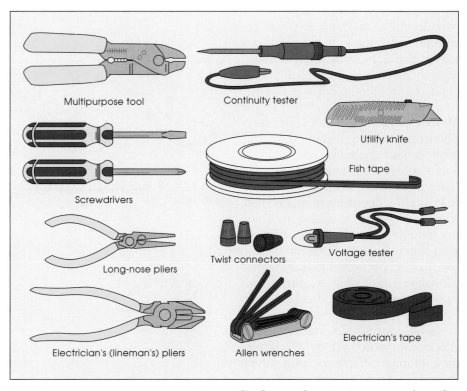

TOOLS FOR ELECTRICAL WORK. Start with voltage and continuity testers and a multipurpose tool; add the others as needed. Be sure that all the tools you choose for electrical work have special-tested insulated handles; most tools have grips insulated only for comfort. Always turn off the power before using any tool on electrical wiring.

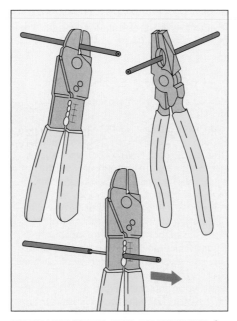

PREPARE WIRE FOR FASTENING by cutting it with a multipurpose tool or electrician's pliers *(top)*. Then strip off about ⅝ inch of insulation *(bottom)*.

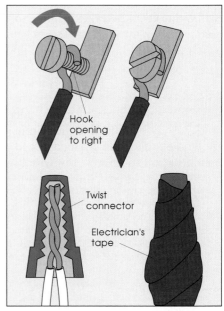

FASTEN WIRES under screw terminals, with their ends hooked as shown. Fasten fixture leads and/or cable wires together with twist connectors.

(Labels in figure: Multipurpose tool, Continuity tester, Utility knife, Screwdrivers, Fish tape, Long-nose pliers, Twist connectors, Voltage tester, Electrician's (lineman's) pliers, Allen wrenches, Electrician's tape; Hook opening to right, Twist connector, Electrician's tape)

TOOLS AND TECHNIQUES

MAKING TESTS *Continued*

grounded hot receptacle, the tester will also light when one probe is in the righthand slot and the other is in the ground prong hole or is touched to the cover plate mounting screw (scraped clean of paint).

To test whether a wall switch is hot, remove the cover plate and touch the probes to the switch terminals where the circuit wires are connected. If the tester lights, the circuit is hot.

To identify the hot wire in a box after a fixture or device has been disconnected (with the circuit turned off), make sure bare wire ends are not touching each other or metal, then turn the circuit on. Touch one tester probe to a black or red wire and the other probe to the white wire or the grounding wire of that same cable. If the tester lights, that colored wire is the incoming hot wire.

Use a continuity tester only with the power turned off and the fixture or component disconnected. To check a fuse, connect the tester to the contacts. If the fuse is good, a battery-powered light in the tester handle will come on. To check a disconnected switch, clip the tester wire to one terminal and touch the point of the probe to the other terminal. If the switch is good, the tester will light only when the switch is on. See page 432 for ways to test sockets, cords, and plugs.

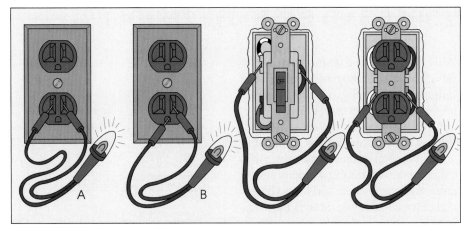

USE A VOLTAGE TESTER WITH CIRCUIT POWER TURNED ON. In the configurations shown, the tester will light if there is power present. *A* applies to receptacles in both ungrounded and grounded circuits, *B* only to grounded circuits. See text for details.

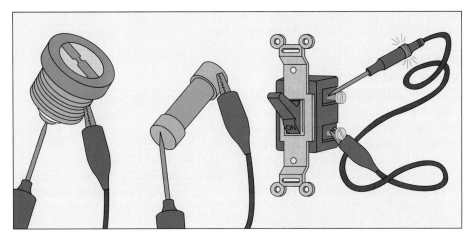

USE A CONTINUITY TESTER ONLY WITH CIRCUIT POWER OFF and the device disconnected; this is essential. The tester will light in each case shown if the device is good. See page 432 for continuity tests with lamps and cords.

REPLACING A PLUG

If a plug shows any signs of cracking or discoloration, or feels warm when a lamp or appliance is operating, replace it immediately.

Lamps and many low-wattage devices often have zip cords—the familiar flat plastic cord that can be pulled apart into two insulated wires. For zip cord, use a simple plug that has a pull-out core with screw terminals. (Plugs that simply clamp on the cord end do not meet National Electrical Code standards.) If the original plug is *polarized* with one wide blade, be sure the replacement plug is also polarized. For heavier cords use a standard plug with screw terminals. If the original plug has a grounding prong, get a matching replacement.

Cut the old plug off, along with any brittle cord. For zip cord, remove the core of the new plug and insert the cord through the hole in the case. Pull the two wires apart for about 1 inch and strip about 5/8 inch of insulation from each one. Twist the strands of each wire together and bend the ends into hooks. If the plug blades are different widths, attach the wire that is silver, or has silver strands or ribbed insulation, securely to the wide blade. Attach the copper wire to the other, narrow blade. Slip the core into the outer case of the plug.

With a larger cord, carefully cut away about 1 1/2 inch of any outer sheathing. Then strip 5/8 inch of insulation from each wire. Feed the wires into the plug and tie the two conductors in an Underwriters' knot (see page 432; do not tie a green grounding wire into the knot). The knot will take the strain when the cord is pulled during use.

Now fasten each wire under its screw: silver or white-insulated wire to the wide blade; copper or black-insulated wire to the narrow blade; green grounding wire to the ground prong. Pull the cord to seat the knot within the plug, then slip the flat insulator in place over the blades.

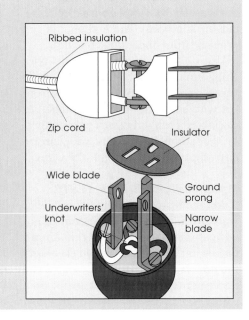

REPAIRING A DOORBELL

When a doorbell or chime acts up, the problem usually can be repaired in short order. Because everything but the transformer uses low-voltage power, there is little shock hazard.

If the bell or chime makes no sound at all, first check the push button. Remove the button, unfasten the wires, and touch them together. If the bell rings, the problem is in the button. Either replace the pushbutton unit entirely (perhaps with an illuminated button, which needs no extra wiring), or clean the old contact tabs and bend them farther apart. If the bell did not ring when you touched the wires together, look for damaged wires or for a loose connection at the bell or transformer.

If a bell sounds, but in muffled tones, the problem is likely to be dirty or pitted contact points. Remove the cover from the bell and inspect the points. If they appear dirty, polish them with fine-grit abrasive cloth or paper.

If a chime sounds in muted tones, look for dirt on the striking plungers or for degraded rubber grommets that support the tone bars. Remove the cover and check for dust accumulations on the plungers. Use an old toothbrush and lighter fluid to get them clean. Do not oil them.

If the rubber grommets under the tone bars are hard, brittle, or missing, replace them. You can get new ones at well-stocked electrical supply outlets.

TRANSFORMER REPLACEMENT

If the bell or chime is dead silent and the button and wiring are all right, check the transformer. It is usually located on a junction box in the basement. Disconnect the low-voltage wires and connect a 12-volt automotive light bulb to those terminals. If it does not light, replace the transformer.

To make the replacement, turn off the power to that circuit and undo the 120-volt wires at the transformer. Undo the mounting nut or screws, mount the new transformer, and make the 120-volt connections with the like-colored circuit wires. If you have more than one bell or chime on a single transformer and they all are weak or sound intermittently, install a transformer with greater low-voltage output. Your supplier can help you select the right unit.

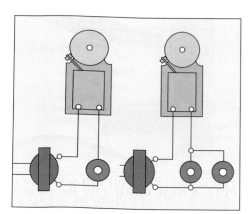

COMMON HOOKUPS use a button and bell at each door with a signal *(left)*, or buttons at two doors for one bell *(right)*.

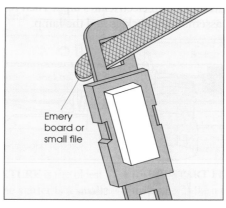

CLEAN PUSHBUTTON CONTACTS and wires. Wet weather and condensation commonly cause corrosion buildup.

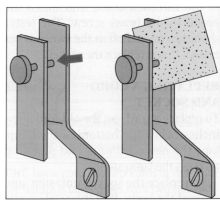

BURNISH BELL CONTACTS with fine-grit abrasive. Dirt and sparking often create problems here.

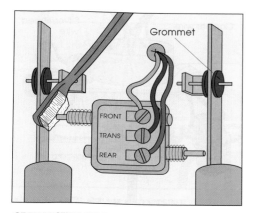

CLEAN CHIME PLUNGERS so they move freely. Replace cracked or brittle grommets in the support holes of the tone bars.

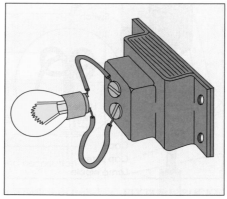

CHECK LOW-VOLTAGE TRANSFORMER OUTPUT with an auto bulb. Use short wires to make contact if necessary.

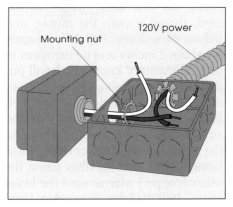

REPLACE A TRANSFORMER with circuit power off. Undo twist connectors and mounting nut; reverse to install new unit.

THERMOSTATS

A home thermostat is a temperature-sensitive switch that controls a furnace or air conditioner. Some models include a thermometer, a clock and timer, and provision for making two or more temperature settings. Thermostats may have separate controls for heating, cooling, and fan-only operation, and may include a humidistat to control a central humidifier. The most sophisticated units are programmable electronic models.

THERMOSTAT OPERATION

The sensor in a thermostat is a bimetal loop or coil that expands and contracts with temperature changes. This movement makes or breaks a 24-volt electrical circuit connected to a start-up relay in the equipment that the thermostat controls.

In some thermostats, the bimetal sensor moves a contact arm directly, or it moves a magnet toward or away from contacts in a glass tube. However, most home thermostats use a mercury switch —a glass tube attached to one end of the bimetal coil. When the coil moves it tilts the tube so that mercury either touches or moves away from two electrodes in the tube, closing or opening the circuit as required.

THERMOSTAT MAINTENANCE

A room or central thermostat seldom needs more than occasional cleaning unless it is defective.

To deal with dust and dirt, remove the front cover. Most covers snap off, bottom first; some have a small retaining screw in the bottom. Remove dust with canned air or a small, soft brush.

Clean and burnish exposed contacts by drawing clean white paper between them several times. Use TV/radio tuner cleaner and a cotton swab to clean other contacts.

To check connections, take out the mounting screws in the front assembly and remove it from the wall plate. Tighten any loose wire terminals.

A mercury-switch thermostat must be level in order to operate properly. Frequent handling and occasional bumps can knock a thermostat out of alignment. When you have the wall plate exposed, place a small level across the top, or hang a plumb bob down the center of a circular wall plate. If necessary, loosen the mounting screws to adjust the plate.

If the thermostat starts the furnace at other than the set temperature, recalibrate it. With some models, use a calibration wrench to turn the nut behind the bimetal coil slightly left or right, as marked. With other models, turn the shaft at the center of the coil with a screwdriver while holding the dial shaft from moving. Do this with the power off, and do not warm the coil by breathing on it. In still other models, or if the furnace stays on too long after the room has reached temperature, move the anticipator indicator one notch higher or lower. Wait 30 minutes between adjustments.

If the system fails to come on, get to the wall plate and touch a small jumper wire between the power terminals, usu-

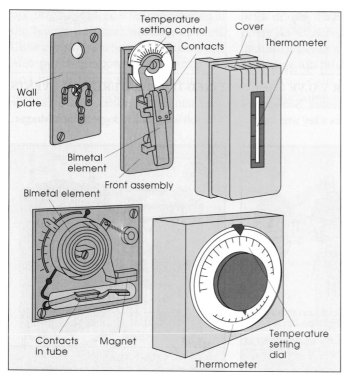

OLDER THERMOSTATS have exposed contacts, one attached to a bimetal strip or coil, or a magnet that activates contacts sealed in a glass tube to keep them free of dirt.

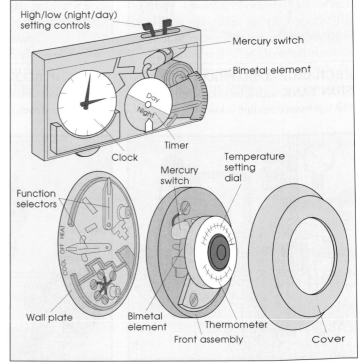

MERCURY-SWITCH THERMOSTATS, the most common type in homes, have various shapes and features. There may be separate sensors and switches to control heating and cooling.

ally the red and white wires. If the furnace starts, the thermostat is faulty.

REPLACING A THERMOSTAT

If you decide to replace your present thermostat for any reason, install a programmable thermostat. It will let you set several different temperatures for various times of day, weekends, and even vacation periods.

The thermostat must match your system, so take the make, model numbers, and electrical ratings of your central air conditioner and humidifier with you when you shop. Get a model with manual override, so you can temporarily change settings without having to reprogram the unit.

Installation is simple. Disassemble the old thermostat and disconnect the wires from the wall plate. If they do not have colored insulation, tag the wires with the initials marked beside the terminals. Wrap them around a dowel or pencil to keep them from slipping into the wall as you remove the wall plate.

Slip the wires through the new wall plate and mount it. Get the plate level. Follow the instructions that come with the thermostat to connect the wires. Then install the front assembly and the cover, and follow the instructions for entering an operating program on the keypad. Because the control circuits are in microchips, the thermostat will be virtually maintenance free.

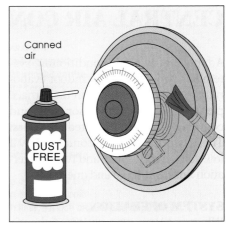

REMOVE DUST from the front-assembly components with low-pressure compressed air from at least 6 inches away, or a soft brush.

CLEAN AND BURNISH FLAT CONTACTS by drawing white paper between them. Use tuner cleaner on a cotton swab for other contacts; do not spray them directly.

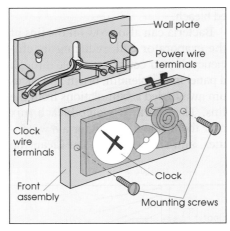

CHECK FOR LOOSE WIRES on the wall plate. Remove the front assembly to gain access to the terminals; there are usually two mounting screws.

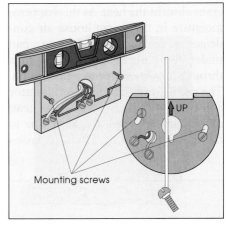

CHECK WALL PLATE ALIGNMENT if a mercury-switch thermometer functions erratically; it must be level. Use a plumb line with a circular plate.

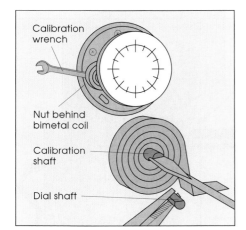

RECALIBRATE A THERMOSTAT that starts the furnace at the wrong temperature. Use a wrench or screwdriver as required; make only a slight change, then test.

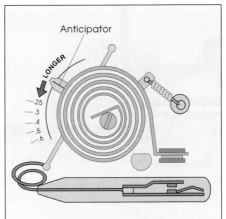

MOVE THE ANTICIPATOR one step at a time, with the power off, to fine-tune the start-up and shutdown response. Wait 30 minutes between changes to test operation.

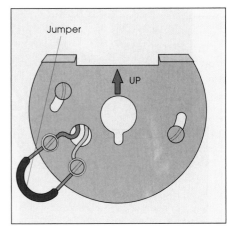

HOLD A JUMPER WIRE across the power terminals on the wall plate when the thermostat does not operate. If the furnace starts, get a new thermostat.

THERMOSTATS

36 FIRE PROTECTION

ire is a hazard every homeowner must protect against. Each year more than 5,000 people die in residential fires, nearly 30,000 more are injured, and billions of dollars worth of property is destroyed. To avoid becoming part of those grim statistics, you must make sure your home is fire-safe. This chapter explains how to do six fundamental things to protect your home. Most are both easy and inexpensive; all are important.

The six fire-protection steps are:
1. Identify and correct current hazards
2. Install smoke detectors on every level
3. Plan escape routes and try them out
4. Put fire extinguishers on every level
5. Store flammable materials safely
6. Install a lightning protection system.

FIRE PROTECTION ANALYSIS

The best way to avoid a tragic fire loss is to prevent fires from starting. Fires need fuel, heat, and oxygen. Break that trio and a fire can't ignite. To react safely to an actual fire emergency you need early warning, the means to extinguish a small fire, and at least two ways out. The illustration at the right includes the most common home fire hazards, based on a survey by the National Fire Protection Association (NFPA). Use it to determine whether your home is at risk. Then develop a plan for fixing the problems, working from the information in the following pages.

Correcting some hazards will be simple, such as installing fresh batteries in your smoke detectors or removing attic insulation from around your bathroom exhaust fan. Other corrections, such as upgrading your electrical service or lining your chimney, will involve more costly home renovations.

HOME FIRE HAZARDS

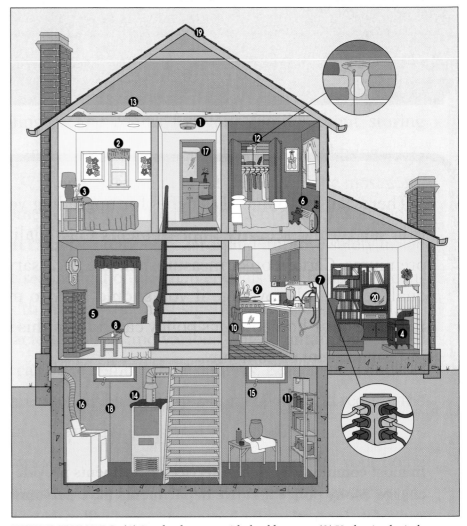

KEY TO HAZARDS. *(1)* Smoke detector with dead battery. *(2)* Undersized window provides poor secondary egress. *(3)* Smoking in bed. *(4)* Wood-burning stove vented through dirty, unlined chimney. *(5)* No screen in front of fireplace. *(6)* Careless use of portable heater. *(7)* Over-loaded electrical circuits. *(8)* Matches or lighters within reach of small children. *(9)* Cooking left unattended. *(10)* Combustible items near cooking appliance. *(11)* Improper storage of flammable liquids. *(12)* Unshielded porcelain fixtures in closets. *(13)* Insulation against recessed electrical fixtures. *(14)* Poorly maintained heating system. *(15)* Inadequate ventilation when using flammable substances. *(16)* Lint-clogged vinyl dryer duct. *(17)* Bulb wattage too great for fixture, overheats socket and wiring. *(18)* Exposed rigid foam insulation. *(19)* No lightning protection. *(20)* Inadequate ventilation around electronic equipment.

SELECTING A SMOKE DETECTOR

Fire officials consider smoke detectors the best protection you can buy to escape a fire in your home. According to the National Fire Protection Association more than half of the fatal home fires in America occur at night while people are asleep, and about two-thirds of the victims die from suffocation rather than burns. Unless something wakes your family soon after a fire starts, your odds of surviving plunge.

Smoke detectors use either of two proven technologies. *Ionization* smoke detectors sense the charged particles that are created when things burn; *photoelectric* detectors react when smoke obscures an internal light beam. Both can be powered by your home's AC electrical system, by disposable batteries, or by a combination of the two. Each kind of detector can provide adequate protection as long as it is properly certified, installed, and maintained.

Smoke detectors are widely available at home centers and hardware stores. Look for a label stating that the design has been approved by a testing organization such as Underwriters Laboratories (UL). Next, consider the power source. Finally, think about where the unit will be installed and whether the location favors a particular sensor technology or special feature.

BATTERY-POWERED DETECTORS

Battery-powered smoke detectors are the least expensive and easiest to install. If you plan to put several devices around your home and your budget or electrical wiring skills are limited, this may be the way to go. However, a battery-powered unit won't do any good unless you diligently replace the battery at least once a year and resist the temptation to remove the cell to silence a false alarm or borrow it for another use.

AC-POWERED DETECTORS

Smoke detectors that are connected to household current cost a bit more, but they are probably more reliable. In new construction, some fire codes require AC-wired devices on each level of the home and outside each sleeping area. AC-powered devices are particularly convenient when the unit will be difficult to reach. What's more, they can be interconnected so all sound if one senses smoke. This is particularly valuable in a large, multilevel home.

DETECTOR CHOICE

Although both ionization and photoelectric sensors can detect fire, one may be slightly better for a given application. A detector with a photoelectric sensor mounted near a sleeping area will react to the slightest trace of smoke. But it will also react to steam from a hot shower, dust from woodworking, or cooking smoke, so it would not be well suited for installation near a bathroom, workshop, or kitchen. A detector with an ionization sensor will not be fooled by steam or dust. And it will detect the invisible ions from a fire even if no smoke is evident.

SPECIAL FEATURES

Some smoke detectors have features beyond just sounding an alarm. You can check some models by shining the beam of an ordinary flashlight at them, so you don't need a stepladder to reach the test button. If false alarms are liable to be a nuisance (such as from cooking smoke or a wood stove), consider a model with an override button that will desensitize the alarm for up to 15 minutes without removing the batteries or turning off the power. Another feature is an integral security light, a real plus for marking stairway escape routes.

Finally, some detectors can be integrated into a whole-house security alarm system (see Chapter 38).

INSTALLING A SMOKE DETECTOR

All smoke detectors come with mounting and installation instructions. With a battery-powered detector, all you do is fasten the base plate to the ceiling or wall with two screws, install the battery (9-volt in most models), and snap the cover in place.

120-volt AC-powered detectors can either be plugged into wall outlets or permanently wired ("hardwired") to the electrical system. Manufacturers recommend that hardwiring be done by licensed electricians. If you feel you can do the job, wiring techniques are covered in Chapter 34. The basic procedure is: Turn off power to the circuit. Connect the detector's black lead to the black wire in the circuit cable and the white lead to the white wire. Make connections by twisting the wire ends together, screw on a wire cap, and then tape the cap in place. Some hardwired alarms can be interconnected so all will sound if one unit detects smoke. These models feature a third (yellow) lead. The yellow leads must be connected by a separate conductor, which will have to be installed. Never connect an AC-powered detector to a wall switch. Put it on an unswitched circuit with other fixtures so a loss of power will be noticed immediately and so it cannot accidentally be turned off.

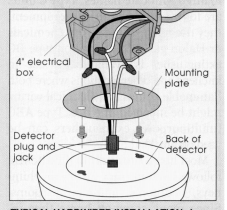

SECURE THE PLUG of an AC-powered smoke detector in a wall outlet so it cannot be unplugged accidentally.

TYPICAL HARDWIRED INSTALLATION. A separate conductor is required for the yellow lead on units that can be interconnected.

37 HOME SAFETY AND HEALTH

A home is not just a building that must be maintained, it is an environment—a complex of living space and conditions in which you and your family spend a major part of your lives. This chapter focuses on some of the most important things you can do to make sure it is a safe and healthy environment.

EVALUATING HOME SAFETY
Most accidents happen at home, primarily because that is where people spend most of their time. Even a modest effort in making your home safer can greatly reduce the chances of a serious or even fatal accident.

To evaluate the present situation in your home, first identify the places where accidents are most likely to occur—the bathroom, stairs, and unlighted areas, for example—and the kinds of hazards that exist. Loose carpeting, inadequate railings, dark stairways, and unprotected electrical outlets are common hazards.

Next, make a list of what needs to be done and get to work. You can't do everything at once, so give priority to those things that put young, elderly, or handicapped family members at special risk.

COMMON SAFETY HAZARDS
Protection against fire, perhaps the most devastating accident in a home, is covered in Chapter 36. Installing ground fault interrupter (GFI) protection to reduce the danger of electrocution or severe shock is covered on page 435. Supplement GFI protection by replacing metal wall plates on switches in sink and other damp-work areas with plastic plates and mounting screws. To prevent toddlers from sticking things into electrical outlets, put plain plastic inserts in unused receptacles and use extension cords with safety caps.

While the hazards of fire and electricity usually come to mind first, the most common home accidents involve falls and serious bumps, burns and scalds, and accidental poisoning.

FALLS AND BUMPS
Be sure carpeting is secure. Fasten stair runners at the rear of each tread. Put nonslip mats under throw rugs on polished floors and under the bathmat in a tiled bathroom. If your tub or shower does not have a matte-surface floor, add adhesive nonslip strips or a rubber mat with suction cups on the underside. Install full-depth nonslip material on the treads of basement and attic stairs.

Provide true grab bars—not just towel bars—in the shower or tub, and perhaps beside the toilet for an elderly person. Provide handrails on all stairs. The elderly often need rails on both sides, and sometimes along hallways as well. Children need a rail at a proper height for their size; it can be removed when they grow. Mount all grab bars and railings with screws long enough to reach into wall studs.

Make sure that halls and stairways have adequate light at all times. An easy solution is to use small lights that plug directly into a receptacle. They come on automatically at night or during the day whenever the ambient light drops below a certain level, and they consume only a quarter-watt of power or less.

Wherever things are stored on overhead shelves, provide a sturdy step stool or short stepladder with a built-in hand bar at waist height. Group items on high shelves in boxes or plastic baskets to prevent them from falling.

Round off sharp corners on counters, tables, and fixtures, or cover them with stick-on rubber or plastic bumpers. A corner at hip height for an adult is at eye or throat height for many children.

Outdoors, proper step, porch, and deck railings are essential (see Chapter 30). A ground-level swimming pool must be enclosed by its own 4-foot-high fence with a locking gate. This is the law in most places, and a liability requirement in home insurance policies.

Cover basement window wells with gratings or plastic domes so a child cannot fall in. Cover outdoor basement steps with a door or doors at surface level. Make sure it can be securely fastened both closed and open. If your garage door has an electric opener, adjust the safety stop/reverse sensitivity carefully to make sure that a child cannot be trapped under it (see Chapter 26).

Install swings and play equipment over earth, sand, or other soft material. Make sure they are securely fastened against tipping over. Keep trees well pruned, so that when youngsters climb they have solid limbs to hang onto.

BURNS AND SCALDS
In the kitchen, keep pot handles turned out of the reach of children and where they cannot be bumped accidentally. Equip drop-in ranges and pull-out cooktops with anti-tipover brackets. Some models have them; older models can be retrofitted easily. Many microwave and wall ovens have double-latching doors to childproof them. Accessory latches are available for older models.

Glass-paneled tub/shower enclosures must have shatter-resistant safety glass. You can have existing sliding panels reglazed, or get new replacements.

Modern building codes require the use of tub shower valves with antiscald protection. One kind has a high-limit stop that restricts movement so a certain amount of cold water is always mixed with the hot, to keep it at a safe temperature. However, that does not protect against a sudden pressure drop if someone flushes a toilet. A pressure-balancing valve does maintain a certain temperature even when the pressure in either the hot or cold water line varies, but it does not respond to temperature changes in the lines. Only a true temperature-control mixing valve will mix the proper amounts of hot and cold water to maintain a constant temperature. If you do not want to change mixers, you can replace the shower head with one that contains a heat-sensitive alloy. When the water temperature exceeds 120°F, the alloy expands and immediately cuts off the flow.

POISONING
Poisonous substances in the home must be clearly marked for adults, and made inaccessible to children. Locking cabinets are suitable in the basement, workshop, or garage, but impractical in the bathroom, kitchen, and laundry. In those locations, one solution is a latch that interlocks adjacent cupboard door handles. Another is a double-acting latch that opens the door only an inch or two when first tripped and requires a second action to open fully. A third is a latch with no handle on the outside of the door. It is activated by an accessory magnet that is kept nearby, out of the reach of a child. These and similar devices are available at home centers, houseware stores, and kitchen and bath suppliers.

HOME SAFETY IMPROVEMENTS

USE PLASTIC WALL PLATES and plastic mounting screws on switches in bathrooms and kitchen wet areas. GFI protection may cover only the receptacles there.

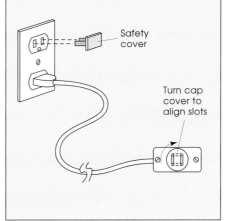

COVER UNUSED RECEPTACLES with plug-in plastic covers, and use extension cords with safety caps, to prevent children from sticking things into the slots.

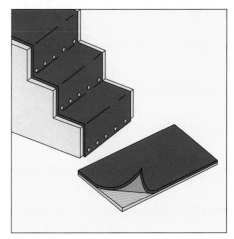

KEEP CARPETING SECURE. Fasten stair runners at the back of each tread. Place thin nonslip mats under throw rugs on polished or tile floors.

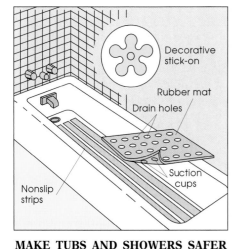

MAKE TUBS AND SHOWERS SAFER with stick-on strips or decorative cutouts of nonslip material, or a waterproof mat with suction cups on the underside.

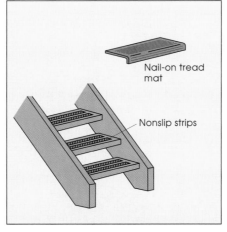

IMPROVE BASEMENT AND ATTIC STAIRS with nonslip adhesive strips, or rubber mats nailed to the treads. Or use paint containing nonslip abrasive particles.

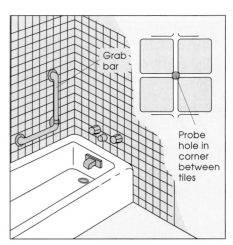

SCREW GRAB BARS INTO STUDS in tubs, showers, and elsewhere. To probe for a stud, drill a small hole between tiles (see page 155); it can be filled easily.

HOME SAFETY

HOME SAFETY IMPROVEMENTS Continued

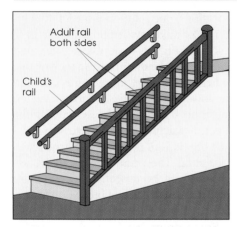

PROVIDE SECURE RAILINGS on all stairs, indoors and out. Double railings are helpful to the elderly or handicapped; children need a rail at their own height.

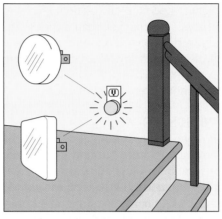

PROVIDE ADEQUATE LIGHT in halls and on stairs at all times. Small plug-in lights come on automatically when needed and consume almost no power.

USE ONLY LADDERS OR STEP STOOLS with safety bars to reach high shelves. Store items in plastic baskets or boxes so they cannot spill down on you.

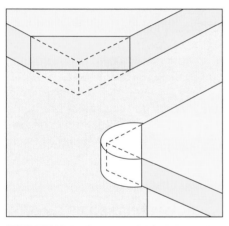

ELIMINATE SHARP CORNERS. Cut them off at an angle, or round them with a sander where feasible. In other cases, cover them with adhesive-backed bumpers.

ENCLOSE AN OUTDOOR POOL with a fence (rails on the inside) and locking gate. Post safety signs. Install a ground fault interrupter on the pool pump (see page 435).

COVER EXTERIOR BASEMENT STEPS with a door that can be locked shut and fastened safely open. Cover window wells with grates or plastic domes to keep toddlers out.

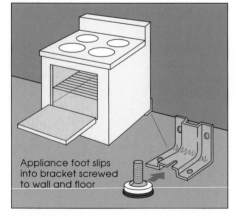

MAKE RANGES AND PULL-OUT COOK-TOPS TIP-PROOF with security brackets. If not included with your unit, brackets are available from appliance dealers.

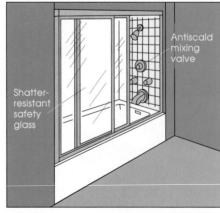

INSTALL AN ANTISCALD MIXING VALVE or showerhead in the bathroom. Be sure panels or doors are glazed with shatter-resistant safety glass.

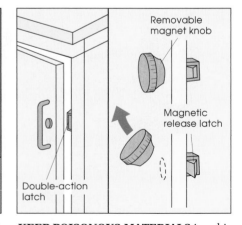

KEEP POISONOUS MATERIALS in cabinets with childproof latches. Even ordinarily safe substances are dangerous to a child who drinks them or gets them in the eyes.

HOME SAFETY

CHILD SAFETY

It's virtually impossible for any parent to exercise constant vigilance over their children for the entire day. During brief interruptions of supervision, children can wander into lethal situations. The best way to insulate children from the hazards of the home is to childproof the home environment. Childproofing a home is a way of adding special safeguards throughout the home environment—safeguards that protect the child without inhibiting his/her ability to explore and learn. This also includes buying and using products that are rated with a stamp of approval from an accredited organization, such as the Juvenile Products Manufacturers Association or *Consumer Reports*. Their approval means that those products meet the safety standards set by a panel of experts.

Childproofing the home begins with an inspection of the entire home, or rather those areas where the child is apt to roam. Rather than simply walking about the house, conduct the inspection on your hands and knees and look for potential hazards. This will help you to see the home environment from a child's point of view.

OUTLETS AND APPLIANCES

Electrical outlets and appliances are especially dangerous because curious children often experiment by poking metal objects into outlets. It's easy to safeguard the outlets with outlet plugs. These are nonconductive plastic inserts (available at hardware stores and home centers) that fit into and block the outlet holes. For receptacles that are often needed for an appliance, you can mount spring safety caps that cover the plug and outlet yet snap back when the receptacle is needed.

Children like to chew on and yank appliance cords so these pose a danger to the curious toddler. Never allow an appliance cord to dangle where a child can pull on it. Make cords as short as possible with telephone cord shorteners or coil them and tie the coil with twist ties. If this is not possible, tape the cord out of the reach of the infant. Be sure to unplug all appliances that are not being used so they can not be turned on.

LOCKS AND DOORS

Lock all doors that you don't want your children to open. This is especially true of doors to a stairway entrance. It is not necessary to install a key lock; a hook and eye or locking catch located high on the outside of these doors will suffice. Doorknob covers, loose-fitting attachments that make it difficult for a child to grip and turn the knob (you can also use a loose sock for this), are another way to safeguard a door.

Some doors, such as closet doors, should not lock because a child could easily get trapped inside. Tie a dish towel from knob to knob to keep the door from locking. This will also prevent the door from closing completely and pinching a child's hands.

The bathroom door should have a special lock so adults can lock it, yet parents must be able to open it from the outside if a young child accidentally locks himself in. Such locks are available; they have a push button on the inside knob and a small hole in the center

Continued

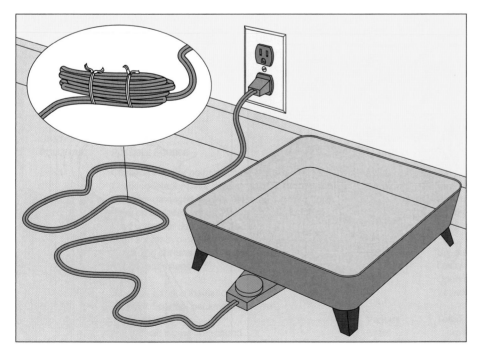

USE TWIST TIES TO TAKE UP THE SLACK in an appliance cord and keep the cord as short as possible. Remember to unplug the appliance when it's not in use to prevent children from accidentally turning it on.

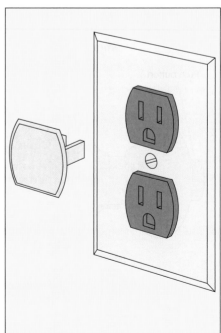

PLACE PLASTIC PLUGS in all unused outlets. These will prevent children from inserting small objects into the outlet holes.

CHILD SAFETY

38 SECURITY

Burglary and vandalism cost home-owners many millions of dollars each year. Every effort you put into making the security improvements discussed in this chapter will repay you many times in increased protection against loss and damage, and greater safety and peace of mind for you and your family. As a bonus, adding security measures may reduce your homeowner's insurance premiums.

DETERMINING SECURITY NEEDS

A burglar has to approach a home un-noticed, gain entry, and remain unde-tected once inside. So, in assessing your present security and what to do about it, consider the following points.

Approach. Is the house isolated or out of the view of neighbors or passing motorists? Do fences, walls, shrubs, or inadequate lighting at night provide concealment? Will exterior conditions or a lack of interior lighting reveal an empty house?

Entry. Are doors and windows equipped with true security locks, or only convenience latches? Pay special attention to sliding doors and windows. Do trees, trellises, decks, or other features make upper-story entry possible? Are basement windows and doors secure? Is the garage secure? Does it contain tools that could be used in a break-in? If it is attached to the house, how secure is the connecting door?

Detection. Is there an alarm to scare off an intruder before entry is attempted? Are there detectors to signal that entry has occurred? Most burglaries take place when no one is home, or at a time when no one is awake to hear a break-in.

Many police departments offer free assistance in making a security survey.

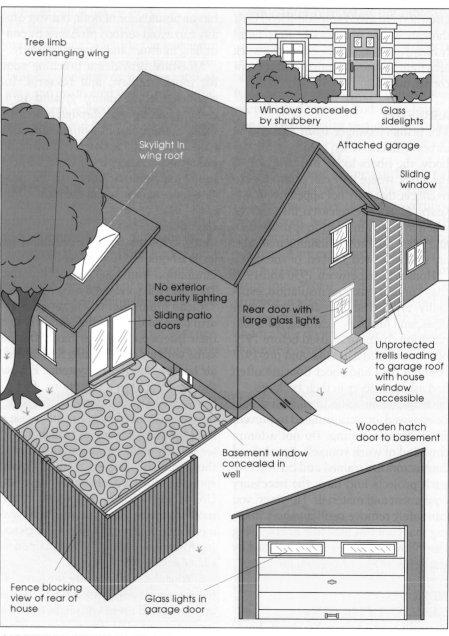

Tree limb overhanging wing

Windows concealed by shrubbery

Glass sidelights

Skylight in wing roof

Attached garage

Sliding window

No exterior security lighting

Sliding patio doors

Rear door with large glass lights

Unprotected trellis leading to garage roof with house window accessible

Wooden hatch door to basement

Basement window concealed in well

Fence blocking view of rear of house

Glass lights in garage door

CAREFULLY CHECK EACH OF THE FACTORS SHOWN ABOVE. In addition to inade-quate locks and latches on doors and windows, they are the weak points in most homes. See the following pages for information on dealing with these and other problems.

SECURING DOORS

A good door lock is very important (see pages 476–479), but only if the door itself is strong and secure. Here are some ways to secure hinged doors (see pages 480–481 for sliding door security). For working techniques, see chapters 19 and 24.

• Use only solid-core doors at least 1¾ inches thick for exterior entries, including into an attached garage. Choose metal-clad doors if possible, especially for side and rear entrances. Many have handsome designs suitable for front entries.

• Be sure frames are solid. Pry between the door and jamb on each side. If the jambs move or the gaps widen at all, remove the inside casing, insert solid blocking, and nail through it into the studs.

• Replace glass in sidelights and the door with shatterproof plastic (see page 480). If you want to see the exterior, install a peephole door viewer.

• Be sure hinge screws in the door leaf are at least 2 inches long, and that those in the jamb leaf reach well into the studs behind—a minimum of 3 inches.

• If the barrels of ordinary hinges are on the exterior side of a door, the pin can be driven out and the door opened. You can install either hinges that have nonremovable pins, or security stud hinges. With the latter, when the door is closed a stud attached to one leaf projects into a hole in the other leaf. You can make your own security studs by replacing one

screw in each existing hinge with a lag screw. Drive it 2 inches into the door, and cut off the head to leave a ¾-inch stud. Remove the opposite screw in the jamb leaf for the stud to enter, or drill a hole if the leaf holes do not match.

• Replace glass in garage doors and windows with shatterproof plastic. Cover the inside to block the view of the interior. Change the factory-set frequency of a remote-control door opener. When you leave on vacation, or any other extended period, turn off the power to the door opener or fasten a padlock through the track just above one of the rollers.

• Use metal or metal-clad doors over exterior basement steps. Sink the hinge barrels flush in a concrete curbing. Put security crossbars at two points on the underside of the door or doors.

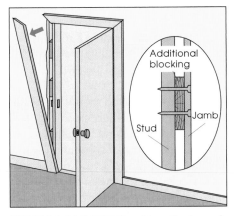

INSTALL BLOCKING, with nails through the jambs into the studs, if the frame flexes when you pry between it and the door.

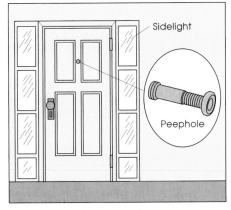

REPLACE GLASS LIGHTS with shatterproof plastic so the lock and hinges cannot be reached. Install a peephole to see outside.

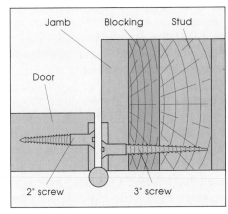

USE LONG HINGE SCREWS: 2-inch screws into the door, 3 inches or longer to reach through the jamb well into a stud.

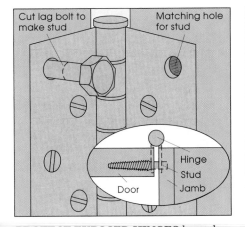

PROTECT EXPOSED HINGES by replacing one screw in each hinge with a stud that fits into the jamb leaf when the door is closed.

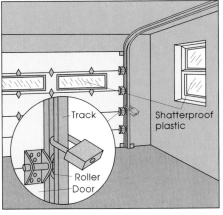

USE SHATTERPROOF PLASTIC in garage windows. Padlock the track or turn off the power for long-term security.

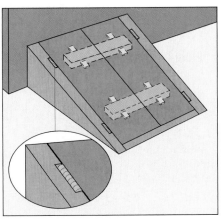

SECURE BASEMENT DOORS with sliding crossbars on the underside. Recess hinge barrels in concrete to protect them.

LOCKS FOR DOORS

A door is held shut by a spring *latch* that moves when you turn the handle or that is pushed back when its slanted face hits the *strike plate* on the jamb. A door can be locked securely only by a *bolt* that engages the strike plate. A *deadbolt* has no spring and is moved by turning a key in a cylinder lock, or an equivalent lever. To provide real security a deadbolt must extend at least 1 inch into a substantial strike. An exposed key cylinder should be protected with a guard plate if possible (see page 478).

There are four major kinds of key-operated locks used on exterior doors: locksets, mortise locks, rim or surface-mounting deadbolt locks, and cylinder deadbolt locks. Two other kinds, cross-bar and brace locks, are more cumbersome and less attractive, but offer even greater security. These locks, and related fittings, are covered on these two pages. Most models come with do-it-yourself installation instructions.

LOCKSETS
In a lockset, also called a cylindrical or key-in-knob lock, the entire mechanism is built into the doorknob. The outer knob has a key cylinder and the interior knob has a pushbutton or turn lever to operate a deadlatch—a spring latch plus a deadbolt plunger that prevents opening the latch with a plastic card.

While very popular for their trim, modern appearance, all but the most substantial (and most expensive) locksets offer only limited security. The outer handle containing the key cylinder can be sheared off with a few blows from a sledgehammer. Then the mechanism often can be operated with a screwdriver. Exterior-door locksets are installed in the same way as tubular locks for interior doors (see page 246).

INSTALLING LOCKSETS
Use the template provided to locate the position of the holes for the cylinder (on the door face) and the bolt (on the door edge) and all pilot holes for mounting screws. Use a ⅛-inch drill bit to drill the pilot holes. Use a hole saw to cut the large hole for the cylinder. Start the hole on one side of the door and bore halfway through. Remove the hole saw and finish the hole from the other side.

From the edge of the door, drill the hole for the latch bolt with a spade bit. Insert the bolt mechanism into this hole and mark the outline of the latch plate on the door surface. Remove the plate and the bolt, then cut a mortise for the plate with a chisel. Replace the bolt-plate mechanism and screw the plate into the mortise. Insert the exterior knob and cylinder into the large hole. Mate the cylinder mechanism with the latch bolt. Place the exterior knob and rose plate on the opposite side of the door and secure it with screws.

Mark the position for the strike plate on the door jamb; be sure it aligns with the latch bolt. Use a sharp chisel to cut a recess for the plate, and a spade bit to bore a hole to accept the latch bolt. Fasten the plate in place with screws.

MORTISE LOCKS
The mechanism of a mortise lock fits into a pocket cut into the edge of the door. The spring latch is operated by a doorknob on both sides, or by a thumb lever above a fixed handle on the outside. Pushbuttons in the edge of the door can block operation of the latch from the outside. Security locking is provided by a separate deadbolt that is operated by a key from outside and a lever from inside.

The pocket for a mortise lock can be a weak spot in the frame of a conventional wood door. Adding a reinforcing plate (see page 478) is a wise measure.

RIM LOCKS
A rim lock—a surface-mounting deadbolt, or night latch—fastens on the back side of a door stile and has a deadbolt that engages a strike mounted on the jamb. It is operated by a small knob (thumbturn) on the inside and by a key from the outside. The key cylinder extends through a hole in the stile.

The deadbolt may move horizontally

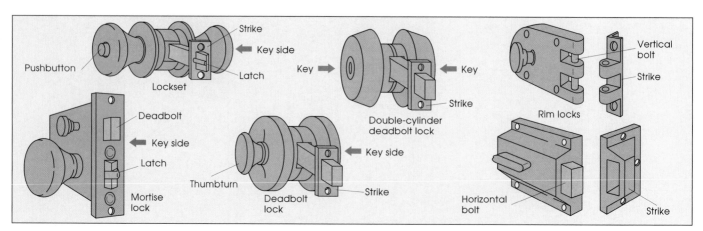

FOUR KINDS OF LOCKS COMMONLY USED ON RESIDENCE EXTERIOR DOORS. Many models of each kind are available, to suit any style door. All can be installed with an electric drill, chisels, and a screwdriver or two. Installation instructions usually include templates for marking hole and mortise positions.

into the strike, or vertically. A vertical bolt is more secure because it engages holes in the strike and cannot be popped out by prying the door away from the jamb. The strike should have an L shape that mounts with screws from two directions. Rimlocks are easy to install and provide good security if bolted rather than screwed to the door, and if strike screws reach into the studs.

INSTALLING RIM LOCKS

Tape the template to the door and use an awl to make the centerpoints for each hole. Use a hole saw to bore a large hole for the cylinder mechanism. Drill four smaller holes ¾-inch deep with a ⅛-inch drill bit. These are pilot holes for the lock mounting screws. Slip the cylinder into the large hole and attach the reinforcing plate. Position the lock case over the reinforcing plate, making sure that the tailpiece from the cylinder fits into the corresponding slot in the lockcase. Secure the lock case to the door with mounting screws.

Close the door so the bolt mechanism on the lock case rests against the edge of the door frame. Use a pencil to mark the outline where the lock case mates with the door frame. The strike plate will be positioned within this outline. Hold the strike plate in position and mark the location of the screw holes.

Drill two pilot holes, then screw the strike plate to the door frame.

For added security, you can buy a cylinder guard at a locksmith's or hardware store and mount it over the cylinder on the exterior side of the door. Place it over the cylinder and bolt it in place with four carriage bolts.

CYLINDER DEADBOLT LOCKS

A cylinder deadbolt lock is installed in the same manner as a cylindrical lockset. A *single-cylinder* lock is operated with a key from the outside and a thumbturn from the inside. A *double-cylinder* lock requires a key on both
Continued

HOW TO INSTALL A RIM LOCK

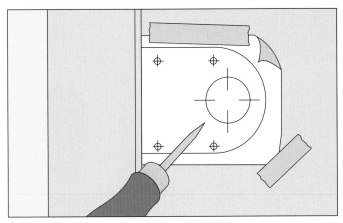

THE LOCK SHOULD COME WITH A PAPER TEMPLATE. Tape this template on the door and mark the places where the holes should be drilled.

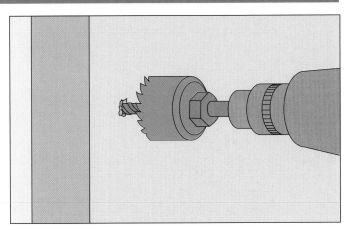

USE A HOLE SAW TO DRILL THE CYLINDER hole in the door. Drill screw holes with a ⅛-bit, or follow the manufacturer's instructions for the preferred size.

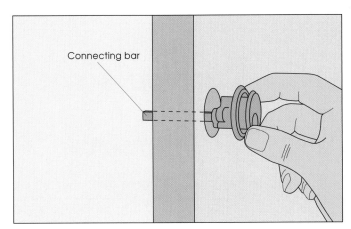

Connecting bar

FROM THE EXTERIOR SIDE OF THE DOOR, insert the cylinder into the large hole making sure it aligns properly. Secure it with the reinforcing plate.

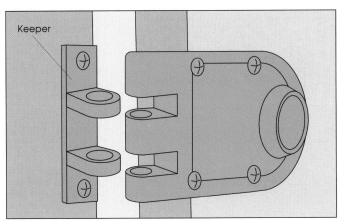

Keeper

POSITION THE LOCK CASE on the door. Align the slot in the case with the connecting bar from the cylinder. Screw the lock case and keeper in place.

LOCKS FOR DOORS

LOCKS FOR DOORS *Continued*

sides. This prevents anyone from operating the lock after making a hole to reach inside. However, in an emergency, anyone inside can get trapped. For this reason, some communities ban double-cylinder locks in residences.

Cylinder deadbolt locks offer excellent security when they are properly mounted in a substantial door. Depending on the design of the lock and the thickness of the door, some cylinders protrude on the outside. They must have tapered guard rings of case-hardened steel to protect them from being gripped with a wrench or attacked with a hammer. A cylinder deadbolt or a rim lock is often used in addition to a mortise lock or a lockset, for increased security.

INSTALLING CYLINDER DEADBOLT LOCKS

Installing a cylinder deadbolt lock involves drilling two holes for the lock mechanism. The one through the face of the door contains the locking mechanism within the cylinder. The bolt mechanism will slide into the other hole, which is drilled perpendicular to the first, through the edge of the door.

Use the paper template provided with the lock to mark the position of the holes. Use a hole saw to drill the first hole. Start cutting the hole from one side of the door. Drill halfway through, then finish the hole from the other side. Use a spade bit to drill the second hole. Start from the door edge and drill into the cylinder hole. It is important to drill the holes precisely, otherwise the cylinder and the bolt mechanism will not be properly aligned.

Insert the bolt mechanism into the appropriate hole and mark the outline of the bolt plate on the edge of the door. Use a sharp chisel to cut a mortise for the plate. Insert the cylinder into the hole—you may have to pull the bolt out first. Bolt the retaining plate to the cylinder, then position the thumb turn (or key lock) and bolt it to the cylinder. Make sure the bolt mechanism is engaged in the cylinder, then turn the key and thumb turn to test for operation.

Position the strike plate on the jamb and mark the position for the bolt hole and mounting screws. Drill pilot holes for the screws and use a chisel to cut a recess for the bolt. Secure the plate to the door jamb with screws.

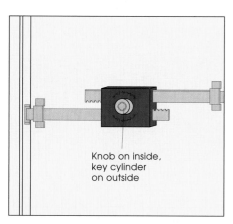

A CROSSBAR LOCK mounts on the back of a door. Operating the center lock moves bars into brackets on the frame.

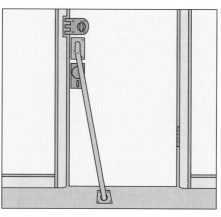

A BRACE OR POLICE LOCK provides triangular bracing. Like a crossbar lock, it is very secure but not very attractive.

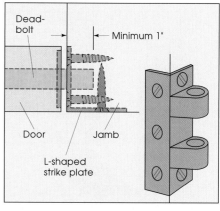

DEADBOLT ESSENTIALS: 1-inch minimum throw into a strike; L-shaped rim lock strike plate, for screws in two directions.

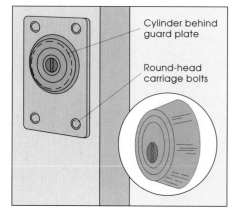

PROTECT THE KEY CYLINDER with a guard plate over a flush mount, or a tapered guard ring over a protruding mount.

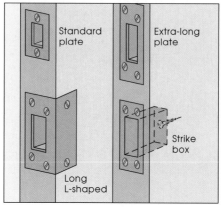

REPLACEMENT STRIKE PLATES can improve security. All should be mounted with screws that will reach into studs.

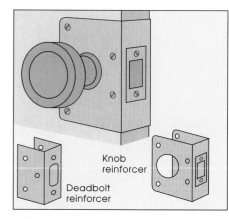

REINFORCING PLATES protect the knob or deadbolt area of a door against damage when a break-in is attempted.

OTHER LOCKS

A *crossbar lock* mounts on the back of the door, with a key cylinder in the center. Turning the key or an inside knob extends two hardened metal bars into metal braces bolted to the framing on either side, or above and below. A *brace lock* or so-called *police lock* mounts on the lock stile of the door, above the handle. A removable, heavy-duty metal rod fits into a socket on the floor to provide triangular bracing. It is operated by a key from the outside and a lever from the inside. Both kinds of locks offer substantial security.

Interior *chain locks* or *door guards* permit opening the door only partway, but offer no security. Surface-mounting *sliding bolts* offer various degrees of security depending on their size, design, and materials. The same is true of *padlocks* in hasps, which may be suitable where appearance is not important.

ADDITIONAL FITTINGS

A hardened metal *guard plate,* or escutcheon, covers a flush-mounted key cylinder on the outside of a door. It is secured with round-head bolts or tamperproof screws.

Extralong or L-shaped *replacement strike plates* can hold a deadbolt more securely than a standard, short plate. So can a *strike box*, which has a metal box that fits into the deadbolt mortise. All mount with four or more screws, some or all long enough to reach into the door studs. Various wraparound *reinforcing plates* fit over the edge of the door to protect the area where a lockset, mortise lock, or deadbolt lock is installed.

LOCKING CONVENIENCE

Some homeowners install *keyed sets* on two or more doors. These are locks with matching cylinders, so that the same key operates them all. This does not increase security, but avoids having to keep track of separate keys for each entrance. You can buy keyed sets and install them in existing locks of the same make.

HOW TO INSTALL A DEADBOLT

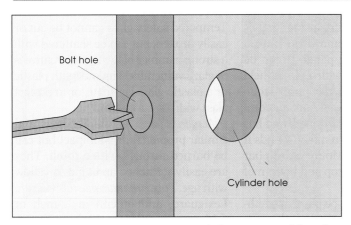

USING THE LOCK TEMPLATE, mark the positions of the cylinder holes and the bolt hole, then drill the appropriate holes using a ⅛-inch drill bit.

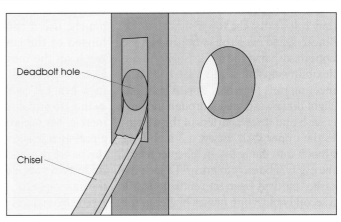

MEASURE OUT THE SPACE FOR THE BOLT HOLE on the edge of the door. Then cut out the mortise for the bolt plate with a sharp chisel.

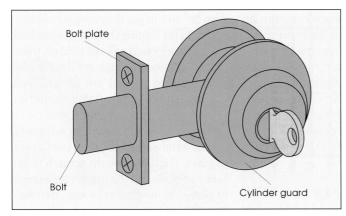

INSERT THE BOLT THROUGH THE HOLE in the edge of the door. Secure it with screws. Insert the cylinder guard from the exterior side of the door.

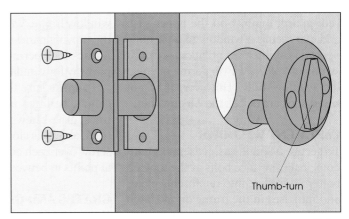

SECURE THE CYLINDER GUARD WITH SCREWS. Install the thumb turn and secure it in place with screws. Test the handle to make sure it operates smoothly.

LOCKS FOR DOORS

EXTERIOR SECURITY LIGHTING

Effective outdoor lighting is a major component of good security. The last thing an intruder wants is to be visible while approaching a home or attempting to break in. If bright lights suddenly come on, a burglar will probably be scared away. (Interior lighting is an important deterrent, too; see page 484.) Good lighting is also a convenience and safety factor for you and your family—for example, when you come home after dark with a trunkload of groceries, or late at night when no neighbors are likely to be awake if you should need help.

OUTDOOR LIGHTING

You can choose to have full security lighting on all night long, but that could be expensive to operate, and bright enough to annoy your neighbors. Many homeowners prefer to have inexpensive low-voltage, low-intensity lighting (see page 439) for convenience and safety along sidewalks, steps, and similar places. This is supplemented with bright security lighting in areas such as the back door and garage and the concealed sides of the house. The security lighting is controlled by sensors and comes on only when triggered by someone entering a protected zone. This will surprise and scare off most prowlers.

POWER SYSTEMS

The bright lights used for outdoor security lighting are usually powered by 120-volt household current. To ensure lighting even if household power is lost, you can use lights powered by conventional batteries, which must be replaced periodically, or by batteries that are recharged by the sun. Solar-charged batteries do not have to be replaced, but are not effective where sunlight is scarce in the winter or where they might become covered with snow.

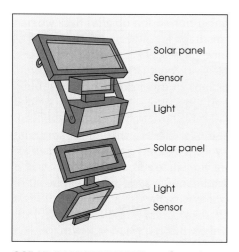

SOLAR-BATTERY UNITS need no wiring, but stay on only a few minutes, to conserve power. Panel tilts for best angle toward sky.

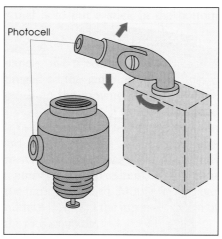

PHOTOCELLS operate lights at dusk and dawn. A screw-in socket installs quickly; a box-mounting sensor is widely adjustable.

A PASSIVE INFRARED SENSOR turns on security lights whenever a heat-radiating object comes into its field of view.

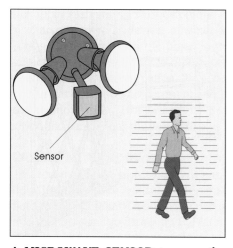

A MICROWAVE SENSOR turns on the lights whenever movement in its field disturbs the pattern of the signal it emits.

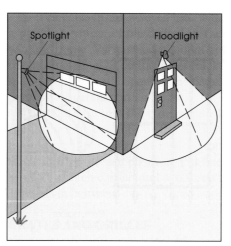

USE FLOODLIGHT AND SPOTLIGHT BULBS where each will be most effective. Place lights well out of reach if possible.

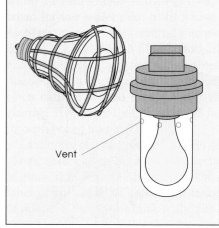

PROTECT OUTDOOR LIGHT BULBS. Wire cages are inexpensive; shatterproof plastic housings also give weather protection.

EXTERIOR LIGHTING

SENSOR-ACTIVATED LIGHTING

Outdoor lighting can be activated in several ways: by a hard-wired switch; by a timer; by a remote radio-frequency switch; or by a sensor. The most widely used and effective sensors are a photoelectric cell, a passive infrared sensor, and a microwave sensor.

A photoelectric cell, or photocell, acts as a switch to turn on a light when the surroundings become dark. You can get exterior light fixtures with built-in photocells, or you can buy accessory photocontrols that either screw in or are hardwired (directly connected) for use with existing fixtures. If you want your general outdoor lighting to go on at dusk and stay on until dawn, choose photoelectric control. If you want the lights to go on and off at other times, choose timer control instead (see page 484).

For lighting that comes on only when someone enters a protected zone, choose an infrared or microwave sensor. As with photocells, you can buy fixtures with built-in sensors, or you can purchase separate sensors and connect them to existing fixtures. Most include a photocell so that they will operate only after dark.

A passive infrared sensor detects heat sources, such as people or car engines, within an unobstructed field of coverage. A microwave sensor detects any movement within a field of high-frequency energy that it emits. (For more about sensors, see pages 485–487.) Many units can be set to either flash on and off or to remain on continuously for a preselected length of time. You also can adjust the sensitivity so that a passing cat or swirling leaves will not turn on the light. The exterior units that are least prone to false triggering use a combination of passive infrared and microwave sensors.

Of course you can power an alarm as well as lights from an exterior security fixture. Or exterior fixtures can be connected to a whole-house electronic security system (see pages 485–487). Then they can be set to flash or sound an alarm at any time when triggered by sensors inside the house as well as outside. Some systems also let you operate the lights from a central control panel or by remote control, from a Touchtone telephone, for example.

LIGHTING PLACEMENT

The primary security function of exterior lighting is to deny would-be intruders the shroud of darkness. Additional functions are to ensure good visibility if you should have to exit in an emergency, and to clearly illuminate your house number to aid emergency response personnel.

Before installing any security lighting, consider fixture choices and their locations carefully. Then prune shrubs and move obstacles that would cast concealing shadows at sensitive points.

All entrances to your home, garage, and outbuildings should become well lighted as soon as anyone comes near, because those are a burglar's most likely points of entry. The same is true of any areas that are not clearly visible from the street or neighboring homes. High-wattage floodlight bulbs are best for illuminating areas directly below a fixture. Use spotlight bulbs to reach an area from any height or distance. Use exterior or weather-resistant bulbs, to minimize the need to replace them.

Ordinary entrance lights with 40- or 60-watt bulbs are usually mounted just above the door, or alongside. Place security lighting fixtures higher—high enough on walls or poles to be out of reach. Protect bulbs at any level against breakage with wire cages or tamper-resistant plastic housings. Exposed 120-volt wiring must run through metal conduit. This is a safety requirement of electrical codes. It also protects the wiring from being cut to black out exterior lighting, or from being tapped into as a power source for a burglar's drill, saw, or other tool.

INSTALLING A SECURITY LIGHT

There are many types of security light fixtures with either passive infrared (PIR) or microwave (MW) sensors, or a combination of the two. Most are designed to be hard-wired to a circular, weatherproof electrical utility box. The base of the fixture becomes the faceplate of the box.

If you have existing exterior boxes in suitable locations, you can replace the present fixtures with security units. Otherwise, have boxes installed where needed. Choose each location so that most movement will be at an angle across the field of coverage, rather than directly toward or away from the detector. PIR sensors in particular are most effective with that orientation. The control switch for a security power circuit should be inside the house, inaccessible to prowlers.

To replace an existing light with a sensor-equipped model, turn off the power to the circuit. Then remove the bulbs and the two screws that hold the faceplate to the utility box. Unscrew the twist connectors that join the black (hot), white (neutral), and green (ground) circuit leads to the fixture leads. Most security fixtures are preassembled and have only two or three leads that need to be connected. If there are more, check the installation instructions to identify the sensor/detector leads. Connect them to the power circuit wires: white to white, black to black, green to green. (If the fixture does not have a grounding wire, connect the grounding wire in the circuit cable to the ground terminal in the utility box.) Use screw-on caps, and tape them in place (see page 429). Fasten the base of the unit onto the box and turn the power on again.

A photoelectric sensor in most units deactivates them in daylight, so wait until dark to aim the motion sensor and adjust the sensitivity control. Follow the unit instructions carefully; have a helper walk in and out of the coverage zone while you make the adjustments.

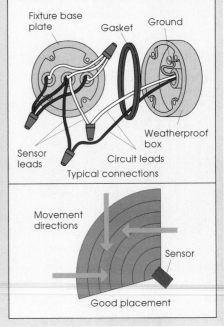

Typical connections

Good placement

EXTERIOR LIGHTING

INTERIOR LIGHTING

The primary security function of interior lighting is to make your house look occupied when you are away. That means having lights come on and go off in various parts of the house in what seems to be a normal pattern of use. (Lights can also be part of an alarm and signaling system; see pages 485–487.)

You can equip lighting fixtures with screw-in photocell sockets into which you screw the light bulbs, but they will stay on all night—hardly a normal pattern. For a varied pattern of light use, you need timer control.

MECHANICAL-SWITCH TIMERS
A basic lighting timer is a combination of an electric clock and a switch. The clock drives the timer dial. Timer operation is set by placing pegs or levers at desired times marked around the rim of the dial. As the dial rotates they trip the switch on and off.

A *receptacle timer* plugs directly into an outlet (or has a short cord). The lamp, radio, or other device to be controlled plugs into the timer. A *socket timer* plugs or screws into an outlet or fixture and has a socket for a bulb.

Some mechanical-switch timers can be set for only one On and one Off time; others permit two or more pairs of settings. Many operate at exactly the set times every day, but better models have

optional random operation that varies the times by up to 20 minutes a day, for a more normal pattern. Almost all have an override switch so you can turn the light on or off independently without disturbing the timing.

ELECTRONIC PROGRAMMABLE TIMERS
Electronic timers can be programmed for multiple settings. They have a control ring, pushbutton, or keypad for entering timing settings, which are recorded on a magnetic chip that controls switch relays. Some provide a digital display of the settings as they are made. One such device is a *timer switch* that mounts in a wall box, in place of a standard switch, for automatic control.

The most versatile and sophisticated timing is provided by a solid-state master unit that controls individual appliance modules throughout the house. From a central location, it can operate lights or appliances plugged into the modules without the need for special wiring.

The control unit is plugged into any electrical outlet. Lights or other appliances are plugged into individual modules, which plug directly into existing outlets. Various control units can handle from four to ten or more modules.

Settings for each module are entered on the keypad of the control unit. At the

programmed times, it transmits on/off signals either over the existing electrical wiring or by a radio frequency. Override switches on the modules permit manual operation of the lights when desired, and the control unit permits independent manual operation as well. Some control units can also be operated by a remote control, or by signals from a Touch-tone telephone.

(Some garage-door openers can act as control units for up to four modules. When the opener receives a signal from its remote control, it transmits signals to modules in the house to turn lights or other devices on or off.)

BUYING LIGHTING CONTROLS
Before you purchase a light-controlling device or system, decide what functions you need—for instance, programming to the nearest minute or the nearest hour; fixed vs. variable day-to-day cycles; and remote control.

If you decide on a programmable system, the control unit and modules will each cost a good deal more than simple manual-set timers. However, security is not an expense, it is an investment. The flexibility and sophistication of a programmable electronic system make it worthwhile to get a large-capacity control unit and just a few modules as a start, and to buy additional modules when necessary or convenient. The best systems can integrate lighting controls with security sensors and alarms.

SET LIGHTS TO GO ON OFF at times that imitate a normal pattern. Adjust according to the time of year.

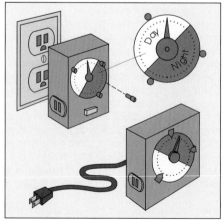

INDIVIDUAL TIMERS are inexpensive and easy to use. Those with a random-timing option are most useful.

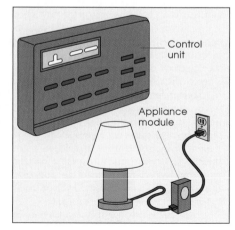

A PROGRAMMABLE CONTROL UNIT offers great flexibility. Lamps and appliances plug into individual modules.

ALARMS AND ALARM SYSTEMS

In addition to physical security for windows and doors, and security lighting, a well-protected house should be equipped with security alarms to signal when a break-in is attempted or takes place.

KINDS OF PROTECTION

Alarms should be used for three levels of security: perimeter protection, space protection, and point protection.

Perimeter protection is provided by alarms placed at points of entry—windows and doors. The alarms may react to detect vibration or noise, the opening of a door or window, or physical damage to a screen or glass. *Space protection* is provided by alarms that monitor an area, such as a room, a hallway, or a stair. *Point protection* is provided by alarms set at specific, high-priority areas, such as a wall safe, a jewelry box or silver chest, and a gun cabinet. Various kinds of devices are used: motion or vibration detectors, narrow-field area sensors, pressure switches, and others.

KINDS OF ALARMS

A security alarm has two major components: a sensor or detector, and a signal unit. The signal unit may be an audible device such as a siren, bell, or horn; it may be a flashing light or beacon; or it may be a device that transmits a signal by telephone line or radio to an outside monitoring point.

Many signal units are activated when the circuit between it and the sensor is broken; others are activated when a circuit to the sensor is completed—by a switch being closed, for instance.

Some alarms are self-contained and battery powered, such as a telescoping arm that is placed between a sliding window or door and the adjacent jamb, or the meeting rail of the bottom sash and a bracket on the top sash in a double-hung window. Any sash movement sets off a piercing whistle-siren alarm built into the rod. A similar doorstop can be wedged between the floor and the back of the door. Another device hangs over the doorknob on the inside; it goes off in response to any movement of the handle.

Other alarms have sensors that are connected to nearby signal units or transmitters. The most common sensor for windows and doors is a two-piece magnetic switch. A small magnet is mounted on the window sash or door, and the switch unit is mounted on the casing, no more than $3/8$ inch away. The switch is connected to an alarm or transmitter and is held shut by the magnet. If the window or door is opened, the switch opens and the signal unit goes off. The illustrations on page 487 show various ways of installing the switches.

Glass alarms include a vibration/breakage-sensitive disk that is adhered to a pane, and metal-foil tape that is applied to the glass all around its perimeter and makes a complete circuit as long as it is unbroken. Both are connected to a signal unit. Windows can also be protected by screens that have sensor wires woven into the mesh. Cutting the screening cuts the wires and breaks the circuit to the signal unit.

Area sensors/detectors use either field or beam coverage. A passive infrared unit detects the heat from a body that enters its field of coverage. An active infrared unit emits a beam that is reflected back to a receiving cell in the unit. Anything passing through the beam breaks the circuit, which sets off the associated signal unit. An active microwave or ultrasonic unit emits a field of energy and reacts if anything moves within its area, disturbing the overall reflection pattern.

Some pressure-sensitive sensors are thin switch assemblies that are held closed until a lid is raised or an object is lifted. Others are floormats or similar pads with multiple switch contacts inside. When they are stepped on, the circuit is completed to the signal unit.

Continued

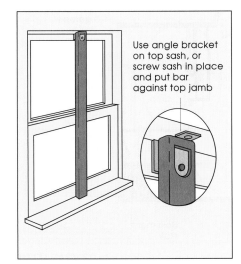

A TELESCOPING BAR ALARM can be used in a double-hung window, as here, or between a sliding window and the side jamb.

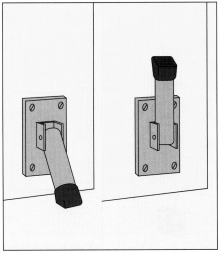

A DOORSTOP ALARM is similar to a window bar alarm: pressure sets it off. It folds up out of the way for normal door use.

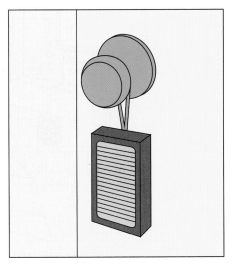

A DOORKNOB ALARM hangs on the inside; any movement will set it off. It is good where nothing can be fastened to the door.

39 INSPECTING THE STRUCTURE

Inspecting a house for defects and problems is not difficult. The trick to making a thorough home inspection is to work systematically, from the bottom of the house to the top, and from side to side. You should record your findings along the way. The following sections will tell you where to look, and what to look for, as you move through and inspect each part of the house.

USE A SEASONAL APPROACH

Plan your inspection by scheduling a certain amount of time, then penciling in those times on the calendar. A complete home inspection is not that difficult because it can be done over time. Interior inspection and maintenance can be accomplished in the winter when the weather is cold. Outside inspection and maintenance can wait until the warmer weather of spring or fall.

Of course, there are some systems in the house that demand seasonal inspection. Consider the heating system for example. The time to inspect it is in the early fall before the cold weather sets in. This way, you have time to do the required preventive maintenance before it gets cold outside and you need heat. This will also give you enough lead time in case you discover any malfunctions that require ordering replacement parts.

The air conditioning system is another component that requires a seasonal approach. Unlike the heating system, the air conditioning system should be inspected and, if necessary, repaired in the early spring so it is ready for the hot days of summer. Likewise a termite inspection should be conducted in the early spring because that is when the insects start to swarm. If the inspection is delayed until the winter, there is apt to be little or no sign of termite infestation (since termites do not nest in a house, but only forage there) and the homeowner may be lulled into a false sense of security.

ESTABLISH A PLAN

This book starts the home inspection at the foundation, because it is the supporting structure for the whole house, but you can start the inspection anywhere and establish your own route. Just be sure to take notes as you inspect and record your findings as you progress through the house. Keep track of the areas covered. In this way you can stop anytime, then pick up again later as time permits, without having to worry about missing any nook or cranny in the house.

Unless you spot a major problem, such as structural damage—an electrical hazard, a plumbing leak, or insect infestation, to name a few—it is better not to stop for maintenance until you have completed the entire inspection. This way, you will be in a better position to compose a complete maintenance schedule and establish a list of matters that need to be addressed first.

USE YOUR SENSES

A house inspection does not require any sophisticated building skills or arcane architectural knowledge. Often it is only a matter of looking at surfaces and materials to see if they look solid and sound. In many cases, problems will be immediately self-evident: boards may be warped or split, masonry surfaces will have cracks, pipes will be leaking. These are visible signs. In some cases, you may get an audible sign, such as water dripping or a squealing drive belt around a drive motor pulley.

In other cases, your nose may alert you to problems that you cannot see or hear. If you detect a strong musty odor it is probably caused by mold or mildew that has accumulated on hidden surfaces or in a wall cavity. If you smell the odor of ozone around an electrical component, it may mean there's a loose connection that is arcing. Remember, if something looks bad, sounds bad, or smells bad, it probably is bad, and needs to be fixed!

Keep in mind, though, that it is not only important to find and correct a problem; in many cases, it is also important to find the underlying cause for that problem. This must also be addressed, otherwise the problem is likely to reoccur.

Although you really only need your senses—sight, hearing, touch, and smell—to locate problems, it helps to have a few other tools handy as you make your inspection. Probably the most important tool is a flashlight that can throw a beam into dark recesses you may find in the attic or basement.

Another handy inspection tool is a pocket knife. You can use this to probe wooden beams for structural soundness or dry rot. It can also be used to scrape rust or test the depth of crumbling concrete. The pocket knife is not used here as a repair tool, but simply as a diagnostic instrument to help you to probe and evaluate the extent of damage.

Goggles, a dust mask, and gloves will protect you if you venture into dusty places or if you want to examine fiberglass insulation. It is not necessary to wear them all the time, but they should be within reach if you need them.

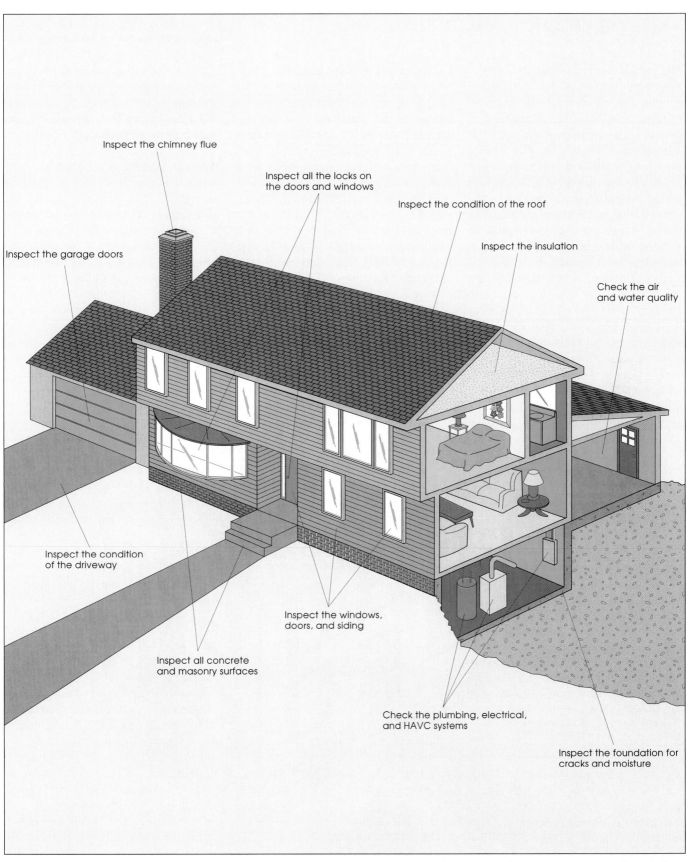

Inspect the chimney flue

Inspect all the locks on
the doors and windows

Inspect the condition of the roof

Inspect the garage doors

Inspect the insulation

Check the air
and water quality

Inspect the condition
of the driveway

Inspect the windows,
doors, and siding

Inspect all concrete
and masonry surfaces

Check the plumbing, electrical,
and HAVC systems

Inspect the foundation for
cracks and moisture

INSPECTING A HOUSE is not difficult, but it should be done systematically, working from the top down (or vice versa) and inside then out. Make a list of all the areas you need to look at, and check off the items on the list after you inspect them. Schedule outside inspection for the warmer months and do the inside inspection when the weather is cold and you must remain indoors.

FOUNDATION CHECKUP

The foundation is the link between the house and the ground. It is designed to support the whole house (a load that weighs hundreds of thousands of pounds) and hold it away from the ground so water and insects do not penetrate or attack the framing. In addition, the foundation is built so it can withstand the pressures exerted by the surrounding earth. It must do this for the life of the occupants and beyond.

In order to support the house, now and into the following centuries, the walls of the foundation must be verti-cally straight within marginal toler-ances. The tops of the walls must be level and even, and the structural in-tegrity of the masonry must remain sound. There is little the homeowner can do if the walls are not plumb (verti-cal) except call in a contractor to see if this is a serious enough problem to warrant correction. Still, a periodic in-spection is important because it can help you identify smaller defects that could, if left uncorrected, develop into major problems that compromise the structural integrity of the foundation.

Fortunately, most small problems can easily be corrected by the average do-it-yourselfer.

The three most common problems that occur with foundations are: water in the basement, damage to the mortar in the floor or walls, and insects or ani-mals entering through the foundation.

WATER IN THE BASEMENT

Water in the basement is usually caused by poor grading around the foundation (remedies for drainage problems are discussed on page 331). The ground should slope away from the foundation, ½ inch to a foot, for at least 6 feet. An easy way to check this is by

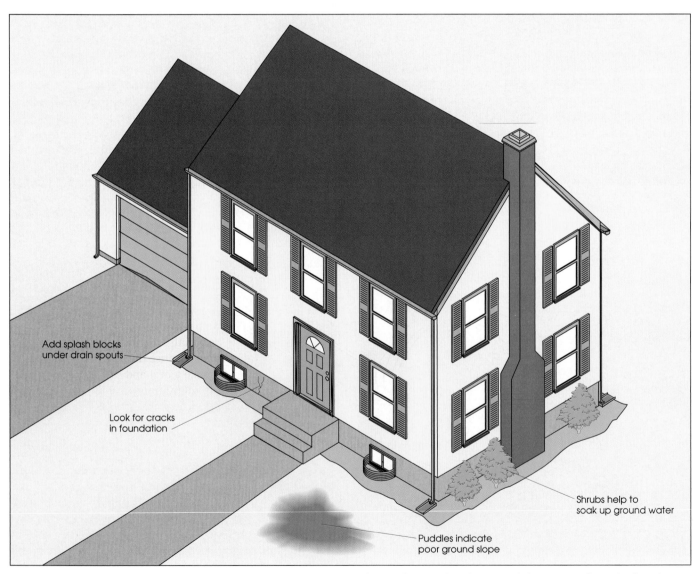

Add splash blocks under drain spouts

Look for cracks in foundation

Shrubs help to soak up ground water

Puddles indicate poor ground slope

WATER IN THE BASEMENT is usually caused by poor grading. Check to make sure that the ground slopes away from the foundation, ½ inch to a foot for at least 6 feet. Check the foundation for cracks or splaying concrete, and repair defects as soon as possible.

walking around the house after a heavy rainstorm. If you see a number of puddles around the foundation walls, it is an indication that the ground is not graded properly.

Another common cause of wet basements is runoff water from the roof that is not diverted away from the foundation. Check to make sure that the gutters are clean and there is no blockage in the downspouts. The downspouts should be positioned so that rainwater is directed away from the house. Installing splash blocks can help.

House location can also be a factor. If the house is located at the foot of a hill, runoff water from the slope could penetrate through the foundation. The solution is to install a French drain to direct water around the house.

Inside the basement, check for moisture on basement walls. This may be caused by moisture seeping through the basement walls or from internal humidity condensing on the walls. To keep groundwater from entering through the basement walls, it may be necessary to seal the walls and possibly add a drain system (see pages 114–122).

Moisture condensing on the walls from humidity can be eliminated by improving the basement ventilation, either with fans or by installing a dehumidifier.

CRACKS IN WALLS OR MORTAR JOINTS
Inspect all the wall surfaces for developing cracks. Hairline cracks in the walls or in mortar joints are usually the result of the concrete settling. These cracks are natural and are no cause for alarm. However, they should be monitored to see if they open further. Wider cracks are caused by ground stresses due to excessive water pressure. These should be repaired (see page 350). However, the cracks will reopen unless underground water pressure in the surrounding soil is relieved. This can be done with improved grading and drainage.

Another masonry problem caused by water pentetration is splaying. The water seeping through causes the faces of concrete blocks to disintergrate. The solution, after correcting the water problem, is to chip away the face of the block and replace it with a paver tile (see pages 352–353).

INSECTS AND ANIMALS ENTERING THE FOUNDATION
The foundation inspection should include checking and sealing all gaps around outside faucets and water pipes, telephone and television lines, electrical conduits, and vents—particularly the dryer vent—to prevent insects and animals from having an accessible pathway into your house.

Termites and ants can be a troublesome problem, but so can animals and birds. When they nest in your home, they eat anything that they can get for food, destroy bedding and insulation for nesting materials, and leave fecal matter around the house. Once an animal lodges in the house, it is difficult to remove the creature. Understand that you cannot kill animals or birds. Federal and state laws prohibit individuals from killing, trapping, or tampering with the nests of animals without special permits. The best strategy is to take preventative measures and secure the house so they cannot gain entry.

Walk around the house and look for overhanging trees and shrubs. Cut back branches and limbs that might allow animals a path to the house. Look for any holes or openings in the walls or foundation that a small creature could enter. Remember that any hole, no matter how small, can be a potential entry point. Mice or birds, for example, can squeeze through a crack that is as small as ¼-inch wide.

Put mesh screening over all exhaust vents. Block the gaps around water lines with steel wool, then caulk over them. Do not rely on caulk alone to keep rodents out since they can eat through caulking.

Animals are usually attracted to a home because they find it a good place to make a nest and find food. Raccoons visit many homes to assault garbage cans. The best possible protection is place the cans in an enclosure that has a roof and latched gate. Place this enclosure away from the foundation to keep the animals away from the house. If this is not possible, fit the garbage cans with tight-fitting lids and connect springs from the lids to eye hooks in the sides of the cans.

Mice and insects also like to make their homes in stacked firewood. Keep stacked firewood several yards away from the foundation to be safe.

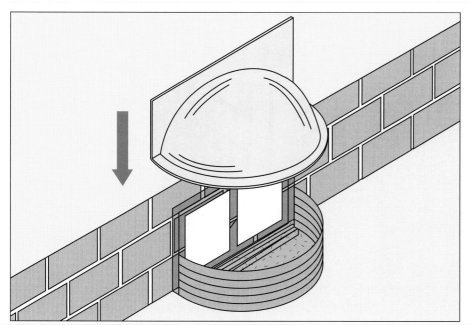

BASEMENT WINDOW WELLS can collect water during a heavy rainstorm and allow water to run into the basement. Install plastic domes over the wells to keep out rainwater.

FRAMING CHECKUP

The house frame is its skeleton. It is the wood structure that supports the floors, walls, ceilings, and roof of the house. Most frame problems are caused by the wood in the frame shrinking as it dries. These problems are relatively minor and easy to fix. Other problems may be caused by boards cracking under the weight of the house, or harm caused by dry rot or insect damage. These problems are more severe and, if not corrected, can result in major damage to a large section of the frame. If the frame deteriorates, part of the house will go with it.

Some parts of the frame, such as the joists and rafters, may be open and visible for inspection. Other parts of the frame, the wall studs for example, will be enclosed within wall board and out of sight. Nevertheless, these can be checked indirectly, because problems are apt to create defects in the walls, floors, or ceilings that enclose the frame. Knowing what to look for, and where, can help you to detect framing problems even though you cannot see the studs, joists, or other members.

FLOORS

Unless you have a finished basement, the joists supporting the first floor are visible from below (and above in an unfinished attic). Make a visual check of all the joists and beams. First look for warped or cracked pieces. Distortion may occur as the wood dries and shrinks over the years. If this is the case, only one or two isolated boards should be warped. The solution is to attach another joist (called a sister joist) to the cracked one and add additional support if necessary. It may also happen if the floor is supporting too much weight. The solution is to add more support from below. It is wise to consult with an architect to determine the best type of support to add.

Check the bridging between the braces. These are the diagonal cross pieces that span between the joists.

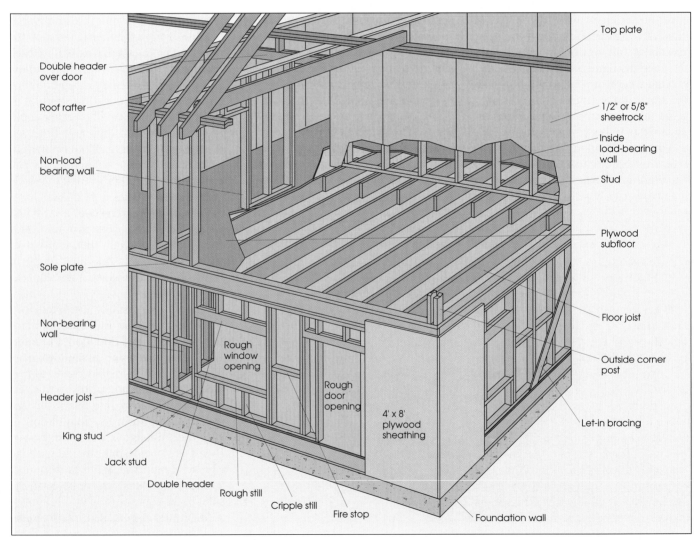

Labels on the diagram:
- Double header over door
- Roof rafter
- Non-load bearing wall
- Sole plate
- Non-bearing wall
- Header joist
- King stud
- Jack stud
- Double header
- Rough still
- Cripple still
- Fire stop
- Rough window opening
- Rough door opening
- 4' x 8' plywood sheathing
- Top plate
- 1/2" or 5/8" sheetrock
- Inside load-bearing wall
- Stud
- Plywood subfloor
- Floor joist
- Outside corner post
- Let-in bracing
- Foundation wall

THE FRAME IS THE SKELETON of the house. Frame damage can cause sections of the house to sag or even collapse. Inspect the framing members for cracks, sags, and rot. Repair or replace all damaged timbers as soon as possible.

Over time, they shrink and loosen. The best remedy is to replace them if you suspect damage.

Look also for rot or insect damage. Unfortunately, this is not always apparent to the naked eye, because the core of the wood may be damaged, while the shell remains intact. Use an awl or sharp knife to probe the boards for soundness.

If pipes or electrical lines run through notches cut into joists, look to see that the notches do not exceed a sixth of the joist's depth. Holes drilled to allow wires through should not exceed a third of the joist's depth. The holes should be at least 2 inches from the edge of the joist. If this is not the case, nail additional bracing to reinforce the joist.

Inspect the floors in all the rooms. This will give you some idea of the joists and subfloor beneath. If the floor boards are buckling up, it is an indication that the subfloor does not have enough clearance to expand or contract with humidity. The solution is to replace the subfloor with underlayment plywood (a major job and one best left to a professional).

If the floor bounces or flexes when you walk on it, the joists are spaced too far apart. The best solution is to add another support beam midpoint between the joists. If the floor bounces severely, it is because the floor lacks proper structural support. Consult a structural engineer for advice.

WALLS
Structural problems with the walls usually show up at the points where the walls meet with the floors, ceilings, or other walls. Look for gaps at the joints where the two surfaces meet. Often these problems are evident in the center of the house, because the central truss has less support and uplift forces are stronger. These forces are generated whenever the house settles or moves in response to ground conditions. Little can be done to counteract them except to make sure the ground around the house is properly graded.

Extreme fluctuations in temperature and humidity conditions can also cause

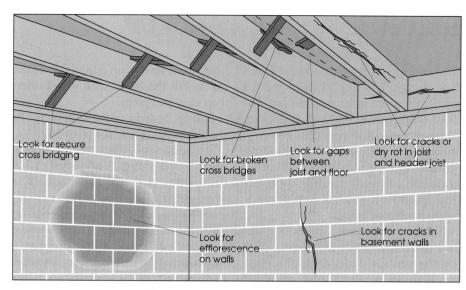

IN AN UNFINISHED BASEMENT, the joists can be inspected from below. Inspect the joists and walls for gaps, cracks, and other warning signs of structural problems.

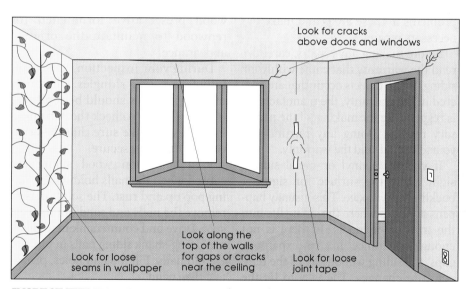

INSPECT THE WALLS FOR CRACKS and gaps. Also inspect for loose joint tape and loose seams in the wallpaper.

gaps to open. They are most likely to occur in late autumn when the heating system is turned on and some framing members expand. The problem should correct itself by springtime.

In some houses, gaps may occur because the framing was constructed with unseasoned wood. As the framing members dry, they pull the ceiling up or distort the walls. Correct ceiling gaps by installing crown molding around the ceiling. Gaps around the floors can be closed by adjusting the shoe molding around the foot of the wall.

Other structural problems show up

as cracks in the walls. The most obvious, especially in new houses, occurs in the walls directly above a doorway. These cracks are a natural result of a house settling. Tape over the cracks with fiberglass joint tape, then spackle.

CAUTION
Severe distortions and warpage occurring in frame alignment are indicative of stress forces that may compromise the structural integrity of the entire house. Before attempting any corrections, consult an architect or structural engineer to see what is causing the problem and what is the best remedy.

DOORS AND WINDOWS CHECKUP

The logical place to inspect the doors and windows is at the entrance door. You will want to check the finish and look for gaps around the trim—all gaps should be caulked (see page 327). Look closely at the hinges; since they support the door, they should be solidly anchored to the frame.

DOORS

Consider how secure the entry door is. Many entry doors are made of wood, a few are hollow-core doors. Hollow-core doors invite heat loss and they offer virtually no protection against break-ins. For maximum security, replace all hollow-core entries with solid-core wooden doors.

Solid-core wooden doors are more formidable and are less likely to warp, however, they must be sealed or they will absorb moisture. This could cause them to expand a bind in the door frame. If you have a solid-core wooden door, inspect it carefully to make sure all surfaces have an adequate coating of varnish or paint. This inspection should include the edges of the door as well as the front and back faces. Perhaps the most important edge is the bottom of the door. It is hard to make a visual inspection of the door bottom because it is so close to the floor. You can try to feel if there is a film of finish on the bottom edge by slipping your fingers under it. You can also place a small flat mirror under the door and catch a glimpse of the bottom edge in the reflection.

LOOSE HINGES or hinges deep in the doorjamb will cause a door to bind. Before planing the door, check the hinges.

If your front door is made of wood consider replacing it with one made of fiberglass or a metal door with a fiberglass core. These doors are expensive but they offer solid protection against break-ins and they have good insulating properties. Metal doors should have a "thermal break" to keep the cold edges of the door away from the metal threshold. Fiberglass or metal doors can also warp if they stand exposed to the hot summer sun. They will return to their original shape when they cool. You can minimize warpage by repainting the door a light color.

Inspect the door hinges. Entry doors are heavy, so they should be supported by no less than three sturdy hinges, and, of course, they should be fastened tightly to the door frame.

All entry doors should have a good lockset with a deadbolt. Exterior locks can collect moisture from rain and snow. Eventually, this moisture will cause the internal parts to corrode and bind. Protect external locks by lubricating them once a month. Do not use graphite lubricants for this because the graphite will eventually collect inside the lock and gum up the works. It is better to use a lightweight machine oil (sewing machine oil is good for this job) to lubricate the locks. Place a few drops on the key; pull it in and out of the key slot a few times, then try opening and closing the lock a number of times.

Over time, some dirt and metal may collect in the oil film and make the lock a little sluggish. You can clean the lock with kerosene. Apply a few drops to the key and repeat the lubrication maneuvers to work it into the mechanism. This technique should be a part of the annual inspection.

The front entry door should be fitted with a sturdy chain lock so you can crack the door open, yet still maintain security. All entry doors should have weather-stripping to cover the gaps around the frame and a gasket or sweep on the threshold (see page 318).

Next, inspect the interior doors. Unlike the entry doors, interior doors should not have weather-stripping. They should have a slight gap (at least ¾-inch) at the bottom to allow for ventilation. If

TIGHTENING A HINGE SCREW

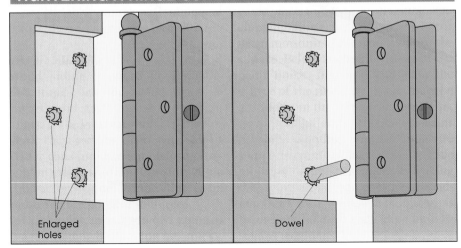

TIGHTENING A HINGE SCREW is difficult if the holes have become enlarged. Insert a glued dowel into the hole. Let the glue dry, drill a pilot hole, then drive the screw into place.

there are locks on the interior doors, make sure you can unlock the door from the outside. This will allow you to open the door and help someone, such as a small child or an elderly person, should they get locked in the room.

Open and close all doors to make sure they latch when closed. If the door does not latch properly, the lockset may need lubrication. Disassemble it, clean and lubricate the moving parts, then re-assemble it. If the lockset is working properly, check to see if the bolt is aligning with the faceplate. The solution is to adjust the faceplate, but before doing this, make sure the hinge screws are tight. Loose screws allow the hinges, and subsequently the door, to sag.

During hot and humid weather, a door may not close properly because it has absorbed moisture and swelled. If this happens, remove the door and sand or plane all the edges until the door closes properly.

Check all sliding doors and bifolding doors to make sure they open and close properly. If the doors stick or slide with difficulty, clean the door track with a toothbrush and a damp cloth, then lubricate the track and rollers with silicone spray. If this does not correct the problem, inspect the rollers to see if they need adjustment (see pages 240–241). A bent or worn mechanism should be replaced. Problems with bifolding doors can usually be traced to improper alignment; this can be corrected by loosening and adjusting the top pivot bracket (see pages 240–241).

WINDOWS

Look at the glass panes in the sashes. Obviously you will want to replace broken panes, but also look for cracks in the glass. Cracked glass is dangerous and inefficient because it allows cold air to penetrate through the window. Look around the edges of the glass at the condition of the glazing compound. It should form a continuous bead around the perimeter of the sash. If there are any gaps or cracks, replace the compound to keep moisture from penetrating into the frame.

After examining the glass, check the condition of the frames. Wooden

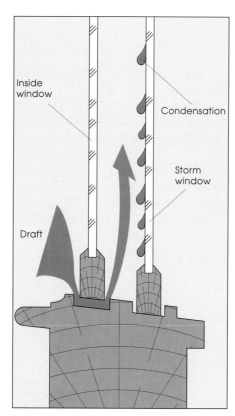

INSPECT THE WINDOWS during the winter for signs of excessive condensation. If warm interior air creeps past the inside window, condensation will form on the interior side of the storm window.

frames with worn paint or bare spots should be sanded and painted. Inspect vinyl clad or aluminum frames for cracks and warpage. Usually these defects cannot be corrected, and it may be necessary to replace the sash.

Open and close the windows. If a window sticks, the tracks are probably dirty or coated with paint. Clean them with a stiff brush and damp cloth. Use soap to lubricate the channels or wooden windows, and silicone compound to lubricate metal window tracks.

Jalousie and casement windows have a crank mechanism to open and close them. The metal gears (do not lubricate plastic gears) in crank housings should be cleaned and lubricated yearly to keep the windows operating smoothly (see page 234).

If a window fails or won't stay open, the operating mechanism may be broken. This is usually a problem with older windows that have sash cords,

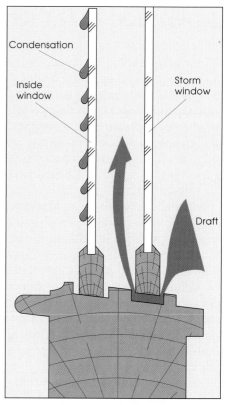

IF COLD AIR LEAKS past the storm window, condensation will form on the interior side of the inside window. Add weather-stripping to the window to prevent the leaks of air.

pulleys, and counterweights inside hollow pockets on the sides of the window.

Look also for condensation build-up on the inside of the window. If condensation forms on the inside window, then cold air is coming around the storm window. It needs better weather-stripping. If condensation forms on the storm window, then warm moist air is flowing past the inside window to the storm window. Add more or better weather-stripping to the inside window.

Inadequate weather-stripping can also allow cold air to enter from the outside and create cold drafts. Slip a dollar bill under the sash and close the window. If you can pull the bill out from under the closed window, there is a gap that needs weather-stripping. You can also test for cold drafts by moving your hand around the perimeter of the window to feel incoming cold air. If either of these tests indicate the presence of incoming air, add weather-stripping.

ROOFING CHECKUP

The average roof is designed to last about 30 years; after that it begins to deteriorate and may need to be replaced. Some roofs last longer, others need to be replaced after a couple of decades. A good roof inspection is important to determine its condition, since making repairs is necessary before it's too late.

Sometimes you can get an idea of the condition of your roof by looking at it from the ground with field glasses, but at some point you will have to climb onto the roof for a careful examination of all areas. A roof inspection can be dangerous because you will be high off the ground. Be sure to inspect your roof on a clear, dry day and wear shoes with nonslip soles. Read the caution panel at the end of this section and understand the risks of climbing on a roof before you venture up.

A typical roof is made up of several elements: the shingles, flashing, gutters and downspouts, the fascia, and the soffits. A thorough inspection should include all of these elements.

SHINGLES

Look at the shingles for damage such as buckling, cupping, cracks, or broken pieces. A few damaged shingles can be repaired or replaced (see page 274) but if there are large areas of damaged shingles, the entire roof should be replaced and reshingled.

During the winter after a snowstorm, ice dams may form. These dams trap water as it runs down the roof. Eventually the captured water works up under the shingles and penetrates through the roof into the attic. The primary cause of ice dams is inadequate roof ventilation. One way to prevent the problem is by adding soffit vents and a ridge vent to the roof (see pages 262–263). Periodically, check the soffits from inside the attic to make sure the vents are not obstructed.

Metal flashing will be placed around a chimney, vent, dormer, or even between two parts of the roof. Flashing keeps water from running under the shingles at those points. Inspect all the flashing to make sure it is sound. Corroded areas may be patched with roofing cement. Flashing with extensive damage should be replaced.

GUTTERS

Gutters and downspouts need to be inspected twice a year, in the early spring and late fall. In the fall, they may be filled with leaves. These should be removed (see pages 280–281). Check also to see if there is evidence of tiny gravel in the gutter debris. Tiny gravel deposits come from deteriorating shingles and are a warning sign that the roof covering is wearing and may soon need to be replaced.

In the spring, inspect the gutters to see if they sustained any damage from the winter snow and ice. Look to see if the gutters are sagging or leaking. Realign sagging gutters and replace the

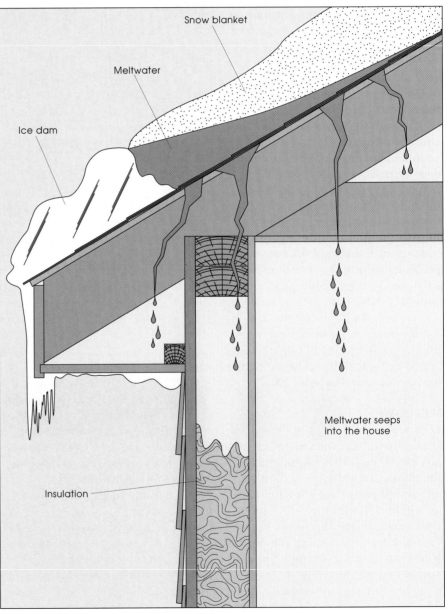

ICE DAMS OCCUR when the snow at the roof ridge melts into water. The water freezes at the eaves and forms a dam to trap additional meltwater. This water will eventually seep through the roof into the attic.

hanging strap to secure them in place. The gutters are attached to the fascia boards. Inspect them for cracks or rot. Replace the damaged fascia boards and remount the gutters with new hanging straps.

Gutters leak if the seams open up or if the gutter is rusted. Fix seam leaks by applying a liberal bead of caulk to the joints. Repair rust holes in the gutter with fiberglass and resin (see pages 280–289).

Inspect the downspouts for clogs and debris. Remove the obstructions by forcing a plumbers' snake through the downspout or by directing a strong jet of water into the downspout with a garden hose. Install downspout strainers and gutter guards to prevent future clogging.

Look at the ground around the outlet pipe of the downspout for signs of soil erosion or for puddles of water (after a rainstorm). These are indications that the runoff water is not being directed away from the house. Install splash blocks under all of the outlet pipes to divert the water.

Finally, it is important to examine the soffit boards for decay or rot. Decay and rot are caused by inadequate soffit ventilation. Replace the boards and install soffit vents for increased ventilation (see pages 262–263).

Base flashing

Up–roof flashing

Step flashing

Counter flashing

LEAKS FREQUENTLY OCCUR around the chimney because the masonry settles at a different rate from the roof and the two pull apart. Check the flashing around the chimney for wide gaps. Chimney flashing consists of base flashing, step flashing, and counter flashing.

CAUTION

Climbing onto a roof for an inspection can be dangerous. If you have any doubts as to your ability to walk on a roof, leave the job to a roofing professional. Do not attempt a roof inspection or any other roof work if you are unsteady working at heights. Do not attempt to climb onto a roof if it has a steep pitch. Wait for a clear day when there is little wind and no rain in the forecast. Wear shoes with nonslip soles and make sure the roof surface is dry before venturing onto it.

Choose a sturdy ladder that is the right height for the roof—the ladder should extend at least 3 feet beyond the edge of the roof. Do not use the ladder if any part is damaged or not working properly. Make sure the ladder is properly positioned against the house and that the base is on solid ground and secure. Working with a partner is also a smart idea. One person can steady the ladder as the other person climbs to the roof. Watch out for power cables and do not take any foolish chances.

PROTECTING GUTTERS

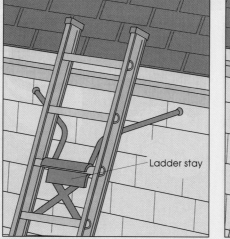

Ladder stay

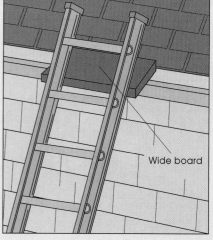

Wide board

USE A LADDER to inspect and clean the gutters. Placing a ladder against the gutters can dent or damage them. Protect the gutters by using a ladder stay or by placing a wide board across the top of the gutters.

ELECTRICAL CHECKUP

The electrical inspection begins at the service panel. Look at the panel to make sure the metal casing is not rusted or corroded. Rust indicates possible water damage that may affect the wiring inside. If any part of the box is rusted, have it inspected by a professional electrician. In addition to a visual inspection, place your ear close to the panel (but not in contact with it) and listen for any buzzing sounds. A buzzing sound can be caused by electrical arcing or vibration and is indicative of a loose connection inside the box.

If your service panel has fuses, there should be an ample supply of spare fuses nearby in case of an emergency (Never insert pennies or any other metal object in the fuse socket in an attempt to bypass a blown fuse. This could cause an electrical fire.) As an added safety precaution, you should always keep a spare flashlight by the service panel in case you have to check the fuses or breakers in the event of a major power overload.

PROPER GROUNDING
Next you will want to check the receptacles throughout the house to see if they are properly grounded. For this, you will need a circuit analyzer, a small hand-held device that is available at any electrical supply store for less than five dollars. Plug the analyzer into the outlet and read the pattern formed by the lights across the display panel of the instrument.

Match the light pattern against the chart on the body of the instrument to see if the outlet is grounded. Do not assume that an outlet is grounded just because it has a three-hole receptacle. Circuits without proper ground connections should be corrected by a licensed electrician.

When checking any outlet, see if it is warm to the touch or if there is a humming sound. Sometimes this is caused by an internal fault in the receptacle. It should be replaced (see page 434). Dust or debris in the electrical box or loose wires can also cause the outlet to hum or overheat. Shut off power to the circuit, then pull the receptacle from the box. Vacuum the box and check all wires to make sure they are secure.

If the outlet is installed in a paneled wall, remove the cover plate and look at the outlet box. It should be flush with the wall surface. Sometimes when do-it-yourselfers panel a wall, they neglect to pull the box forward and there is a gap between the edges or the box and the cover plate. This is a code violation. An easy way to correct this is by buying an electrical box extender at an electrical supply store. This is simply a metal sleeve that fits within the box and extends to the cover plate.

In the bathroom and kitchen, you will have special receptacles called Ground Fault Interrupters (GFI). GFI outlets should be tested weekly to make sure they are functioning properly. Fortunately the test is simply and does not require any special equipment. Simply plug an appliance, like a hair dryer, into the GFI and turn it on. Press the test button in the center of the GFI—the appliance should go off. Press the reset button on the GFI and the appliance should start up again. If not, replace the GFI (see page 435).

LIGHT FIXTURES AND WALL SWITCHES
Check all wall switches to make sure that they operate without humming and that they are cool to the touch. Replace any switches that you suspect are damaged (see page 434).

Check all installed incandescent light fixtures by turning the wall switch on and off. The light should come on without flickering. Flickering indicates a

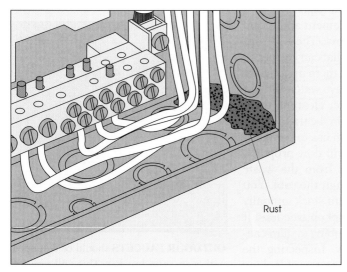

INSPECT THE MAIN SERVICE PANEL for rust spots. These might indicate that water has leaked into the box and could possibly cause a short circuit.

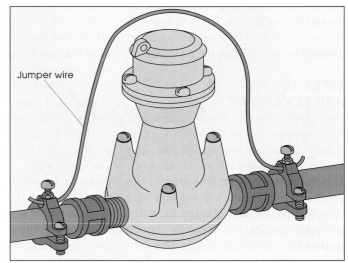

Jumper wire

WHEN A WATER METER is connected to the incoming water line, it can break the electrical ground connection. Install a jumper wire around the meter to restore ground continuity.

loose bulb or faulty wiring in the socket. Tighten the bulb, then check the wiring in the socket (see page 436).

There is no need to open up every light fixture to inspect the wiring unless you suspect a malfunction. If, however, you have reason to check out the wiring, check to see that all connections are made with solderless connectors (also called wire nuts) and not electrical tape. Electrical tape is dangerous because it disintegrates over time and leaves bare wires exposed. This is usual-ly not a problem in newer homes, but it can be prevalent in older homes. If you find a fixture with taped over connections, switch off the power, remove the tape, and install solderless connectors. Then inspect the other fixtures in the house for the same problem.

Inspect all fluorescent light fixtures. Black deposits around the ballast indi-cate that the ballast is worn and should be replaced (see page 433). If the light flickers or hums it could mean that the light tube is defective or it may not be properly seated. These are easy problems to correct. In some cases flickering or humming may be caused by cracked sockets. In this case the entire lamp should be replaced.

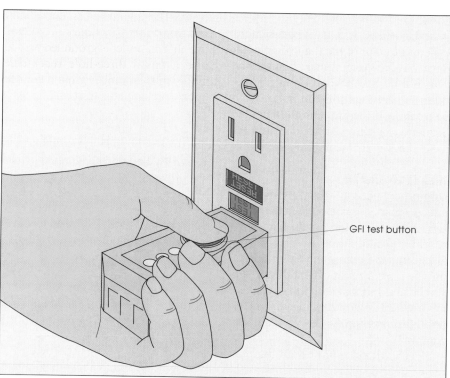

USE A CIRCUIT ANALYZER to test outlets for proper ground connection. Some circuit analyzers have a button to make a GFI test.

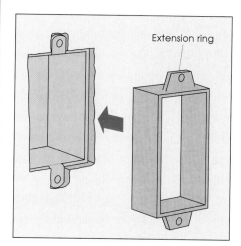

IF AN ELECTRICAL BOX IS RECESSED below the wall surface, install an extension ring to bring it flush with the surface.

THE GROUND FAULT INTERRUPTER (GFI) has a small internal transformer that senses current leaks.

HAVC CHECKUP

The heart of a heating system is the burner unit, so check it first. In general, it is best to have a service technician look at the unit every year to clean it and make any adjustments. Still, you can inspect it by yourself from time to time to familiarize yourself with the unit and make sure it is functioning correctly.

If the heater is a gas-fired heater, look at the color of the flame. It should have a blue-green inner flame surrounded by a yellowish flame. If the flame is all yellow, the air orifice may be clogged. If the flame is all blue, the burner is getting too much air. (To make these adjustments, see page 443.)

HEATING UNITS

Oil burners need a little more maintenance. Again, it is a good idea to have a service technician inspect the unit every year. He should clean the firebox and also clean and adjust the flame orifice on the burner unit. In addition, he should also lubricate the motor (unless it is a sealed unit) and change the oil filter; if not, you can do this yourself (see page 445).

Electric units require little maintenance since they have no moving parts. However, the electrical connections can loosen or break over time. At least twice a year, check all terminal bars (do this with the power off) for loose or damaged connections. Tighten loose terminal screws and replace worn or frayed wires (see page 446).

The burner heats the medium—air, water, or steam—that distributes the heat through the house. You will next want to inspect the heat distribution system for your unit.

For a forced hot-air system, you need to first check the blower assembly then the heating ducts. At the blower assembly, check the drive belts for proper tension. Adjust the belt tension, if necessary, and replace the belt if it is worn or frayed. Next, check the blower fan (also called the "squirrel cage"). Use a vacuum cleaner to remove any dust or debris. For stubborn dirt or oil deposits

clean the unit with a degreaser. Finally replace the air in the return duct (see page 441).

Next look at the registers in the individual rooms. Use a vacuum cleaner to remove any dust that may be lodged in them. Check all the dampers and registers to make sure they are positioned correctly The position of each may vary depending on the amount of heat being delivered to a particular area. If that area is too warm or cool, you can re-adjust the damper.

A hot-water heating system will not operate efficiently if sediment and sludge accumulate in the water lines, or if air builds up in the radiators or convectors. At least once a year, you should drain water from the boiler system. Go to the boiler and place a pail under the drain faucet. Close the water inlet valve, then open the drain valve and allow at least a gallon or two of water to flow in-

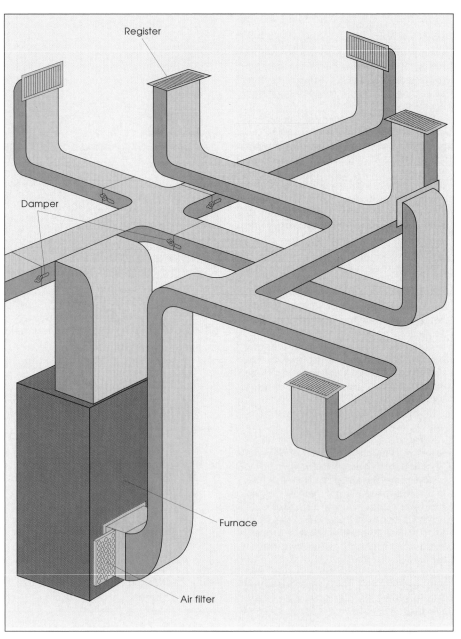

Register

Damper

Furnace

Air filter

FORCED-AIR SYSTEMS should be inspected each year. Make sure the registers are clean and warm air is coming from them. Air filters should be changed when they are dirty.

to the bucket (be very careful because this water may be boiling hot). At first, the water may be dirty or rusty. Continue draining until the water runs clear, then close the faucet and open the faucet on the supply line to replace the drained water in the system (see pages 448–449).

Next, bleed the radiators or convectors. Position a pan under the bleeder valve, then open the valve. At first, air will come out of the valve, then water will flow. At that point, close the valve. Follow this procedure at each radiator or convector.

Steam systems are also susceptible to sediment and rust accumulations in the water supply. They should be drained yearly. The drainage procedure is the same as for a hot-water system (see instructions above).

Steam radiators can also collect water if they are not leveled properly. This water makes the system extremely noisy (commonly called "knocking") and inefficient. The radiators should be pitched so they incline toward the inlet valve. The yearly inspection should include a check of each radiator with a level. Units that are level or inclined away from the valve can be corrected by placing a wedge under the legs at the opposite end of the radiator.

AIR CONDITIONING UNITS

Whether you have an air conditioning system that consists of several window units or a central air conditioning system that runs throughout the house, both should be checked in the spring before the heat of summer arrives. Individual air conditioning units are very heavy. If you need to remove a unit from the window, enlist the aid of a helper.

To inspect, remove the housing and check the filters and vents. Be sure they are intact, then brush and vacuum out all dust and debris. Before attempting to clean and prep the air conditioner, make sure that it is unplugged from the socket. Clean the drain pan and inspect the drain hole. If the hole is clogged, clear it by running a stiff wire through it. Wash or replace dirty filters and oil the fan motor (see pages 454–451).

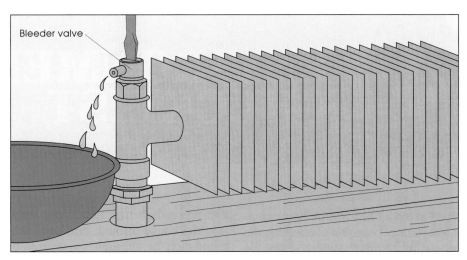

BLEED THE TRAPPED AIR from a hot-water radiator by opening the bleeder valve. Close it when water flows from the valve.

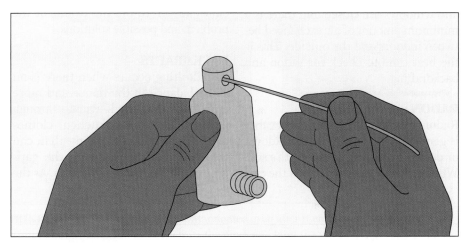

A CLOGGED VENT will prevent steam from entering the radiator. The air vents in steam radiators can often be cleaned with a wire. You can sometimes clean mineral deposits from the port by boiling the valve in vinegar. If these methods fail, replace the valve.

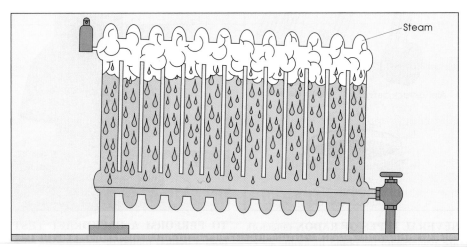

THE RADIATOR SHOULD BE PLACED on an incline toward the valve so that condensed water can return to the boiler. To prevent knocking, open the valve all the way.

HAVC CHECKUP

CHECKLIST *Continued*

of their presence in the form of mud tubes or tunnels up the side of the foundation. More often, however, there is no sign of termite infestation because the termites do not nest in the house. They work their way underground and penetrate the house through hairline cracks in the foundation. You are usually not aware of termites until you discover badly damaged framing members.

The only sure way to find termites in your home or in the surrounding soil is by having a pest control expert make an inspection. Pest control experts know where to look for termites and they have a variety of instruments and detectors to determine the extent of infestation. One device is the fiber optic borescope that can peep beneath flooring, and behind panels, to see if termites are present. You should have the inspection performed every few years.

Animal pests can also invade your home at any time. Raccoons, mice, and squirrels commonly enter through the chimney or dryer vent. Sometimes squirrels will eat through a weak soffit panel to make a nest in the attic. Checks consist of looking in potential nesting places throughout the home. Inspect the dryer vent every year—do this as a matter of routine to remove accumulated lint as well as mouse nests.

Before lighting the fireplace in the late fall, make a thorough examination of the chimney flue. This is a favorite nesting place of raccoons and squirrels. Also look at the insulation in the attic, because rodents invading the attic will nest in the soft fibers. Look in the far corners of the attic under the eaves. Indications of nests are rounded depressions with animal droppings. Birds will also nest in the chimney and in the rain gutters around the house, so inspect these areas in the late spring.

MOLD AND MILDEW

Other serious biological pollutants in the home are mold and mildew. Some may seem like minor annoyances, such as the blackish stains that form on shower curtains, but when the infestation grows into large accumulations, it can become a serious health hazard. Often homeowners believe that as long as they do not see any signs of mold—that is, patches of green, blue, or black discoloration on surfaces—their environment is free of contamination. What they don't realize is that mold colonies can be growing in areas that they cannot see, such as in air ducts, remote attic or basement spaces, or in the wall cavities. Left to grow and multiply, mold infestations may produce enough organic compounds to cause allergic reactions, sickness and, in extreme cases, death (a possibility with infants and others with breathing problems).

You should make an annual inspection of the house for possible mold and mildew contamination. The only tools you need are a strong flashlight and your eyes and nose. The flashlight and your eyes will help you to see in dark corners and recesses throughout the house. Your nose will help you to detect any musty odors present in the air. You may not be able to see the mold if it is growing in enclosed areas, such as a wall cavity, but you can detect it because the odor-laden spores will drift out through an electrical outlet or through a crack in the wall.

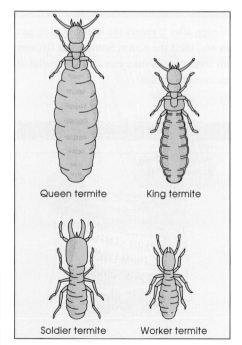

KING AND QUEEN TERMITES produce offspring. Workers are responsible for wood damage and feeding the young. Soldiers protect the colony against predators.

Queen termite   King termite

Soldier termite   Worker termite

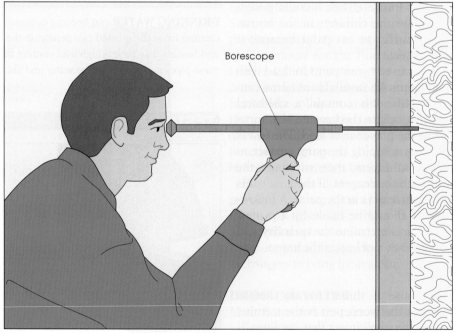

Borescope

WITH A FIBER-OPTIC BORESCOPE, a pest control expert can look into walls and beneath flooring to find termite infestation. If your house has a history of termite problems, you should have this inspection performed every few years in the springtime when termites tend to thrive.

MOLD AND MILDEW

SEASONAL CHECKLIST

Inspecting your home should be a year-round activity. It is important to schedule your inspections at the right time of year in order to maximize your results and also to make the most of your time. For example, interior inspection and maintenance should be carried out in the winter when the weather is cold. Outside inspection and maintenance should wait until the warmer weather of spring or fall. The following list contains information on what should be inspected, and at what time of year, as well as what you should look for when inspecting.

WINTER

Appliances	Check for clean parts and lubrication
Door jambs	Check for proper closing and air leaks (see pages 498-499)
Door locks	Check for proper action (see page 498)
Environment	Check radon levels and water quality, and paint for lead (see pages 512-513)
Faucets	Check for leaks and corrosion (see pages 506-507)
Floors and stairs	Check for squeaks, stains, cracks, and gaps (see pages 494-495, 503)
Hot water heater (body)	Check for leaks and corrosion (see page 507)
Hot water heater (burner)	Check for proper flame color and flame height (see page 507)
Hot water heater - (pressure relief valve)	Check for proper functioning (see page 507)
Household tools	Check for sharpness and integrity
Ladders	Check for defects (see page 501)
Sink drains	Check for proper draining action, leaks, and corrosion (see page 507)
Sink supply valve	Check for leaks
Smoke and CO detectors	Check for proper operation and batteries
Toilet (tank)	Check condition of internal flush mechanism and handle for proper action (see pages 506-507)
Toilet (supply valve)	Check for leaks (see pages 506-507)
Walls and ceilings	Check for cracks, dents, holes, and loose joint tape, and condition of paint or wallpaper (see pages 495, 502)
Windows	Check for proper action, leaks, and drafts (see page 499)

SPRING

Air conditioner	Check for clean filters, interior and exterior (see page 511)
Attic (inside)	Check for leaks (see page 500)
Chimney	Check flue for damage, cleanliness, and creosote deposits (see pages 500-501)
Driveway	Check for cracks and holes (see page 504)
Floors	Check for scratches and proper finish (see page 503)
Gutters and downspouts	Check for damage and proper placement of splash blocks (see pages 500-501)
Masonry, exterior	Check for crumbling mortar or splayed concrete (see pages 492-493)
Masonry, interior (basement)	Check for condensation on walls (see page 495)
Pest control	Check for termites (see pages 513-514)

Roof	Check for overall condition and curled, broken, or missing shingles (see pages 500-501)
Siding (metal or vinyl)	Check for cracks, dents, warps, and defects (see pages 496-497)
Siding (wood)	Check for cracks, dents, warps, and defects, and condition of paint (see page 496)
Walls and ceilings	Check for cleanliness and integrity of paint (see page 502)
Windows	Check for broken panes, cracked glazing compound, and cleanliness (see page 498-499)

SUMMER

Doors	Check for lubrication of hinges and general condition (see pages 498-499)
Floors	Check finish (see page 503)
Furniture	Check finish
Home security	Check quality of locks and lights, trim shrubs, hedges, and trees
Lawn furniture	Check for cleanliness and needed repairs
Lawn mower	Check for overall condition, and cleanliness, and sharpness of blade
Windows	Check for cleanliness and integrity of screens (see pages 498-499)

FALL

Attic	Check condition of insulation (see pages 500-501)
Chimney	Check for cleanliness
Exterior windows and doors	Check for cracks and gaps in caulk (see pages 498-499)
Gutters and downspouts	Check for clogs (see pages 500-501)
Heating system (hot water)	Check radiators for repairs; bleed them and drain sediment from boiler (see page 507)
Heating system (steam)	Check for proper pitch and unclogged valves, and drain sediment from boiler (see pages 510-511)
Heating unit (electric)	Check for broken wires, loose connections, and clean contacts (see pages 510-511)
Heating unit (forced air)	Check air filters for cleanliness, drive belts for integrity, all ducts for leaks and gaps, and position of all dampers; clean all registers and clean and lubricate blower motor (see pages 510-511)
Heating unit (gas)	Check flame for color and height; have burner unit cleaned (see pages 510-511)
Heating unit (oil)	Check for filters cleanliness; lubricate motor and pump; have technician clean and tune (see pages 510-511)

APPENDIX: WORKING WITH PROFESSIONALS

If you have a large-scale home improvement project, an experienced professional designer can provide specialized information and advice that can save you money in the long run.

ARCHITECTS AND DESIGNERS

Architects have a college degree in architecture, have passed a rigorous state examination, and have apprenticed with an established firm before being licensed to practice. They can plan every element of a complex project, provide detailed working drawings, obtain building permits, and even serve as general contractors. An architect is legally responsible for the quality of work done under his or her supervision. An architect's fee is usually a percentage of the total cost of the work.

House designers or *architectural designers* are less rigorously trained than architects. Many have backgrounds as home builders or architectural draftsmen and can provide many of the same planning and supervision services as an architect, at less cost. But because they are not licensed, they may have little legal responsibility for the quality of work done.

Kitchen designers specialize in kitchen and bathroom remodelings. *Interior designers* typically select color schemes, cabinets, furniture, and other furnishings. *Landscape designers* can develop a plan for your entire site and suggest appropriate plants for the soil and climate as well as for appearance. Designers can simply develop a plan, or can also secure materials and/or labor for the job. Some charge an hourly rate or flat fee; others receive a commission for work done by their company or for materials and furnishings purchased through them.

CONTRACTORS

Various projects can require the services of one or more contractors. In some cases, you may lack the time or skills for a particular kind of work. In other cases, building codes require that certain work—notably electrical and plumbing installations and alterations to the load-bearing structure—be done by or under the supervision of a licensed specialist. You may choose to hire individual *subcontractors* for the parts of a job you decide not to do yourself. However, for a large or complex project you may do better to hire a *general contractor*.

A general contractor takes responsibility for the entire job, from ordering materials and securing building permits to final inspections and cleanup. He or she hires and coordinates the efforts of all subcontractors, oversees the budget, and inspects the work to ensure that it is done carefully and correctly.

BIDS AND CONTRACTS

Whether you hire a general contractor or act as your own, begin by getting bids. Select possible contractors by asking for recommendations from friends, co-workers, neighbors, and—if you are financing the project—your lending institution. Go over your plan with four or five candidates and ask for rough estimates of the money and time involved. Also request references and proof that each contractor is bonded, insured against property damage, and covered by workers' compensation.

Ask for written final bids from at least three contractors. Be sure that everyone is bidding on exactly the same specifications, so comparisons are valid. Analyze each bid with the contractor who submitted it. Be wary of a bid that is substantially lower than the others. The bidder may be overlooking something, planning to cut corners, or expecting to ask for more money later.

Once you have decided on a person for the job, insist on a written contract. Read it carefully before you sign, or have an attorney look it over for you. In discussing the contract with the bidder, remember that you are not adversaries, but are attempting to arrive at a cooperative agreement. Be sure the following points are covered.

- The starting and completion dates.
- The payment schedule—commonly one-third at the beginning, one-third when the work is well along, and the balance when all work has been inspected and approved.
- Who is responsible for obtaining permits, inspections, and approvals.
- Change orders: What kind or number of new or different specifications not included in the plan can be made without additional charge, and what charges will be made for others.
- Penalty fees: The reduction in cost if work is not completed on time except for reasons beyond the contractor's control, such as weather. The increase in cost if you cause the work to be delayed.
- Completion details: Removal of debris. Completing the job "in a workmanlike manner" (a standard phrase) to a specified state. Restoring surroundings disturbed or altered by the work to their original condition.

ZONING, CODES, AND PERMITS

Various community laws govern what you can do to your home and how the work must be done. *Zoning ordinances* regulate improvements that affect your home's relationship with its neighbors. *Building codes* mandate construction safety standards and specify what work must be done by licensed professionals. A *building permit*, based on plans submitted to community authorities, ensures that major improvements will conform to zoning and code provisions.

Most zoning ordinances regulate setbacks, the distances from a structure to the street and adjacent property lines. They may also regulate the height and size of structures, how many people may reside at an address, the types of business that may be conducted there, and even matters of appearance such as landscaping and architectural style.

Building codes typically fall into three categories: general construction, plumbing, and electrical. You may need to secure permits for each kind of work and have the work inspected one or more times to ensure that it has been completed according to the approved plan and code requirements.

Do not ignore zoning ordinances and building codes. If you violate them, you will be fined and required to tear out or modify nonconforming work. If a project you have in mind would be at odds with a zoning or code provision, an architect or structural engineer may be able to help you gain a variance that sets aside the conflicting regulation.

MEASUREMENT CONVERSIONS
(For standard lumber sizes, see page 67; for nail and screw sizes, see pages 70–71.)

Units of Length
in: inch; ft: foot; yd: yard   12 in = 1 ft; 36 in = 1 yd; 3 ft = 1 yd
mm: millimeter; cm: centimeter; m: meter   1,000 mm = 100 cm = 1 m

Units of Weight
oz: ounce; lb: pound   16 oz = 1 lb
g: gram; kg: kilogram   1,000 g = 1 kg

Units of Liquid Measure
oz: ounce; pt: pint; qt: quart   16 oz = 1 pt; 32 oz = 1 qt; 2 pt = 1 qt
gal: gallon   128 oz = 1 gal; 8 pt = 1 gal; 4 qt = 1 gal
mL: milliliter; L: liter   1,000 mL = 1 L

CONVERSIONS

MULTIPLY	BY	TO GET	MULTIPLY	BY	TO GET
Length					
in	25.4	mm	mm	0.039	in
in	2.54	cm	mm	0.003	ft
in	0.025	m	mm	0.001	yd
ft	304.8	mm	cm	0.394	in
ft	30.48	cm	cm	0.033	ft
ft	0.305	m	cm	0.011	yd
yd	914.4	mm	m	39.37	in
yd	91.44	cm	m	3.28	ft
yd	0.914	m	m	1.09	yd
Weight					
oz	28.35	g	g	0.035	oz
oz	0.028	kg	g	0.002	lb
lb	453.6	g	kg	35.27	oz
lb	0.454	kg	kg	2.2	lb
Liquid Measure					
oz	29.57	mL	mL	0.034	oz
oz	0.029	L	mL	0.002	pt
			mL	0.001	qt
pt	473.2	mL	mL	0.0003	gal
pt	0.473	L			
			L	33.8	oz
qt	946.4	mL	L	2.11	pt
qt	0.946	L	L	1.06	qt
			L	0.26	gal
gal	3,785	mL			
gal	3.785	L			